Labour market theory

Labour markets have been going through dramatic changes over the past two decades. Women have been participating in the work-force in unprecedented numbers. Skills and earnings have been raised for some through the impact of new technology, whereas it has meant insecurity, casualisation and poor conditions of employment for others. Globalisation, flexibility, de-industrialisation, the new industrial relations and human resource development as a branch of management science have all shaken up the functioning of labour markets.

Labour Market Theory: A Constructive Reassessment is the first text to address these issues on a theoretical level, with a commanding assessment of labour market theory across the social sciences. Beginning with macroeconomics and human capital theory, it demonstrates how the existing literature, rooted in mainstream economics, has been forced to acknowledge that there is a multiplicity of labour markets, even though labour market theory has not developed the capacity to address this coherently. Alternative approaches through segmented labour markets, the new institutional theories, or notions such as flexibility have substituted theoretical eclecticism and descriptive categorisation for sound analytical principles. Paradoxically, even though it is flourishing, labour market theory is shown to be in profound disarray.

An alternative and radically original approach is offered which draws constructively but critically on existing literature. The book argues that different labour markets are structured, reproduced or transformed differently according to the way in which underlying economic and social relations interact. The arguments are illustrated by reference to empirical studies, such as the South African labour market and the impact of equal pay legislation, and the implications for policy are drawn out in a discussion of the minimum wage debate.

Ben Fine is Professor of Economics at the School of Oriental and African Studies (SOAS), University of London. He served as an expert adviser to the South African Presidential Labour Market Commission in 1995/96. His recent co-authored books include *Consumption in the Age of Affluence: The World of Food* (Routledge, 1996) and *South Africa's Political Economy* (Hurst, 1997).

Routledge frontiers of political economy

Labour market theory
A constructive reassessment

Ben Fine

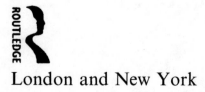

London and New York

First published 1998 by Routledge
11 New Fetter Lane, London EC4P 4EE

Simultaneously published in the USA and Canada
by Routledge
29 West 35th Street, New York, NY 10001

Typeset in Times by BC Typesetting, Bristol
Printed and bound in Great Britain by
Antony Rowe Ltd, Chippenham, Wiltshire

British Library Cataloguing in Publication Data
A catalogue record for this book is available from the British Library

Library of Congress Cataloging in Publication Data
A catalogue record for this book has been requested

ISBN 0–415–16676–4

For Naomi

Contents

List of figures and tables

FIGURES

TABLES

Acknowledgements

I would like to thank those who have read and commented upon various parts of this book, especially, Costas Lapavitsas, Alfredo Saad-Filho, and Mushtaq Khan. Peter Nolan read the whole manuscript and offered suggestions for improvement which are to be found on every page.

List of abbreviations

DLM	dual labour market
ECJ	European Court of Justice
ILO	International Labour Organisation
IMP	income maintenance programme
ISCUWB	Industrial and Staff Canteen Wages Board
NAIRU	non-accelerating inflation rate of unemployment
NCE	New Classical Economics
NIE	New Institutional Economics
NRU	natural rate of unemployment
NUM	National Union of Mineworkers
RPE	radical political economy
SCELI	Social Change and Economic Life Initiative
SLM	segmented labour market
SOP	system of provision
TFP	total factor productivity
TTWA	travel to work area

Part I
The state of play

1 Introduction and overview

This book is concerned primarily with the economics of labour markets. As such, it is devoted to theoretical considerations and the critical deployment of ideas about the workings of labour markets. The writing has taken place over a period of more than a decade, although much of the text is recently written and the whole text has been revised over the past year.

During this gestation period, however, labour market theory has changed substantially. The oldest part of the work is the critical assessment of segmented labour market theory. Ten years ago, it was dominated by radical political economy, and it was treated with contempt by orthodox economics; it was more comfortably accommodated within mainstream industrial sociology. However, as demonstrated in detail in Chapter 5, the theory was permanently open to question in terms of its content and validity. The literature was prospering if success were to be measured by quantity of output alone, for it did generate an extremely diverse set of empirical case studies. But its rich contribution in terms of empirical content has to be set against theoretical deficiencies and lack of firm analytical foundations.

As shown in Chapter 6, this situation has changed quite dramatically over the intervening period, if not through the resolution of the difficulties within the radical theory. Rather, it is mainstream neoclassical economics that has progressed, positively embracing a role for segmented labour markets. And, to a large extent, the more radical approach has set aside much of its traditional content and has compromised with, indeed has become subordinate to, the orthodoxy. This remarkable change has come about through the capacity of neoclassical economics, despite being based upon a particularly narrow form of methodological individualism, to develop a theory of market structures. Its apparent inability to do so previously had been the basis both for the support by others for critical alternatives as well as the orthodoxy's hostility to them.

By providing an explanation of how the aggregated behaviour of optimising individuals might give rise to socioeconomic structures within equilibrium, neoclassical orthodoxy has realised three significant accomplishments, certainly from the perspective of just a decade or two before.

First, it has broadened its own scope of analysis to incorporate structures and institutions on the basis of methodological individualism. Second, as argued elsewhere (Fine 1997a), new developments within mainstream neo-classical economics are bringing about a reversal of one of the fundamental features of the marginalist revolution of a century previously. At that time, the orthodoxy was established in part by retreating into the most peculiar methodology from the standpoint of other social sciences and which isolated it from them. Methodological individualism in the form of optimisation by individual economic agents has been at the core of neoclassical economics but, at most, on the margins of other social sciences. Consequently, despite its continuing emphasis on individual rationality, mainstream economics is now colonising the territory of the other social sciences rather than aban-doning them as barren or, in the vernacular as 'unscientific' or lacking 'rigour'. Third, then, other social science disciplines have been faced with an analytical challenge to which they have been forced to respond.

These more general shifts in economics' position within the social sciences, its thrust for hegemony over rather than apart from the others, has been no more prominent than in labour market theory, and especially prominent in segmented labour market theory. There has even been, as dis-cussed in Chapter 6, what has been described as a marriage between radical political economy and neoclassical orthodoxy. However much the former may claim to have transformed the latter, the marriage is undoubtedly an incorporation of a few structural insights into the orthodoxy and the casting aside of those methodological and theoretical elements offered by radical political economy that prove incompatible with the new orthodoxy.

This assessment is established in detail in Chapters 5 and 6, but it is also shown that much of the literature, even the majority, continues to occupy a position that straddles the various strands that have just been identified. Indeed, the Cambridge school of segmented labour market theory, one which can hardly be described as having embraced either methodological individualism or neoclassical economics, is identified as being the most developed and accomplished. Similarly, many sociological analyses have remained genuinely and consciously committed to the notion that socio-economic structures, agents and processes determine labour market out-comes. But, given their failure to progress theoretically and the continued reliance upon an ever-expanding mass of diverse case studies whose descrip-tive and empirical content barely conceals their conceptual limitations, the orthodoxy from within neoclassical economics has been able to push its own research programme forward with relatively little effective opposition.

This has not been simply a parallel manoeuvre with the initiative from within orthodox economics developing side by side with radical alternatives. Rather, at times insidiously and unnoticed, the latter have been tainted by the former's conceptual content. This is clearly revealed by the notion and theory of human capital. Twenty years previously, this concept would have been flatly rejected by radical social theory. Yet, today, it has become a standard item across the social sciences as well as within common discourse. Consequently, Chapter 3 is devoted to providing a timely reminder just how unacceptable is this now commonly accepted way of thinking, for it depends, however much it might be amended theoretically or empirically in particular contributions, upon two facile notions: on the one hand, it treats the individual capacity to work as something that is simply produced by the resources devoted to that purpose and, on the other, it treats the labour market as simply rewarding workers according to those capacities. This means that the socioeconomic relations by which labour markets are structured occupy at best a secondary position in the analysis, as divergences from the norm that would be ground out by a perfectly harmonious system of creating and rewarding human capital. This is made explicit in what is the standard, if bizarre, empirical procedure of correcting for human capital effects before examining the impact of other factors such as discrimination.

Chapters 2 and 4 which, along with the chapter on human capital, complete the first part of the book, contain a wide-ranging overview of the state of labour market analysis, if with an uneven and far from comprehensive coverage. Chapter 2 addresses macroeconomics and how it has evolved, focusing in particular upon the notion of there being a long-run natural rate of unemployment, around which there have been short-run variations. In this context, the discussion of macroeconomics is organised around three related themes. First, even from within the orthodoxy itself, the validity and usefulness of the notion of a natural rate is highly questionable. Second, it depends upon a division of factors into 'short-run' and 'long-run' determinants. This division is open to doubt in principle and is arbitrary in practice. Third, whilst macroeconomics is primarily concerned with the economic aggregates, it is pushed to disaggregate the economy. This is equally so for the labour market, whether dealing with the employed or the unemployed and whether in theory or empirical work.

This last theme is crucial throughout the book, for it necessarily points to an important and central conclusion – that labour markets are different from one another, not only in outcomes in the sense of rewards in the form of wages, conditions and careers, but also in the way in which they are structured and reproduced. There is no single labour market, although labour markets are intimately connected to one another, and no single generally applicable labour market theory. Whilst it is possible to identify appropriate abstract analytical principles, how they apply will differ across labour markets. This simple, even elementary, insight appears to have been implicitly rejected by the vast majority of the literature. This is especially so where a general theory of markets is applied to the putative labour market in particular. Even those attempts to differentiate labour from other markets, as discussed in Chapter 10, have often sought to do so on the basis of general principles which, on close inspection, prove not to have addressed labour markets specifically.

Once accepting that there are labour markets and that each is differentiated from the others in terms of structure and functioning, this still leaves open two questions. First, what are the appropriate analytical principles to be employed in addressing labour markets, especially if neoclassical economics is rejected in favour of an approach that emphasises socio-economic relations, processes and structures as a starting-point? Second, if such principles are unable to serve as the potential source of a general theory of labour markets, how are they to be applied in practice to delineate one labour market from another and to uncover the presence, distinctiveness and workings of particular labour markets?

Chapter 4 searches for answers to these questions by taking a critical look at other, mainly new, approaches to or studies of labour markets, covering industrial relations and some popular concepts that have emerged recently to straddle different disciplines. Broadly, three different analytical elements can be identified. First, as previously discussed, theory has increasingly been influenced, sometimes only implicitly, as in human capital theory, by dependence upon methodological individualism. This is true of the new, or newly used, organisational theory, but has a longer tradition within the economics literature on trade unions by treating the latter as if they were rational (individual) economic agents with well-defined objective functions – although this also opens up the potential, even if again on an individualistic basis, to explore how trade unions derive their objectives from the collected, not collective, motives of their members (and non-members).

Second, much labour market analysis has fallen back upon a descriptive, particularly an empirical, mode of study. This is not so much a case of 'so and so did this' and then 'this and that happened', as in older forms of institutional approaches to industrial relations, as an increasingly sophisticated statistical analysis of data-sets, especially those drawn from large data-sets, in which associations are found between various select variables. As such, there is little theoretical and methodological progress, but this does not mean that the work is entirely atheoretical. For the particular choice of variables to explore and the way in which the empirical relations between them are interpreted are the consequences of theoretical predispositions. But this is not itself conducive to analytical innovation nor to critical reflection, except on the basis of empirical refutation or confirmation. Perhaps the strongest representative of this treatment of labour markets is to be found in the Social Change and Economic Life Initiative (SCELI) research programme, some of whose results are considered in this chapter as well as elsewhere throughout the book.

The third broad approach to labour markets that has informed recent work is much more theoretically inventive, and has given a continuing momentum both to theoretical and empirical work. To be more explicit, social as well as labour market theory has been revived by use of concepts such as flexibility, post- or neo-Fordism, Japanisation and globalisation. In general, each of these concepts has a particular intellectual history.

First, an empirical anomaly, however widespread and however legitimate, is presumed to be identified relative to existing hegemonic and inflexible theory – as in the decline of, or counter-examples to, Fordist mass production, for example. Then, a new conceptualisation is developed to correspond to these empirical observations – as in flexible specialisation, to continue the example. Each of these approaches is then embodied in its own theory and evolves accordingly within more or less arbitrary and broad empirical and analytical frameworks – many recent developments in social theory in general and in labour market theory in particular have displayed a predilection for eclecticism, and especially for crude synthesis across different ideas and schools of thought. The next step in the evolution of each new analytical framework is that it is found to be applicable to a range of empirical studies including, not surprisingly, the ones that inspired it, but often overlooking those that do not comfortably correspond to its outlook. Finally, such modes of producing theory and interpreting evidence are subject to popularisation as well as to substantive criticism from a variety of perspectives, lending both legitimacy (it is subject to debate) and sophistication (it needs to develop and be refined in the light of the debate or to incorporate other factors) to the analytical enterprise.

Interestingly, then, labour market theory has proved relatively immune, like most academic endeavours with a strong component of mainstream economics, to the influence of postmodernism that has swept across the more interpretative disciplines and even the social sciences (and history) wherever, for example, cultural or ideological concerns come to the fore. For the 'harder' social sciences, such as economics, concerned with the material and empirical realities of labour markets, the descent (or ascent) into critical discourse theory has proved far from palatable, alien in effect. Although mildly influenced by, and borrowing terminology from, postmodernism in some approaches, as in notions of post-Fordism, recent developments within labour market analysis are marked by a general lack of critical conceptual reflection.

Instead, there have been three major influences over current labour market studies: first, colonisation by economics through methodological individualism, either by treating social agents as if they were optimising individuals or by treating optimising individuals as if they were the source of social structures; second, by relying upon organised descriptive analysis, whether as narrative or more or less sophisticated statistics, but drawing predominantly upon well-worn hypotheses; third, the highly inventive creation of abstract categories that are deemed to correspond to and address the most recent transformations in modern capitalism but which are themselves limited in terms of their clarity of theoretical definition, their scope of application beyond the empirical material that has inspired them and the analytical pertinence of the content with which they originated. Only the first and last of these compete actively over theoretical terrain, and it is hardly surprising that the steady march of methodological individualism should prevail over or, at least, progress side-by-side with, what is often a shifting and chaotic set of alternatives. Otherwise, the empirically based option offers secure if analytically unexciting opportunities.

Against this background, it is suggested in Chapter 4 that industrial relations is caught between offering descriptive analyses coupled with theoretical stagnation and being increasingly subordinated to the formalism and individualism of neoclassical economics. The new theory of industrial organisation and institutions, which adopts the labour market as a special case, has been much more subordinated to, and dependent upon, the colonisation of the new neoclassical orthodoxy. Theories of flexibility and globalisation have been innovative but do themselves vary too rapidly in analytical content to establish a firm theoretical or empirical foundation on their own terms, let alone one that is acceptable to the narrower and more conservative criteria of the orthodoxies which have increasingly drawn upon elements of methodological individualism, even if in heavy disguise.

From a critical review of existing literature, the more challenging and controversial aspect of this work is the theoretical alternative that it offers in response to the questions outlined above. This is to be found in the final chapter of Part III. Its location in the part of the book devoted to labour market segmentation is particularly appropriate as it reflects the previously mentioned analytical theme that persists throughout this volume. By drawing critically upon the literature reviews that have gone before, the following conclusions are drawn. First, the capitalist economy is fundamentally based upon a division between capital and labour, and the pursuit of surplus value (or profitability) which give rise to underlying economic laws, tendencies or forces whose complex resolutions or outcomes in turn give rise to a whole variety of economic structures which are open to reproduction and transformation. These include processes such as skilling and deskilling, rising capital-intensity and monopolisation. In addition, the pure division between capital and labour opens the way for and influences other labour market structures as in self-employment, 'unproductive' labour as for many state employees, 'sweated' employment, and professionals or functionaries for capital.

However, the (re-)creation of such separate labour markets and their distinct mode of functioning cannot be reduced to these abstract principles alone. Rather, there is dependence upon how these labour markets and the capital–labour relation are reproduced both within the economy (and not just in production) and within society more broadly. To address these influences, which have frequently been acknowledged in social theory previously, a much more exacting notion of the concept of the value of labour-power is developed and deployed. The analysis focuses on a number of different aspects.

First, the value of labour-power is examined in terms of its economic aspect – how much value is received in return for the capacity to work. However, this correct general definition of the value of labour-power has usually been developed no further. In particular, the value of labour-power has most often been conceived of as a quantity, bundle or vector of goods for which a given amount of labour-time is required to produce them – with surplus labour left over to make up the profit and other revenues attached to exploitation. This, however, is essentially an equilibrium concept. It takes no account of the dynamic content and intent of the concepts involved. In particular, as productivity increase is associated with the accumulation of capital, the labour-time required to produce commodities, including the putative wage bundle, is reduced.

This raises the age-old question, whether addressed in Marxist terms or otherwise, of who benefits from the increased net output associated with productivity increase. At one extreme, the value of labour-power remains the same, implying that labour is the sole beneficiary; at the other extreme, the wage bundle is unaltered with capital accruing all the gains. The outcome cannot be determined merely by posing the question, since it relates to the whole structure of economic processes and relations through which the productivity effect is created and incorporated. Moreover, these aspects will be uneven, both within and across different sectors of the economy, and this will prove an important element in the differentiation of the labour market into separate and separately functioning labour market structures.

Such primarily economic analysis needs to be complemented by a second aspect of the value of labour-power: the notion that the consumption bundle so provided suffices for social reproduction of the work-force. In the vast majority of the literature, this has rightly been seen as a corrective against economic reductionism – the work-force does not depend solely upon a wage but is engaged in activity outside the place of employment, thereby involving the state, the household and other social relations, structures and processes more generally. There is a further emphasis here, however, the role of consumption as a third aspect of the value of labour-power.

It is argued, first, drawing upon previous work, that the way in which various items enter into consumption differs from one item to another according to the whole chain of activities constituting and surrounding the path leading from production to consumption itself. Second, norms of consumption, as in the definition of the wage bundle, do not constitute some sort of average across the working class as a whole but are to be interpreted as varying systematically across different sections of the population, and hence the structured work-force, according to socioeconomic variables, such as age, income, occupation, etc. Third, then, there is a link between differentiation in consumption and differentiation, and hence structuring, within the labour market. Whilst this is readily recognised in case of income – labour market structures defined by differences in levels of remuneration – the approach offered here is more refined by differentiating consumption by separate sections of the work-force and by differentiating this aspect itself from one consumption good to another: housing standards differentiate the work-force, as do food habits and other items of consumption, but in ways that themselves are intimately and uniquely associated with these items of consumption.

Three aspects of the structuring of labour markets have now been identified by refining the notion of the value of labour-power – from the general economic laws of capitalism, and their negation by way of exception; from the social reproduction of the work-force; and from differentiation by consumption and consumption goods. How these all interact to give rise to specific labour market structures cannot be predetermined theoretically. Rather, labour market structures are defined historically by the creation and reproduction of definite socioeconomic structures in correspondence to the three aspects of the value of labour-power just identified. Only in this way is it possible to distinguish labour market structures, whether these be by sector, occupation or socioeconomic variable, as opposed to variation within a labour market structure. It is the integral nature of the way in which socioeconomic processes create a labour market structure and its mode of operation that are crucial. These are, as previously emphasised, necessarily various both within and without the confines of the labour market itself and the wages and conditions that it provides.

The final part of the book is concerned with policy issues but, once again, very much from the theoretical point of view around how labour markets function. One of these chapters is concerned with minimum wages and, drawing implicitly upon the arguments that have gone before, exposes the weaknesses of the conventional understanding of the relationship between wages and employment as either being one of more or less simple negative (the conventional view) or positive (the revisionist view) correlation. The other policy chapter addresses the issue of equal pay for work of equal value, or comparative worth, in the context of gender differences in wages. Once again, conventional views are critically assessed and, as for minimum wages, the analysis essentially revolves around an application as well as an affirmation of the earlier more general analysis. Significantly, each of these chapters was prepared in different form for a definite purpose – for the South African Presidential Labour Market Commission and as evidence for the UK National Union of Mineworkers (NUM) in pursuit of an equal pay claim. To some extent, these purposes have continued to influence the content and style of the arguments. But the arguments remain dependent upon, as well as helping to inform, the more abstract analysis that precedes them in the book. I hope that this demonstrates the practical significance of more abstract theory in general and of that offered here in particular.

The final chapter of the book serves as a summary, but it is organised around one particular theme. What is it that distinguishes labour from other markets? Addressing this issue is often the analytical goal claimed by many labour market theorists, although there is a strong tradition within neoclassical economics that is committed to treating labour like any other asset or factor endowment. For those with a more catholic, some would say more realistic, approach, the labour market is not the same as any other market, because of the various uniquely human attributes of those engaging on both sides of the market, with the focus being primarily on the labour side, although greater if not equal emphasis is now being placed on the management side in terms of business organisations, human resource development and various principal–agent problems in the context of less than perfect information.

In the final chapter it is shown that many of these attempts to develop a distinct theory of the labour market fail, not because they do not distinguish labour, or labour-power, from other commodities by the active role that the labourer plays as a human agent, but rather because there has been insufficient attention given to the nature of the market itself or the commodity system. Quite clearly, there is no problem distinguishing work and wage from an orange or a banana and their prices – nor, indeed, the latter two from one another. So, the distinctiveness of labour within labour market theory must arise out of how the market is understood and how the market translates into real effects differences in the nature of the commodities that are bought and sold.

Generally, the market is seen as a social institution coordinating transactions with greater or lesser success and efficiency. But what exactly is coordinated? The answer is not to be found in the difference between human attributes and those of fruits, but in the socioeconomic relations that are expressed through the market. In addressing the issue of the specificity of labour markets in this way, attention is drawn once again to the fundamental schism between capital and labour, to the need to address the relationship between economic processes, structures and agents, and the dependence of the labour market on differently structured and functioning labour markets.

Throughout the book, the use of statistics and of statistical methods is avoided as far as possible. There are no tables of data nor regressions. But empirical issues are not set aside, for a number of reasons. First, much of the theory is itself inspired by empirical and policy questions: What is the natural rate of unemployment? How many labour market segments are there? Why do wage differentials persist, what would be the effect of a minimum wage or equal pay legislation, etc? The substance of much of the theory that has been used to address these questions is understood much better, possibly is only understandable, when set against the empirical or statistical issues that have motivated it. For example, theories based on the notion of a natural rate of unemployment were faced with the problem of explaining how, in the light of such an equilibrium concept, the actual rate of unemployment could have grown so much.

Second, although this is not the primary objective, some attention is given to the theory of labour markets in the history of economic thought, and why the latter has developed in the way that it has. To some extent, not surprisingly, the theory has been responsive to economic events and the empirical interpretation of them. Consequently, in order to chart as well as to explain the theory's evolution, reference has to be made to empirical developments. Thus, one of the factors behind the emergence of dual labour market theory was the explosion of riots in the black urban ghettos of the United States. This certainly had an effect on how the theory was formulated initially, even if the continuing influence is questionable. Yet, it is natural to wonder to what extent a theory derived in this context, however valid on its own terrain, would be generalisable to other circumstances.

Third, in order both to illustrate the arguments and to clarify the exposition, use will occasionally be made of particular examples, although, as in the other uses of empirical material, the analysis will not be pursued in any depth. Rather, broad reference will be made *inter alia* to different sectors of the economy, to the gender division of labour, the impact of trade unions, as these will prompt consideration of different factors and raise different theoretical issues in the functioning of labour markets.

Despite the absence of direct treatment of empirical issues, however, it is intended that the book should prove of considerable use to those engaged in applied analysis of labour markets for two reasons. First, as observed above, there is one strand within labour market analysis which is increasingly reliant upon empirical studies of one sort or another. I hope that the insights offered here will allow these contributions and contributors to rely upon and set their work within more considered theoretical propositions and hold back, or even reverse, the tide of methodological individualism and 'new wave' *ad hoc* theory.

Second, as has been argued, empirical studies are the way forward in prompting theoretical contributions in the analysis of labour markets precisely because of differentiation in the structuring and functioning of labour markets. There may be those who share my misgivings about the theoretical direction of labour market studies and who 'degenerate' into empirical work by default, waiting and hoping for an alternative theory within which to work or to set their applied work. According to the arguments here, whilst there is a place for abstract theory, it cannot legitimately be grounded in the study of labour markets or of a particular labour market without developing the theory in conjunction with the specifics of the labour market concerned. Labour market theory cannot be picked off the shelf and applied; it must respond and correspond to the specific combination of socioeconomic relations, processes, structures and agents through which the market coordinates the underlying relationship between capital and labour. It is ever both a theoretical and an empirical task.

Part II

Critical assessments

The purpose of Part II is to review the standard literature on how labour markets function. In this, as in much socioeconomic theory concerned with other issues, there is a tension between macro-level and micro-level approaches. This serves as a useful context within which to begin to approach the material covered here.

Chapter 2, for example, is concerned with the macroeconomics of labour markets. It examines how the Keynesian revolution established a macro-level analysis for determining the levels of employment and unemployment. Aggregate effective demand, the consumption function and the liquidity trap were all conceptually pitched at the systemic level. However, no sooner was the Keynesian analysis established than it became targeted for a range of interpretations that sought to reconstruct it on micro-foundations, primarily at the expense of its macro-level content other than the latter being treated as the aggregated market-coordinated outcomes of the stylised behaviour of individual economic agents. Systemic analysis is increasingly discarded. Unemployment is explained by imperfections in the availability of information, in the competitiveness of markets or in the failure of prices to adjust fast enough to clear what would otherwise be temporary imbalances between supply and demand. The macro-economy is simply the more or less efficient coordination through the market of optimising, representative individuals, one of whom stands for households, another for firms. Micro-foundations, and its inherited analytical baggage and techniques, imply that methodological individualism rides roughshod over truly macroeconomic analysis – that involving the systemic impact of productivity increase, monopolisation or class conflict between capital and labour other than as a pricing or contracting relation on the basis of imperfect information.

In this vein, three different approaches can be delineated within mainstream macroeconomics. The first two are entirely confined to micro-foundations. One seeks to explain fluctuations in aggregate economic activity, and hence employment, on the basis of markets that work perfectly and harmoniously. Problems arise merely out of what are termed 'exogenous shocks' or from informational uncertainties. Real business cycle theory, for example, argues that when productivity increases faster than usual, wages are correspondingly higher and workers are more willing to enter the labour market. When productivity is sluggish, however, some workers will become voluntarily unemployed. The second approach emphasizes how market and informational imperfections can lead to the persistence of involuntary unemployment – unable to monitor their work performance perfectly, for example, employers might hold wages above the market-clearing level in order to induce workers to sustain work effort as in efficiency-wage models.

The third approach is more eclectic, appealing both to micro-level and macro-level analysis without necessarily combining them consistently. This is characteristic of the literature around the non-accelerating inflation rate of unemployment (NAIRU), and also structuralist or post-Keynesian models which appeal, for example, to the role of distributional conflict between profits and wages and monopolisation as well as at times to the optimising behaviour of individual economic agents.

Whatever their differences, these three approaches are all oriented around equilibrium defined by the long run and around which short-run deviations occur. This allows for a whole range of variables to be set aside as belonging to the long run, especially those involving institutions and technical change, for example. But there must be doubts about such a division of variables between the short and long runs as well as the notion of the long run as equilibrium itself. This is especially so for the labour market where unemployment persists and at distinctly higher levels between different periods. At best, such blatant empirical refutations of equilibrium as an organising concept have been addressed by reference to hysteresis, the notion that particular levels of unemployment tend to persist once established. Essentially, however, this is merely a technical device that enables persistently high levels to be explained empirically, like any other statistical time series that is treated as path-dependent. Specific understanding of the labour market itself in these terms remains limited, although hypotheses can be postulated about the unwillingness or inability of the long-term unemployed to work and of employers to hire them.

If macroeconomic treatments of labour markets have become increasingly tied to micro-foundations, the mirror-image of this process is to be found in the case of human capital theory, the subject of Chapter 3. Human capital theory was initially formulated to explain why individual labour market rewards should differ despite or even because of the perfect working of (labour) markets. To explain why the more skilled are paid more, and by how much, it is necessary at least in principle to correct for, or incorporate, all other causal factors in the labour market analysis. Consequently, human capital has become a standard component of labour market analysis, standing alongside other variables, such as class or sex, even though these are in conflict with the individualistic foundations of neoclassical economics. Whilst the economics of education to which human capital theory is attached has increasingly addressed the twin issues of how skills are provided and how they are rewarded, its capacity to do so adequately is always circumscribed when reduced to the measurement of human capital and its rate of return as if it were a physical asset.

Chapter 4 covers material more like that of Chapter 2 addressing systemic or macro factors. It addresses two apparently unconnected branches of the literature – that concerned with flexibility and that with (non-market) institutions. But the two subject-matters do have something in common – each is an analytical response to the recognition that the market necessarily interacts with non-market factors. The market does not exist in a vacuum. The flexibility literature has arisen out of the empirically inspired suspicion that non-market factors were being driven out by market forces, signalling the end of the Fordist, Keynesian and/or welfarist post-war boom. As such, it has spawned both a descriptive literature with limited theoretical content and grand theory in the attempt to define and examine flexibility.

On the one hand, is the labour market becoming more flexible and, if so, how? What are the institutions that affect the functioning of labour markets, why do they emerge, and with what effects? For each of these issues there is a vibrant research programme. But, taken together, they constitute an incoherent amalgam of theoretical and empirical insights. Descriptive accounts of flexibility, whatever their general validity, induce corresponding conceptual innovation of limited analytical depth by reference, for example, to casualisation, subcontracting, marginalisation, etc. Or, on the other hand, traversing in the opposite direction to descriptive narrative, grand theoretical schemes around modes of regulation, globalisation, etc. are perceived to locate flexibility as part of a new phase of capitalism. This, as will be shown, is more ambitious but little more successful in advancing our theoretical let alone our empirical knowledge.

In contrast to the flexibility literature, which tends to accept the decline of the non-market, the institutional literature bases itself on the necessity of a division between market and non-market institutions and an equilibrium or even an evolving relationship between the two. In this respect, it is the *alter ego* of flexibility analysis. The latter, prompted by contemporary empirical developments, sets itself the task of identifying the extent and consequences of the triumph of the market. Institutional theory, drawing upon long-standing empirical knowledge of the presence of large-scale corporate firms and other institutions, emphasises the irreducible presence of the non-market. Trends to flexibility, if valid in practice, cannot be absolute.

Thus, in institutional analysis, it is recognised that the market does not and cannot exhaust nor stand for the full range of socioeconomic relations. This opens up two issues: How are the inadequacies of the market made up for by the emergence and evolution of other institutional forms? How does the market evolve and function in the context of pre-existing non-market institutions? In face of this simultaneity, the literature has run from pillar to post, like a dog chasing its own tail in ever-widening circles. On the one hand, answers are sought through tracing the emergence of institutions through time. On the other hand, an ever-expanding range of factors, such as law, custom, ideology, culture, etc., is perceived to be important. The strengths and weaknesses of this literature derive from the same source. It correctly recognises that the market cannot exist in a vacuum and, consequently, must be analysed in conjunction with its non-market complements. Yet, this involves theoretically privileging the market, whether for labour or more generally, by constructing an analytical framework on the basis of market and non-market (or non-market alone in 'pre-history', as it were), rather than examining whether the market itself differs, as in Marxist theory, from one mode of *production* to another. Only regulation theory, initiated by Aglietta (1979) began to broach such considerations. But it has abandoned the project by increasingly embracing a theoretical eclecticism that tends to mirror the empirical developments that it identifies, however correctly, and seeks to explain. Unless labour market studies can successfully fill the lacunae in theoretical and empirical studies, and the interaction between them, then its fate will be to be swamped by mainstream neoclassical labour economics, with its optimising agents and econometric number-crunching. As is shown for the discipline of industrial relations, the process is already well advanced!

Although, especially in the detail of the exposition and critical assessment, there are many different conclusions to be drawn from this Part of the book, two in particular are central to what follows. The first is to suggest that, whilst there is considerable innovation in labour market theory, which is thriving as never before, this represents a highly misleading intellectual prosperity. For, despite its range and sophistication, each theoretical fragment is often flawed by reference to broader questions – the relationship between long and short runs, between micro and macro, with the empirical evidence, etc. Moreover, taken together, whilst often highlighting particular aspects of labour markets, these theoretical fragments are incompatible with one another. It is as if mix-and-match in labour market theory has created the most horrendously unacceptable plaid designs. Just contemplate whether the separate broad areas covered here are compatible with one another – macroeconomics, human capital, and flexibility and institutions. Whatever the answer in principle, the answer in practice is one of negligible overlap between these areas of study. Each tends to take the others as given in order to be able to proceed.

The second conclusion is to reject the possibility of a general and an aggregate theory of labour markets. It is wrong to consider that the labour market as a whole and individual labour markets function in the same way. There are not only different labour markets but each is structured and is reproduced differently. This view is supported by a close examination of the literature from this perspective. For, whether dealing in the micro-foundations of macro (and the imperfections of markets, information, and competition), the provision of, and rewards to, human capital, or the forms and incidence of flexibility and institutions, how these factors interact with one another is highly diverse.

These two conclusions can be considered to be confirmed unconsciously by the studies from SCELI (Anderson *et al.* 1994; Gallie *et al.* 1994; Gallie *et al.* 1996; Penn *et al.* 1994b; Rubery and Wilkinson 1994; Scott 1994a).[1] The SCELI research was based on surveys in six different local labour markets between 1986 and 1987, initially covered around 1,000 individuals in each location, including information on experiences of employment and unemployment, attitudes to work, and household strategies and activities. In addition, surveys were undertaken of local employers. Consequently, the research programme was provided with a sound empirical basis from which to explore the dynamics and structures of labour markets.

For the gendering of labour markets, as addressed by Scott (1994a), the following multiplicity of factors emerge as important: attitudes, skills, work experience, class, marital and life-cycle status, public and private and part-time and full-time employment, interaction with domestic roles, and geographical mobility. Sloane (1994) uses an augmented (i.e., throw in as many variables as possible) Mincer equation to measure returns to human capital and residual discrimination. He concludes:

> We can divide the explanatory variables . . . into four groups – personal characteristics (education, experience, father's socio-economic group), job variables (training, shiftwork, merit payments, and job security), establishment and industry variables (whether union member, white-collar employee, engaged in the public sector and size of establishment), and location . . . The reasons then for the lower pay of women relative to men are multifarious.
>
> (Sloane 1994: 198)

Such conclusions are reinforced by more qualitative sectoral studies for retailing, finance and textiles – Scott (1994c), Crompton and Sanderson (1994) and Penn *et al.* (1994a), respectively. Not surprisingly, Scott (1994b: 33) is forced to the confession, 'there is no SCELI theory of gender segregation as yet'.

Rubery and Wilkinson (1994) focus on employers' strategies ranging over the formation and response to internal and external labour markets, flexibility, skills, gender, and industrial relations more generally, and interaction with product markets. Rubery concludes:

> at theoretical and empirical levels . . . a more integrated approach to the analysis of labour markets is needed than that which juxtaposes the internal to the external, the bureaucratic to the spot market, the core, to the periphery or the primary to the secondary.
>
> (Rubery 1994: 66)

Yet, surely, for this long list of attributes to be combined along with others, there can be no prospect of a *general* theory appropriate to the variety of labour markets and labour market factors?

Skills and their consequences are the subject of Penn *et al.* (1994b). There are processes of deskilling, enskilling and reskilling. Gender differences are crucial, as are the distinctions between full- and part-time work. The changing composition of the work-force, with the rise of services and computerisation, is important. The relative weakness in theoretical advance, and its direct ties to empirical findings, is illustrated by the approach of Penn *et al.*, even if, to be fair, the quotation is torn from its context: 'The revised theory also argued that *some* production skills were increasing whilst *some* were decreasing and many other production skills remained more or less constant' (Penn *et al.* 1994c: 134; emphasis in original). The variability in outcome depends upon the form taken by technological innovation and whether it is full- or semi-automation.

Gallie *et al.* (1994) are concerned with unemployment, but much more with the consequences than with the causes and, specifically, whether the unemployed constitute an underclass and, if so, whether they are responsible for their own fate. The underclass thesis is rejected, especially in so far as it suggests that the unemployed are increasingly unemployable as a consequence of the support they receive from the welfare state. However, the evidence that, once removed from employment, the unemployed experience recurrent difficulties through the welfare system, the household, their work histories, and psychologically, also suggests that these factors are of importance for the employed even if in varied ways. This is addressed in the context of household arrangements by Anderson *et al.* (1994). The main theoretical hypothesis is put forward by Gershuny *et al.* (1994) with the idea that the revolution in domestic labour lags with considerable inertia behind that required by the increasing participation of women in the labour market. Necessarily, however, outcomes will be highly differentiated, given an analytical structure, as in the diagrammatical form provided by Gershuny *et al.* (1994: 186), which includes the following variables in the inter-generational transmission of behaviourial norms: socialisation, domestic division of labour, employment experience and public policy.

Finally, the study by Gallie *et al.* (1996) of the role of trade unions reinforces conclusions concerning the multiplicity and heterogeneity of factors and effects in and around the labour market. Variables include full- and part-time working, size distribution of establishments, technical change and work practices, unemployment (especially in local labour markets), product competition, public or private sector, legislative framework, etc.

In short, the SCELI studies support the propositions that the variables that affect the labour market are multifarious and derived from economic and non-economic factors, and that labour markets are liable to function differently according to which factors are significant and how they interact with one another. Traditionally, such conclusions have been pursued further in the context of segmented labour market theory. Consequently, this is the object of Part III of the book.

NOTE

1 For use of the SCELI surveys to study the characteristics of low-paid women in Britain, see Dex *et al.* (1994).

2   The macroeconomics of labour markets

1 INTRODUCTION

The purpose of this chapter is to review the understanding of labour markets that arises out of macroeconomic theory. It has been difficult to write, predominantly because of the varying background knowledge of the potential readership. For economists, there will be yawning familiarity with much of the technical material that is covered, and its corresponding jargon – IS/LM, efficiency-wages, rational expectations, etc.[1] For this reason, accounts of the details of such concepts and the models in which they are embedded will be kept to a minimum, and a certain familiarity with them will be assumed. Those interested in acquiring greater familiarity can consult the standard texts. On the other hand, familiarity with such concepts has not bred contempt, only uncritical use. Much more attention here, then, is devoted throughout to revealing the weakness of macroeconomic theory in general and its treatment of labour markets in particular. As a result, this is the most specialised and advanced chapter in the book with regard to the economics content.

It is shown that, despite considerable ingenuity and change in analytical content, macroeconomics has remained riddled with inadequacies that are transparent to those who are prepared to look. For those inadequacies can be and have been revealed even on the theory's own terms or within its own methodologies. Consequently, the critical account offered here is based in large part upon reference to the work of those, relatively few in number, who have been prepared to engage in more circumspect assessment of the standard material. Necessarily, an account of this sort does depend upon the use of the standard terminology and concepts. These may be particularly mystifying to those studying labour markets from the vantage-point of other disciplines. However, the central message that is being delivered here is that the technical and statistical wizardry of macroeconomics, intimidating in itself, is based upon the most nebulous of analytical foundations if, indeed, there are any foundations at all that are able to stand up even to the most cursory critical scrutiny. Those willing to challenge the theory from a more radical methodology than its own, even one which would be far from radical within other social sciences, can point to the following fundamental features: its methodological individualism (i.e., that the economy is seen as being made up of the aggregated behaviour of otherwise atomised individuals); its dependence upon equilibrium as an organising concept; the artificial division between the short and the long run; and the equally sharp and artificial division between exogenous and endogenous factors.

These issues are taken up in the concluding remarks, together with the argument that a macroeconomics of labour markets, certainly as conceived by orthodox economics, is a false objective, since labour markets are too heterogeneous to be lumped together for the purpose of a common treatment. This is a major theme to be taken up in the remainder of the book. The review of macroeconomics offered here suggests that this conclusion might be accepted readily, for recent theoretical developments provide support for the view that labour markets function in a variety of different ways from one another – although particular ideal types are often taken as representative of the economy as a whole. But, even if to insist upon the heterogeneity of labour markets is to push against an open door, it remains important to have a clear idea of the chamber we are leaving behind in entering and occupying new analytical space. The intellectual dynamic by which macroeconomics is now accommodating labour market theory is far from satisfactory, even if it is more varied in what will be seen to be a microeconomic eclecticism.

The next section begins, then, by suggesting that there is a trend characterising the evolution of macroeconomics, comprising three elements – the increasing use of general equilibrium, of micro-foundations, and of competitive, informational and market imperfections. Rather than then following a chronology of macroeconomic theory from its origins with Keynes's contribution in the 1930s, attentions shifts forward to the New Classical Economics (NCE) of the 1970s. This is because the NCE represents an extreme and decisive moment in the development of macroeconomic theory, one which sheds considerable light on what went before and what was to follow. Unfortunately, this means that the earlier macroeconomic theory, to which the NCE was in part a response, has to be taken for granted to some extent, even though it is itself discussed in later sections.

This breach in a chronological account of macroeconomic theory is justified in view of the assessment made of the NCE. It is argued that, far from heralding a (supermonetarist) revolution in macroeconomic thought under the banner of rational expectations, it has inspired an interim period of transition within macroeconomic theory in which the role of methodological individualism has become consolidated. The following sections chart that transition and examine the connections between the neoclassical synthesis (IS/LM framework), the reappraisal of Keynes (quantity-constrained, fixed-price models), the vertical Phillips curve (lower unemployment than the natural rate only at the expense of ever-accelerating inflation), and the most recent understandings of the natural rate of unemployment and its dependence upon hysteresis. In a detailed discussion of NAIRU, the rationale for these approaches is found to be entirely spurious.

2 SHIFTING THEORETICAL EMPHASES

The theory of aggregate employment and unemployment has formed a central part of macroeconomics. Consequently, macroeconomic theory offers particular ways of understanding how labour markets work both in and of themselves and through their interaction with other macroeconomic markets and variables. However, macroeconomics has itself evolved continuously since the Keynesian revolution which sought to establish that unemployment could result from deficient aggregate effective demand for goods, whether this be due to excessive saving (as in the simple multiplier model) or to excessive demand for liquidity as in standard IS/LM representations of the Keynesian system and the liquidity trap.

Broadly, three separate influences can be identified as having informed the content of this evolution of macroeconomic theory.[2] The first has been to tie the theory more consistently to what can be termed 'general equilibrium considerations'.[3] This itself has had two components. On the one hand, because macroeconomics is concerned with the functioning of the economy as a whole, it follows that there must be overall consistency between the markets that are incorporated into the theory. In the simplest terms, any purchase (or intended purchase) must be matched by a corresponding sale. This facile observation has not, however, always been honoured, especially with the arbitrary bundling together of what are presumed to be a number of separate, if interactive, macroeconomic relations. Decisions to save, spend or hold money are interdependent. Consequently, saving, consumption and demand for money functions should not be constructed independently of one another as macroeconomic aggregates, as they have often been. By the same token, it has been standard in the past for a government's economic interventions to be insufficiently and inadequately addressed from a general equilibrium perspective. If a government taxes, for example, it must do something with the revenue; it is not simply deflationary. A balance of payments deficit is not simply indicative of being out of equilibrium nor is it simply a running down of central bank reserves; it has implications for the movement of capital and for changes in debt repayments, and so on.

These general equilibrium considerations, some of which take the simple form of accounting identities, have been prominent in the design of macroeconomic policies, especially for those developing countries going through stabilisation and needing to cover so-called 'gaps' in budget deficits, balance of payments or between savings and investments. To a large extent, as identities, these aspects are independent of the theoretical content with which they are endowed, even if, in practice, it has often been conservative and deflationary.[4] Even so, such accounting identities are not entirely analytically neutral, despite being tautologous within their own frame of reference, for, they do incorporate a particular *structural* understanding of the economy depending on how the latter is disaggregated into the separate components that are added together to form the identities.[5] In addition, they necessarily suppose that certain variables are contemporaneous with one another, since they have to be added together at one and the same time.[6] Thus, the use of general equilibrium identities in macroeconomic theory presupposes assumptions about both structuring and sequencing between variables. Such issues are of paramount importance, but they tend to be overlooked as conventional wisdom in model building becoming stand-ardised and adopted unquestioningly.

Although these issues will be taken up later in the specific context of the relationship between the short run and the long run, of more direct concern to the workings of the labour market from the perspective of general equilib-rium considerations is what has been termed the 'micro-foundations' of macroeconomics. For a given structure or disaggregation of the economy into its separate constituent components, each of these is analysed in terms of the aggregated behaviour of the individual economic agents con-cerned, usually firms and households – although the government and trade unions can also be involved as special 'individuals'. In this way, macroeconomics becomes based on methodological individualism, usually as a consequence of optimising behaviour to a greater or lesser degree. Macroeconomic relations that are independent of such aggregated indi-vidual behaviour are eschewed, and the distinction between micro and macro is blurred or, more precisely, the macro is reduced to aggregated micro.

A second influence upon macroeconomic theory has been to incorporate different assumptions around competitiveness. Whether in the labour market itself or in product markets, different models are generated depend-ing upon how price–output (or wage–employment) decisions are made and upon the competitive environment within which those decisions are made. If, for example, every product market is assumed to be a monopoly, there is a presumption that the price level will be higher and the output level (and employment) lower than for more competitive conditions. Similarly, a trade union can have the effect of forcing up wages for those in employ-ment but forcing down the number of employees. Of course, what is true for an individual sector might be replicated across the economy as a whole, but it might not be so, depending upon what happens to prices and overall aggregate demand.

How markets respond to being out of equilibrium has been a third factor in the development of macroeconomics. If there is an excess of supply over demand (or vice versa), how fast does the price adjust down (up) to clear the market? If there is instantaneous, or infinitely fast, market-clearing across all sectors, then the economy will always be in equilibrium (should it exist and be stable). Otherwise, it is possible for some markets to adjust infinitely fast and for others to be stickier in their pace of adjustment. Labour markets are often presumed to adjust slowly, for a variety of reasons, whereas money markets, with a large number of dealers benefiting from ease of transactions and rapidly available information, are perceived to clear instantly – especially foreign exchange markets, for example.

The fourth feature of macroeconomic theory has concerned the treatment of information. Who has what information and how is it used? Workers, for example, may have better information than employers about their own abilities and how intensively they are using them. This has an impact on the making and monitoring of labour market contracts. On a rather different tack, economic agents need to employ the information they do possess in order to come to decisions through the expectations they form of the future course of economic events. In particular, how do they form expectations of future prices and how do they use such expectations? As is well known, the last 20 years has witnessed the rise of rational expectations in place of adaptive expectations. Economic agents are now presumed to use information optimally by forming their own consistent model of the economy rather than adopting some behavioural rule based on the extent to which expectations have been right or wrong in the past.

Different macroeconomic models will put these different features together in different ways: how the economy is constructed as a general equilibrium, which competitive conditions are assumed within each market, what micro- as opposed to macro-foundations are provided, how the various markets do or do not clear, and how informational considerations are deployed including the formation of expectations. The character of each specific model will depend upon how these issues are treated and, equally important, how they interact with one another.

From a logical point of view, certainly in retrospect, there is no reason why one sort of model, or one particular stance on the issues outlined, should prevail at any particular time. But the evolution of macroeconomics has a definite history, even if it cannot be reasonably deduced from a logic of forward progress, as some might suggest. There has been a tendency for general equilibrium to become more prominent, and for competitiveness, market-clearing, and informational considerations to be taken more explicitly into account.

3 RATIONAL EXPECTATIONS AND NEW CLASSICAL ECONOMICS: REVOLUTION OR INTERREGNUM?

The determinants of the evolution of macroeconomics as a subdiscipline of economics are complex. First, economic theory does respond to the pressure of external events. By this is not meant the ideal way suggested by the use of econometrics to test theories for rejection, for it is questionable whether this procedure is systematically pursued in practice, despite the growing preponderance of econometric studies. It is, in any case, generally possible for the given theory and/or testing procedures to be amended sufficiently to avoid such a fate. However, the stagflation of the 1970s was sufficiently dramatic that the then Keynesian analysis became untenable since it required that rising unemployment and inflation be mutually incompatible. By the same token, the Phillips curve, suggesting a trade-off between unemployment and inflation, could not survive in its traditional form.

There had to be a change in macroeconomic theory, but it was by no means predetermined that it should have taken the direction that it did, even if, in retrospect, the swing seemed inevitable to what has loosely been termed 'monetarism' in popular parlance.[7] Undoubtedly, the depth of the recession as well as the rise of deeply conservative politics and ideology, Reaganomics and Thatcherism, had a profound influence.[8] But radical economics had previously been strong and could have strengthened further as a counterbalance to the orthodoxy or even spawned heterodoxy, as has happened in other disciplines, in response to reactionary times. Irrespective of the extent to which the left has remained strong in other disciplines, what marks out economics is the increasing stranglehold taken by the orthodoxy and its underlying analytical principles.

The lack of critical reconstruction in economics, even in response to critical economic circumstances, is possibly due to three closely related and mutually reinforcing reasons. First, the technical requirements of economics, both for students and researchers, were already formidable, certainly by comparison with other social sciences. Exercising these skills within a given orthodoxy has proven to be more attractive than questioning conceptual and explanatory content more critically.

Second, despite the emergence of radical political economy in the 1960s, the mainstream within economics has always been dominant in a way that necessarily precludes alternatives. Paradoxically, this is a consequence of its logical weaknesses, in terms of dependence upon restrictive assumptions around given preferences, endowments and technology as well as the focus on equilibrium as an organising concept, even in the context of economic crisis and chronic recession. Precisely because of its vulnerability to almost any breach of its standard assumptions, mainstream economics has always been particularly limited in the analytical scope of its competing schools of thought. Even the long-standing and shifting dispute between monetarism and Keynesianism has always been more a matter of emphasis than fundamental theoretical differences.[9] In short, mainstream economics cannot allow other alternatives to flourish and be confident itself of surviving the experience.

Third, orthodox macroeconomics found a way of turning the economic crisis, and its own disarray, to its advantage. This was done by incorporating expectations into existing models. The coexistence of increasing unemployment and inflation could be explained, where previously there had only been a trade-off, as in the Phillips curve, by the use of self-fulfilling expectations. Initially, this took the simple, adaptive form of explaining expectations of the future price level in terms of existing inflation – in effect, explaining inflation by inflation even if indirectly through expectations. As a consequence, however, the way was opened up for more sophisticated theories, not of inflation as such, but of the way in which expectations are formed. The rational expectations revolution, which is a theory of the optimal use of available information – economic agents are assumed to model the economy correctly within the bounds of statistical variation rather than make guesses by extrapolation – allowed the whole of macroeconomics to be rewritten by incorporating a new technique for forming so-called rational expectations, not only in the model but also by the agents within the model. This ratcheted up the technical sophistication required in terms of the mathematics of the modelling involved, and it drew upon and solicited advances in econometrics and statistical techniques which were only possible for the economics profession as a whole in the wake of the PC revolution in computing power. In conjunction with this advance in the 'means of production of knowledge', rational expectations allowed both standard theoretical and empirical methods of enquiry to blossom.

The rational expectations revolution was initially associated with what came to be termed the NCE. Previously, as popularised by Milton Friedman, the vertical Phillips curve had suggested that unemployment could be reduced by reflationary policy, but only at the expense of ever-accelerating inflation. This result, however, depended upon the assumption of adaptive expectations which implied that economic agents systematically underestimated the actual turnout for the level of inflation within the model. Basically, because prices and wages are being underestimated, certain economic agents consider themselves to be better off than they actually are, and this boosts the overall level of economic activity and employment. But inflationary pressures are continuously sustained as the price level is forever underanticipated.

The premise of incorrect forecasts proved the point of entry for the NCE. Rational expectations would not allow economic agents to make incorrect forecasts indefinitely. Correctly anticipating inflation, subject to random variation, would eliminate any effect on the overall unemployment level, even with accelerating inflation. Even Friedman had proved too Keynesian, as it were, in suggesting that government expansionary policy could positively moderate the level of unemployment, although he would deplore the debasement of the currency involved through ever-accelerating inflation. The NCE, the first to be armed with rational expectations, was able to make a number of other apparently devastating critiques – concerning the complete ineffectiveness of systematic government policy (because it is neutralised by anticipation of its inevitable consequences) and the inadequacy of previous macro models for use in policy-making in view of their failure to take into account the economic agents' anticipation of their effects.

Despite its being first in promoting rational expectations and despite, at least to begin with, the heavy association of NCE with rational expectations, it was soon realised that the highly unpalatable and special results, from the perspective of those who wished to see a role for government intervention, had nothing as such to do with rational expectations. Rather, it is the assumption of instantaneous market-clearing across all markets that is crucial to the *laissez-faire* policy stance of the NCE. More conventional results concerning the potential role and impact of state economic intervention in macro policy were restored once rational expectations were used in conjunction with assumptions other than those of perfectly working markets, which had always been the bread and butter of the Keynesian perspective.

In this light, NCE can be seen as a remarkable interlude in the evolution of macroeconomics. It gave a new lease of life to the subject both by incorporating rational expectations and by opening the way for more sophisticated use of mathematical and statistical techniques.[10] NCE can be seen in retrospect to have turned out to be a shock which knocked macroeconomics away from considering any radical alternative. It has also continued to influence the subsequent evolution of the subject-matter, even if by way of departure. Initially, much attention was devoted to displacing the classical results in the presence of rational expectations but in the absence of perfect markets. Subsequently, with a vibrant research programme in place, previous developments within the field could be resumed, but now around imperfect competition, market-clearing and information within a general equilibrium framework which, equilibrium apart, had been notably absent from NCE.

4 THE NEOCLASSICAL SYNTHESIS

To a large extent, the discussion of the rational expectations revolution has inappropriately preceded earlier developments within the discipline for which there were other definite staging posts. In the post-war period, the IS/LM framework has dominated both the understanding and teaching of Keynesian economics, even if it has fallen into disuse recently on the frontiers of macroeconomic research. In orthodox terminology, the IS/LM system has been known as the neoclassical synthesis, and it is worth examining why this is so.[11]

First, in general, it is a synthesis between pre-Keynesian notions of the workings of the aggregate economy and the insights offered by Keynes. In particular, the focus is upon how persistent unemployment is to be explained. From within the IS/LM framework, three potential reasons emerge: either the IS curve is vertical so that investment is interest-inelastic (this is the simple multiplier model in which investment is given exogenously and does not increase even when the cost of investment falls as it does with a falling rate of interest), or wages and prices will not adjust downwards despite unemployed workers and unsold goods (this prevents the effect of the LM curve shifting to the right, as if there were a reflationary increase in the money supply). Finally, the LM curve may be horizontal, the so-called liquidity trap, so that shifts in the LM curve have no effect on the rate of interest and the inducement to invest. The extra effective liquidity generated by falling prices is held as real balances rather than used to generate effective demand through spending. Whilst the rate of interest needs to fall to restore full employment equilibrium, it does not do so since investors are holding on to cash in anticipation that the rate of interest will rise in the future.

Second, according to the synthesis, Keynes justifiably claimed to have made an innovation by introducing the money market more centrally into macroeconomics. This involves the replacement of Say's Law of Markets by Walras's Law. According to the former, it is impossible to have a general glut or excess supply of all commodities, since this would signify in aggregate that more goods were being supplied than were being demanded. This would be inconsistent with the aggregate intentions of economic agents, who would plan a demand in correspondence with any planned supply. Whilst there might be mismatches between supplies and demands in particular sectors, excess supply over demand could not prevail in aggregate over all simultaneously. This argument falls under Walras's Law, however, since this extends the consideration of aggregate market supply and demand to include the money market as well as commodities. As a result, there can be an excess supply of all commodities, a general glut, if it is matched by an equal and opposite excess demand for money – precisely the situation suggested by the liquidity trap.

Third, whilst Keynes can be credited with having discovered a monetary mechanism for generating unemployment, his claim for a more general theory is invalid. Indeed, he has offered a special case, albeit a potentially important one, of market rigidity within the money market (the rate of interest will not fall) which complements those already outlined for the product market (prices will not fall), the labour market (wages will not fall) and the capital market (investment is interest-inelastic).[12]

Fourth, although this is of less concern here, the synthesis offers scope for debate over the relative efficacy of monetary (shifting the LM curve) and fiscal (shifting the IS curve) policy. This will depend upon the form taken empirically by the two curves and their speeds of adjustment.

Such is the conventional interpretation of the neoclassical synthesis. It raises a number of issues, all of which are germane to the continuing debates over macroeconomics. To what extent was there a revolution in economic thought? What was its impact through policy? Is the IS/LM a correct interpretation of Keynes?

Addressing these issues in turn, it is important to realise that the Keynesian revolution, and Keynes himself, had little or no impact upon traditional microeconomics. The theory of the firm as profit-maximiser and the consumer as utility-maximiser remained untouched. Accordingly, with the focus upon macroeconomic aggregates, much macroeconomic theory became concerned with the direct or indirect determinants of aggregate effective demand, as in the theories of the consumption, investment and demand for money functions. These were more or less loosely based on microeconomic foundations. By the same token, macroeconomic relations that lay outside traditional concern, such as the extent of monopolisation and the distribution of income, also remained unchallenged, even un-addressed. In short, theoretically, the Keynesian revolution in intellectual terms has proved extremely limited in scope, dealing predominantly in pos-tulating and examining the interaction between macroeconomic aggregates.

Although much less acceptable over the last 20 years, for the period of the post-war boom, it became a conventional wisdom that the Keynesian revo-lution had provided the policy basis on which full employment could be and had been achieved. Even in Keynesians' own terms, however, this is scarcely credible. Increases in aggregate demand have come from systematic expan-sion in state expenditure, from the extremely rapid growth in world trade, and from the investment flows arising out the operations of multinational corporations – in other words, not as a result of the short-term manipula-tion of effective demand through macroeconomic policy. In addition, state intervention has been extensive in health, education and various forms of industrial policy, all of which have contributed enormously to the produc-tivity increase that fuelled the post-war expansion. In short, Keynesianism can at most have made a minor contribution to the factors that caused the post-war boom. Further, analytically, the powerful position held by Keynesian macroeconomics only served to draw attention away from those other factors that promoted economic growth, either by assigning them to microeconomics, as in monopolisation, or by leaving them aside, as in distribution, or through industrial policy or other forms of state inter-vention and expenditure.

5 THE REAPPRAISAL OF KEYNES OR THE REPRISAL OF METHODOLOGICAL INDIVIDUALISM

Quite apart from the extent of the Keynesian revolution, and the extent of its influence upon policy and growth, some have challenged the idea that the IS/LM framework truly represents Keynes's own ideas. Such claims have been important in legitimising alternative macroeconomic theories: 'Keynes really said this and so do we.' This is true of radical, left or post-Keynesians. But the most prominent mainstream approach in this vein is what has been termed the 'reappraisal' of Keynes, although it is variously also known as fixed-price, quantity-rationed or quality-constrained, or dis-equilibrium macroeconomics.[13] Here, it is argued that the market system works through an interdependent system of exchanges. As an individual, subject to money holdings, I can only buy if I have already sold. My demand for goods is ineffective unless I have already been able, for example, to find employment and been paid a money wage with which to purchase consumption goods. But if the firm is unable to sell its output, it will not employ. Accordingly, there can be a vicious circle in which the worker is not employed because there is no demand for goods, and there is no demand for goods because the worker is unemployed.

Macroeconomic models constructed on this basis clearly have an affinity with the notion of ineffective demand and, crucially, they can be shown to be a generalisation of the neoclassical version of a competitive equilibrium with money. This is not surprising, since the latter's optimisation is complemented by a constraint over and above those imposed by levels of factor endowments and prices, namely, the extent to which individual economic agents have been able to make sales and purchases, with an inability to do so tending to be self-replicating. But would an unemployment equilibrium persist over time in these circumstances?

If prices and wages remain rigid and do not adjust in the light of the frustrated intentions in the supplies and demands of individual economic agents, then such a result is possible. The assumption of fixed prices does have the benefit of incorporating the idea that macroeconomic quantities might adjust faster than prices in the short run. But it is hardly plausible that prices and wages would not adjust at all over time, even if an assumption of instantaneous market-clearing is not made. As acknowledged in one of the names given to the approach, quantity-constrained or rationing models, agents on the short side of the market are unable to buy and sell as much as they would like and must remain in this position indefinitely if the same (dis)equilibrium is to persist.

This issue will be taken up later in the context of theories seeking to explain why prices (and wages) might not be adjusted by individual agents even though they are free to do so and markets are not clearing. First, however, it is important to recognise a broader methodological point about the reappraisal of Keynesian economics. Whilst, in some respects, appearing to be revolutionary itself in criticising the IS/LM interpretation – by emphasising the role of aggregate demand, of money in lubricating the coordination of exchanges through the market system, and of quantity as opposed to price adjustment – the reappraisal is also deeply conservative in tying the interpretation of Keynes entirely to methodological individualism. The macro-economy emerges out of the aggregated behaviour of individuals even if these individuals are now quantity-constrained by the market as well as by prices and their factor endowments. In other words, this is just the old theory with the addition of quantity constraints which, when added up across individuals, must be mutually consistent in giving rise to less than full employment equilibrium or, somewhat inappropriately, 'disequilibrium', as it has come to be called. Significantly, in later versions of such models, the economy tends to be reduced to just two representative economic agents – a firm that supplies goods and employs labour, and a household that buys goods and supplies labour – who fail to coordinate their mutual sales and purchases effectively!

Some economists, especially those hailing from Keynes's own analytical turf and traditions in Cambridge, have been dismissive of the reappraisal's interpretation, even though they are far from satisfied with the synthesis as an alternative. The reason is precisely because of the methodological individualism upon which the two are based, the reappraisal more so and more explicitly so, whereas Keynes is seen as having emphasised the systemic nature of advanced capitalism's malfunctioning irrespective of, or as the context within which, individual agents were forced to conform. This explains, for example, Keynes's emphasis on the impact of waves of pessimistic expectations and the potentially damaging implications for overall effective demand of the speculative functioning of the financial system. The alternative, post-Keynesian, tradition to which this has led emphasises broad macroeconomic relations concerning the role of the distribution of income (in wage–profit conflict and in influencing aggregate demand given different class propensities to consume) and of the degree of monopolisation within the economy (which affects pricing and the level of output).[14]

6 CONSOLIDATING MICRO-FOUNDATIONS, WEAKENING COHERENCE

Radical alternatives such as those offered by post-Keynesianism did not prosper, despite the collapse of the post-war boom, as the NCE filled the analytical void that had previously been occupied by the debate between monetarism and Keynesianism – with monetarism increasingly in the ascendancy in the wake of the vertical Phillips curve. Rational expectations proved to be the only analytical novelty employed by the NCE, although the results were dramatically negative, especially from a Keynesian perspective, as a consequence of the assumption of instantaneous market-clearing. But the position of theoretical prominence occupied by the NCE has proved both temporary and short-lived – hardly surprising, given that it is a one-idea innovation.

Yet, as argued above, it played a crucial, if perverse, role in tiding over the crisis in macroeconomic theory. It stimulated debate by provocatively basing itself on the perfect workings of markets, when they were demonstrably working terribly, and by suggesting that state intervention was essentially futile even though it was desperately needed. All unemployment was essentially voluntary as, with market-clearing, anybody who wanted a job could get one by lowering the wage required.[15] But the NCE played a further, less obvious role in the subsequent evolution of macroeconomic theory, one that contributed to a consolidation of the position of methodological individualism, even if in a way that was at odds with the New

Classical school. The latter's own input came in the form of the individual's optimal use of the available information, and rational expectations have now become more or less standard within macroeconomics theory. But the reaction against the results of the New Classical school necessarily induced an intellectual challenge to reveal that they constituted a special case dependent upon market-clearing.

This, in itself, is simple to demonstrate by assuming that one or more markets do not clear instantaneously. But this had to be justified. If markets do not clear, why do rational economic agents, those on the short side of the market, not adjust their prices. And, just as the assumption of individual optimisation in the case of rational expectations seemed to present the challenge posed by the NCE, so there was a natural inclination to explain lack of market-clearing equally on the basis of individual optimisation. Hence, the reappraisal could be picked up, never having been particularly prominent before except for a short period, and complemented by theories seeking to explain inflexible prices. These could depend upon imperfect competition, either in product markets or in the labour market, or a number of ingenious microeconomic devices based on less than perfect and asymmetrical access to information. This has given rise to what has been termed 'new Keynesianism'. It sees itself as resurrecting old Keynesian propositions on more secure micro-foundations.[16] As Greenwald and Stiglitz put it, this is neither a break with the old nor even with Keynes himself – it is the perfection of both![17]

> Some new Keynesians are wont to claim that this insistence on micro-foundations distinguishes them from Keynes and older Keynesians. Though much macroeconomic analysis in the Keynesian tradition in the 1950s and 1960s did stray from a solid grounding in micro-foundations, Keynes himself clearly argued each of his macroeconomic relations on the basis of microeconomic analysis. In fact, we would argue that Keynes did the best he could with the micro-foundations which were available at the time. Macroeconomists of the 1950s and 1960s faced a dilemma: the microeconomics that was fashionable at the time – assuming perfect information, complete markets, and so on – was obviously inconsistent with the spirit of the Keynesian model. It made sense for them to ignore that kind of microeconomics.
>
> (Greenwald and Stiglitz 1993: 25)

Specifically, within the labour market, for example, efficiency-wage theory argues that wages are not reduced, even if unemployed workers are prepared to work at a lower wage, because this would attract workers with lower skills, contributing less effort and loyalty, and increasing turnover and hence personnel costs. Insider-outsider theory suggests those in employment have some power to disrupt and hence to share in profitability, thereby pushing the wage above the level at which the unemployed would work. And implicit contract models suggest that less risk-averse employers essentially offer their workers insurance over the business cycle, thereby reducing the average wage but holding it above the market-clearing level in a recession (and below by a larger margin is a boom).

Now the theoretical narrative is complete. Macroeconomics has become based upon a variety of eclectic microeconomic foundations, generally with rational expectations and optimising, often representative, individual agents, with a variety of mechanisms for generating unemployment both in the short and the long run.[18] Thus, in his survey of theories of unemployment, in which appropriate policy design needs to be targeted to the presumed cause of unemployment to be cured, Snower (1995) distinguishes five different causes of unemployment, each corresponding to a different micro-foundation. These are: the determinants of the natural rate of unemployment (on which see section 7); the role of the demand-side for which prices might not be flexible in view of 'menu-costs' (the cost of changing prices), the cost of decision-making, and the staggering of contracts over time; the supply-side due to search and match by firms and employees, worker discouragement effects after long bouts of unemployment, efficiency-wages, and labour market mobility in view of housing, health and pensions; the interaction of supply and demand, in imperfect product and labour market competition, and in handling market imperfections as in training and skill and the more general provision of infrastructure; and the role of institutions such as trade unions – how strong they are and whether they are decentralised or not.

A more telling, if less comprehensive, account from a critical point of view is provided by Hahn and Solow, and it is worth discussing their contribution in a little detail. Theirs is a considered piece of work, having evolved over a long gestation period, reflecting their unease as economists, borne of the Keynesian era, with the results of the NCE: the new macroeconomists were claiming much more that could be deduced from fundamental neoclassical principles (Hahn and Solow 1995: vii). Hahn and Solow are looking for what they term a 'respectable' response which in part reflects their wish to engage in debate on the chosen grounds of their opponents. But it also conforms to their own analytical tastes within economics: 'we also both regarded ourselves as neoclassical economists in the sense that we required theories of the economy to be firmly based on the rationality of agents and on decentralised modes of economic communication among them' (ibid.).

As two of the leading economic theorists over the post-war period,[19] Hahn and Solow provide *A Critical Essay on Modern Macroeconomic Theory*. Whilst posing as adopting a critical stance, this is only in their point of departure from the special results of the NCE. Otherwise, they remain profoundly uncritical and surprisingly eclectic. They are attached to methodological individualism as the source of macroeconomic relations, and the macro-economy is understood in terms of a general equilibrium, from which there can be short-run deviations. For them, the goal is to construct a theory of unemployment equilibrium, on the basis of methodological individualism – 'in the modern spirit, however, resistance has to begin with alternative micro foundations' (ibid.: 3). This does not necessarily imply that Hahn and Solow accept all the assumptions involved, since their strategy is, in part, to employ their opponents's assumptions as a 'technique of subversion', modifying them slightly in order to start 'boring from within'. The two aspects which they find most objectionable are the use of a representative individual, as this undermines certain possibilities for coordination failures through the market, and the use of intertemporal optimising by such agents subject only to budget, price and technology constraints.

However, the criteria by which these assumptions are perceived to be unreasonable are far from precise or justified – representative individuals might be used subject to the scope, realism, flexibility and tractability of the analysis. There is also the stated objective of creating models which are 'capable of doing what is required of them', such as generating fluctuations in output and employment in which the latter can be positively correlated with the real wage. This, together with their strategy of subversion by boring from within allows enormous freedom in the assumptions that can be made – even adopting those that are recognised to be unrealistic, if standard, as in an overlapping generations model in which individuals live for just two periods, working only in the first and living off savings in the second. In short, Hahn and Solow can pick and choose whatever assumptions they like to get their preferred results. Even objectionable assumptions might be justified as seeking to be persuasive on the chosen analytical terrain of opponents!

In these terms, Hahn and Solow are able to construct the models that they require, employing the microeconomic insights previously mentioned. In one model, for example, with increasing returns to scale and imperfect competition, there is the potential for multiple equilibria. Consequently, real wages and employment are not necessarily inversely related, as in standard labour market analysis since, at high levels of employment and output, average unit costs and prices can be lower, thereby raising the value of a given or even lower money wage. More generally with imperfect competition, equilibrium depends upon the conjectures that agents make about one another's decisions, and these too can be self-fulfilling in a variety of equilibria.[20] In short, neither is equilibrium unique nor are valid the intuitive neoclassical results concerning comparative statics (for example, the association of higher real wages with lower employment and higher unemployment).

Finally, Hahn and Solow accept that macroeconomic models can legitimately be built without providing the micro-foundations necessary to justify the assumptions made at the aggregate level.[21] For, micro-foundations have already been found to rationalise inflexibility in markets on the basis of optimisation by individuals. For the sake of plausibility, flexibility and, one suspects, tractability, they claim that macro without firm micro-foundations is worthwhile, even if at the expense of purity (ibid.: 105), i.e. methodological individualism.

The contribution of Hahn and Solow is remarkable, for it effectively represents a manifesto for macro of 'anything goes' as long as it remains within the bounds of now standard micro-foundations and arbitrary macro assumption by which inflexible prices can be assumed in some markets. In the end, macroeconomics needs only to throw down a few or even numerous equations based on micro-foundations, a few macro judgements, and accounting identities based on general equilibrium in adding up across markets. As long as Keynesian results are possible, and the abhorred NCE at most a full market-clearing special case, the rest can be left to the econometricians to tidy up. This is exactly the stuff of which the natural rate of unemployment is a natural consequence and organising concept.

7 THE NATURAL RATE OF UNEMPLOYMENT AS EPIPHENOMENON[22]

The characteristics of modern macroeconomics outlined in the previous paragraph have been crucial in the formulation not only of theory, but of macroeconomic models for empirical testing. The construction of the macro-economy as a general equilibrium has rationalised the notion of the natural rate of unemployment, that level of joblessness that is warranted even where the market is working 'ideally' because, for example, of the need for workers to look for new jobs or, increasingly, because of random and unforeseen shocks to the economic system to which adjustment needs to be made (including correction of expectations). The inverted commas are in place because the definition of when the market is working or can work well is vague. For example, if there are increasing returns to scale or informational deficiencies, the market could be working as well as can be expected but not yielding an ideal outcome. The ambiguity arises, then, around how the market works (often, for example, in terms of competitiveness) as opposed to the results that it secures.

The natural rate of unemployment was also originally identified as that point at which inflation would not accelerate, or decelerate, along the vertical Phillips curve – as unemployment is held too low or high, respectively. With unemployment having increased so much over the past 20 years compared to the same length of period before, the task was posed of explaining the levels and persistence of unemployment. Quite clearly, two interpretations are available. Either the natural rate of unemployment has increased over time or short-run fluctuations around it have been large and persistent. This involves, respectively, identifying shifts in exogenous parameters, which raise the natural rate of unemployment, and the transmission mechanisms through which exogenously given shocks move the economy around a given natural rate.

Despite the scale and persistence of unemployment, there have been theories to suggest that it has arisen because the market has worked well. Real business-cycle theory, for example, argues that individual agents respond to shocks by adjusting their intertemporal allocations. If productivity, and hence wages, are particularly favourable in one period, workers will seek greater employment at that time at the expense of greater voluntary unemployment at a later date. A similarly motivated approach is provided by search and matching, or flow, models.[23] Here, the idea is that workers and jobs are highly heterogeneous but can be matched to a greater or lesser extent according to a variety of characteristics. The extent to which they are matched depends upon the time taken to search out better jobs, itself an optimal decision to be made in the light of the higher wages that might be earned at the expense of those foregone whilst searching. As Romer concludes:

> Search and matching models offer a straightforward explanation for average unemployment: it may be the result of continually matching workers and jobs in a complex and changing economy. Thus, much of observed unemployment may reflect what is traditionally known as *frictional* unemployment.
>
> (Romer 1996: 480; emphasis in original)

But this does seem incapable of explaining the persistence of long-term unemployment.

A rather different explanation, from the monetary side, has arisen out of informational imperfections, originating with Lucas's 1974 price-misperception model. Essentially, we all occupy separate economic islands and when prices rise, for example, in our vicinity, we have to decide the extent to which this represents a localised price rise, in which case we ought to go off trading elsewhere more than before, or a general price rise in which case we should stay at home. A shock increase in inflation, for example, will lead us to underestimate it by attributing it in part to a purely local increase, only applying to our own prices and not all in general. Accordingly, as is well known, any misperception of the price level leads to deviation from equilibrium – in this case, for example, the real wage might be too low, with workers underanticipating inflation, and employment levels too high.

These examples are highly significant. Whilst one, the theory of real business cycles, focuses on the supply-side (productivity shocks or whatever), another, that of Lucas, focuses on the demand-side through monetary and informational factors, and the third, of search and match, focuses on the interaction of supply and demand, they are generally considered to be extreme for limiting themselves to circumstances in which the market works effectively, if not always ideally, as a result of random and unforeseeable events beyond the scope and immediate control of the market. More catholic analyses create the space for a greater role for market imperfections for the sorts of reasons previously discussed. Yet, of greater importance than the more or less extreme positions adopted towards the workings of the market, is the extent to which all of the analyses share an approach in common. Each adopts a different view about what factors are allowed to cause deviations from the natural equilibrium and the mechanism by which they do so.

This point is well-illustrated by the work of Phelps,[24] who was responsible, along with Friedman, for positing the natural rate in the first place in the context of the vertical Phillips curve. His motivation is to construct a theory of the natural rate of unemployment as an equilibrium that is invariant with respect to monetary factors. He sees this as a logical requirement: 'Natural rate models, to repeat, are so constructed that, if they contain nominal variables at all, the equilibrium path from every initial condition is invariant to "money" and to the purely monetary effects of disturbances generally' (Phelps 1994: 23). The natural rate is perceived as an equilibrium in the sense that expectations are correct, model-consistent according to rational expectations, once the economy attains this rate.

Phelps (1992: 1480) dubs his approach as '*structuralist* theory to draw attention to four features' (emphasis in original). First, the natural rate equilibrium is structural in the sense of being free of cyclical factors creating deviations around the equilibrium path. Second, unemployment is the consequence of structural inefficiencies in the labour market due to informational and institutional imperfections. Third, the natural rate is structural in being non-monetary, with no influence from the supply of money relative to more or less sticky prices and wages. Finally, his approach is structural in so far as the structure or composition of output affects the way in which the natural rate evolves.

For many, these might constitute an extremely weak basis on which to employ the term structural but Phelps is less concerned with the name than to distinguish his approach from what he dubs collectively the 'Keynesian/monetarist/New Keynesian class of models' (ibid.). For these consider deviations around a given natural rate of unemployment. Phelps on the other hand, is concerned with the path of the natural rate as well as deviations around it: 'The equilibrium path of the unemployment rate always approaches the natural rate, as before. But something has been added. The natural rate moves!' (Phelps 1994: vii) Crucially, the analytical basis on which the natural rate moves is exactly the same as the factors which cause deviations from it for others. Drawing upon the whole gamut of micro-foundations, Phelps recognises that these are incorporated into intertemporal optimisation, thereby affecting the 'structure' of the economy. This is most obviously seen in terms of what happens to the capital stock, whose level is usually assigned to the long run, but whose level and composition may be permanently affected by a sustained slump in terms of the future growth path. For Phelps, the natural rate is endogenous, a product of the economy itself and not simply given by exogenous factors such as tastes, technology and endowments. His own emphasis is upon what happens to the real rate of interest and the allocation of investment by firms to customers (building up markets), functional employees (human capital) and physical capital.

The importance of Phelps's contributions is that they take the natural rate as far as it can be taken without discarding the notion altogether, for it has become a moving target around which deviations take place. The exclusion of monetary factors reflects in part an intellectual and inherited bias in seeking to move on from the vertical Phillips curve for which the natural rate figured as a constant around which monetary factors merely determined the rate of inflation.[25] But, in part, it also reflects a logical requirement to enable the theory to sustain the concept of the natural rate of unemployment. For, a moving natural rate has become essential in order to be able to explain the persistence of much higher levels of unemployment. If, however, monetary factors were allowed to influence the natural rate as well, then the short run becomes hopelessly entangled with the long run. The deviations around the equilibrium path move that path faster than the economy moves towards it. The equilibrium target could be moving faster than adjustment to it.

Nor is it clear why monetary factors should be excluded from affecting the equilibrium path of the natural rate, unless they are interpreted in the very narrow context of the quantity of the supply of money. For exactly the same imperfect information theories that have been used to explain non-clearing in the labour market have also been used in, and have even been inspired by, the study of money markets. How these are functioning will affect the path of the level and composition of the capital stock as much as the underlying real factors preferred by Phelps.

Some of these issues will be explored in greater depth below. Initially, it is worth reviewing some of the misgivings about the natural rate that have been made from within the orthodoxy, some of which have been covered already, if only implicitly.[26] First, there are conceptual problems with the definition of the natural rate itself which leave it loosely and not necessarily consistently defined both within and across different contributions unless particularly powerful assumptions are made. The simplest definition is one which takes it as the level of unemployment ground out by given tastes, technologies and endowments. This carries with it the standard assumption that these remain fixed over time. However, broader definitions of the natural rate include other factors such as how the market coordinates these underlying 'fundamentals'.[27]

Essentially, what is involved is the assignation of different factors to the long or to the short run and, similarly if not identically, to whether they are endogenous or exogenous. Unless this is done, it becomes impossible to construct a theory of short-run deviations around the long-run equilibrium path of the natural rate. Where the actual divide is made between short/long and exogenous/endogenous is a matter of taste and, often, conventional wisdoms within theory and around stylised facts (tastes do not change over time, for example). This is all inadvertently brought out neatly by Snower in two successive explanatory footnotes:[28]

> Some economists use the term 'natural rate of unemployment' more broadly, letting it stand for any short-term equilibrium unemployment rate, regardless of whether the labour market clears . . . and regardless of the underlying institutional structure . . . In that view, the natural rate rests on much more than tastes, technologies, and endowments: it could also depend on the existence of credit constraints, degree of competition in labour and product markets, the nature of wage-bargaining institutions, the level of labour turnover coasts, and the size of the incumbent work-forces, just to give a few examples. Then, however, the natural-rate theory becomes so all-inclusive, that it can no longer be distinguished from labour union, insider-outsider, efficiency-wage and other theories.
>
> (Snower 1995: 111)

Thus, the theory is much the same – it's just a matter of whether changes in unemployment are perceived as part of the natural rate or deviations from it. Empirical plausibility is the ground on which factors are assigned to the short or long run in explaining cyclical movements:

> Taking the wider view of the natural-rate theory, summarized in the previous footnote, it is worth observing that the degree of competition and the economic institutions governing behaviour in the labour, product, credit, and international markets are generally not subject to cyclical fluctuations either. Thus cyclical fluctuations in unemployment remain to be explained (by perfect market-clearing theorists) by fluctuations in expectational errors.
>
> (ibid.: 112)

In short, the definition of the natural rate is bound up in a complicated way, belied by the rigour of mathematical models, with assumptions about what makes up the short and long runs, what is endogenous and exogenous and what are the empirical and theoretical conventional wisdoms informing the stance on these. Some assumptions are highly implausible, such as fixed tastes, etc., and none is generally subject to serious statistical testing, as opposed to the narrower hypotheses within the models.

A second problem is the existence, uniqueness and stability of the general equilibrium derived from the supply-side (and tastes) which is supposed to underlie the natural rate. In terms of micro-foundations in a perfectly competitive general equilibrium of price-takers, this may not hold (unless the sufficient assumption of all goods being gross substitutes is made). The problem is that much worse in the context of imperfect competition and increasing returns to scale. It is relatively easy to show how these give rise to multiple equilibria so that there is not a single natural rate, and one may have both higher wages and employment in one equilibrium compared to another with correspondingly counter-intuitive results for comparative statics (increasing the real wage may increase the level of employment).

Third, as is now generally recognised, the real wage is not a directly nego- tiated variable. Rather, the money wage and the price level are determined in separate markets (the labour and product markets, respectively). Conse- quently, rational economic agents such as workers (capitalists) have to take a view about what the price (wage) level is going to be when bargaining over wage levels (setting product prices), as they must when theory moves beyond the Walrasian world of all agents being price-takers. As Hahn (1995: 48) observes, this is not simply a matter of forming rational expectations about other prices, it involves forming a strategy around reactions to your own bargaining. In such a game-theoretic context, this implies that the natural rate as an equilibrium cannot be defined without considering the impact of being out of equilibrium (since agents need to assure themselves it is worth remaining as they are). But strategic game-playing does not figure in the conventional definition of the natural rate, and this has the effect of precluding a source of multiple equilibria.

Fourth is the treatment of productivity change (and at least the capital– labour ratio) which can be crucial in defining the long-run equilibrium path and its associated natural rate of unemployment. At one level, eco- nomic theory does not appear to connect the two sides of the same brain, or at least the theories of the short and long run, for, over the past decade and more, endogenous growth theory has been prospering – the notion that the growth rate depends upon the path taken by the economy (i.e., the short run) because, for example, of increasing returns and extern- alities of various sorts.[29] This implies that short-run deviations in the econ- omy will potentially affect the subsequent path of the natural rate. As Hahn (1995: 52) points out: 'One can only be amazed at the neglect of investment and of the capital stock in theories of the natural rate'. More generally than through changes in the capital stock alone, there is the issue of the path- dependence of the economy, what is known as hysteresis, how the future path is affected by the path taken in the past so that adjustment from the same starting-point may differ according to how that starting-point was attained.[30] This can take two different forms. The more fundamental is that posed, for example, by Phelps as discussed above, in which the path of the natural rate is itself endogenous and dependent on the route pre- viously taken. Less fundamental is the notion that the natural rate remains the same but adjustment around it responds differently according to the past path of the economy. Only the adjustment mechanism and short-run equilibrium are affected, not the long-run natural rate.

8 THE SHORT JOURNEY FROM NRU TO NAIRU

In short, even within the confines of neoclassical economics itself, the notion of the natural rate of unemployment poses considerable problems in terms of three overlapping and interrelated issues – its dependence upon equilibrium, its division of variables and the economy's path between the short and the long run, and the division between exogenous and endogenous variables. A more critical discussion of these issues follows in the final section. Beforehand, consider a highly influential use of the natural rate, the one associated with Jackman, Layard and Nickell.[31] Their work has evolved over longer than a decade and is a particular and particularly apt illustration of the more general commentary already provided. Its popularity derives from: its relative simplicity; its being readily elaborated in non-technical language; its capacity to be used in empirical work in which changes in the actual rate of unemployment can be divided down into short- and long-run contributions as well as disentangling the impact on unemployment of the changes in particular variables (such as welfare benefits, trade unions); and its ready use for suggesting a variety of policy measures which might alleviate if not cure unemployment.

A first, striking feature of the approach is terminological, the replacement of the natural rate of unemployment, NRU, by the non-accelerating inflation rate of unemployment, NAIRU. The apparent distaste for the term 'natural', however, merely reflects a dependence upon a broader notion of the determinants of the natural rate than technology, tastes and endowments to include a variety of other factors, such as institutional arrangements, which are appropriately seen as open to change, especially through policy, and hence are not predetermined to the same extent as technology, etc.

Second, the approach sees itself as being confronted by eight stylised facts, five derived from time series data and three from cross-section:

1 unemployment fluctuates over time with large secular changes (the postwar boom compared with the past 20 years, for example);
2 unemployment varies more between than within business cycles – this is perceived to reflect institutional change between business cycles as opposed to adjustment to shocks within them;
3 there has been a large recent rise in the proportion of long-run unemployed;
4 unemployment has risen relative to the number of vacancies;
5 unemployment does not exhibit a long-run trend – suggesting it is not the consequence of variables with a trend such as productivity;
6 there are differences in unemployment across countries, presumed to reflect differences social institutions and wage/benefit ratios;
7 few unemployed have chosen unemployment through quitting rather than being subject to redundancy;
8 there are huge differences in unemployment by age, occupation, region, race and especially by levels of skill.

Third, there is a profound belief in hysteresis in the path of unemployment for various reasons. But this only applies to the short run or in the weak sense as discussed above in the context of Phelps' theory. Consequently, unemployment can be due to adjustment to short-run shocks, including their lagged persistence from hysteresis, as well as shifts in long-term parameters determining the NAIRU, on which see below. Unemployment is seen as path-dependent because, at a given level of unemployment, rising unemployment, for example, moderates the influence and bargaining power of those in jobs. There is also liable to be fewer long-term unemployed in the labour market, which discourages employers from hiring as a result of the lower presumed standards on average within the supply of labour, and the recently unemployed are presumed to be more active within the labour market.[32]

Fourth, the details of the model are remarkably simple in principle: firms price by a monopoly mark-up on costs, subject to the overall level of aggregate demand;[33] workers negotiate wages according to insider-outsider and efficiency-wage considerations with the outcome dependent upon trade union power, the level and change in unemployment, the wage–benefit ratio (which when higher causes more unemployment because of the voluntarily unemployed and because of the lesser pressure on those in jobs), and any other number of exogenously given worker characteristics. With prices and nominal wages set separately, these core relations are wrapped up in a standard IS/LM framework. Inflation is provided for through more or less self-fulfilling expectations.

Fifth, the monetary sector in the economy is essentially passive with the inflationary impetus coming entirely from cost pressures and a wage-price spiral, although this needs to be accommodated by increases in the money supply. Indeed, both the long-run NAIRU and the short-run dynamics are highly dependent upon the parameters that capture the wage- and price-setting pressures. As Phelps observes in a review of their work:[34]

> The authors' approach is remote from the radical pessimism of Keynes's *General Theory* on the capacity of agents to arrive quickly at equilibrium expectations, and Keynes's corresponding emphasis on 'effective' demand . . . It is perhaps a mark of how far Keynesian influence has sunk in the profession that the standard elements in Keynes's conception of nominal demand – propensity to consume, marginal efficiency (of capital), and money rate of interest – do not appear.
>
> (Phelps 1992: 1478)

Sixth, the model also includes what Phelps terms 'social policy variables', such as unemployment insurance and the power and structure of trade unions. For Phelps, this is a distinctive feature, especially in the empirical domain:

Evidently the authors are primarily interested in a specification of the modern-equilibrium framework allotting to *social policy* parameters the major part of unemployment determination. The development of this *aspect* of . . . the modern-equilibrium framework and their work at making it *empirical* constitute the value added on which the success of this venture will largely be judged.

(ibid.: 1481; emphases in original)

Seventh, it is not only the social policy variables that can be incorporated into the empirical analysis, they can be assessed alongside other factors such as the level of aggregate demand, and the effects of hysteresis. Causes for the current levels of unemployment can be disaggregated into their constituent components relative to the short- and long-run NAIRUs.[35] Interestingly, Layard *et al.* accept that there is considerable affinity between their model and that of the NCE, although the direction of underlying causation is different: 'Although our interpretation of the structural model differs so sharply from the new classical model, it remains true that the reduced forms are *indistinguishable*' (Layard *et al.* 1991: 21; emphasis added).

Eighth, on the basis of the theoretical and empirical results, policies can be devised to amend the NAIRUs and the adjustment path. In light of the previous point, not surprisingly, these are at times reactionary from the perspective of labour, both for those in employment (since their bargaining power and wage pressure needs to be moderated to bring down the NAIRUs) when sympathy lies with the unemployed willing to work at the going real wage, and for those in unemployment since there is a gain from lowering the level and duration of unemployment benefit. Their antipathy to labour corresponds to their view on the negative effect of insider (the employed) strength in itself and in its being in conflict with the interests of outsiders (the unemployed). Most of their proposals come from the supply-side since this is what most affects the NAIRUs; Keynesian demand management is suggested only when unemployment is particularly high and the dangers of hysteresis especially damaging. Even then, there is a negative impact, since those in employment will be strengthened and exert undue wage pressure:[36] 'If there is significant hysteresis, then, . . . demand (policy) should ensure that unemployment is prevented from rising too far after a temporary shock – even if this means that it has to remain higher for longer' (ibid.: 509).

In short, from this account and relative to those given previously, the NAIRU approach is extremely crude, and has been criticised as such. As Cross has confirmed: 'The "hysteresis" in such models, however, was nothing more than persistence in deviations of actual unemployment from the natural rate' (Cross 1995a: 7). The NAIRU model does not allow shifts in the fundamentals (the determinants of the long-run NAIRU) as a result of the path taken. As such, it is a particularly weak version of the dependence (in fact independence) of the long run on the short run. There is, as it were, path-persistence as opposed to path-dependence.

In part, this is a consequence of the neglect of the possibility of multiple equilibria, for which one path will lead to one equilibrium and another elsewhere. Layard *et al.* address and dismiss this possibility within the space occupied by a single page, concluding:

> It should, however, be noted that multiple equilibria of this type are rarely looked for, and never found, in any empirical investigation . . . So we shall proceed with an investigation of the dynamics of our standard linear model and ignore the possibility of multiple equilibria from now on.
>
> (Layard *et al.* 1991: 369–70)

The logic is, to say the least, escapable. Ignore something because it has not been looked for and, hence, found. Even if seriously investigated, the search would be biased. For, on the assumption that economies are around a relatively stable equilibrium most of the time, there is a bias towards observing absence of multiple equilibria even where they do exist. Moreover, Manning (1992) has investigated empirically the presence of multiple equilibria in the UK economy, and concludes that they do, indeed, exist, and the economy is trapped in the low wage and high unemployment equilibrium![37]

Another reason reflecting, concealing and, hence, implicitly justifying the lack of genuine hysteresis follows from the omission of what are crucial variables not only in their own right but also as ones which potentially affect the long run through their short-run impact. As Hahn observes of the neglect of investment and of the capital stock:

> Theories of the natural rate are amongst the class of shaky and vastly incomplete theories. This has been recognised by some of the practitioners . . . [Hahn cites Nickell 1990] . . . Unfortunately, if understandably, he and others are none the less keen to get down to econometrics long before an integrated and reasonable theory has been assembled . . . The capital stock is ignored as is investment, which is one of the more peculiar aspects of these theories.
>
> (Hahn 1995: 54)

Phelps (1992), from his own rather different perspective, is also concerned about the failure of the real interest rate, taxes and relative international prices (oil crises, etc.) to play a more prominent role in the model both in the short and long run and so in tracing the genuinely hysteresis path of equilibrium unemployment. For him, these involve both wealth effects and movements in the distribution and levels of the capital stock across sectors and countries.

The omission of such factors and the more general weakness of the relationship between the short and long run is usefully discussed in the context of productivity change. This is summarily dismissed as a potential causal factor in generating unemployment over the long term, as Layard *et al.* (1991, p. 47) note: 'If productivity, or living standards generally, had a long-run effect on unemployment, unemployment could not be untrended'. This is a remarkable argument. First, it is not confined to productivity but, essentially, suggests that any trended variable can be set aside. It is purely a statistical argument and has nothing to do with economics. As such, it is unwittingly if popularly conflating two different notions of the long run – one which is, indeed, attached to economics, namely, when some notion of equilibrium is reached, and one which is not, namely, the passage of time. Quite clearly, over very long periods, productivity could affect the level of unemployment in one way and, then, over another period equally long, not do so for other reasons.

This can be made more specific in a number of ways which serve to reveal how both common sense and intuition have been totally abandoned. First, employment has also had a trend over the last 100 years. Should this lead us to conclude that, over the long term, unemployment has nothing to do with the amount of employment generated? Quite clearly, the same factors that generate employment may induce a growth in the labour force (not least rising living standards, especially in a Malthusian context). However, with minor exceptions, demographics are left aside, despite concern with the long-run level of (un)employment. Changes in productivity, for example, have completely changed the way in which the economy functions with respect to employment and unemployment when it comes to women's waged work. Without engaging in detailed analysis, it is possible to see that the rise in women's labour market participation (and, hence, potential for employment and unemployment) would have been impossible without the rises in standards of living that have been experienced in advanced capitalist countries (Fine 1992).

Second, we know that productivity increase can cause unemployment since fewer workers are required to produce the same level of output. Of course, this has to be set against increases in the level of output – as employment equals labour productivity multiplied by output. Suppose, simply for the sake of argument, that the trend growth in state expenditure provides the mechanism by which the productivity effects on employment are neutralised, thereby leaving unemployment unaffected (with taxes also funded out of the increase in incomes provided by higher productivity). Then, by the argument quoted above by Layard *et al.*, growth in both productivity and state expenditure are not significant in generating long-run (un)employment. And the same would apply to all the other trended variables that we know to be crucial to the performance of economies, especially in the postwar period. We must consider that they do not affect the long-run NAIRU – the unprecedented growth in world trade, the rise of multinationals, the higher levels, direction and composition of foreign direct investment, the internationalisation in new forms of the financial and commodity trading systems, and the continuing impact of new electronic and information technology. These are all trended in the long run and hence have no impact on the NAIRU. Well, as we are often reminded in the quotation from Keynes, in the long run we are all dead. By the same token, the NAIRU approach to the impact of these factors on unemployment is absolutely correct in the null or trivial sense that the long-run NAIRU does not exist and so cannot be affected by anything! In short, trended variables do count, even if they might net out one another's effects. And they may count differently over different, possibly extended, periods of time, which should not be overlooked in using the long run to brush these considerations aside.

Third, even setting all of this aside, unemployment might be affected by trended variables in their first differences. Unemployment might well be affected if productivity grows much faster or slower than normal around its putative long-run trend. This point might be dismissed as a short-run effect for which almost any economic variable is allowed to play a role. However, the trend argument is allowed to dismiss productivity from short-run considerations altogether other than as a random shock. However, if changes in productivity are, for the sake of argument, untrended, why are they excluded but other untrended variables included?[38] Thus, lagged unemployment, for example, is included to accrue the feeble hysteresis effect. On a slightly different, but similar, point, monopolisation and trade union membership are trended, but they figure in the determinants of both the short- and long-run NAIRUs through their impact on wage and price pressure. But empirical study after empirical study has shown that these and wages are all closely correlated to changing productivity! Consequently, there must be a case for the rate of productivity increase feeding into the model through the adjustment parameters that already define the short- and long-run NAIRUs.

Fourth, again reflecting a conflation within economics between conceptual convenience and material realities, in the short run, trended variables are taken as given. They change only between and not within short-run periods. As has already been seen, this has been heavily criticised for ignoring what is happening to the level of investment and the capital stock. It raises the issue more generally of how trended variables get to change and what is their relationship to the short run. For example, trade unionism, monopolisation and productivity can change rapidly in the short run, in conjunction with one another and other variables, and might better be considered to constitute part of it.[39]

Finally, it is important to ask why these apparently facile procedures have been adopted despite the use of relatively sophisticated technical and statistical methods. In part, the answer has to do with the common tradition within economics of netting out the short run and the long run from one another both in theory and statistically. In part, it reflects the goals of the research in terms of empirical and policy outcomes. In part, it is a consequence of the way in which technical detail in productivity is modelled, with the impact through wage costs exactly matching the impact through monopoly pricing – with similar results for the impact of taxes and (inter-national) input prices. However, Layard *et al.* cannot have been dis-contented with this apparently fortuitous result because it allows them to proceed to their theoretical, empirical and policy conclusions. As Phelps perceptively, possibly ironically, observes:

> We do not want the natural rate to trend down as productivity trends up . . . The authors clearly want the natural rate to be invariant to productivity in the 'long run' but not in the short! This must have created a modelling crisis and it is interesting to see how they coped with it.

> (Phelps 1992: 1484)

9 CONCLUDING REMARKS

The answer from Layard *et al.*, as has been seen, is unsatisfactory.[40] The same applies more generally to macroeconomics, wriggle as ingeniously as it has across the analytical elements previously identified. It has signally failed to construct a satisfactory theory of the functioning of labour markets, even on its own terms. This is because, as is now apparent, it is tied to a number of debilitating, but continuing, methodological and theo-retical foundations.[41] These are, first, dependence upon methodological individualism which severely limits, if it does not preclude, the extent to which and the way in which both socioeconomic structures and agents can enter into the analysis.

Second, equilibrium plays a major organising role even if by way of the dynamics of deviation from it. As Lawlor argues of the most recent macro-economics:

> But note that this left the benchmark of the New Classical Economics intact. Unemployment would not occur if only markets were perfect as Beveridge and Pigou said 60 years ago . . . Perhaps the definition of the perfect benchmark is what needs to change.

> (Lawlor 1993: 19)

If not thrown out altogether! In its present form, the analysis becomes one of short-run (dis)equilibrium from which there is subsequent movement to the next (dis)equilibrium. This has the effect of treating the interaction of underlying socioeconomic forces or imperatives (derived from the drive for profitability) as essentially harmoniously, if not always fully effectively, coordinated through the more or less imperfect market.[42]

Third, there is the arbitrary and ambiguous division between the short and the long run, with the latter serving both as the passage of time and the depository of ultimate equilibrium. At worst, the short and long runs are rendered mutually compatible by treating them as independent of one another so that the short run represents deviations around a long-run trend that can be netted out. At best, the two are run together through hysteresis. This still requires a hierarchical division between variables in terms of their potential speeds of adjustment, including ones which must remain invariant otherwise the analytical structure collapses. Otherwise, the basis on which the long run is constructed potentially changes faster than movements relative to it. Within most recent analyses, based on inter-temporal optimisation and game-theoretic assumptions about competitors' strategies, short-run decisions can only be made on the basis of conjectures about the totality of the future – leading to further doubts around the validity of the distinction between the short and long runs, quite apart from the problem of multiple equilibria. Theoretically, then, the short-run–long-run distinction serves to order variables causally and chronologically in ways which are rarely examined, let alone justified. In addition, even with path-dependent hysteresis, the relationship between the short and long runs, with the former signifying fluctuations around the latter, also tends to be taken. But, as Stock and Watson (1988) have shown, there is evidence to suggest that, from a statistical point of view, economic series do not simply divide into trend with fluctuation.

Fourth, there is the arbitrary division between exogenous and endogenous variables. In conjunction with the particular theory and model structure employed, the exogenous variables, generally parameters within a system of equations, determine both long-run equilibrium and short-run dynamics. These parameters can be estimated, the theory tested statistically, comparative analysis within and between countries undertaken, and policies proposed in the light of their impact on the parameters and/or dynamics. Some of the factors taken as exogenous border on, or deeply invade, the ludicrous, especially those concerning tastes, endowments and technology. Others reflect the need to integrate the short and long runs, even if not simply netting out the latter. Either way, there is the prospect of explaining the path of the economy over the long term (in the chronological sense) on the basis of a few equations and parameters.

Fifth, this entails a particular understanding of the history of economies. Distinct periods can only be addressed in terms of the particular dynamics of a given model and set of parameters or through an exogenous shift in the model and parameters. This is made explicit in the NAIRU work where broad social and institutional change, as in the strength and organisation of trade unions or the benefit system, are reduced to parameter shifts. As Phelps reckons: 'The authors have taken a huge risk in throwing out nearly the whole corpus of general equilibrium theory in favor of a focus on some social and political parameters' (Phelps 1992: 1489). The weak conceptual basis with which such parameters are understood (and that they should not be seen as economic) is indicative of how they are left out altogether (or presumed to be neutral) in the vast majority of macroeconomics.

All of these points can be understood in a slightly different way. Just over a decade ago, as the NAIRU analysis itself was emerging, Fine and Harris (1985) were suggesting an account for the long-term weakness of the British economy. They characterised it empirically in terms of the 'three lows' – low wages, low investment and low productivity. An explanation for this was located in the lack of coherent industrial policy, itself a consequence of the strength of multinational corporations in undermining domestic industrial restructuring, the nature of financial institutions and their lack of commitment to long-term industrial investment and supervision, and the weakness of the trade union and labour movement in pressing successfully for alternatives. These factors have been important in the extent of Britain's deindustrialisation, and the rise of women's employment in the form of casualised, part-time and low-paid service jobs, as discussed in Fine (1992) against much broader historical and socioeconomic changes and their particular outcome in Britain.

The particular details and veracity of this account need not detain us. What is important is that such considerations as are brought to bear, and their impact on the functioning of labour markets, simply do not figure, except in very oblique ways, in the studies that are attached to more or less standard macroeconomics. At the time, this was the basis for a critique of the NAIRU approach: How could they be addressing the issue of unemployment without considering major features of the British economy, such as its financial institutions, its lack of coherence in industrial policy, its dominance by multinationals using it as an assembly point for serving the markets of Western Europe, its long-standing poor performance in growth and productivity, and the particularly severe form taken by deindustrialisation? The answer is to be found in the earlier discussion in terms of the setting aside of trends or interpreting such changes simply as shifts in parameter values. It is one of the paradoxes of the recent development of macroeconomic theory that the drive to consistency – in micro-foundations, in general equilibrium and in intertemporal optimisation – should require that consistent solutions be found simultaneously both for the short and the long runs, even though the scope of explanatory variables incorporated and the methodology employed are so demonstrably inadequate to the task that this presupposes.

The rest of this book is designed to consider and offer alternative ways of understanding the way in which labour markets function, ones which break with the features of the orthodoxy outlined at the beginning of this section. It does not, however, suggest an alternative macroeconomics. Rather, emphasis is placed on the different ways in which different sections of the labour market are structured and reproduced. In many respects, this is an acceptable conclusion to the orthodoxy, both in theoretical principle and empirical practice. The increasing reliance upon micro-foundations, for example, except where employing a representative worker, and the significance of trade unionism, monopoly in product markets, informational asymmetries and imperfections all suggest a varied labour market outcome from one sector to another. Theories of unemployment, especially in the insider-outsider version, suggest a division between the employed and the unemployed. The latter are themselves differentiated by a variety of categories and processes, the skilled underemployed as opposed to the unemployed, the voluntary and involuntary, short and long run, discouraged and searching, frictional and structural, etc., suggesting that, however the unemployed are counted in practice,[43] a very broad and clumsy mingling together of separate effects is involved.

Disaggregation is also a characteristic feature of the analysis of those in employment. Much emphasis has been placed recently on differentiation by skill, with the US achieving much less aggregate unemployment through a widening of pay differentials and less generous unemployment benefit, compared to the Western European model, other than Britain. Part of the argument derives from the extent to which technical change has favoured the more skilled and absolutely disfavoured the unskilled.[44] Layard *et al.* (1994: 64) suggest that the primary labour market is subject to job-rationing but that the secondary sector is market-clearing (despite high levels of unemployed especially amongst black youth). The notion of a wage curve, as sponsored by Blanchflower and Oswald on micro-foundations, also disaggregates, arguing that there is a remarkably stable inverse relation between wage rates and *local* levels of unemployment, once correcting for other, standard labour market variables.[45]

This is not to suggest that the mainstream's acknowledgement of the specificity of disaggregated labour, or other, markets is about to inspire a new round of theoretical endeavour that breaks with the inadequacies and simplicities of the past. On the contrary, as shown especially in the assessment of Hahn and Solow, the new macroeconomics is flourishing on the basis of an eclectic amalgam of methodological individualism, micro-foundations, and more or less arbitrary macroeconomic judgements – how to disaggregate, which prices to take as more or less flexible, etc. Despite this eclecticism, however, its application to the empirical evidence persistently reveals the differentiation between labour markets and how they function.

To sum up, interrogation of the limited understanding of labour markets that is offered by conventional macroeconomics offers two conclusions as the basis for further study. First, there must be a complete change in method and theory. Second, separate labour markets function differently from one another, and theory should be sensitive to such variations.

NOTES

1 For a standard macroeconomic text, see Carlin and Soskice (1990) or Chrystal and Price (1994). For more critical presentations, see Weeks (1989) and especially Dow (1985, 1996) for contrasts with other approaches. For a more advanced and contemporary macroeconomic text, see Romer (1996). Note that his final chapter is devoted to (the microeconomics of) unemployment and stands alone from the rest of the book rather than, for example, serving as the culmination of the earlier chapters.

2 For overviews of developments in macroeconomics, see Fischer (1988) and Mankiw (1990) and, in the context of labour markets, see Sapsford and Tzannatos (1990), Sapsford and Tzannatos (1993), Lawlor (1993) and Manning (1995), for example.

3 See Nickell's Royal Economics Society centenary survey of unemployment: 'Not surprisingly, a good deal of this survey is concerned with macroeconomic issues because unemployment is a general equilibrium phenomenon' (Nickell 1990: 393). This is frequently complemented by the distinction between short- and long-run equilibria, with the latter netted out, subject to hysteresis, to examine the former independently of trends. All of this is discussed in detail below.

4 For a critique of the associated stabilisation programmes, see Fine and Stoneman (1996) and references cited there.

5 An excellent example is given by the different versions of Keynesian economics offered by Keynes himself (disaggregating national income by consumption and investment) and Kalecki (disaggregating by wages and profits).

6 For example, (neo-)Ricardian theories of distribution assume that profits and wages are the simultaneous division of net output, whereas Marx's theory of exploitation presumes that wages precede production which results in profits. See Chapter 7, but note that the simplest version of Walrasian competitive equilibrium depends upon everything taking place simultaneously over an infinitesimally small moment of time.

7 Note that Keyssar (1993) argues that economic theory does not necessarily have to respond to change in order to accommodate the facts, rather the facts can change to accommodate the theory! Hence, as unemployment rose, this promoted the idea that it was voluntary even more than when unemployment was less severe.

8 Corry (1995) considers that the New Classical Economics arose out of the need to serve a shift to the right and that its appeal has declined, opening the way for less extreme use of rational expectations, in the more recent period.

9 See Dow:

> Among many economists also there is a deep-seated and genuine wish that all economists might agree on a range of general principles and argue only about the details. Hence Friedman's attempt to pour oil on waters he had troubled with his monetarism: 'We are all Keynesians now' . . . echoed more recently by Laidler . . . 'We are all monetarists now'.
>
> (Dow 1985: 1)

10 By way of parody with hysteresis within macroeconomics itself, to be discussed below, NCE can be seen to have had a path-dependent impact upon the evolution of macroeconomic theory despite having been surpassed itself!

11 For discussion of these points in greater detail, see Fine (1980). Coddington (1983) refers to the IS/LM framework as hydraulic Keynesianism as a result of its use of effective demand as a mechanical lever on the economy.

12 Note that one message of the Keynesian system is that money matters in the short run to the outcome of the macro-economy. This was formalised by Patinkin (1965) in 1956 in his refutation of the classical dichotomy. It is illegitimate to separate the economy into a real sector that grinds out equilibrium quantities and *relative* prices and a monetary sector that determines the level of absolute prices. More formally, the homogeneity postulate, the classical dichotomy and Walras Law are mutually inconsistent. For a discussion, see Fine and Murfin (1984).

13 Coddington (1983) uses the term "reconstituted reductionism" because, as discussed below, it explicitly restores methodological individualism to macroeconomics and for the purpose of interpreting Keynes.

14 Note, however, that such models have now been constructed in a standard way on microeconomic foundations, with a representative monopolistic firm, and a representative monopsonistic trade union supplier of labour. See Dixon (1991) and Dixon and Rankin (1994) for example.

15 The denial of involuntary unemployment even as it is glaringly and increasingly obvious has remarkable parallels with Lionel Robbins definition of economics, 50 years or so earlier, as the allocation of scarce resources between competing ends – this even though both capital and labour were massively underutilised during the 1930s.

16 For reviews of new Keynesianism, see for example the special issue of *Journal of Economic Perspectives*, edited by Mankiw (1993).

17 Note that this takes for granted that micro-foundations for macro is the appropriate methodology and the appropriate prism through which to judge the macroeconomics of the past. It writes out the possibility of macro as distinct from micro except as depending upon inadequately developed micro.

18 Phelps suggests:

> Looking back it is now clear that rapid changes in both focus and method have been overtaking macroeconomics in the past dozen years. In the second half of the 70s the New Keynesian economics of nonsynchronous wage and price setting . . . was given a rational expectations formulation and coupled with the standard Keynesian/monetarist demand side to become in a few years' time the model of choice in most macroeconomic textbooks of the 80s. It replaced the purely qualitative, expectational-disequilibrium Old Keynesian models from the late 60s and effectively beat back the elegant New Classical equilibrium models from the early 70s.
>
> (Phelps 1992: 1476–7)

19 Solow is a Nobel prize winner.

20 Another model is one in which a social norm is internalised and institutionalised. This is discussed in Chapter 10.

21 In their case, they assume that the nominal wage is exogenous and fixed in order to ease comparative statics.

22 See Solow:

> The proper conclusion is not that the vertical long-run Phillips curve version of the natural-rate hypothesis is wrong. I would suggest instead that the empirical basis for that story is at best flimsy. A natural rate that hops around from one triennium to another under the influence of unspecified forces, *including past unemployment rates*, is not 'natural' at all. 'Epiphenomenal' would be a better adjective; look it up.
>
> (Solow 1987: 33; emphasis in original)

23 For an account and assessment, see Romer (1996).

24 See especially Phelps (1992, 1994, 1995).

25 Obviously, the interpretation of Phelps' motives are in part speculative, but see the preface to his 1994 book.

26 See Cross (1995b) and especially Hahn (1995).

27 The term 'fundamentals' here refers to what are taken to be the exogenously given factors such as tastes, endowments and technology. Note the term tends to take on an opposite meaning in more informal and journalistic macroeconomic

and financial assessments, where it refers to what are highly variable economic and political influences.

28 See also Dixon, who suggests that:

> The concept of the natural rate . . . in its simplest form . . . consists of two hypotheses:
> (a) There exists a unique equilibrium for the economy determined by real factors in the economy (classical dichotomy).
> (b) Equilibrium output, employment and the real wage are determined in the labour market (decomposability).
>
> (Dixon 1995: 69)

Once moving beyond the generally invalid properties of dichotomy and decomposability, we enter the chaotic conceptual world recognised by Solow:

> The usual, if casual, interpretation of the 'natural rate' has very little basis either in theory or in data analysis. In a sense, it is not clear what we are talking about when we talk about the natural rate.
>
> (Solow 1987: 24)

29 Endogenous growth theory was inspired by the empirical anomaly of non-convergence of growth rates, leading to amendments in standard growth theory – just as the theory of the natural rate has been amended to handle the empirical anomaly of persistently higher levels of unemployment.

30 The term 'hysteresis' is borrowed from physics. The standard example is given by a spring which retrieves its initial elasticity properties (no hysteresis) as long as it is not unduly stretched (hysteresis). As will be seen, hysteresis has been used to suggest that very high and persistent levels of unemployment will lead to a lack of elasticity in adjustment to lower levels.

31 See especially Layard *et al.* (1991, 1994).

32 Capacity to work deteriorates and, according to Snower (1995) being unemployed becomes addictive, and hence cumulative, as analysed by Becker (1992). If this is so, however, employed workers would taken this into account in their optimisation just as Becker suggests that (potential) addicts set current satisfaction against lesser utility later as a result of changes in preferences (as addiction is understood). For a critique of Becker's understanding of addiction, see Fine (1997b).

33 For consideration of macroeconomic effects in the presence of strategic oligopoly, see Damania and Madsen (1995) and Madsen (1995). Because higher interest rates, generally thought to be deflationary, can raise the incentive to breach collusion and expand output, results can be counter-intuitive to those of standard models.

34 Phelps's (1992) review is highly perceptive, not least because it is written from a very clear perspective of his own as laid out above. On the other hand, this is also a weakness as he necessarily interprets other's work within a framework of conforming to, or diverging from, his own stance. In particular, he sees their work as specifying the path of the natural rate (he has no problem with the term) even if with deviations, although their emphasis might be more on the deviations. Preceding the quote offered in the text:

> Such general equilibrium models of the equilibrium unemployment rate path present a moving equilibrium-rate theory of actual unemployment if we add the supplementary hypothesis that the actual unemployment rate, though possibly displaying disturbances, tends closely to track the equilibrium rate. The volume by Layard and company can be said to belong to this new equilibrium category of macroeconomic modelling.
>
> (Phelps 1992: 1478)

Note how often 'equilibrium' appears in this assessment!

35 Apart from their own empirical work, and those collected in Bean *et al.* (1987), see Anderton and Mayhew (1994) for example.

36 Other reactionary proposals include an aversion to public sector employment, employment protection laws and free collective bargaining - they strengthen the power of insiders and wage pressure.

37 Alan Manning appears to have devoted himself to refutation of standard neo-classical results by use of its own techniques. Apart from multiple equilibria in the presence of economies of scale, he has also argued, for example, against the supposed negative effects of a minimum wage on employment and of equal pay legislation on employment of women. See Chapters 8 and 9, respectively.

38 For a similar argument, see Manning:

> It is possible that the unemployment rate is affected by the rate of productivity growth but not the level of productivity . . . The faster the rate of growth, the higher the returns to being in a job tomorrow. The best way to be in a job tomorrow is to be in a job today and the best way to do this is to moderate your wage demands today . . . this opens up the possibility that there has been a permanent rise in the unemployment rate as a result of the fall in productivity growth that seemed to occur in the mid 1970s in many OECD countries.
>
> (Manning 1995: 264)

39 Layard *et al.* (1991) do allow for variations in monopoly mark-up over the cycle.

40 Phelps (1992: 1484) suggests his own resolution: 'In my view the best solution is the introduction of wealth (or, better, the income from wealth) into the wage-setting block of structuralist models'. Thus, productivity effects are neutralised over the long run through their impact on trended income rather than trended costs.

41 To a lesser extent, this is also true of genuinely, rather than Phelps-type, structuralist models most of which can be reconstructed on microfoundations as they differ only by offering deviations from conventional equilibria. See Fine and Murfin (1984) for a critique of post-Keynesian macroeconomics from this perspective.

42 Note that Heckman and MacCurdy are highly critical of the distinction between equilibrium and disequilibrium, suggesting that the latter reflects a lack of theory to specify the mechanism by which unemployment is generated or distributed. Either the mechanism must be historical, as in insider-outsider models, for which there is then an equilibrium, or employment is on the basis of random selection for which one needs to specify the rationing mechanism for jobs. They are also deeply sceptical about whether such different interpretations of unemployment can be tested against one another effectively: 'A protective belt of logically possible equilibrium alternatives and the absence of any clearly stated disequilibrium alternative make impossible a sharp test of disequilibrium in the labor market' (Heckman and MacCurdy 1993: 133).

43 This is as much determined ideologically and politically as by economic concepts. See Bartholomew *et al.*'s report on the measurement of unemployment in the UK, pointing to heterogeneity within the employed and the unemployed: 'The situation is now more fluid and it is no longer possible to make the simple dichotomy into employed and unemployed' (Bartholomew *et al.* 1995: 363). They also reproduce a table detailing the 32 changes that have been made in measuring unemployment from 1979 to 1989. Of these, only the first seems to have increased the count – by 20,000. The others seem to have reduced the count by at least one million!

44 See Freeman (1995), for example, and also Nickell (1996), who finds that widening differentials in pay and unemployment is more common across than within sectors and enterprises, including more and less technically innovative, concluding that this is due to widening general effects of unequal distribution of human capital. This, however, leaves unexplained why relatively high levels of unemployment should have persisted amongst the more highly educated than previously.

45 See especially Blanchflower and Oswald (1994, 1995) and Card (1995) for a critical assessment.

3 Human capital theory
Labour as asset?

1 INTRODUCTION

In principle, neoclassical economics focuses on the optimising individual agent. In the context of the labour market, this involves the specific characteristics that each worker has to offer in terms of the supply of labour and, in formulating demand for labour, the productive services that are sought by employers. The labour that is offered by individual workers reflects the capabilities for work which are either innate or acquired over a lifetime through upbringing, general or specific education and training, and work or other experience.[1] For neoclassical economists, 'human capital' is designated as the flow of productive services that can be provided by a worker. It is a term used as a parallel with, some might say a parody of, 'physical capital', which is equally perceived as providing a stream of productive services over time. Human capital theory, then, is concerned with the extent to which human capital is accumulated, through education, training and work experience, and how it is used and rewarded.

In this way, use of the notion of 'human capital' has now become acceptable and even standard across a wide range of applications in economic and social analysis. In particular, it has been seen to be crucial in explaining differences in rates of growth between countries, in levels of fertility across the population, in economic comparative advantage, and so on.[2] It is also important in arguing for the presence of market failure, whether in schooling or training, and for legitimising a continuing role for the state, although this is still open to challenge by die-hard free-marketeers,[3] in an ideological climate where its interventions have increasingly been challenged. It can be argued that social and private rates of return diverge, with the former higher and in excess of the cost of capital. In other words, as the private market system does not provide sufficient education and skills, the state should intervene to do so. Further, we all tend to favour education in principle and as a potential lever for egalitarianism and for promoting economic development. The idea of human capital offers us the opportunity to argue coherently for such positions. In its range of applications and in its analytical and ideological acceptability, human capital is an idea whose time has come in a big way, even if surreptitiously rather than with a big bang.

It was not always thus. Becker (1993: xix), one of the founders of the human capital theory, observes that the term has become popular enough to be incorporated into presidential campaigning, yet notes that 'a dozen years ago, this terminology would have been inconceivable'. It is hardly surprising that there should have been an antipathy to the concept, whether in its formal analytical clothes or in its more informal popular usage. For, in both cases, it signifies the reification of the human – that the results of education, or learning more generally from whatever source, should be considered akin to the creation and possession of a physical asset. Thus, it is as if workers can be clothed, fed, housed *and* educated by expenditure of the corresponding costs of provision. The only major difference is that education seems to hold out the prospects of longer-lasting productive benefits for the economy as a whole as well as for the individual worker in terms of higher rewards.

There is, in a sense, especially in the hands of neoclassical economists, a double reification. First, capital in general – and not just human capital – is treated as a physical asset, as opposed to a social relation of production as in Marxist theory, for example. Issues of power and conflict are set aside for narrow notions of capital as a fixed input into the production process. There must be doubts about whether the neglect of power and conflict is appropriate for what are primarily commercially provided goods. The doubts must be even greater for the provision of education where the state and politics are heavily embroiled, often with a non-commercial content. Second, then, as already observed, when addressing education and skills, the notion of capital as a physical asset is superimposed on a human activity, or set of human activities, that do not generally and directly fall within the orbit of capital.

Consequently, human capital treats education, training, etc. as a stream of costs of provision which are to be set against the stream of benefits which accrue. The incidence of these costs and benefits, whether attached to the state or individuals, is of secondary conceptual importance. It is, however, crucial in practice in seeking greater efficiency, equality and appropriate levels of educational provision. As argued at length in Agbodza and Fine (1996), it follows that human capital theory is entirely without a theory of educational provision. The latter remains an unopened 'black box',[4] sufficiently specified, as far as it is itself concerned, for the purposes at hand merely by specifying its associated streams of costs and benefits.

This account of human capital theory is confirmed by the response of one of its leading practitioners, Psacharopoulos, to criticisms of calculations of rates of return to public investment in human capital. Many of the criticisms are empirical, but some are conceptual along the lines already broadly suggested. The reaction is akin to that of the practical scientist seeking pragmatic solutions to urgent problems on the basis of limited resources:

'If you do not like my calculations, do your own and justify them as better.'[5] Such bluster can neither conceal nor excuse the limitations of the conceptual basis of the standard approach. It involves the principles of comparative advantage, which are sacrosanct, applicable to education as for any other investment, and open only to empirical dispute, like any other prospective return on investment:

> This is all there is in the human capital concept – a simple trade-off between sacrificing something today for the sake of having more tomorrow . . . Such a trade-off has been documented extensively around the world and, pending another revolution in economic thought, it remains valid today . . . Such rate of return is very similar to the one firms use to decide whether or not they would enter a particular investment venture, and it can be compared with the interest rate on bank deposits or the yield of equities in the stock market . . . As with all scientific tools, the rate of return has been subject to controversy centred on its empirical application . . . Yet, to blankly deny its validity, or shy away from its estimation, is equivalent to an investor throwing money at a venture without having some notion of the anticipated yield.
>
> (Psacharopoulos 1996b: 278)

On this basis, Psacharopoulos parodies his opponents as daydreamers who imagine that educational needs in some absolute sense can be met without regard to cost or rate of return on alternative uses of the resources concerned.

Leaving behind the businessmen of education, the economics of education more generally, as a specialised field, is not so blinkered. It does attempt to examine in greater detail the uses and effectiveness of the various economic resources devoted to human capital.[6] This distinguishes it from the work of the founding 'fathers' of the field, like Becker (1993), who deal primarily in principles and pay little attention to the practical details of education itself. The main concern is with only more slightly developed notions of the productivity of time as materialised in education and work experience. The economics of education proper goes beyond this by throwing in other variables in order to provide a more accurate assessment of how human capital is produced. Carnoy observing that the empirical performance of production functions for human capital models has been limited suggests that:

> Moving away from the assembly line model of educational production adds a completely new dimension to the production function models of schools and educational systems and even those micro models of education that attempt to analyze the achievement productivity of classrooms in terms of time use.
>
> (Carnoy 1995a: 5)

Broadly, with much detail to be filled in, he sees teaching and learning as an activity, involving processes, interactions and relations between people.

What is peculiar in this, and much of the more aware literature in the field, is that such deeper understandings are perceived as requiring modification in the ways in which human capital is produced, measured and even understood, but it is not that the concept of human capital itself is totally undermined. Carnoy (1995c) himself, for example, correctly rejects the notion that the school can be understood as a private firm, and seeks to understand it as a hybrid of a public and private firm. This is to accept the validity of a particular notion of a private firm, even if it is understood as inappropriate for schooling. The specific economic and social relations governing the provision of schooling are not necessarily directly addressed; the orientation remains one of measuring how the nebulous output, human capital, is created.[7] It is as if the addition of teacher–pupil ratios and other qualitative and quantitative indices of schools, schooling and pupils suffice to amend or refine the notion of human capital and to measure it more accurately. More generally, in the special issue of the *Economics of Education Review* edited by Carnoy (1996a), the comparative contributions bring out how diverse is the production of 'human capital'.[8]

Exactly the same considerations apply to analysis of the *use* of human capital. Carnoy observes: 'Thus the pay off to education is conditioned not only by technology, but by information, ideology, political power, property rights, citizenship rights in the workplace, and the willingness of organisations to innovate constantly' (Carnoy 1995a: 3). It is a moot point whether such a broad range of such all-embracing causal factors should be used to modify the calculation of the pay-off to education or, rather, to reject its basis in human capital theory altogether. Does it really make sense in the presence of these factors to treat the attributes of the worker as embodying a well-defined set of productive properties comparable to a physical asset? There is an irreconcilable conflict between the defining and core notion of human capital as a physical asset and its refinement to take account of other factors and corresponding processes and relations which are clearly not asset-like. Paradoxically, the incorporation of other considerations into the understanding of human capital, especially those which are specific to schooling, seem to have rendered it more acceptable, even though they highlight the concept's glaring inadequacies on close scrutiny.

It is against this background that the role of human capital in analysing segmented labour markets will be considered in this chapter. Apart from the more general ideological acceptability that it has enjoyed, the gross conceptual deficiencies in human capital theory have been papered over or set aside by its relatively limited role in theoretical advance, with effort consolidated by its pervasive presence in empirical, applied and policy work.[9] It is almost impossible to consider labour market issues, and differentiation in pay and conditions, without reference to skills. And skills are inevitably examined by reference to some notion of human capital. In other words, human capital is perceived to be blessed with being empirically and practically useful as a tool for which its conceptual inadequacies can be excused, even forgotten. Conceptual and other criticisms of the use of human capital theory tend first to be met with the response of reluctant acceptance and, then, with a more aggressive challenge of what to put in its place, as at least it gives a figure or two with which to understand the world and to design policy. However, as will be shown below, its usefulness as a tool is thrown into doubt by its conceptual inadequacies, not only in theory but also in practice.

To a large extent, then, the discussion here is oriented around issues linked to empirical applications associated with human capital theory despite the main concern being with theory in this book. However, this is more or less inevitable because of the superficial nature of human capital as a concept, so that its fuller development, as well as its inadequacies, emerge most sharply in applied statistical work. It displays just how simple is the understanding of what constitutes skills, how they are produced and with what effects.

2 THE BASIC MODEL: THEORY AND PRACTICE

Essentially, the purpose of human capital theory in the first instance, as far as labour markets are concerned, is to be able to explain why there should be differences in wages for different workers, even in the context of a perfectly functioning market. If workers have different productive capabilities, however they may have been gained, then they should receive correspondingly different rewards. These capabilities, warranting wage differentials, might arise from innate abilities or upbringing, or they might have been positively pursued in order to gain economic advantage. Thus, all abilities constitute human capital, but education and training build it up deliberately through the use of economic resources. Human capital can also be gained through work experience.

The arguments in the preceding paragraph do not effectively go beyond a situation in which there is a single job at which some workers are more productive than others. There are two further issues to address. First, who gets what education and training and, second, who gets allocated to which jobs. Taking work experience into account, these two questions are not necessarily independent of one another. For the perfectly functioning economy, free of market imperfections, individual workers would be allocated to appropriate jobs, and efficient levels and types of education and training would also be distributed across the work-force, equating marginal products, costs and benefits in human capital in exactly the same way as supply and demand are equalised for a general economic equilibrium across goods and services.

Now, we have a model which sets out to explain the skill and occupational distribution of the work-force as well as the corresponding rewards. In some respects, it is very much analogous to a theory of supply and demand in which resources are devoted to product differentiation in the form of higher or lower quality. A high-quality product costs more to produce but yields more output in the form of utility – hence it commands a higher price, contingent upon the relative demand for higher- and lower-quality products. The same applies to labour, only it contributes more indirectly to final utility through the contribution that it can make to output, whether quantitatively or qualitatively – human capital as a source per unit of labour of more or better output.[10]

To this basic model, further angles can be added that do indeed draw upon the specificity of the labour market, that distinguish it from bananas, cheese or motor cars. For labour itself is produced in a very different way than these commodities, which are generally dependent primarily upon commercial supply alone. Labour, on the other hand, has a will of its own and can choose to work or not, whereas other commodities are the playthings of human agents. Whether by virtue of culture or, as some would have it, innate biological differences, men and women have to allocate their time not only between work and leisure but also between working in the domestic and in the commercial sphere. If there are economies of scale in the acquisition of human capital, it would make sense for those with a comparative advantage in the commercial (domestic) sphere to specialise in that sphere, both in gaining work experience and in education and training. Consequently, it can be argued that it makes sense for men and women to specialise in paid and unpaid work, respectively, on the basis of initial talents that are consolidated over a lifetime.

Of course, such differences will be modified by the shifting productivities of the commercial and domestic spheres and by the rise of real wages, which may induce women to participate more in the labour market. These factors will also affect the incentives to have children and the ways in which they are brought up (fewer higher-quality children through bought-in goods and services). Even the rise of divorce in the light of women's independent careers may be explained by the lesser benefits of the economies of co-operation and specialisation in a marriage contract with a man.

This brief overview of the role of human capital theory is intended to illustrate a number of points.[11] First, it can purport to explain why there are extremely complex variations in wages, occupations, human capital and conditions of work across the population, even in the context of perfectly working labour (and other) markets. Second, the capacity to explain this variation involves the incorporation of a whole range of variables and economic and social processes, not all of which are directly associated with the labour market or even the formal economy. Third, almost any outcome may be said to conform to human capital theory following tautologous reference to exogenously given preferences or technology. Thus, for example, women enter the labour market because the income effect of their higher wage is greater than the substitution effect of the higher income that can be earned by their husbands (and it would be the other way round if women did not enter the labour market). Alternatively, as more features of the labour market emerge over time or at lower levels of disaggregation, more and more factors or ingenious processes can be suggested in order to explain why these apparent paradoxes do conform to the model of a perfectly working economy, despite initial appearances to the contrary.

On this basis, human capital theory can suggest models for econometric estimation. In principle, these ought to incorporate the roles both of the supply of and the demand for labour.[12] In practice, this is rarely done. Rather, the wage of different workers is expected to be related in a simple regression to independent variables that represent the level of human capital. In addition, other variables, such as gender, might be added and these can also be interpreted as reflecting differences in productivity due to innate or acquired capabilities. Such an interpretation may be advanced, however, only if it is presumed that the labour market is working perfectly; otherwise, a significant coefficient for gender differences may be interpreted as reflecting sexism in the labour market in one form or another.

But, if as is more usual now, the labour market is interpreted as working imperfectly, then the role of an independent gender variable takes on exactly the opposite role. If differences in human capital are accounted for as far as possible by other independent variables, such as education, training and work experience, then gender can be used as a variable to measure the extent of labour market discrimination against women (although some still might argue that a significant difference is due to unmeasured differences in human capital between the sexes). Thus, for Carnoy:[13]

> The human capital model predicts that the main factor explaining changes in the relative earnings of different groups in society is the change in the relative level of education amongst the groups. All the papers in this collection begin with this hypothesis and the empirical results suggest that this is at least partially true.
>
> (Carnoy 1996a: 209)

However, once it is admitted that the labour market is no longer working perfectly, this opens up the possibility of introducing a whole range of other factors that might affect outcomes. Traditionally, it is observed that the functioning of the labour market involves a wide range of factors. Higher wages, for example, can be associated with particular sectors, capital-intensity, trade unionism, market concentration, etc. The rationale for including such independent variables in a wage equation is twofold. They may be interpreted as proxies for human capital or other factors that would induce wage differentials in an ideally working labour market, or, on the basis of some alternative analytical insight, these factors could be seen to represent the effect of an imperfectly working labour market – as in the ability of a trade union to create a wage relativity or to share in surplus profits however they might have been created. In addition, another set of variables might be thrown into the estimation of a wage equation:

those reflecting the personal characteristics of the workers – such as age, gender and race. Again, these might be proxies for sources of wage differentials, even in an ideal labour market, or they might be perceived as connected to the consequences of labour market imperfections.

The foregoing all provides what might be termed 'the basic model' within human capital theory for estimating wages. To repeat, it divides variables into those that might be expected to influence outcomes and create differentials even in an ideal world of perfect competition and those that have the same effect but through an imperfectly functioning labour market – although, of course, it is possible, especially between theories and given limitations of data, for the same variables to figure on both sides of this analytical divide.

This ambiguity is extended once the significance of such wage equations for labour market segmentation is addressed. For segmentation implies imperfectly working labour markets in this context.[14] In the case of gender, for example, a difference in the estimated coefficient for men (higher wages) and women (lower), would suggest that women belong to a separate labour market segment representing sexism or discrimination. This now, however, involves a rather different notion of what is a normally functioning labour market from which discrimination is being measured. Initially, the idea is that perfect competition is the standard from which deviations should be measured and which would itself, in any case, allow for wage differentials according to a set of factors representing human capital. But in looking at wage differentials between men and women, the effect, for example, of trade unions needs to be netted out (since men may belong to trade unions more than women) in a way that is statistically comparable to the netting out of 'genuine' human capital effects. In other words, the normal functioning of the labour market, from which differentials, and hence segmentation, are being measured, is no longer the ideal of perfect competition. Essentially, what is being construed as the standard against which to measure a legitimate source of wage differentials is potentially, and even surreptitiously, being extended to incorporate factors associated in the orthodoxy with deviation from perfect competition.

Of course, the segmentation could be interpreted in a different way altogether, as a mirror image of the previously discussed example. It could focus on the differences between those workers who belong to trade unions and those who do not, correcting wage outcomes for gender differences – so that the wage differences between men and women are taken as a standard against which the trade union differential and segmentation can be measured. A further extension could be the refinement of segmentation into the four groups defined according to gender and trade union membership. A similar extension could be made on the basis of other socioeconomic characteristics which, in principle, could be extended more or less indefinitely.

None the less, the fundamental logic remains the same, irrespective of the number of socioeconomic variables and segments employed. There is a

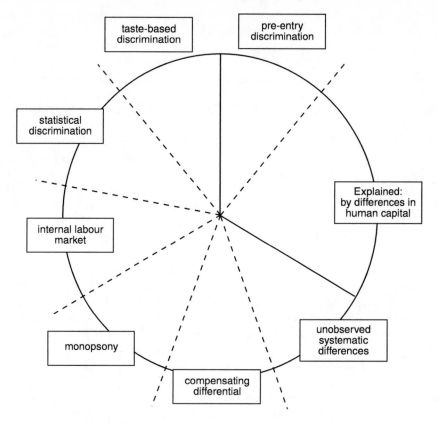

Figure 1 Pay differentials explained with human capital as one component
Source: Paci *et al.* (1995: 91)

'normal' labour market outcome (not necessarily perfect competition), including differentials, for which the distribution of human capital provides a core if not exclusive part, from which other deviations represent plausible evidence for the presence of segmentation. Two implications follow from such an analytical schema. First, as more variables are introduced and are assigned to the normal workings of the labour market, so the measured importance of segmentation tends in practice, if not of necessity in principle, to be whittled away, as it is detached from segmentation variables and attached to other explanatory factors. Thus, women are paid less not because of sexism but because of lack of human capital, work experience, trade unionism, occupational advantage etc., although these might themselves be imbued with structured and systemic disadvantage. If so, however, the sources of such inequalities can be interpreted as not necessarily belonging to, or originating within, the labour market but as being due to what are termed 'pre-entry factors'.

A second implication of constructing and measuring the effects of segmentation through corrected human capital equations is that, as the number of variables increases, so does the number of potential segments.[15] In principle, it would be possible to have as many segments as individuals, as long as the number of characteristics that distinguish between individual workers were expanded sufficiently. This *reductio ad absurdum* is a reflection of the individualistic methodology underlying human capital theory and its empirical application – even if it can be concealed by the use of social or group variables, such as class or gender, which are none the less applicable as individual characteristics. Essentially, each individual worker is rewarded according to a set of characteristics, even if some of them are shared in common and each is not a genuine or legitimate index of productive contribution. It is almost as if there is a points system, some plus and some minus, for which you get rewards in the form of higher wages. The estimation of a human capital equation is designed to determine the number of points corresponding to each labour market, or other, attribute.

Both this and the previous point are reflections of the underlying methodological individualism and, in particular, a sharp illustration of the absence of any proper economic modelling, even from an orthodox stance. This problem can be put in another way: What exactly is the equation being estimated even from an orthodox, neoclassical point of view? Is it the supply of labour or is it the demand for labour? Or is it some reduced form of the two? For human capital theory, the answer would appear to be the demand for labour, further warranted by the notion that there is general excess supply of labour (so that outcomes are always on the demand curve). Further, this would also be legitimate should it be assumed that supply-side effects are statistically independent of those on the demand-side, given the frequent reliance upon cross-section household data. However, this would all need to be taken into account in deriving the form of, and restrictions on (signs of parameters), the equation to be estimated. Obviously, for some variables, the sign of parameters in the labour equation will be different (even of opposite sign) according to whether they reflect supply or demand, especially for wages but also for other working conditions. Should part-time working, for example, exhibit a positive coefficient (potentially reflecting employer's wish for a cheap, flexible work-force) or a negative one (workers' wish for full-time, secure employment).

The lack of a specific, or well-specified, theory is reflected in a number of different ways. First, there is generally no alternative hypothesis against which the theory is tested, other than the trivial one of significance for test-statistics. What is meant here by 'alternative theory' is a different view of how the labour market works. In human capital theory, it is perceived to be more or less distant from an ideal, perfectly competitive labour market according to the extent to which unjustified wage differentials persist. These differentials or residuals after correcting for other variables tend, in turn, to be 'explained' by a collective set of factors gathered under the umbrella of institutional structure or other factors, such as sexism, trade unions, etc., which occur to the researcher and which have not previously been specified within the initial theory and equation to be estimated. In this respect, there is a shift to a norm for the working of the labour market which is no longer that of perfect competition – quite the opposite. The labour market norm is now intended to be realistic, reflecting how real labour markets actually work, with all their standard imperfections incorporated. In addition, whilst there may be commonly recognised factors to include as part and parcel of a typical labour market, each researcher can freely select or design the norm. Paradoxically, the standard against which labour market deviations come to be judged is no longer itself a standard of any general applicability!

In this procedure, not only is there no structure to the analysis in the sense of carefully distinguishing supply and demand, but labour market structure itself is only identified with differences in parameter values as estimated in a single equation. This leads to the conclusion that if men and women, say, with the same labour market characteristics are paid the same wage, then there are no labour market structures. This is absurd, given that it is consistent with heavy, even total, occupational segmentation by sex. Further, although this is a corollary of the previous point, there is theoretical deficiency in failing to explore the potential connections between the variables that are included in the wage equation and which are taken to be independent of one another for the purposes of such single equation regressions. To have rectified this would be to give some structure to the 'model'. It surely can be argued that there are definite mutually determining relations between variables such as gender, occupation, capital-intensity and sector, etc. The failure to recognise this is not merely a theoretical error, but it implies that no confidence can reside in any of the empirical results since they are based on mis-specification of the underlying model from whatever theoretical perspective it might be drawn. In principle, there is no problem in specifying a set of equations to estimate how the labour market works. In practice, in human capital theory, this is extremely rare.[16]

In short, the analytical procedure can be summarised as follows. A tripartheid division of variables is made into:

1 those that are included in a more or less standard regression;
2 those that are included in the analysis but outside the regression;
3 those that are excluded altogether from the analysis but which might be relevant.

Concern, here, is not with (3), although it can be serious given the wide range of variables that are known to affect labour market outcomes. Taking (1) and (2) together first, (1) is used to construct a set of statistics, to measure decomposed changes in wages, incorporating a role for variations in human capital after taking account of other variables. At the same time, the impact of these other variables can also be measured, whether indicating a normal working of the labour market or not, together with an unexplained part of wage variations. These measures can then be explained by (2) – market imperfections, possibly unspecified, serving as an explanatory factor of last resort.

The typical human capital equation might be written in the form:

$$w = a + bH + cX + e$$

where w is wage; e is an error term; a, b and c are vectors of parameters; H a set of human capital variables; and X a set of variables that affect labour market outcomes but not as human capital. The H variables ought only to involve those factors that affect the wage through greater reward for greater productivity. The X variables reflect market imperfections such as trade unionism. These represent a standard if imperfect working of the labour market. It is a moot point whether personal or other characteristics, such as age, gender and geographical location, should fall under H or X. For they can constitute variables that simultaneously reflect the perfect and the imperfect working of the market according to the underlying theory employed. Gender, for example, may be used either to measure discrimination or as a taste for discrimination or comparative advantage in domestic as opposed to commercial labour.

The procedure, then, is to derive a set of statistics to explain the wage relativities (from variables (1)) and to explain those statistics by an informally defined set of factors and, presumably, a complementary set of what are usually ill-specified theoretical propositions, around variables (2). This begs the questions of why the supplementary set of variables (2) were not included in the initial regressions and whether the two sets of theoretical propositions are consistent with one another. There may be data reasons for the first issue: How are we to quantify institutional change and market imperfections, for example? But this can hardly justify confidence in the results of empirical work. For it depends upon the following sort of logic:

> We believe that such and such a variable is a crucial determinant of the workings of the labour market but we are excluding it from our calculations because we do not have data on it. However, we will use it to explain the results that we do get in more informal discourse.

This is open to the immediate objection that the empirical results that you are seeking to explain would themselves have been dramatically different if the initially excluded variables had been included in the first place!

The issue of theoretical compatibility between (1) and (2) is also serious, for the estimates from (1) are based on a human capital theory in which the institutional factors of (2) are presumed to be absent (unless inadvertently captured statistically in the independent variables included in (1)). As previously observed, the single equation estimation implies that labour markets are only structured by shifts in the parameter values. Consequently, to the extent that labour markets are more fundamentally structured by institutional or other change, there is an inconsistency between the way in which the estimates are made and the way in which they are explained, for, as already argued, the estimates depend upon the absence of the institutional change which are then used to explain them! Consequently, when discrimination by race or sex, or a trade union, mark-up is measured by the extent of a residual in an estimated labour market equation, something very peculiar is going on especially, as is usually the case, when the residual is found to be substantial even after the removal of other factors. In this instance, the conclusion that such residual factors are important undermines the basis on which the extent to which they are important is being calculated.[17] The only valid conclusion that can be drawn is that theory, and empirical work, needs to start over again.

3 CONCLUDING REMARKS

In many respects, these criticisms of the way in which labour market equations are theoretically understood and estimated are not specific to human capital theory. However, as already observed, the inclusion of human capital variables is now extremely common, adds a tinge of (false) realism and is closely related to explaining wage differentials, in terms of both justified and unjustified components relative to some labour market norm that has often wandered away from its intellectual origins in a perfectly competitive market. More specifically, though, there are two major and broad criticisms that can be made of human capital theory. The first is a criticism in theory. By reducing the production and use (and definition) of skills to a factor akin to a physical asset, that can be created and employed in production like any other (even if with certain difficulties around contractual arrangements), the distinctive features of education and training and their deployment are simply set aside – or merely introduced as complicating rather than determining factors. The second is a criticism in (statistical) practice. Even if human capital were acceptable in theory, in practice it has been used in empirical work in the most casual and simplistic fashion, as if the functioning and outcomes in a labour market could be specified adequately with a single equation with a greater or lesser number of variables thrown in to represent normal or abnormal functioning of the labour market.

More sophisticated treatments can be made within the human capital tradition. The social content of education and training can be introduced as a form of market imperfection. The labour market equations can be given a structure – to take account of both the supply- and demand-sides.[18] But, for the purposes of this book, these two underlying weaknesses have been mutually reinforcing in undermining the potential for a genuine theory of segmented labour markets. Whilst the human capital approach can explain wage differentials, and even impute labour market structures on the basis of differences in rates of return to such human capital or, more generally, in the wage equation for different labour markets, the underlying theory is one in which all labour markets behave in exactly the same way. Irrespective of the number of variables that are employed, they contribute more or less to the level of wages for the individual employee or even for groups of employees. The analytical thrust of this book, however, is less to deny the relevance of a wide variety of causal factors than to argue that different labour markets are structured and function differently from one another. Consequently, a homogeneous theory of any type and however general, such as that of human capital, whatever its other deficiencies and merits, will be inappropriate to the study of labour market segmentation. In short, it is less a matter of what is the quantitative and cumulative weight of the causal factors, and more an imperative to examine how they interact with one another in potentially different ways. Without this perspective, labour markets will simply and erroneously be seen as more or less minor variations of the same species. In addition, the analytical issue of how to address the interaction of variables such as gender, trade unionism and capital-intensity cannot even begin to be broached other than as simple quantitative effects. The following chapters attempt to move beyond such limitations.

NOTES

1 Of course, the distinction between innate and acquired skills is impossible to sustain since all capabilities evolve over time.
2 See Sweetland (1996) for an uncritical review of the wide variety of applications of human capital theory, tracing its origins to Adam Smith and 1776.
3 Notably in the policy proposal of a voucher system for educational provision or, more generally, the introduction of market-type forms of organisation at all educational levels.
4 See also Samoff (1996).
5 See the reply to Bennell (1996a) by Psacharopoulos (1996a: 201): 'We all hope that Bennell will soon give us estimates of the returns to education in just one country of sub-Saharan Africa, that will be as rigorous and painstaking as his critique of past studies'.
6 An outstanding coverage of the literature is supplied by Carnoy (1995b). See also Blaug (1987) and Johnes (1993). The concern in this chapter is less with the detail and more with the principles concerned both in theory and empirical application.
7 See also Carnoy (1995d) who points out that there are problems with education as production functions in view of doubt around what is learning, what is the decision-making unit and who makes the decisions, and the nature of the agencies and organisations involved in the 'production' of education. Hanushek (1995) has a different response to the failure for there to be regular production functions for human capital. He suggests, rather than rejecting the theory, that schools must vary in efficiency. For a critique of Hanushek, see Kremer (1995).
8 See overview in Carnoy (1996a) but also Morris (1996).
9 There was an academic reaction against human capital theory in the 1970s, drawing upon Bowles and Gintis (1976). Note that they substitute the notion of a capitalist factory for the neoclassical production function, with schooling managing the reproduction of classes rather than commodities. See Blaug (1987) but also Agbodza and Fine (1996).

10 It is worth recalling within neoclassical theory (and this often motivates individuals in pursuing education) that human capital can be a more direct source of utility than in the productivity that it putatively engenders. It is a consumption good itself and enhances the consumption of other goods. However, calculations have set this aside so that education, like training, becomes purely vocational.

11 For a more extended discussion, see Fine (1992).

12 The following discussion depends to some extent on a more specific critique in Fine (1994a).

13 See also his own contribution (Carnoy 1996b), where it is made clear that the starting-point is always the absence of discrimination and the equality of wages once correcting for the differences in human capital.

14 It need not do so in models involving imperfect information, for example, on which see Chapters 2 and 6.

15 For a dummy with two values, for example, the number of potential segments increases by two times.

16 A rather different way of incorporating structure is through estimation of sample selection bias in which, for example, the unobserved characteristics of the more highly qualified can be taken into account by their access or self-selection, for example, to preferred employment. Along with omitted variables, the omission of sample selection bias is heavily emphasised by Bennell's (1996a, 1996b) criticisms of calculations of rates of return to human capital. These are exaggerated because no account is taken of the fact that the more talented or otherwise advantaged gain more education and higher rewards as a result. As such, they are not appropriate for extrapolating rewards for others.

17 There is often an analogous practice in the calculation and explanation of total factor productivity (TFP). This is constructed on the basis of full employment and perfect competition for factor inputs, but then its changes over time are explained by such factors as excess capacity, strength of trade unionism, etc, which contradict the initial basis on which TFP has been measured.

18 As discussed in later chapters, neoclassical theory has been able to provide models of self-segmenting on the basis of individual optimisation. This does involve the theory and estimation of structures through self-selection, whether on the supply- or the demand-side.

4 Flexibility and institutions in labour markets

1 INTRODUCTION

The common theme running through this chapter is that the theory of markets in general, and labour markets in particular, requires consideration of the impact of non-market factors. Traditional supply and demand analysis, however sophisticated, is unacceptable when non-market relationships slip into the background and, ultimately, beyond the horizon. The market and non-market interact and mutually condition one another. Neither one can be legitimately taken as exogenous in order to examine the other.

The first port of call within the chapter is the recent literature on flexibility. It has generated two separate literatures. One has been prompted by the empirical observation that labour markets have become more flexible. By this is meant, however consciously, the practical removal of impediments to market adjustments governing wages and working conditions. In other words, flexibility is understood as allowing the market to function as freely as possible without interference by what are perceived to be non-market interventions, whether emanating from trade unions, customs or government regulation. Here, it is concluded that this simple dichotomy between the market and the non-market, and its putative correspondence with flexibility and non-flexibility, respectively, is totally chaotic. At most, it merely allows previous disputes about how labour markets work to be revisited with little advance other than onto a new terminological terrain.

The second approach to flexibility is made of sterner stuff and can be interpreted as the mirror image of the more descriptive approach. It draws contemporary developments within capitalism on an abstract theoretical canvas, understanding flexibility as systemic and marking the transition between phases of capitalism. Fordism has given way to post-Fordism or, at least, to what is termed 'flexible specialisation' in production whereby skilled workers supply quality products to niche markets through use of machinery, work and other processes that have escaped the dull monotony of uniform mass production and consumption.

In this view, the interaction between market and non-market is, and needs to be, fundamentally transformed. Indeed, this simple dichotomy is driven deeper in pursuing changes both in and around production through flexible specialisation and in consumption and the organisation of political and cultural life within the non-market, most notably in the formation of industrial districts. It will be shown, however, that this world of flexible specialisation is profoundly romantic, with limited empirical foundations and a dependence upon an economic theory that simply reverses the traditional and crude ranking of secure work in large-scale industry as against insecure employment in the small-scale sector.

Despite their separate origins, motives and methods, the two flexibility literatures have converged upon, and even merged with, one another. The most recent contributions employ the term 'flexibility' freely as a descriptive device, as a systemic economy-wide factor, or at all points in between. Like human capital, as discussed in Chapter 3, despite well-documented and continuing conceptual and analytical deficiencies, the term is currently deployed at will in a wide range of empirical, theoretical and policy studies as if it were well-founded and coherent. As such, the flexibility literature has tended to address the role of non-market institutions obliquely, as constituting or reflecting sources of (in)flexibility. Institutional analysis, which is covered in this chapter after flexibility, confronts institutions directly. Its intellectual pedigree is more long-standing. But the outcome is, in some respects, very similar. A number of different lines of thought, more or less abstract in content but of dubious validity, are run together around what are taken to be common and acceptable notions such as rent-seeking, transactions costs, informational asymmetries and imperfections, and the interaction between markets and hierarchies. Apart from the wealth of such theoretical fragments, new institutional theory draws upon a variety of theoretical traditions, not least neoclassical economics, with its optimising individuals. The new rub is that the optimisation takes place within and across both market and non-market institutions, with the latter themselves becoming endogenous as a result.

One consequence has been to launch a profound challenge by economics against more traditional approaches to institutions that have been located within other disciplines or the older, more descriptive and theoretically informal (i.e., non-mathematical) field of institutional economics.[1] The concluding section briefly examines how these theoretical developments have had a major impact upon the field of industrial relations, exposing its continuing weaknesses and threatening to cast it asunder in deference to the rampaging axiomatics and econometrics of the new neoclassical labour economics.

2 FLEXIBILITY IN THEORY?

In his review of labour market flexibility, Brodsky (1994: 53) suggests that OECD countries 'have experimented over the past 30 years with a variety of policies to promote flexibility in the labor market'. Brodsky observes how these policies have shifted and varied across countries and over time according to differences in economic and political conditions. The stagflation of the 1970s witnessed a deregulatory reaction against the measures taken in the 1960s and earlier which were designed to support the labour market through state interventions such as employment protection and provision of unemployment benefit, i.e., welfarism applied to the labour market. Undoubtedly, however, this reading is necessarily retrospective, for the account is heavily dependent upon the notion of flexibility that itself only emerged to prominence in the literature in the 1980s. The use of flexibility as such as a rationale to promote the policy shifts away from active interventionism would have been most unusual at the earlier time, if not impossible. Much more prominent would have been a more or less conservative macroeconomic stance and the deployment of notions such as efficiency, equity and market imperfections at the microeconomic level. Atkinson's (1984) contribution essentially marks the first concerted attempt to deal with the notion of flexibility in a coherent fashion from an orthodox stance. His was an *ad hoc* conceptual response to what was perceived to be contemporary developments within labour markets and the shifting mode of determination of wages and labour market conditions.

From that point, two key and interrelated issues have been to the fore, although each incorporates a number of aspects. The first issue is the definition of flexibility itself. What do we mean by it? The second issue is whether flexibility is a good thing or not. Will economies, especially labour markets, work more efficiently if they are more flexible – however it, or efficiency for that matter, is understood.[2]

What connects these two issues is the manner in which they relate to the theoretical norms of neoclassical economics. For this, flexibility is initially understood narrowly in terms of absence of wage-rigidity, especially in the context of unemployment and otherwise perfectly working labour markets. The notion of flexibility was brought forward in order to justify reductions in real wages and, more fundamentally, to undermine the capacity of labour to defend them through trade unions and government legislation and policy. In this case, the neoclassical approach is both well-defined and it is understood as a good thing – at least by the criterion of Pareto-efficiency. With respect to the definition of flexibility, this opens the way for a much wider range of factors to be considered, even if, on a narrow reading, wage (in)flexibility can be construed as a metaphor for other labour market conditions. It is not simply whether wages will adjust to clear the labour market but also if all other conditions of employment, such as hours, tasks, employment rights, etc., are equally flexible, thereby providing a rationale for what is termed the 'deregulation' of labour markets and the reform of labour market institutions that are perceived to be impediments to the free market. Not surprisingly, even within the metaphor of Walrasian market-clearing, empirical experience from the functioning of labour markets provides a host of definitional ammunition for the flexibility armoury.

Thus, Beatson (1995: 3), having drawn simple upward-sloping supply and downward-sloping demand curves for the real wage against employment, sees this as a 'useful metric': 'In this framework, a flexible labour market is one that behaves, at the aggregate level, like a competitive labour market.'

He then, even if within more sophisticated frameworks, considers empirically the shifting extent of part-time, temporary and self-employment, engagement and dismissals, working time, functional flexibility, labour mobility, wage determination, relative wage flexibility by region, occupation and human capital, and aggregate employment, hours worked and wages. But the essential point remains the same. A labour market restriction, such as an effective minimum wage, leads to Pareto-inefficient unemployment as labour supply is increased and demand decreased compared to the outcome in the unrestricted equilibrium where supply and demand are equal. As mentioned, the graph can stand as a parable for any labour market condition, and not just for the wage level.

The benefits of flexibility, however defined, become questionable once departing from this simplest of norms within neoclassical economics. If the conditions are not in place for markets to be able to work perfectly, or if account is taken of factors and analysis that lie outside the neoclassical orthodoxy, as in consideration of technical change and non-market relations, for example, then there can be no presumption that greater flexibility, in whatever aspect, is a good thing. A most obvious example is provided by the provision of training. It may be beneficial to require all firms to provide training, in order that skills are not poached thereby leading to overall underprovision. Further, this inflexible requirement within the labour market may not only enhance efficiency, it can also induce a higher level of *systemic* flexibility, since the higher level of skills across the economy will raise the potential for adjustment to economic shocks or, for example, to new technology.[3]

The last example involves a more general point. Once the analysis moves out of the Walrasian metaphor, flexibility itself becomes both a more ambiguous and a more complex concept, as has been amply reflected and acknowledged in the literature referred to below. For the neoclassical norm is based upon the aggregated behaviour of individuals in which there is a presumption that the expansion of the opportunities or flexibility for one or more is replicated at the aggregate level. Although there can be individual losers – those made redundant for example – they can be compensated, which is in part a practical issue in gaining the acceptance of greater flexibility subject to distributive judgements and policies. However, once this connection between the individual and the aggregate is breached, then the notion of flexibility becomes elusive as it varies from one level to another and across the economy as a whole. There is potential for fallacy of composition – increasing flexibility for individuals may reduce overall flexibility.[4]

The result of these definitional and theoretical conundrums has been to create an acknowledged conceptual chaos. As Brodsky (1994: 54) observes in quoting US Secretary for Labour, Robert Reich: 'The term "labor market flexibility" has taken on a variety of meanings, prompting the observation that "rarely in international discourse has the term gone so directly from obscurity to meaninglessness without any intervening period of coherence".' Yet, 10 years ago, even shortly after the concept had been introduced, the extent of coherence was already implicitly in question. In the International Labour Organisation (ILO) review volume edited by Meulders and Wilkin (1987a), the contributions go beyond specifying wage (remuneration), numerical (numbers employed) and functional (tasks performed) flexibility, and flexibility in other conditions of work (such as security of tenure and hours of work). For, in surveying the literature, Meulders and Wilkin (1987b) observe that flexibility has simultaneously been promoted as a miraculous solution to labour market problems and as a means of legitimising any proposed change.

They discuss five themes: the meaning of flexibility; the form it takes; its relative impact in the relationship between the short and long runs (a potential case of conflict with short-run being at the expense of long-run flexibility as in cost-cutting through non-provision of training, for example); variations in national contexts and institutions (as in the system of industrial relations); and the variety of instruments for policy. They conclude by suggesting five areas for further study: the detailing of typologies; the ideal combination of policy mixes at micro- and macro-levels and at national and international levels; differences across sectors of the economy; how labour market flexibility relates to factors such as consumption, leisure and other social activities; and the appropriate institutions for formulating and implementing decision-making. The simple point is that individual and systemic flexibility vary along a number of lines which do not correspond with one another and which interact in varied ways. Possibly the easiest way to envision this is in acknowledging how flexible have been Japanese workers because of the inflexibility of their guaranteed employment contracts.

The case studies in the volume edited by Meulders and Wilkin display an equally wide range of considerations. Atkinson (1987) discusses the role of subcontracting (or 'distancing' more generally) and how this is perceived to have created flexibility in the form of a segment of peripheral workers as opposed to the inflexible core work-force. Not surprisingly in view of the discussion of segmented labour market theory which follows in this volume, he finds that such a simple dichotomy proves, 'as slippery in theory as it has become all pervasive in practice' (Atkinson 1987: 87). Further, he notes that flexibility at one level may be at the expense of flexibility at another. Indeed, this paradox is already a feature of the neoclassical norm for which, for example, increasing the powers to throw workers out of employment is considered to increase overall employment, since employers are no longer bound to retain employees in case of a slump and are, therefore, more willing to take on workers since they can always be readily sacked again. Boyer (1987) offers five definitions of flexibility – organisational, internal job and task allocation, legal restraints, wages, and state regulation and reorganisation. Rubery *et al.* (1987) discuss flexibility in terms of interactions with financial institutions (availability of funds for investment) and the structure of product markets (extent of product differentiation and competition, for example).

In short, the orthodox debate over flexibility is characterised by the following features. First, it concerns the functioning of the economic system as a whole, including interactions between micro- and macro-levels and between the labour market and other markets. Second, it ranges over the relationship between the economy and socioeconomic relations more generally, necessarily incorporating industrial relations, the state and other institutions. Third, and by way of one conclusion, it follows that descriptive approach to flexibility has simply served both as a terminological device for arranging a chaotic array of empirical material and as a means to replicate theoretical debates over how the economy works without adding any new analytical content. Finally, as another conclusion, whilst there have been empirical changes in capitalism with and since the breakdown of the post-war boom, and these have eventually prompted the notion of flexibility by way of analytical empirical and policy response, it is a concept that it totally inadequate in its theoretical and empirical content to deal with the tasks with which it has been confronted.[5] Have more ambitious and less orthodox approaches been any more successful?

3 FLEXIBLE SPECIALISATION AND POST-FORDISM[6]

From completely different analytical origins, flexibility has also been prominent in more ambitious attempts to understand the changes in the ways in which labour markets, and the economy more generally, have been functioning. At times, drawing upon French regulation theory initiated by Aglietta (1979), capitalism is divided into distinct periods. Oversimplifying, the post-war boom was characterised by Fordism, a stage dependent on mass production and consumption of uniform commodities, with continuing growth sustained by a mode of regulation associated with Keynesian welfarism. This has now given way to a new stage of neo-Fordism or post-Fordism in which both production and consumption have become more customised. In particular, flexible specialisation is now perceived to be at the cutting edge of competitiveness. By the same token, post-Fordism has become the more popular term, not least and appropriately because of its resonances with the term, and putative era of, postmodernism. More substantively, neo-Fordism has been seen to be too deterministic with the new stage of capitalism driven by the imperatives of flexibility in production at economic, political and ideological levels. By contrast, post-Fordism suggests that flec-spec is the new route to competitive success, but its progress depends upon relatively autonomous outcomes both in other economic and political and social aspects. Marketing and design come to the fore, for example, as does the degree of decentralisation between local and national government (as well as in relations between local and central collective bargaining in labour markets).[7]

Whilst regulation theory provided the intellectual stimulus to notions of neo-Fordism, it has been much less prominent in the recent literature, in which flexible specialisation has, not surprisingly, taken on an analytical life of its own. In part, this reflects the abandonment of the Marxist content of regulation theory, even by regulationists themselves,[8] even though this was an important component of Aglietta's initial contribution – with its concern with periodisation of stages of capitalism, Marxist value theory and reproduction schema, etc. Flexible specialisation has departed from regulation theory which has itself departed from Marxism. It has become more eclectic and has drawn upon, as will be seen, different intellectual origins. As a result, regulation theory has served as a sort of grand but mystical theoretical rationale for flexible specialisation, but with a decreasing analytical impact in practice.

Consequently, the concern here will be with flexible specialisation primarily and less with regulation theory.[9] Although the notion of flexible specialisation (affectionately dubbed flec-spec) is little more than a decade old, it has already experienced a leap forward in sophistication and scope. Indeed, it has exhibited a degree of analytical flexibility and heterogeneity to match that of the economic developments that are taken as its object. It has encompassed subjects as diverse as changes in technology and the organisation of production, (sub)contracting, the size distribution of industry, retailing, distribution, industrial districts, skills and training, retailing, automation, consumer tastes for difference and niche markets, computer-aided management and design, and flexibility within labour markets as well as within production levels, composition and quality, etc. By the same token, the theoretical scope of flexible specialisation has grown significantly and chaotically. It can be married with notions of post-Fordism and regulation theory to give rise to particular views of the relationship between economics and politics, or it can form a partnership with postmodernism to give new meanings to production and, ultimately, consumption. At other times, shifting notions of flexibility and any variety of theoretical fragments can be and have been drawn together under the general umbrella of flexible specialisation or some other terminology.

This has led to a counter-reaction so that much of the burden of the literature critical of flec-spec is to point to how limited is the extent to which Fordist production has been replaced by flec-spec production. Further, even where there is evidence of flexibility in output composition, such flexible batch production has become more like mass production rather than displacing it. In addition, the virtues of flec-spec for commercial success and for the benefits of the work-force have been heavily exaggerated – depending upon a limited number of success stories, such as the Third Italy (regionally) and clothing (sectorally), which are themselves heavily contested in interpretation.[10] This is not simply a matter of the empirical validity of appealing to one form of production or another (although the flec-spec school has tended to depend upon isolated case studies and to fail to engage with the presentation of the more extensive contrary empirical evidence). Rather, an ideal type of Fordist production is constructed as mass, factory production through deskilled labour of uniform commodities for mass consumption.[11] Partly because of its intellectual flexibility, any variation from this ideal type is construed as conforming to flexible production. In other words, the conceptual balance is tipped in favour of viewing as flec-spec any divergence from an ideal type of Fordist production. Consequently, to defend analytically the importance of mass production, factory techniques, tendencies to deskilling, etc. is not to be blind to the pervasive significance of new technology and organisational change. Rather, it is to reject the idea that there is only one immutable form of Fordist production (and that all production must be Fordist for mass production to be in the ascendancy).[12]

Flexible specialisation, then, holds to a view of the world in which the economic and social conditions associated with Fordism or mass production are in crisis and are possibly drawing to an ultimate close. In the future, building on existing trends, there is an alternative path of development associated with smaller-scale batch production, satisfying more specialised demand and offering more skilled and varied work.

But, as has now been recognised in the prolific debate over flec-spec, even amongst many flec-spec sympathisers, a simply dichotomy between Fordist and post-Fordist forms of production is unacceptable. As Gertler (1988, 1989, 1992) argues from a relatively critical stance to flec-spec, 'flexibility' itself needs to be unbundled into a range of separate components – not least those mentioned above in terms of the increasing sophistication, scope and flexibility and heterogeneity of flec-spec itself as a concept. It is not necessarily the case that the separate components will always have shifted in the same direction, towards or away from the new forms of production, Indeed, it is apparent that flexibility in one component of an economic system may *require* rigidity in another component – a large, inflexible dedicated machine, for example, can embody capacity for flexibility in product mix. This is obviously the case for the car industry, for example, which is why it can be claimed by both sides in the debate over flec-spec. Significantly, once the concepts attached to flexible specialisation are interrogated analytically and empirically, particularly as in opposition to Fordism, and whether sympathetically or not, the material covered, if not always the terminology, is more or less identical to that treated in the more empiricist notions of flexibility discussed in previous sections.

For this reason, as mentioned above, those opposed to the flec-spec stance are reasonably drawn to pointing out the limited extent to which all of its features are empirically realised in all but a few select industries and localities. Those favouring flec-spec, as illustrated by Schoenberger (1989) in debate with Gertler, argue that not all of its elements need to be in place for its presence to be empirically verified. There only has to be a movement towards them. Schoenberger adds to her case by a further appeal for support from regulation theory, claiming a systemic shift in the 'regime of accumulation'. For her, it is a matter of the early days in the transition towards a new stage of capitalism so that the empirical evidence is liable, as yet, to be limited. Evidence against the flec-spec case can even be taken to be in its favour since it represents the wrong side of the cutting edge as it moves forward!

Gertler reasonably concludes that the theoretical debate has only rendered the empirical questions more impenetrable. Given there is no rigid distinction between Fordism and post-Fordism, how is it possible to identify a shift from one to the other, whether tied to a regime shift or not, especially if acknowledging that flexibility is intrinsically subject to contradictory and opposing developments across the separate components that mark the supposed Fordist/post-Fordist divide? When is an industrial district to be distinguished from a spatial conglomeration of producers? What is a small as opposed to a large firm? When is flexible technology at the leading or lagging edge, signifying a continuity or rupture with the past, overhauling or overthrowing what has gone before?

Apart from these theoretical/empirical conundrums, Gertler points to a number of factors that have been insufficiently incorporated into the debate. How are inter-sectoral boundaries established and restructured? What is the significance of gender and class relations, national systems of innovation, and the reconstruction of space in the light of the pace and nature of technological change? No doubt these could be added to, or developed within, a continuing debate, even if at the expense of continuing erosion of the Fordist/post-Fordist divide. There is, however, an alternative option, one that is both readily suggested by the increasing eclecticism of the flec-spec debate and which breaks with it entirely. Rather than basing theoretical and empirical analysis upon the putative dichotomy which can only be sustained by increasingly complex analytical acrobatics, why not abandon this as a starting-point?[13]

Of course, this raises the problem of what to put in its place. But this is a false problem, since the flec-spec claim of discovering previously unanalysed, and now leading-edge, economic developments is itself totally fallacious once the simple dichotomy between Fordism and post-Fordism is rejected. All the components that make up the diode have long been the subject of theoretical and empirical investigation. The debate may, rightly or wrongly, have brought some of these more to our attention than previously and have prompted theoretical innovation and flexibility, whether in support of the flec-spec stance or not. It is arguable, however, that whatever the role of the debate previously in stimulating intellectual progress, its 'market' niche is now exhausted and it has passed its sell-by date.

Quite apart from the conundrums identified by Gertler, this conclusion is confirmed by a particular way in which empirical evidence is now being handled theoretically. Corresponding to the different, empirically identified, aspects of (non-)flexibility, it is possible to argue that they constitute contradictory tendencies. These theoretical constructs, in turn, can be used to 'explain' the empirical trends from which they have been induced. Thus, where flexibility is contradicted empirically, this can be interpreted as an impediment to, or even reaction against, leading edge development, as in Hirst and Zeitlin (1989).[14] In other words, evidence, either in support of or against either stance, can be interpreted favourably in view of contradictory tendencies. Gertler is, himself, notably guilty in this respect, suggesting the concept of 'glocalisation' to signify the contradictory interaction of globalisation and localisation.

4 FLEC-SPEC'S INTELLECTUAL ORIGINS

Hyman (1991) comes to some similar conclusions to those offered here, arguing that the pertinent question is why flec-spec should have gained such analytical prominence (rather than how valid is it).[15] To a large extent, the answer is to be found in the flexibility of the theory itself, not only in response to the inconvenient weight of empirical evidence but also in its capacity to incorporate and appear compatible with a whole range of other, generally orthodox, theories and analytical fragments. In addition, an answer is in part to be found in the intellectual appeal of new ideas, despite the weight of contrary evidence. For this reason, it is worth uncovering what has been an initiating and persistent theme within the favourable literature. In this respect, the classic statement is to be found in Piore and Sabel (1984).

The fundamental position adopted here to that work is that the flec-spec school, even if subsequently diluted by sophistication and a range of other considerations, has retained at its core a faithful reproduction of an earlier theory, that attached to dual labour markets. This theory was advanced in the early 1970s and argued that the labour force is divided into two strata, the primary and the secondary, in correspondence to an industrial structure based on mass production and casualised production, respectively. Those in the core or primary sectors enjoyed well-paid, secure jobs with career ladders. Those in secondary or peripheral labour markets suffered poor wages and working conditions and the immanent threat of unemployment. This theory was developed to explain black riots in the US city ghettos – as a consequence of employment deprivation. It has since blossomed into a much more sophisticated understanding of the structure and causes of labour market segmentation, just as the flec-spec school has incorporated more considerations. Dual has given way to segmented labour market theory, with many more segments and explanatory factors.[16] What the flec-spec school has done is simply to reverse the ranking of the primary and secondary sectors, with the latter potentially providing the key to economic progress and favourable working conditions. Indeed, this strong link between dual labour market theory and flec-spec is not difficult to discover, for it stands out in the person of Piore who co-authored the classic work both on dual labour markets with Doeringer at its (modern) outset and on flec-spec with Sabel subsequently.[17]

But the parallels between the two positions still have to be identified. Begin with the economic theory involved. First, there is the question of industrial structure. Of necessity, flec-spec offers a duality between mass production and flexible production, and these are core concepts. It is argued that mass production won out in the struggle for ascendancy at the end of the nineteenth century, although this was not an inevitable outcome if economic and political conflicts had been resolved differently. But once half-way established, whether as a paradigm to be copied or by the inertia embodied in fixed capital and institutions, the mass production model's dominance was guaranteed – at least for the better part of a century.[18]

Even so, flec-spec's fundamental viability is demonstrated by the otherwise presumed anomalous survival of small-scale and flexible methods of production. These have themselves been given a new lease of life by the crisis of Fordism and by the potential opened up by new technology. The historic choice between mass and flexible production is to be offered once more. Hence, the *Second Industrial Divide* is the title taken by Piore and Sabel (1984) and the divide re-opens before us.

Significantly, the division between mass and flexible sectors is not determined by economics and certainly not by technology alone. Here the parallel is with segmented labour market theory in so far as the latter depends on contingent supply and demand factors, in which sexism and racism, for example, assume a prominent role.[19] For flec-spec, more emphasis is given to the more orthodox factors of social theory, such as trade union organisation, the community and government support (predominantly at the *exceptional* local level for flec-spec to prosper, since central and *normal* local governments serve the needs of mass production).[20]

None the less, there is an economic theory at the core of flec-spec and it is identical to much that is to be found in segmented labour market theory. This is explicitly recognised by Sabel (1982: 34), who refers to Piore's earlier work. Central is the division of demand into a stable and a variable component with the allocation of each, respectively, to the mass and flec-spec sectors. All that is now added is that the former of these is restricted by the extent of the market (Piore and Sabel 1984: 55), whilst the latter can become more secure by frequent innovation to satisfy specialised market niches (ibid.: 27). Stable demand around mass production/consumption is now insecure; unstable demand is more secure through innovation to serve market niches.

But what is it that has opened up the second industrial divide? At a theoretical level, as has been seen, the relative merits of mass production and flec-spec are presumed to be ever present. Mass production's historically contingent success lies purely in its initially gained lead which ultimately moulded economic and social institutions to its advantage. Otherwise, the choice is between dedicated low unit cost, high fixed cost unskilled mass production and high unit cost, low fixed cost, skilled, specialised production. Much less is made of the impact of new technology in swinging the balance in favour of flec-spec than might be expected in view of later literature.

Accordingly, a search is made for the economic and social causes of the decline of Fordism and for the social factors promoting flec-spec. The economic crisis and slow-down of the 1970s certainly signals for the flec-spec school that mass production is down if not necessarily out. Explanations in terms of 'shock factors', such as oil crises, etc., are viewed with suspicion and linked more to the timing of the crisis (ibid.: 168). More systematic and secular within the economic plain is the exhaustion of demand, for 'the crisis of the last decade is a crisis of underconsumption, rooted in the saturation of core markets for consumer durables' (ibid.: 252).

Of course, within political economy, an unresolved issue has always been whether underconsumption – crudely put, lack of sufficient aggregate Keynesian, effective demand – is a cause rather than a symptom of crisis. Certainly, the one must be accompanied by the other and, similarly, mass producers are expected to form cartels, seek out guaranteed markets and to suffer excess capacity from time to time. Such symptoms cannot be taken to be an adequate explanation for, or characterisation of, the crisis of Fordism. But flec-spec theory also examines the cost side of mass production. Here, it is argued that 'hidden costs' have imperceptibly crept up on transnational and multi-plant producers. These are predominantly concerned with management responses to the underlying and determining conditions of demand. Thus, for Piore and Sabel (ibid.: 200), there are problems of managing dispersed sites of production, maintaining inventory and quality control, bending standardised products towards fragmenting tastes and dealing, more generally, with instability when constrained by large-scale, dedicated, production methods.

In the case of labour, mass production yields a systemic compromise in which workplace control and wage costs are stabilised in return for security of employment (ibid.: 64). Both the organisation of work and the levels of wage costs become increasingly inflexible relative to the market demands that are placed upon them, although the whole of this argument depends upon setting aside the superior productivity (gains) associated with mass production (for which the notion of stable wage unit *costs*, as opposed to wage *levels* becomes problematic). Again, it is questionable whether pointing to the notion of inflexible labour in wages and conditions is a recognition of a (management perspective) symptom of the crisis rather than the identification of a fundamental cause.[21]

But whether in looking to the labour or the product markets, the trans-national corporation is perceived to be the, increasingly pressurised, micro-economic regulator of the Fordist economic system. This represents a welcome break with orthodox neoclassical economics, for which trans-nationals might just as well not exist. At the macroeconomic level, however, the orthodox notion of Keynesian demand management, coupled with wel-farism, is adopted as the regulator, increasingly powerless to satisfy the economic and social demands placed upon it. It must again be observed that the crisis of Keynesianism is more a symptom than a cause of crisis and, for that reason, a common ingredient to every analysis of the last decade or more.

As such, this not only reflects limited analytical perception, it also seriously understates and distorts the economic role of the state, for its economic policies have been equally concerned with microeconomic regulation, in supporting and promoting the model of transnational and large-scale cor-porate growth – through industrial and other policy measures (not least public ownership) – and these are arguably as significant to mass production as manipulation of aggregate demand. No doubt, such points are to be warmly embraced by the flec-spec school as supporting their view that mass production has an institutionalised advantage. But it leaves open the unanswered question of why such advantages should have proved insuffi-cient to sustain the Fordist model. It also serves to accentuate the (false) idea that Fordism involves more of a separation between economy and society than flec-spec, so that the latter becomes a novel model with poten-tial derived from the evaporating boundaries between economic and social organisation.

In short, the crisis of Fordism is perceived as a structural crisis of labour and corporate and social organisation which has been brought about by the inflexibility of the system to respond to volatile, faltering and increasingly sophisticated demand. The mirror image of this is to be found in conditions favourable to flec-spec. Apart from the demand conditions and new tech-nology, the most important factor is the contingent political conditions that have been created, predominantly at the regional or local level, to which progressives have turned, following curtailed or disillusioned activity at the national level. The stereotype is provided by Third Italy, Mondragon and, as some would have it, London, with particular emphasis on fashion-able, flexible demand goods such as clothes and furniture.[22]

The ideology of the second divide depends then on a ready identification with each other of different instances of the paradigm or principle of the craft worker, forged not only across space and sectors, but also historically to create a connection with the first divide. In addition, this homogenising of flec-spec production into a single principle is heavily romanticised. Thus, for Sabel (1982: 107–8), we have the 'fusion of conception and execution', 'with a bright idea', 'he begins to attend night-school classes', 'the ability . . . to make virtually any tool in his shop do new tricks', and each firm is 'jealous of its autonomy', 'overproud of its capacity', 'linked to the collective efforts of the community', whilst the 'relations between firms resembles the collegial relation between good doctors, good lawyers, or good university teachers'.

Such paradises are few and far between, certainly as rare as the good professionals last named. Flec-spec is also well aware that the secondary sector and/or labour market can become the site of subcontracted, sweated work as the source of flexibility for the corporations reeling under the crisis of Fordism. Indeed, this trend is a symptom of the crisis. Only progressive forms of local economic and political organisation to create industrial districts/communities are perceived to offer any guarantee against this. On the other hand, flec-spec can develop within the corporations themselves, by reorganisation of work and marketing. The idea is that production is geared towards small-batch production, with more flexible fixed capital and a greater diversity of skills and job content for teams of workers enjoying greater job autonomy and control. Examples offered include mini-steel mills, chemicals and machine tools (Piore and Sabel 1984: 205), but the most stunning convert is to be found within the car industry, with the decline in the strategy for a world car and greater emphasis on offering model selection (Katz and Sabel 1985).

This hardly conforms to craft production (and concentration within the car industry has increased since the seventies as transnationals such as Chrysler and British Leyland have fallen behind into a lower league). As Katz and Sabel fully recognise:

> The emerging strategy is to group automobile components into modules, each produced in high volume, and then combine the modules into a wide variety of finished products . . . the entire manufacturing set-up becomes strikingly flexible by the industry's previous standards.
>
> (ibid.: 298)

This conclusion is not analytically obvious. The distance between the car industry and the flec-spec industry of the first divide and even of small-scale production of the second divide constitutes a gaping chasm which is hardly bridged by some abstract notion of their sharing a common response of flexibility to market uncertainty.

Thus, as has been so often emphasised in the subsequent literature, flec-spec in the modern world seems way off the mark both analytically and empirically. But it should not be dismissed too easily and purely on academic grounds. For it does, despite its utopian vision for the future,[23] support more immediate policies, certainly as far as industrial relations and economic intervention are concerned. Underlying flec-spec proposals for each of these is the idea that compromise can be reached between capital and labour so that each can benefit from the high-quality, variable production and the enhanced and varied work. Conflict between the two sides of industry is not absented, but it is required that labour make concessions, particularly at the level of national agreements, so that the plant-level work-force can bargain flexibly with management, even if within a broader framework of higher level bargaining:

> Unions will have to exchange the rights to impose uniform conditions for rights in decision making . . . the unions will have to find ways of tying the interests of particular companies to the interests of their industry and even of the economy as a whole . . . Under extraordinarily favourable circumstances, national unions might even help structure the strategy of whole industries . . . and have a say in macroeconomic decisions.
>
> (ibid.: 314)

Although derived from different arguments and considerations, the flec-spec approach reaches similar conclusions to those put forward by cautious social democrats who seek limited state intervention and wage increases. Capital and labour need to reach an accord in order mutually to benefit from the attached productivity or commercial gains. In conjunction with the rosy picture that is potentially painted of small-scale enterprise – in contrast to what is often the sweated, casualised and exploitative reality – this opens the way for employers to pick and choose from the portfolio of policies offered by the flec-spec perspective. The workers must compromise and the state must offer industrial support; possibly the benefits to labour will follow but they are liable to be hostage to commercial and precarious business fortune.

Leaving aside these policy issues, it is crucial to recognise the substantial shift that has taken place through flec-spec in the analytical content with which economic restructuring and its implications for labour markets are considered. This is so even relative to its own intellectual origins. As already suggested, the influence of regulation theory is now at most ghost-like; even the radicalism of dual labour market theory has long-since evaporated along with questions of power, class and conflict. Indeed, even though this and the previous sections have broached the issue of flexibility from two entirely different perspectives – the empirical and orthodox tradition and that of grand theory – they have increasingly merged with one another so that theory and evidence can be flexibly chosen at will from both and as if each were well-grounded both analytically and empirically.[24] Although concerned with how and which institutions are formed, and with what effect, the focus has not primarily been upon whether institutions are more or less conducive to flexibility. None the less, unfortunately, in a parallel literature, much the same mix-and-(mis)match across theory and evidence is to be found in institutional approaches to labour markets which are now briefly considered.

5 INSTITUTIONAL APPROACHES TO LABOUR MARKETS

As has long been recognised in many disciplines other than economics, not least industrial relations and sociology, the labour market is heavily influenced by the presence of non-market factors and activities. Trade unions and the role of political, ideological and workplace relations lie outside the standard neoclassical treatment of the labour market, as does the role of the state. Institutional approaches to the labour market explicitly recognise that more is involved in labour markets than the buying and selling of labour through the market. In addition, there has recently been a growing interest in the theory of institutions, although its focus has not necessarily been primarily upon labour markets. None the less, the trend is increasingly towards acknowledging theoretically, rather than just descriptively, the role played by institutions in the functioning of labour markets. Consequently, this justifies dealing with emerging theories of institutions, even where they have not been often applied to labour markets, not least because doing so anticipates future directions liable to be taken by labour market theory.

Much of the new theory of institutions has common elements, the exception being the neo-Austrian approach which is the least influential, if only within the academic environment.[25] Most important is that neoclassical economics, especially general equilibrium theory, is taken as a point of departure. Because the market is recognised not to be perfect, it is presumed that non-market institutions are generated in response, or that they necessarily coexist and interact with the market. Fine (1980) has lampooned this as a unicorn-type theory: we invent a fiction, the perfectly functioning market by analogy with the unicorn, and then seek to explain economic realities by its divergence from the fiction. It is as if we were to explain the anatomy of the horse by comparison with the unicorn. In short, the use of market imperfections as representing a divergence from competitive equilibrium offers only the most limited explanatory content. But in much of the new institutionalism, one general equilibrium unicorn is simply replaced by another which is just a little more general.

A second element in new institutional theory is its rapidly widening scope and eclecticism. This follows from the capacity to depart from the fiction of competitive equilibrium in a vast number of different directions, especially through engaging with behaviour other than utility-maximisation (too informationally demanding in complex situations), with non-economic institutions other than the market and, corresponding to each of these, with other disciplines.

A third element, though, is the continuing commitment to theory being based upon methodological individualism, even where institutions and collective action are concerned. This does, however, present certain problems. Either a generalised equilibrium is the outcome, incorporating institutions other than the market, in which case there is a division between exogenous and endogenous variables with the former remaining unaddressed – where do information, technology, preferences originate if not from the very institutions they are supposed to explain? Or there is a historical, even an infinite, regress in which causation is simply pushed back to some unexplained initial conditions. For, by beginning with individuals whose behaviour is not, as in utility-maximisation, intrinsic but which is socially formed through institutions, then there is an inconsistent acceptance of the priority of the social. It follows that the new institutional theory inevitably, often surreptitiously, falls back upon social causation despite, or even because of, the priority it endows to individual agents.[26]

But enough by way of initial, abstract posturing, the significance of which is sharper in the detail. To be more specific, Rowthorn and Chang (1995b) suggest that much new institutional theory, especially that critical of state intervention, draws its analytical inspiration from three different sources. First, there is the new political economy which has its origins in counter-posing the failure of the state to the failure of the market. Within neo-classical economics, there has been the long-standing tradition within welfare economics that stresses that market imperfections, such as external-ities, would justify state intervention to rectify those inefficiencies, and pos-sibly the injustices, that result from relying upon market forces alone.

The new political economy challenges this conclusion in two different ways. On the one hand, it correctly recognises that the role of the state has been unexamined and idealised. The state must do this because it is desirable for it to do so. But where does the state come from and why should it act in this way? On the other hand, much more controversially, the new political economy constructs a theory of the state in which its actions are governed by the self-interest of those who hold or can potentially influence state policy. The analytical and terminological symbol of the new political economy is the notion of 'rent-seeking'. It is argued that inter-ventions by the state will not only create rents for those who benefit by them but will also encourage economic agents to incur unproductive expen-diture of resources to establish policy in their own favour. Consequently, the new political economy seeks to minimise the role of the state, both to limit the distortions that arise directly from the state's interventions and those distortions that arise from those seeking to persuade the state to adopt distorting policies.[27] Rent-seeking leads to state or regulatory failure that can be as bad if not worse than the market failures that they are designed to cure.

The new political economy is extraordinarily weak analytically. It does, however, raise a very important question, even if not in these terms; namely: Who holds and exercises state power and how? But it does so from a position of methodological individualism in which socioeconomic structures are simply the product of self-seeking, optimising behaviour. In a sense, the division between the market and the state, or between the economy and politics or society more generally, is bridged by treating non-market relations as though they were an extension of the market but necessarily with relatively unfavourable consequences. Even with this method, the new political economy tends to assume arbitrarily that favour-able conclusions can be drawn about the efficacy of the market and the inefficacy of state intervention. In short, though this is rarely made explicit, the new political economy is essentially a regurgitation of the virtues of the static model of perfect competition, setting aside even the criticisms that can be made from within neoclassical orthodoxy, such as the theory of the second best and the need to respond to market imperfections however imperfectly.[28]

This static analytical basis on which the new political economy is constructed tends to be concealed by the (terminological) innovation that it has promoted. The notion of rent-seeking is, in principle, open to interpretation in a wide variety of contexts and not just as a distortion from competitive equilibrium. Thus, there can be the attempt to gain from the excess profits that arise out of technological innovation, from monopolisation or from any process of change in which an economic agent can play a promoting or an obstructing role, whether with or without state support. Paradoxically, the very process of apparently withdrawing state intervention in deference to the new political economy, as in privatisation, does itself induce its own army of rent-seekers in the form of the merchant bankers, who arrange the sales, and the managers and work-force of the enterprises whose co-operation is required, at a cost, to a greater or lesser degree.

In short, whatever its analytical basis, rent-seeking can be discovered everywhere, and not least in labour markets. Inevitably, this leads to the view that labour market regulations and those who pursue them, such as trade unions, are damaging to the economy. Thus, if the turnover or monitoring of labour is costly to employers, trade unions can have an incentive to make it more so in order to accrue the 'rents' attached to the hiring and firing of labour. In other words, wherever trade unions have some market power, they have an incentive to engage in the use of resources to strengthen it. This can also arise for firms which are innovating or adding to their capital stock to gain a commercial edge. Cooperation from the work-force will require trade unions to be paid a 'rent' in the form of a wage differential to the extent that they can influence or even block the firm's behaviour.

But arguments of this type do not necessarily have to be exclusively supportive of reliance upon market forces. More generally, whatever are identified as the potential sources of profitability, the work-force is able to engage in rent-sharing with employers, and this can be advantageous to all concerned. A particularly simple example is provided by the 'hump-shaped' hypothesis around the impact of different forms of collective bargaining.[29] For a highly centralised bargaining system, trade unions will be sensitive to the effect on employment of exploiting their monopsony power and will moderate wage demands accordingly in the general interest of those that they represent. For a highly decentralised system, wage demands will be held down by competition within the labour market. Only at intermediate levels of (de)centralisation in bargaining will trade unions have both the power to raise the wage above the market-clearing level and the will to do so, in the interests of their membership at the expense of externalising employment effects to the rest of the economy. Similarly, as Freeman and Medoff (1984) have argued following Hirschmann (1970), trade unions may prove an effective way of organising and giving voice to their members' concerns, with disgruntled exit otherwise leading to higher labour turnover costs for the firm.

A second influence on institutional theory is the New Institutional Economics which has its origins in the work of Ronald Coase. It takes the market as just one institution through which economic life can be organised. As such, the market is far from perfect in the sense of always being the most efficient form of organisation. In particular, transactions are costly and imperfect in that contracts have to be specified and monitored and information is both imperfect and asymmetrical. As a result, it may be more efficient to engage in transactions other than through the market. This is used to explain the existence of firms, thought of as hierarchies complementing the market. Firms will internalise transactions if it is more cost-effective than undertaking them externally through the market. In other words, there is an efficient allocation of transaction activity between the market and hierarchies as well as within the market itself, as in orthodox economics.

The New Institutional Economics has developed in two different but complementary directions. One is rooted in the extension of neoclassical economics and is more limited in scope in that it takes the structure of information as given and examines how social institutions arise, and the division of activity between them, out of the optimising behaviour of individual agents. Essentially, it may be optimal to structure and internalise the market in the face of imperfect, asymmetrical and costly information.

The way in which this can be done in for labour markets has already been outlined in Chapter 2 in the context of the microeconomics of macroeconomics, as in screening models, for example. Career paths might be offered to attract and retain more skilled workers who cannot be identified in advance. In what follows, a rather different application will be outlined which is only indirectly related to labour markets.[30] It does have the advantage, however, of bringing out very clearly how institutions and structures might arise in the presence of informational imperfections. The policy issue is a standard one within the welfare economics of labour markets: how to support each member of the potentially working population at a minimum level of income at the least cost to the fiscus.

6 INDIVIDUAL OPTIMISATION AND ENDOGENOUS SOCIOECONOMIC STRUCTURE

Suppose the goal is to ensure that every member of the work-force has at least a minimum level of income. To do this, a benefit system must be designed in order to fund those who are unemployed and to push up the income of those who are employed but at too low a wage rate or for too few hours to meet the minimum income targeted. At first sight, the solution seems obvious – just make up the difference to the minimum for those below it for whatever reason. Surely this would provide for the guaranteed minimum at the lowest cost the exchequer. The answer is not necessarily; for the proposed solution takes no account of how individual workers will respond to the benefit system offered. Some earning at a wage rate just below enough to match the minimum have an incentive to become unemployed. Following the introduction of the scheme, they will get as much money as if they were working – in each case, they will be on the minimum. All they have to do is to decide whether to work or not! Social stigma and work experience aside, they will not suffer from the presumed disutility of labour. The scheme introduces a sort of poverty trap, although it is not an income trap so much as a work trap. By guaranteeing a minimum income and no more, the state runs the risk of encouraging some to work – bad enough in itself but with the added drawback of increasing the overall number and expense of the benefit scheme, since it will induce more to be on no or lower wage income than the minimum.

This raises the possibility that the state might do better, i.e., be able to pay out less in total, if it allows some workers' income to rise above the minimum even while they are in receipt of benefit. Otherwise, paying a reduced benefit or no benefit at all may lead these workers to choose unemployment at an even higher fiscal cost. The most sophisticated treatment of this problem is provided by Besley and Coate (1995), whose results are drawn upon here freely. It is first assumed that individuals fall into groups with different earning capacities. If government has full knowledge of these earning capacities for each individual, it can design a 'first best' income support scheme at minimum cost that subsidises those who earn below the minimum level and which does not raise anyone above that level. The fiscus simply makes up the difference between earnings and the minimum required income level. Also, except for those with zero earning capacity, by making a certain level of earned income as a precondition for income maintenance, it is even possible to make recipients work more than they would in the absence of support. The point is to use the income support in part as a mechanism of 'self-help'. The state knows each worker's earning capacity; it offers just enough top up income so that the utility-maximising worker provides the complementary wage component to attain the minimum.

None of this is possible if, realistically, government does not know individual earning capacities, even if it does know the distribution of earning capacities across the economy – that is, the number of individuals potentially able to earn each amount, if not who they are. If, for example, government attempted to operate the first best scheme, those capable of earning just above the minimum level would have an incentive not to do so, to take income benefit and work less. Those earning just below the minimum would also work less and claim more benefit. This leads to the design of a more complex 'second best' income maintenance programme (IMP) by government in which the previous first best of two groups of recipients/non-recipients is supplemented by a third intermediate group who receive benefit which takes them above the minimum, apparently leading to a waste of fiscal expenditure. However, should their benefit be cut to bring them down to the minimum, then they would work less and claim an even higher benefit to bring them up to the minimum. Everybody on benefit would be at the minimum income level but, paradoxically, the scheme would be more expensive than allowing some to be on benefit whilst above the minimum since, without this, there would be more beneficiaries being paid more and working less overall.

This situation arises because of the inability of government to target or 'screen' earning abilities perfectly. Indeed, the only way of screening benefit recipients is in the offer of income support itself. As a result, in order to minimise the fiscal cost of the universal minimum, it is necessary both to support some at a rate that raises them above the minimum and, in addition, some will be supported who could earn above the minimum in the absence of the IMP. Further, some in receipt of benefit will work less than in the absence of the IMP. Clearly, inferring this after the implementation of the IMP might lead to the conclusion that the intermediate group should be denied benefits. But this can only be done by increasing the total cost of the scheme (as members of the middle group switch to less work and join the lower income group) or by lowering the minimum standard.

The political acceptability of the second best optimal outcome to the lower and upper groups must be examined seriously. For both will observe that transfers are being made to those in the intermediate group whom they might consider are undeserving – to the lower group because they are them-selves worse-off, and to the upper group who would prefer fiscal transfers to target the lower group or to be saved altogether. The minimum income target at lowest fiscal cost, however, requires that the natural inclination to cut back these apparently superfluous benefits be resisted. Otherwise, the state will have to pay out even more to the voluntarily unemployed, 'work-shy' individuals. The political drawback of running the least cost benefit scheme is the need to pay benefit to relatively well-placed workers, those with intermediate earning capacity, raising their income above the target minimum.

Besley and Coate (1995) add a further dimension to their IMP by allowing for 'workfare', in which income support is contingent upon undertaking public sector work. This allows the second best to be moved another step closer to the first best, because the offer of workfare can be used as a second screening device to sort between earning capacities of households. In this case, four groupings emerge in the optimal government benefit scheme. The lowest group engages in private and public sector work, remuneration from the latter just bringing them up to the minimum. This implies a 100 per cent tax for them on private sector earnings, but more such work would be compensated for by a reduction in public sector work obligations. The second group with higher earning capacity would not engage in workfare but would receive income support. A third group would not engage in workfare but would receive income support to take them above the minimum. Finally, a fourth group would simply rely upon relatively high private sector earnings. Once again, the political accept-ability of this outcome must be questioned, especially as it can be shown that the public sector wage offered must exceed the lowest private sector wage and must rise with the individual's private sector earning capacity. This is necessary in order to guarantee incentive compatibility – to minimise the adverse effect on the overall cost of the programme due to individuals choosing to misrepresent their earnings capacity by hopping between groups.

As is apparent, such analysis is complex even on the basis of drastic simplifying assumptions – not least the capacity of government to vary the level of income support and workfare requirements and of individuals to vary the level of private sector earnings (by hours worked) whether engaged in workfare or not. For reasons of institutional convenience and political acceptability, much simpler schemes are inevitable, although this carries the implication of only attaining the minimum for all at a higher fiscal cost.

7 THE CHAOTIC THEORETICAL CASCADE OF THE NEW INSTITUTIONALISM

But what are the implications for the New Institutional Economics and for labour markets? The analysis is readily transferable to labour markets. For the beauty of the analysis is that it relies purely upon individual optimi-sation – by workers and even by the state as an agent seeking to attain a target at minimum cost. In addition, the state chooses to sort workers into various groups according to its knowledge of the distribution of earning capacities, if not their individual incidence. In other words, the state segments and institutionalises the labour market. Now, if we substitute a variety of workers' characteristics (such as skills, effort, etc.) for earning capacities, and if we consider employers rather than the state as offering a variety of wages and conditions in return for those characteristics, then exactly the same sorts of structures and sortings can arise as both sides opti-mise. It is possible to see how an optimum, if second best, equilibrium will arise comprising both internal and external labour market structures with corresponding wages and conditions.[31]

The New Institutional Economics has also developed in a less formal and more qualitative fashion by taking much less as exogenous and considering the historical evolution of institutions. In the previous example, the avail-ability of information is taken as given, and the institutional outcome is a consequence of optimising relative to that information on the basis of other institutions that are already themselves taken as given (the household, the state and the labour market). The New Institutional Economics is based on the (re)division between market and non-market forms because of informational imperfections, transactions costs and what is termed 'bounded information' and rationality. But where do these concepts come from in the first place?

This is a dynamic and historical question in terms of the evolution of, and interaction between, institutions and information, etc. For North (1993), for example, institutions have to become credible, which requires time for agents to form a common model of them and to believe in them as secure. Arbitrarily, possibly tautologously, this tends to be attached by North to the creation of well-defined and stable property rights. This is a consequence of the initiating emphasis on imperfect information and trans-action costs so that institutional evolution is understood as 'formed to reduce uncertainty in human exchange' (North 1993: 18). North also places emphasis upon the dynamic impetus to shifting transactions costs, and their impact on institutions, that derive from advances in technology and necessarily restructure the market/non-market boundary. This suffices to endow the historical evolution of institutions with the potential for multiple equilibria and path-dependence. Does society go for a system of pervasive piracy and perfect its presumably inefficient redistribution of resources, or does it solicit mutual benefits through the pursuit of productivity increases? The answer lies in the nature and security of property rights.

What this leaves unaddressed, a factor that is absent within the New Institutional Economics, is the question of power, as is recognised by enthusiastic practitioners such as Bates (1996).[32] This is in part a consequence of the association of non-market institutions with the correction of market imperfections – a sort of evolution by natural selection, with the horse perfecting the deficiencies of the unicorn! For Bates:

> In situations of market failure, people acting rationally generate social dilemmas. Their individually rational choices fail to elicit allocation of resources that maximise social welfare. By providing forms of pre-commitment, altering individual incentives, generating governance structures and so forth, non-market institutions provide mechanisms that enable individuals to transcend these dilemmas and thereby attain higher levels of collective welfare.
>
> (Bates 1996: 35)

A neat solution for him and for others is to allow politics to resolve the problem of multiple equilibria and path-dependence with the apparent added advantage of incorporating the role of the state and collective action. Even this neat resolution, however, gives rise to continuing ambiguity. As Weingast (1993: 305) puts it, echoing the debate over the 'developmental state' which might use its powers to become parasitic and corrupt:[33] 'The fundamental political dilemma of an economic system is that a state strong enough to protect private markets is strong enough to confiscate the wealth of its citizens'. Much the same fear, if not always embedded within institutional economics, is expressed about trade unions and governments supportive of labour:[34] How can the latter's interests be appropriately promoted without their being taken too far and the state become captured by too powerful labour movements – as is often suggested in the context of Latin American populism in the 1970s?

A more fundamental critique of the position of power with respect to the New Institutional Economics is offered by Khan (1996b), who argues that the initial divorce between the economy and politics cannot be rectified by a simply harmonious marriage between the two. This is because the dynamic between institutions and transaction costs presupposes a shift from the initial balance of political power as well as imposing more general political costs and benefits of transition. Power and institutions are not simply complementary, they are interdependent and cannot be analysed separately, with the former determining the outcomes offered by the latter.

The specific confrontation of New Institutional Economics with the issue of politics and power is an example of a more general characteristic, and hence problems, that it faces in its historical and evolutionary as opposed to its equilibrium vein. First, taking general equilibrium as its point of departure, New Institutional Economics counterposes the economy (or market) to other institutions:

> The new institutionalism represents an attempt to build a coherent account of institutions from micro-foundations. It seeks to apply to non-market institutions the same forms of reasoning that neoclassical economics has applied to the analysis of markets.
>
> (Bates 1996: 27)

In the dynamic between the market and non-market institutions, there remains a division between what is included within the analysis (now broader than before by incorporating non-market institutions) and what is excluded (politics, power and the state, for example). As previously discussed for the latter, what was previously absent can be added as new factors in a piecemeal and arbitrary fashion, according to the particular interests and disciplines of the contributors. Not only do agents have to respond to institutions, but they also have to reproduce or transform them. As a consequence, the New Institutional Economics becomes concerned with the role of law, customs, the state, etc. Consequently, the simplicity of the transactions approach to markets and hierarchies is entirely lost, even swamped, by any number of other considerations.[35] And, other than historical or empirical contingency, on which see the next section, the theory is caught in an infinite regress of what is causally prior.[36] With the inter- and intra-institutional determination of activity and outcomes dependent upon methodological individualism (not necessarily optimisation because of its complexity and cost to the individual),[37] this leaves open, as for the conundrum of the chicken and the egg, the informational conditions – or should it be more general social conditions – which individuals take as their starting-point for *forming* institutions or the institutions and information within which individuals choose a strategy.

The alternative to such infinite regress is to appeal to contingency. At such and such a time, these issues were resolved in a particular way as starting-point for subsequent institutional evolution – in a striking parallel with the narrower general equilibrium theory and its appeal to initial endowments. The problem for New Institutional Economics is that it cannot appeal to initial endowments alone, since these are indeterminate until we know the 'initial endowment' of the institutions defining property rights. These conundrums of infinite regress and broadening analytical scope are reflected in the most recent literature. Thus, for Williamson (1993b), apart from credibility and the associated problems with selective intervention, the New Institutional Economics (NIE) is concerned with first mover advantages (as in 'opportunism'), asymmetry of knowledge, and the Fundamental Transformation – how the division between market and hierarchy is first established. Kirchner (1995: 266) correctly summarises conference proceedings by noting 'the broadening of the scope of NIE-analysis', including such factors as ideology which assumes importance once rationality itself becomes endogenous in view of the informational/institutional interaction. Similarly, Joskow (1995) constructs four building-blocks for the NIE – institutional environment, market organisation, governance structures and modern industrial organisation. Each of these is made up of a number of aspects, such as informational asymmetries, transactions costs, property rights, etc. Is this not generalised equilibrium supply and demand extended to the whole world of institutions and behaviour? In short, from the simple problem of allocating activity between markets and firms in the light of relative transactions cost, the NIE has become unlimited in the theoretical and empirical material upon which it can draw, even if its intellectual origins in the initial understanding of markets and hierarchies tend to continue to exert an influence.[38] Further, there is the potential for the close cousin to the New Institutional Economics, the political theory of collective action, to be incorporated also. Following Olson (1965), the micro-foundations of collective action, and the formation of corresponding political institutions, can be based upon the calculation of the costs and benefits of forming institutions promoting the interests of groups of individuals in common. Essentially, this is simply the construction of New Institutional Economics through a journey from politics to economics rather than vice versa.

The third source of institutional theory has been the neo-Austrian school, which has followed the tradition established by Hayek. Like the new political economy, it is strongly in favour of the market and against intervention by the state. But it adopts this stance from a position of liberalism and the maximum exercise of individual freedom for entirely different reasons. For the neo-Austrians, the economy is full of uncertainties and continuing discoveries in which the local or individual access to, and use of, knowledge is preferable to the imposition of outcomes by those more distant from the needs and capabilities of individual economic agents.

Consequently, the market is seen as an ideal but evolving social mechanism for the communication and deployment of knowledge in which other institutions should occupy a subordinate position. As such, the neo-Austrian school is fundamentally opposed to notions of equilibrium and is concerned with dynamic progress through the exercise of individual liberty rather than with the static inefficiencies that may or may not arise through the rent-seeking activity associated with the new political economy.[39] Nor is it concerned with the efficient allocation of activity across institutions for given informational conditions since the market is seen as the best institution for the diffusion and inducement of *new* knowledge in pursuit of self-interest. Indeed, neo-Austrianism is notable for its neglect of consideration of the non-market institutions that it eschews. In addition, as Hodgson (1988) argues, like the New Institutional Economics, the neo-Austrian school depends upon an infinite regress, for it takes as given the institutions within which individuals are supposedly more or less able to pursue their own interests and remake those institutions. In any case, as argued by Chang (1994) in the context of industrial policy, there is no presumption in favour of the market just by virtue of the localisation, uncertainty and evolution of knowledge, even if such factors are taken to be the most crucial.[40] Possibly unwittingly, this is taken up in the labour market context by the literature on the relationship between trade unions and productivity growth. The standard argument, drawing upon rent-seeking, is that trade unions will obstruct change, in work practices for example. However, appealing to the notion of 'voice' as opposed to 'exit', it has been argued, following the empirical finding that presence of trade unions is positively associated with productivity increase and organisational change, that trade unions can efficiently represent their members interests collectively and co-operatively rather than individual workers responding to change by quitting their jobs or resisting innovation in work practices.[41]

The three influences upon new institutional theory – of new political economy, New Institutional Economics and the neo-Austrian school – are often seen as setting it apart from old institutionalism.[42] The latter tends to be disparaged for being descriptive, lacking in analytical precision and rigour, and arbitrary.[43] This is not surprising, as old institutionalists tend to be eclectic, sharing in common the belief that institutions other than the market do matter but that what they are and how they matter is historically contingent and requiring empirical investigation. As Klein puts it:

> The market is a useful instrumentality. No one would deny it. But it does not give direction, it takes orders and reflects orders. Somewhere there must be (and of course there is) debate about the orders, where they originate, what they reflect, and what they lead to. Institutionalists have

always insisted that it is a total abdication of responsibility for economists to argue that this lies 'outside' their discipline.

(Klein 1993: 284)

In many respects, however, this would be acceptable to new institutionalists.
Further, it is arguable that the latter do not break with the old institutionalists but incorporate elements of this tradition alongside the three other elements previously mentioned, for much of their theory is also empirically
contingent, theoretically underdeveloped and arbitrary in its emphasis.

8 NEW INDUSTRIAL RELATIONS FOR OLD?

This is perhaps most notable in the discipline of industrial relations which
might best be considered in its orthodoxy as institutionalism applied to
labour markets.[44] It is now widely recognised, especially in the UK, that
there is a new industrial relations both within the labour market itself and
in its content as an academic discipline.[45] The power of trade unions is considered to have declined, and the focus has switched, for example, to the role
that can be played by employers in human resource management, in part
and has imported emphasis from the USA. The traditional focus has been
upon trade unions, the institutions of formal and informal bargaining,
and qualitative workplace studies. But these seem less appropriate with
the decline of heavily unionised industries and with the majority of the
work-force no longer belonging to trade unions.

However, Kelly (1996) argues that, despite this shift in subject-matter,
there are considerable continuities in the analytical content of industrial
relations as a discipline, especially as far as its weaknesses are concerned.
Revisiting the critical commentary of Bain and Clegg (1974), he finds that
the field has remained descriptive rather than analytical, primarily focused
upon institutions at the expense of other social relations, and is largely
policy- and topically rather than research-driven, and without a formal
and precise conceptual apparatus relying, instead, upon ambiguous notions
such as power, legitimacy, (the industrial relations) system and the drift
between collectivism and individualism.[46] These weaknesses have been com-
pounded not only by the mismatch between the types of analysis developed
for the old (unionised) industrial relations and the new, the latter often
management of human resources in the absence of trade unions, but also
by the encroachment of orthodox labour economics and its techniques
into the field.[47]

This has occurred in two ways. First, empirically, different types of
hypotheses can be tested drawing upon large-scale data-sets that have
eclipsed more qualitative workplace studies. Whether dealing in trends, correlations, the (before and after) impact of policy, or multi-factor statistical
models, the econometric techniques associated with labour economics can
be employed to throw in variables that might affect labour market outcomes

over and above human capital, such as presence of trade unions, form of bargaining, capital-intensity, competitive conditions in product markets, etc. Second, the analytical rationale for the inclusion of such variables is through appeal more or less directly to the various elements of the new institutional theory previously outlined.

In short, as Nolan (1996) has argued, the old industrial relations has long suffered from a lack of substantial input from economic theory, especially that appropriate for dealing with the relationship between how labour markets are organised and function and, for example, the generation of productivity increase.[48] Instead, the industrial relations system tended to be described and judged as good or bad, usually on the basis of the strength and militancy of the trade union movement. Thus, simple correlations are presumed and investigated between trade unionism and productivity increase, as in the debate over whether the reform of industrial relations under Margaret Thatcher in the 1980s gave rise to a sustained increase in productivity.[49] The result is to neglect the broader historical context in which Britain's economic performance has been so weak, as well as the much more complex ways in which productivity is determined both within and from outside the labour market. Far from rectifying these weaknesses, the new industrial relations – drawing from institutional theory, labour economics, sophisticated statistical techniques and large data-sets – will only serve to continue to obscure the processes by which labour markets are structured and function. Thus, Nolan (1996) argues that the popular explanation of Britain's economic weaknesses in terms of obstructive trade union strength, and the solutions offered by Thatcherism in the 1980s, fails to address the more plausible alternative. This is that the UK has suffered from the long-standing *weakness* of the labour movement, and other economic agencies such as the state, industry and finance, in pressing for effective economic restructuring. The lagging performance in productivity has been compensated for by squeezes in wages and working conditions which induce, often to an extent that is exaggerated, industrial action from the labour movement, the suppression of which can only consolidate long-term deficiencies in return at most for short-run gains by cutting wage costs.[50] Trade unions, then, have been a contributory factor in the UK's economic weakness rather than an underlying cause.

One picture that emerges from this and previous chapters is of a vibrant and successfully developing theory of labour markets. It has well-established elements, as in human capital theory, as well as innovative points of departure, as in the use of hysteresis and informational and market asymmetries and imperfections. It is interdisciplinary in drawing upon the various types of institutional theory, and it is sensitive to empirical and historical contingency in so far as the (institutional) outcomes of the past affect those of the future. It deals in grand theory, as in post-Fordism, and in the most immediate descriptive hypotheses, as in the study of flexibility.

Yet, labour market theory, as the same picture viewed from another angle, is in a state of analytical chaos which, perversely, precisely because of its frantic levels of activity, serves to conceal its lack of coherence. Taken individually or collectively, the literature is simply an eclectic amalgam of theoretical (and empirical) fragments. Further, despite the wide range of analytical elements deployed, much of the literature is parsimonious in its use of them. In extreme form, it is not too much of a parody to see orthodox developments in labour market theory as parallel to the sort of methodological stance that is adopted by Gary Becker for his work whether for human capital or not: 'if I am ingenious enough to explain labour market structures and outcomes in terms of methodological individualism, equilibrium, and optimisation, why should I make reference to socioeconomic structures, tendencies and processes?' That others, and other disciplines, might be more eclectic in their choice of explanatory factors and methodologies employed is a substantial advance in logic and realism. But fundamental weaknesses remain. It is not enough to rely upon new political economy for static (in)efficiencies, New Institutional Economics for (static) division between market and non-market activity (even if dynamics is added in the historical version, as in the work of North and others), and upon neo-Austrian considerations for the dynamics of change.

As is apparent from institutional theory, there are central questions concerning socioeconomic structures: How are they created and reproduced and what activity takes place within and between them, and how does this all shift over time? What are the underlying forces that drive the economy and society, and how do these interact with the formation and functioning of social structures and the institutions to which these are attached? New institutional theory has primarily answered these questions in terms of market and informational imperfections and the problems of incentive compatibility and contracting.[51] These are euphemisms, lacking historical precision, for the issues are posed by capitalism for which we know the driving force is the imperative of profitability and preservation of particular types of property. Such analytical features are more prominent in radical labour market literature which, in the form of segmented labour market theory, is critically assessed in Part III, which also seeks to address the concerns just mentioned, those that are scarcely broached let alone answered by the orthodox treatment of the labour market covered in this Part.

NOTES

1 The current invasive tendency of neoclassical economics against other disciplines and approaches is argued in Fine (1997a).
2 A third issue is the empirical extent of flexibility. For a study of the UK, see Beatson (1995) and Sisson and Marginson (1995). See also the detailed study of flexibility in retailing and finance provided by EOC (1995). Significantly for the conclusions in this chapter, and for the book more generally, flexibility is shown to have depended upon worse working conditions for a part-time and

temporary workforce, particularly but not exclusively for women. The incidence of this is, however, different between the two sectors.

3 For such arguments in detail, see Streeck (1992), for example.

4 For economists, the most familiar fallacy of composition is Keynes' paradox of thrift where the result of individuals attempting to save more is to cause a depression through deficient aggregate effective demand and, hence, reducing income and saving.

5 See Hyman (1991) for a discussion of the empirical changes in contemporary capitalism that have provoked the use of flexibility as an explanatory factor despite its lack of sufficient content and originality for that purpose.

6 This section draws heavily upon Fine (1995). This is a response to Rogerson (1994) which provides an excellent overview of the literature on flexible specialisation. The two articles concern the applicability of flexible specialisation to South Africa, an issue not covered here. See also Pollert (1991a) and Nolan and Walsh (1995).

7 For the distinction between flec-spec and post-Fordism, with the rejection of the latter as too deterministic, see Hirst and Zeitlin (1989).

8 This can be traced most clearly in the work of Boyer.

9 For excellent critical expositions of regulation theory, see Mavroudeas (1990) and Brenner and Glick (1991).

10 For a critical review even of flec-spec's most favoured territory, see Amin (1991). Taplin (1996) points to the ambiguity between flexibility and Fordism in the context of the apparel industry. The recent special issue of *World Development*, edited by Humphrey (1995) and devoted to flexibility in developing countries, is remarkable both for failing to recognise how limited is its scope of application and, on which see later, for neglecting the role of underlying economic interests and their political expression. The latter is primarily seen as affecting the form in which flexibility is adopted, conveniently allowing for further analytical flexibility in empirical interpretation.

11 By contrast, Tickell and Peck (1995), for example, identify eight different types of Fordism.

12 For an outstanding critique of the binary opposition between Fordism and flec-spec, and its analytical imposition upon the development of food systems, see Goodman and Watts (1994).

13 As Pollert concludes:

> Further research on restructuring should free itself from unhelpful conceptual convention, and explore the relationships of similarity and *difference* in institutional backgrounds, social structures and current lines of development in economic and labour arrangements.
>
> (Pollert 1991b: 8; emphasis in original)

14 Fine (1994b) criticises a similar method in food systems theory, where empirical trends are treated as tendencies whose contradictions are ultimately perceived to require structural change. See the debate in the same place that this inspired as well as Fine *et al.* (1996).

15 He, however, searches for an alternative in terms of a dialectic between rigidity and flexibility which is itself arbitrary and not analytically rooted.

16 What follows was initially drafted in an appendix to Fine (1987). It is significant that the intellectual origins of flec-spec could have been identified so early and as a corollary of an earlier tradition in labour market theory (rather than as a pure response to the demise of Fordism, however well understood in theory and realised in practice). A comprehensive account of dual, and segmented, labour market theory follows later in the book.

17 As far as the reversal of hierarchy in market structure is concerned, this is also observed by Gertler (1992: 265).
18 For the flec-spec history reported in this paragraph, see Sabel and Zeitlin (1985).
19 In Sabel (1982), however, workers are invariably 'he', and this may in part reflect the central role of crafts*men* in flec-spec analysis, on which see later. The role of ethnic groups is more prominent than gender considerations since they are more liable to form a community for economic as well as for social purposes.
20 Thus, Piore and Sabel assert (incorrectly for classical as opposed to neoclassical economics):

> Flexible specialisation works by violating one of the assumptions of classical political economy: that the economy is separate from society . . . By contrast, in flexible specialisation it is hard to tell where society . . . ends, and where economic organisation begins.
>
> (Piore and Sobel 1986: 275)

21 In more recent work involving Piore, Locke *et al.* (1995), emphasis is placed upon variety in the evolution of industrial relations systems within and between countries. Oversimplifying, but catching the core of the argument, the key issue is seen as one of moving in response to the new international (flec-spec) competition and away from old Fordist norms and modes of organisation. Responses are seen as favourable or unfavourable according to whether they are short-run cost-cutting or long-run skills-building, with the latter requiring state intervention. In short, the rush to flec-spec is tempered by the recognition that it can degenerate into a form of sweating.
22 These areas and sectors are cited so often as to have become clichés of the flec-spec school. For a critique of the notion as applied to the Greater London Council's industrial strategy, see Nolan and O'Donnell (1987), for example. The story of the GLC's interventions based on flec-spec has yet to be fully and properly told. The present author had some involvement and would emphasise how difficult it was to find appropriate investments and how disastrous those that were made were to prove.
23 Thus, in Piore and Sabel:

> A shift away from mass production would restore the neoclassical equilibrating mechanisms . . . the risks of investment will be generally reduced . . . it would be possible to maintain full employment largely through monetary policy . . . there would be much less danger of shocks to the economy touching off inflationary surges . . . Similarly, flexible specialisation is better able to accommodate fluctuations in exchange rates and commodity prices . . . flexible specialisation and mass production could be combined in a unified *international* economy. In this system, the old mass-production industries might migrate to the underdeveloped world, leaving behind in the industrialized world the high-tech industries . . . To the underdeveloped world, this hybrid system would provide industrialisation.
>
> (Piore and Sobel: 276–9; emphasis in original)

Otherwise, the alternative is a resumption of Fordism on the basis of a multinational Keynesianism to provide adequate demand.
24 Thus, the notion of flexibility is commonly, and often critically, assessed from a variety of points of view. See, for example, Harley (1995) and Gilbert *et al.* (1992).
25 On the other hand, the ideological impact of neo-Austrianism on and in promoting the new right has been enormous. For a striking example, see Hanson and Mather (1988).

26 There are other features of the new institutionalism which it is worthwhile listing briefly although they will be reviewed later in more detail. Its core theory draws upon limited explanatory variables (transaction costs and imperfect information); it is generally contemptuous of the older institutionalism for lack of rigour (finance being an exception) despite not yielding any results that it had not yet discovered; its core models are applicable to any market in principle even though they have usually been developed in the context of a particular market such as labour or finance; and it meets with a mixed reception across the social sciences but with an increasing influence over them.

27 The classic example is tax avoidance and evasion which lead to the wasteful use of resources to save individual tax incidence even though the same amount of government revenue still has to be raised in aggregate.

28 The theory of the second best finds that if not all the conditions for perfect competition can be satisfied simultaneously, then policy may not improve the economy by shifting it towards perfect competition in one or other respect alone.

29 For a survey of the theoretical and empirical evidence, see Calmfors (1993). This analysis is a specific application to labour market bargaining of Mancur Olson's more general theory of the external imposition of costs on others by special interest groups or political organisations.

30 This example draws upon a paper on income maintenance programmes, prepared for the South African Presidential Labour Market Commission.

31 Although not revealed here, however, this is all only so in principle, for, even for the relatively simple examples outlined above, the mathematics becomes extremely complex as the number of reward strategies, and screening devices, increases.

32 Evidence of the New Institutional Economics' distaste and discomfort for dealing with power is shown from the response by Williamson (1993a) and Stiglitz (1993) to the relatively mild suggestion from Bowles and Gintis (1993) that exchange is not only institutionally driven but also 'contested'. For Williamson:

> The power hypothesis is typically vague and often reduces to an ex post rationalization . . . Although I seriously doubt that power qualifies for main case standing in the commercial arena, I agree that it can sometimes be brought in as an auxiliary hypothesis.
>
> (Williamson 1993a: 107)

For Stiglitz:

> There are good economic reasons, beyond the exercise of 'power' (whatever that much-used term means) for the existence of hierarchical relationships.
>
> (Stiglitz 1993: 111)

For an assessment of the distinction between the contested exchange model and that of conventional efficiency-wage type, see Costabile (1995).

33 For a critical assessment of the developmental state literature, see Fine and Stoneman (1996).

34 And, to be fair, similar concerns are expressed over industrial policy and the potential for excessive protection of the interests of industrialists.

35 See also the other contributions in the issue in which North's (1993) article appears.

36 For these and other criticisms, see Ingham (1996).

37 As Swedberg (1993: 205) observes: 'In all brevity, since custom tends to interfere with the general model of explanation, it is *eliminated* rather than *neglected* in the historical tradition' (emphases in original).

38 Interestingly, Coase reflects that the NIE is compatible with (neoclassical) 'economic theory' but that further progress in theoretical development is currently dependent upon more evidence:

> As you know, it is impossible to undertake good empirical work without a theory and difficult to formulate theories without good empirical work. Empirical work and the improvement of our theories have to go on simultaneously. But sometimes the need is greater for more theoretical work and sometimes for more empirical. It is my view that at the present time we are so ignorant that it is difficult to formulate theories to explain the working of the economic system, at any rate in that part of our subject termed industrial organization but no doubt elsewhere. The need at the present time, in my view, is for more empirical work.

> (Coase 1993: 361)

It is this author's view that to the extent that this vacuous commentary has any content at all, it is the opposite of the truth. There is a surfeit of theory but it is chaotic and needs to be sorted out and fundamentally transformed in the light of an equally abundant wealth of empirical knowledge.

39 As Nishibe (1996) suggests, this means that the debate over market socialism is less about socialism and more, from a Hayekian perspective, about the inapplicability of notions of equilibrium to economic problems.

40 Indirectly, Khan (1996b) argues the same point on the favoured ground of those in favour of the market and against the state – in the context of corruption. Comparing India and South Korea, he suggests that whether corruption is functional for an economy depends upon the broader context of economic and political power within which it is situated.

41 The standard reference is for the USA (Freeman and Medoff 1984). See also Nolan (1996) for a discussion in the UK context.

42 For a recent overview and optimistic account of the prospects for the revitalisation of heterodox institutionalism, see Samuels (1995). Harriss *et al.* (1996: 5) posit the difference between the old and the New Institutional Economics as follows: 'In sum, the OIE may be presented as descriptive, holistic and behaviourist and the NIE as formalist and reductionist'. See also Tool (1993) for an overview of the 'old' institutional economics.

43 A general exception is provided by consideration of financial institutions. This no doubt reflects the fluidity of its institutions as well as their variability across what otherwise appear to be similar comparative conditions, so that equilibrium analysis is left floundering in explaining why, for example, some financial systems seem to generate and deploy finance for industry more effectively than others. For an outstanding but isolated exception in the case of labour economics, see Freeman's (1989) sterling defence of the older tradition against the new.

44 For a period, as with Marxist political economy around the 1970s, radical industrial relations prospered, not accidentally, alongside theoretical innovation as attention was drawn to the labour process (and the processes and mechanisms attached to the labour market more generally, especially around forms of control and conflict at the place of production).

45 See Kelly (1996), Edwards (1995) and Beardwell (1996).

46 On the latter, see Kessler and Purcell (1995).

47 Kelly considers that the assault from human resource management and labour economics on top of its own continuing weaknesses is sufficient to place the future of industrial relations as a discipline at risk. Somewhat arbitrarily, he considers the incorporation of long wave theory and the role of social movements as a means of potential survival.

48 See also Nolan and Walsh (1995).
49 For a review of this debate, see Nolan and O'Donnell (1995).
50 See also Fine and Harris (1985).
51 There is an extraordinary naivety and lack of scholarship with which institutional theories (and neoclassical economics more generally) have successively been drawn into larger questions without the conceptual apparatus to handle them other than to invent terms as a quick fix, usually around information, individual behaviour and contracting. In addition, as Ingham perceptively observes:

> It is difficult not to share this irritation when confronted, for example, with . . . 'agency theory' which quite simply tries to reduce the complexity of social and economic organisation to the individual propensities of the amoral maximiser . . . The issue is not merely that this form of theorising can easily be made the subject of cogent theoretical and empirical critiques . . . but that the authors were so structurally insulated by the social organisation of intellectual specialisation that they were able to disregard the huge non-economic literature on the very problems that they had posed for themselves.
>
> (Ingham 1996: 262)

For Toye:

> The main weakness of the NIE as a grand theory of socio-economic development is that it is empty . . . the theory adds nothing to what we already have. No new predictions can be derived; no new policies recommended. No historical episodes can be explained better now than they were by the historians who have already studied them.
>
> (Toye 1995: 64)

Part III

Segmented labour market theory

The main conclusion of Part II is that *the* labour market is a misnomer and that labour markets need to be studied from a disaggregated perspective. A natural next step is to assess the literature on segmented labour markets which directly addresses divisions across labour markets, even if usually for empirical rather than for the theoretical reasons adopted here. Contributions to segmented labour market (SLM) theory have usually been motivated by the transparency of the divisions that demarcate separate sections of the work-force and the corresponding inability of standard textbook labour economics to explain them.

Chapters 5 and 6 present a critical review of the literature in chronological sequence. Chapter 5 covers the early radical literature, which was dismissed by neoclassical orthodoxy for its conceptual and theoretical weaknesses from that perspective. To the extent that this rejection was based on, and motivated by, the literature's refusal to accept methodological individualism and its determination to acknowledge the reality of social relations, structures and processes, it was unjustified. To the extent that the rejection was based on the literature's dependence upon an incoherent jumble of theoretical and empirical fragments, it has some resonances with the assessment offered here. Radical SLM theory has always suffered from *ad hoc*ery that is both concealed and reinforced by the multiplicity of case studies that it has inspired.

Chapter 6 examines developments over the past decade during which neoclassical orthodoxy has turned an intellectual somersault in its stance towards the issues involved. Following the emergence of its analytical capacity to explain social structures and inequality of outcomes for otherwise identical economic agents (as a consequence of market and informational imperfections), SLM theory has become part and parcel of orthodox labour market theory. Whilst the radical tradition has not been completely displaced – indeed, case studies continue to proliferate – the dull influence of the orthodoxy has increasingly been felt. Its modes of reasoning have been incorporated alongside other more catholic methods of reasoning, but the grander theoretical goals of labour market theory associated with the radical tradition's understanding of different phases of capitalism have more or less disappeared other than in the flexibility debate discussed in the last chapter.

These two chapters illustrate that it is one thing to demand an analysis directed at labour market segmentation; it is quite another to provide it on a satisfactory methodological basis. Chapter 7 is more constructive and its conclusions, which are disarmingly simple, are worth laying out in advance. First, segmentation of the labour market is the consequence of underlying socioeconomic processes, forces or tendencies that give rise to, and reproduce, specific and historically contingent labour market structures. Second, each labour market segment does not only incorporate and combine socioeconomic factors that set it apart from other segments, the structuring is itself different from one segment to another. Only in a limited sense do labour market segments belong to the same labour market. By analogy, they have no more in common in principle than do markets for apples and oranges or, possibly more apt, fish and fowl. Neoclassical economists would have us believe that these commodities are ready substitutes for one another in generating utility. By the same token, labour is presumed to be fluid across the whole economy under the rubric of labour market mobility and substitutability within production. But, this is all a unicorn-type fiction and should not form the analytical basis on which to address labour market structures, even by way of market imperfections. How labour is structured within and across sectors should serve as the investigative starting-point.

Third, the study of these processes of segmentation extends beyond the narrow economic arena defined by production, distribution and exchange to include social reproduction and differentiation by consumption. The latter refers to the processes whereby different consumption goods enter differently and unevenly into the standards of working-class consumption.

On the one hand, these propositions may appear too general, abstract and weak to command disagreement or controversy; on the other, they may appear to lack clarity. On the first score, it is worth highlighting differences with the existing literature. First, there is a definite causal sequencing between underlying socioeconomic factors and the structures that they yield and reproduce. This not only rejects an equilibrium understanding of labour market structures but also the notion that they are simply the reflection of, or in correspondence with, other structures – most notably for patriarchal or industrial structures, for example. Second, the notion that labour markets are not only distinct but distinctly structured involves a rejection of the idea that all labour markets are simultaneously structured relative to one another as well as the possibility of a general theory of specific labour market segments.

Third, and possibly most innovative, the role of differentiation in consumption in structuring labour markets is a departure from the pervasive tradition of treating wage differentials merely in terms of their monetary equivalent, simply as the amount that can be purchased rather than what is purchased and *consumed*. Emphasis is placed upon the different ways in which consumption goods enter consumption across the population and hence the work-force. In other words, consumption goods link to the labour market in a variety of different ways from one good and labour market to another, and not just as a wage cost or expenditure. Whilst there are working-class norms in consumption – the so-called moral and historical elements in subsistence or the value of labour-power – these do vary both by item of consumption and labour market segment.

To clarify the proposed understanding of labour market structures, consider two influences in earlier work that informed the analysis. In studying consumption, as reported in Fine and Leopold (1993) and Fine *et al.* (1996), very similar methodological arguments have been deployed. First, different items of consumption are attached to their own structures that are the product of underlying socioeconomic relations and forces to yield what are termed 'systems of provision' (SOP), linking production to ultimate consumption through a whole chain of activities as in the food, energy, fashion and transport systems. Second, these distinct sops differ in how they function and are reproduced. Subsequently, this second conclusion can be carried over to labour markets but not the first conclusion, given the extensive mobility of labour, certainly occupationally, across sectors of the economy. This contrasts with consumption, where there are limits to the connections between different items of consumption for which an intimate connection would broaden the content or scope of a particular sop. Without going into details here, whilst consumption is structured 'vertically' through the chain of activities that lead to it, the same is not true of labour which can be structured vertically in the sectors in which it is employed as well as horizontally across sectors occupationally. None the less, with this modification, the notion of distinct and distinctly functioning and historically contingent labour market structures as the outcome of underlying socioeconomic factors can be retained.

In breaking with the existing literature on SLM theory, however, a more important influence was work on the South African labour market. It would be difficult to suggest a more suitable testing ground for SLM theory, with the particularly sharp differentiation between the wages and working conditions of blacks and whites. Surprisingly, however, labour market analysis for South Africa had remained in its infancy until recently, with discussion revolving around the so-called race-class and articulation of modes of production debates.[1] Much of the literature proceeded as if migrant miners or others were the sole or typically representative members of the work-force. Were they a source of cheap labour-power and, if so, was this a consequence of the contribution to social reproduction provided by neighbouring countries or subsistence agriculture in the homelands? More surprising, even to the present day, there has been the limited use of SLM theory for the South African labour market, despite its apparently startling suitability from an empirical standpoint. The major exception was the debate between

Cassim (1982, 1983a, 1983b) and Truu (1983a, 1983b), although this primarily hinged theoretically around the relative merits of neoclassical and radical economics.

The situation with respect to labour market analysis more generally has changed with the political demise of apartheid, although this was preceded from the second half of the 1970s by considerable trade union activity, leading to a narrowing of white–black wage differentials. More traditional labour market analyses have begun to emerge, not least to explain continuing differentials and to suggest how they might be closed. Extremely conservative, and poor, analyses emanating from the World Bank, such as that by Fallon (1992) for example, conclude that the differential is now about right, appropriately reflecting levels and differences in marginal productivities across the work-force. Any rise in black wages, or closing of differentials, would be a source of labour market inefficiency and result in higher levels of black unemployment. Policy needs to restrain black wages and address longer-term pre-market inequalities, especially education.[2]

A more sophisticated and detailed account of recent shifts in South African labour markets is offered by Hofmeyr (1994a).[3] Essentially, he observes a narrowing if not closing of differentials between the wages of blacks and whites and views this as indicative of the labour market becoming more racially integrated. For him to assess this quantitatively, however, it is necessary to correct for 'legitimate' or possibly non-racial sources of wages differentials, such as those attached to education or regional location of employment, respectively. Significantly, according to this approach, as long as wages merely reflect non-racial attributes, then labour markets are fully integrated or non-structured.[4]

Such a conclusion is absurd on closer examination. Suppose men and women were paid the same, correcting for legitimate non-gender differences, but were totally occupationally segregated. We could hardly infer that the labour market had become integrated. In short, assessment of labour market segmentation/integration purely on the grounds of *outcomes* (even moving beyond wages corrected for personal and other attributes) is insufficient. Clearly, and this inspired the alternative approach adopted here, whatever the outcomes, the manner in which the black and white labour markets had been, and were continuing to be, structured and reproduced was entirely different.

More specifically, consider features of the South African labour market that are well-known.[5] First, and historically with few exceptions, blacks have been denied access to sufficient land to enable their basic reproduction without recourse to wage labour, whether as migrant labour or not, or whether employed by mining, agriculture, manufacturing or services. In addition, as a means of enhancing the competitiveness of white farming, the latter has been the beneficiary of a range of supports that have not been available to black agriculture, irrespective of its access to sufficient qualities and quantities of land.

Second, in South Africa, a major aspect in access to employment has been influx control. Apartheid ideology, as much as practice, has been caught on the contradiction between separate development and dependence upon black labour. Structurally, the labour force has been differentiated between those on the homelands (possibly employed on white farms), those oscillating between the homelands and white urban areas and those permanently based in or around white urban areas. Legislation and policy has fluctuated around how to *define* and distinguish these segments and how to control them (and render them functional). In retrospect, the crisis of apartheid from the 1970s onwards, as repression became increasingly futile as a mechanism of control, led to a strategy focused upon the granting of rights to a permanent or commuting work-force whilst intensifying the oppression against those (the majority) excluded from such privileges.[6] Consequently, the distance between urban and rural conditions has widened as education, housing and employment conditions have diverged. The result has been even greater pressures for urbanisation and knock-on effects for agriculture. Because of its higher levels of productivity, capitalist agricultural development in general does tend to undermine the viability of small-scale, subsistence agriculture. But there are countertendencies; small-scale agriculture finds that markets are created for its products, cheaper inputs are made available, and other sources of revenue, most notably wage remittances, can be earned to finance them (including casual labour). For these reasons, we tend to observe both the growth of large-scale agriculture and the survival of small-scale farmers, the exact balance depending on how well their economic interests are represented.[7]

Characteristic of the apartheid system has been the extent to which the tendencies to small-scale, black agriculture have been undermined by apartheid policies, together with the economic viability of the homelands. It is a transparent outcome from the use of wage remittances to support homeland subsistence rather than further economic activity, although this can occur by way of exception. Significant is the lack of vibrant 'informal' sectors in South Africa,[8] the use of wage remittances to buy consumption goods produced by the (external) capitalist sector[9] and, as an exception that proves the rule, the success of the taxi system for transport arising out of economic opportunities provided by the apartheid's system of segregation.[10]

In addition, dependence on wage remittances has given rise to a specifically sharp gender division of labour in which marginal homeland agriculture has been increasingly the responsibility of women.[11] The counterpart to such poor opportunities in agriculture has been women's availability as a cheap, often casualised, source of labour, especially in white agriculture and domestic service, the latter potentially magnified in current conditions of high unemployment and the relaxation of restrictions on urbanisation. In this light, it can be seen, as argued previously at the theoretical level, that there are some common determinants to male migrant mine labour and female domestic service, but the two labour markets are structured entirely differently from one another, something which cannot be captured by reference to differences in wages and conditions alone.[12]

Further, job reservation has structured employment along racial lines, for which the state has played a major role both legislatively and as an employer itself. Such employment hierarchies are neither inflexible nor unchanging and, even to the extent that they are, this has to be explained against the processes and pressures associated with the 'dilution' of white labour by cheaper, or more readily available, black labour, and the recomposition and redefinition of skills as technology changes. The definition of skill, and corresponding grading and remuneration is socially constructed in a number of ways, not least the technically determined requirements of the job, the need for management and control, the access to education and training – whether to acquire formal qualifications or as a screen for social-isation into work habits – and the (ideological) labelling of jobs as more or less skilled according to trade union or other conflicts over grading (with what whites or males do as more readily recognised as skilled over what blacks or women do, irrespective of the inherent skills required). Whilst there has been an upgrading of black skills in recent years, it has given rise to a 'floating' colour bar rather than a breach in the colour bar, as the white–black hierarchies have remained predominantly untouched.[13]

Over the 1970s, a major transformation took place in the way that labour markets operated within South Africa. This is uncontroversial. The issues are how to identify and understand such changes. Consider mining: the dependence of the mines on foreign migrant labour had declined from 80 per cent to 40 per cent; white : black wage ratios in mining had declined from 20 : 1 to 6 : 1 and were closely aligned to wage levels and ratios typical in manufacturing; black trade unions, it is now known in retrospect, had securely established themselves, were rapidly growing in membership and were actively engaged in both industrial and political activity. By the end of the decade, the Wiehahn and Riekert Commissions were, respectively, accepting the need for recognition of black trade unionism and greater rights of residence for blacks in secure urban employment.

In terms of labour's access to employment, the most startling change has been the decline in foreign migrant labour to the mines. As documented by Wilson (1972a, 1972b), through all the vicissitudes of the previous 50 years, the ability of the mining companies to recruit such workers had enabled black wages to stagnate or even to decline in real terms. Consequently, they remained at levels which rendered them too low to attract or to make attractive a majority South African labour force. Undoubtedly, the liberation of the frontline states totally transformed the conditions of the mines' access to labour irrespective of the extent to which mutual economic dependence (the mines' on labour supply, the frontline states' on wage remittances) was used by one side or the other in political conflicts.[14] As Crush *et al.* (1991: 104) put it, the 1970s witnessed the 'break-up of the mining industry's northern empire'.

Obviously, the relative loss of foreign migrant labour strengthened the hand of their domestic counterparts. Similarly, the rising price of gold in the 1970s enhanced the profitability of the mines and more readily enabled mining companies to pay higher wages.[15] Longer-run factors included the growing costs of the migrant system itself, in terms of transport and recruitment, and the need for a more stable work-force as the capital expenditure on the fabric of mines and on mechanisation dictated the need for skills derived from continuous work experience.[16] For the latter, foreign migrant workers often had accumulated higher levels of skills and experience so that the rapid adjustment to use of South African labour must have entailed the loss of much accumulated expertise.

It is also important to recognise, however, how certain structures have remained essentially unchanged. One significant example is the residential housing at the mines which has continued to be predominantly for whites. The legal limitation to 3 per cent of the black labour force has been lifted (and was never a binding constraint) but with only a token response in housing programmes. A second example is the skill hierarchy between whites and blacks, which remains rigid, even if the latter are rising in the skill hierarchy and pushing up whites above them – and as black skills are increasingly recognised in practice through (re)grading. Indeed, job reservation on the mines was only lifted in the late 1980s, and training and skilled posts more fully made formally available to black miners.

Such factors, and changes in them, were not unique to the 1970s. The gold price had risen in the 1930s; the relative strength of white miners had been shattered in the 1920s; labour markets had been tight in and after the Second World War. What appears to have been decisive in restructuring the labour markets in the 1970s was the coincidence of these factors, together with the successful prosecution of struggle by the work-force. There was the growth of the National Union of Mineworkers in the context of broader industrial action, following on from the strikes in Durban in 1972–3; but equally if not more important, was a crisis of control within the mining compounds themselves, as both work and living conditions became contested terrain.[17]

Developments within the mining industry have interacted with those external to it. During the 1970s, conditions in the homelands continued to deteriorate.[18] Although the proportion living below subsistence is estimated to have fallen from 99 per cent to 81 per cent between 1960 and 1980, the absolute numbers have risen from 13 million to 15 million, creating pressure for migration, urbanisation and dependence on wage remittances. Alternative employment opportunities in agriculture have been eroded with an absolute decline in the work-force as farms have increased in size and have relied heavily upon mechanisation.[19] There has also been a heavy increase in unemployment, estimated to have doubled between the 1960s and the 1970s, and standing at a level of 40 per cent or so in the 1990s, depending on how it is defined and how reliably it is measured.[20]

In these circumstances, it is hardly surprising that the mines should have been able to recruit domestic labour in place of foreign migrants. Symptomatic of this was the erosion of conflict between different employers over labour supplies. By 1986, legal protection of black farm workers against recruitment for the mines was withdrawn and urban recruitment became less contentious.[21] However, it would be a mistake to conclude that the systemic structures within the labour market had, thereby, been removed. The 1970s does appear to have witnessed the erosion of some of the disadvantages confronted by the black mining work-force compared to those of manufacturing so that, for the black work-force, wages and conditions are determined in comparable fashions, subject to the variety of 'legitimate' factors that influence each differentially. The change has come about with the reduction in foreign migrant workers. But the same cannot be said of agriculture and female employment or of the racial hierarchies in employment more generally.

More recent literature, such as the work of Hofmeyr, has begun to disaggregate the South African labour markets in ways which confirm the virtues of the analysis offered here but without conforming to it. Bundles of general theories are thrown together at too great a level of aggregation and without otherwise acknowledging that each labour market is structured and reproduced differently. Thus, Chadha (1995) considers that the labour market is divided into skilled (white) and unskilled (black), with one subject to market-clearing and the other to excess supply, respectively. He throws in notions of structural and cyclical unemployment, together with models of efficiency-wage, incentive efficiency and the role of centralised bargaining. He concludes:

> Each (model) is shown to be empirically capable of generating the kind of wage gap observed in the market for unskilled labor in South Africa. At an aggregate level the models are, therefore observationally equivalent. In any given sector, however, one of the models is likely to be more relevant than the others, as the economy comprises various sectors that differ in terms of average levels of wages, industrial structure, and the extent of unionization.

> (Chadha 1995: 643)

On the other hand, to chart significant change in segmentation in the South African labour market over the past 20 years, Kraak draws upon the US and Cambridge segmented labour market schools as well as the post-Fordist literature. For him: 'The examination of recent trends in the South African labour market will be based on an eclectic borrowing from all these influences' (Kraak 1995: 658). Finally, Smit (1996) emphasises the role of product market structures in the formation of South African labour markets, explaining wage differentials as workers share in the oligopolistic rents gleaned from higher product market concentration.[22] Dovetailing such considerations with a segmentation by black (unskilled) and white (skilled), she obtains a fourfold structure for the work-force, also drawing upon capital-intensity as a close correlate of market concentration and skill. What she overlooks, however, is trade unionism, migrancy, gender, public as opposed to private ownership, export and import penetration, access to finance, more or less favourable government policy, and the list could run on, multiplying the number of segments by two for each extra factor added.

Hopefully, even this cursory examination of the more general literature on South African labour markets, as well as of the shifting reproduction of the mining labour market, suffices to demonstrate that labour market structures are the product of underlying socioeconomic factors, and that the labour markets are structured differently from one another whilst sharing some determinants in common. The specific features of the South African mining labour market is blatant evidence of such a conclusion; it is a market that is entirely different from that of domestic servants or agricultural workers, whatever wages and conditions are attached to them all. The ultimate purpose of Part III of the book is to extend such insights to labour market theory more generally.

NOTES

1 For a brief review and for a longer discussion of what follows, see Fine (1994a). An annotated bibliography of studies on the South African labour market is to be published by the ILO as part of its contribution to the Presidential Labour Market Commission.
2 More recently, the South African Foundation (1996) has proposed a two-tier system of wages with lower levels for new black entrants. For a critical review of recent developments and arguments, see Michie (1997) and also ILO (1996).
3 See also Hofmeyr (1990a, 1990b, 1993, 1994b).
4 The difficulties and weaknesses exhibited by Hofmeyr in undertaking this exercise are legion, if not the primary theoretical concern here once the underlying methodology has been accepted. In brief, it is not clear that he has a well-specified theory of the labour market that is being tested against an alternative; there is multicollinearity between the variables concerned; there are absent variables such as capital-intensity, industrial structure and levels of profitability which are known to affect labour market outcomes; insufficient account is taken of composition of employment, particularly between public and private sectors – with faster growth for blacks in the public sector; and, most surprising, no account taken of the impact of trade unions.
5 For an overview of developments in the South African labour market, see Kraak (1993) and ILO (1996). On differentiation by skill, see Crankshaw (1996).
6 See Hindson (1987). For an outstanding account on the contradictions of apartheid ideology in theory and practice, see Posel (1991).
7 See Fine (1994b).
8 See Nattrass (1990), for example.
9 See Wilson and Ramphele (1989) and Lundahl and Petersson (1991), for example, for Lesotho's dependence both on wage remittances and on commodities 'imported' from South Africa.
10 See Khosa (1990).

11 Although, as Sender emphasises in ILO (1996), one of the most important factors for women in rural areas are the conditions governing casualised wage labour rather than the inordinately emphasised, own-account subsistence farming.

12 On domestic workers, see Cock (1980).

13 Kaplan (1990: 32) shows, for the telecommunications industry, that job reservation was not always imposed. For Lewis (1984), white unions employed job reservation to preserve their designation as skilled workers in face of technological change and the threat of 'dilution', a strategy pursued by ISCOR, for example (Clark 1994). See also Webster (1985) and Cross (1993).

14 On the significance of foreign migrant labour, see Crush *et al.* (1991) and Freund (1991).

15 See Spandau (1980a).

16 See Spandau (1980b).

17 See Horner and Kooy (1980) and Crush (1989) for argument that foreign migrants were no more difficult to organise on the mines. See also James (1992), who argues that divisions amongst corporations over industrial relations was an important factor in the rapid growth of the NUM.

18 For what follows, see especially Wilson and Ramphele (1989).

19 See May (1990).

20 See Lewis (1991) but also ILO (1996).

21 See Crush *et al.* (1991) and especially Crush (1993), who shows how the conflict between mining and farming over access to labour has long and unevenly persisted – despite high levels of unemployment and increasing capital-intensity on the land. For a more general and historical discussion of South Africa's political economy, as the background against which to understand the structuring of labour markets, see Fine and Rustomjee (1997).

22 See also Smit (1995).

5 From dual to segmented labour markets

The radical tradition

1 THE HISTORICAL ORIGINS

Although it has its roots in the work of Kerr (1954), on balkanisation of labour, and other US institutionalists,[1] segmented labour market (SLM) theory, at least by that name, is generally acknowledged to be little more than a quarter of a century old. Even so, it already has a history, divided into distinct periods. It began with the dual labour market (DLM) theory of the early 1970s, and this gave way to a more general approach, SLM theory itself, both in terms of number of labour market segments and range of explanatory factors. From the outset, the theory was heterodox, certainly as far as neoclassical economics was concerned, although SLM theory has found more favour within other social sciences in which social structures, institutions and relations are conventionally to be found. By the mid-1980s, neoclassical economics began to abandon its hostility to SLM theory and to contribute a distinctive analysis of its own which has developed alongside and influenced the continuing radical tradition. These most recent developments are covered in the following chapter. This chapter is concerned with the first, radical phase of SLM theory.

As is usual with the more historically minded contributions to the literature, reference can be made to the insights of J.S. Mill (1929) and J.E. Cairnes (1967), originally published in 1848 and 1874, respectively, for whom the division of labour and its associated wages and conditions of work were far from the ideal of hardships matched by compensating benefits as proposed by Adam Smith (1937).[2] He considered wages in chapters 8 and 10 of Book I of the *Wealth of Nations*, suggesting they were liable to be higher or lower at least in part according to the advantages or disadvantages of the working conditions:[3]

> The whole of the advantages and disadvantages of the different employments of labour and stock must, in the same neighbourhood, be either perfectly equal or continually tending to equality . . . The five following are the principal circumstances which, so far as I have been able to observe, make up for a small pecuniary gain in some employments, and counterbalance a great one in others; first, the agreeableness or

disagreeableness of the employments themselves; secondly, the easiness and cheapness, or the difficulty and expense of learning them; thirdly, the constancy or inconstancy of employment in them; fourthly, the small or great trust which must be reposed in those who exercise them; and fifthly, the probability or improbability of success in them.

(Smith 1937: 99–100)

Smith also argued that the immobility of labour would lead to wage differentials, since, compared to other commodities, competition over the wage would be more impeded by transport costs than competition over prices in general: 'it appears evidently from experience that a man is of all sorts of luggage the most difficult to be transported (ibid.: 75).

Mill (1929: 389) accepted the idea of higher wages for uncertainty in employment and for trustworthiness and learning (ibid.: 39), but he was not prepared to accept Smith's first principle:

The really exhausting and the really repulsive labours, instead of being better paid than others, are almost invariably paid the worst of all, because performed by those who have no choice.

(Mill 1929: 389)

In addition, Mill emphasised the role of custom and law in regulating wages, including the exclusion of women from some jobs and their being lower paid even when doing identical work (ibid.: 399–401). Following Smith on another point, Mill argues that too general an education across the population, whilst welcome in itself, may bring down the wages of skilled workers. This is but a special case of the more general principle that wages within an occupation are determined, in a Malthusian fashion, by the rate of increase of the population that serves it. For:

So complete, indeed, has hitherto been the separation, so strongly marked the line of demarcation, between the different grades of labourers, as to be almost equivalent to an hereditary distinction of caste; each employment being chiefly recruited from the children of those already employed in it . . . Consequently the wages of each class have hitherto been regulated by the increase of its own population, rather than of the general population of the country.

(ibid.: 303)

A similar view of 'castes' or non-competing groups is taken up by Cairnes:

Certain industrial circles or groups exist, the workmen composing each of which, while competing among themselves, are, from social circumstances, excluded from effective competition with the workmen of different groups.

(Cairnes 1967: 191)[4]

The supply of labour to these groups is also fixed through social reproduction, as in Mill:

> A man, whatever be his rank of life, brings up his children – I speak of the common case – as far as he is able, according to the ideas prevailing in that rank of life . . . His children once arrived at maturity, no doubt his views and theirs will take a direction more distinctly governed by industrial considerations . . . but at this point the supply of labor *has been already determined.*
>
> (ibid.: 153; emphasis in original)

Against this, workers are more or less powerless against the forces of competition for:

> My conclusion is that, though combination, whether employed by capitalists or by labourers, may succeed in controlling for a time the price of labor, it is utterly powerless, in the hands of either, to effect a permanent alteration in the market rate of wages as determined by supply and demand.
>
> (ibid.: 235)

But there are two exceptions; first should there be a genuine monopoly of a skill (ibid.: 77), or second an artificial barrier to entry to a trade or its training through a trade union (ibid.: 245) – representing privileges for the few against the many.

These references are sufficient to remind us that the elements that make up the subject-matter of SLM are far from new. In the next section, the more recent history of SLM theory is examined through the work of Doeringer and Piore (1971) and Piore and then of Reich, Edwards and Gordon. But SLM has only been prominent in the last 15 years or so. In the following section, it is shown how, from these beginnings, it evolved to what is judged to be its fully mature and ripe *radical* version, prior to its being given a new lease of life by being embraced, rather than dismissed, by neoclassical theory (as addressed in the following chapter). The peak in SLM theory is associated with the work of those at and around the University of Cambridge, Wilkinson (1981) for example, elaborated in section 3, whose SLM theory has been extended subsequently but only with limited *conceptual* advance.

Against this background, in section 4, the development of SLM theory will be traced from its origins up to the point at which it began to be displaced by neoclassical orthodoxy, in part as a consequence of its own deficiencies. This is not to suggest that the current version of radical SLM theory is the inevitable terminus to which it has single-mindedly travelled. Indeed, it will be shown later in section 6 how a major diversion towards a much grander role for SLM theory – the specification of the history and current structure of the US economy, for example – stands alongside the more modest aim of analysing the structure and dynamics of one or more labour markets.

On the basis of this overview of the development of radical SLM theory, section 4 considers the chronic crisis in which it has always found itself, as has often been acknowledged by its own exponents. This poses the problem of how the theory could creditably survive in the face of such a limited, coherent analytical foundation. The answer, covered in section 5, is that it has done so through resort to empirical verification and study of hypotheses which, again acknowledged, have a tenuous connection to an already tenuous theory. The final section summarises the results.

2 INTERNAL OR DIVIDED LABOUR MARKETS?

In this section, the origins of SLM theory are considered by stepping one stage back and by examining the dual labour market (DLM) theory of the early 1970s that preceded it. There were, however, two different schools of DLM theory more or less from the outset. The more conventional is associated with the classic publication of Doeringer and Piore (DP) (1971), whilst the radical version within the Marxist tradition is particularly associated with the various individual and collective works of Reich, Edwards and Gordon (REG). The differences between these two schools is easily exaggerated, and there is little evidence of explicit antagonism. As will be seen, REG is best seen as a more general and more radical version of DP. The discussion begins for convenience with the latter, although this is not supposed to reflect the assigning of any credit for 'discovering' DLM theory.[5]

The DP approach is based on the idea that labour markets do not work perfectly in the standard neoclassical sense. This is because labour is not like any other commodity. Having a will of its own, it is interested in 'enhancing job security and advancement opportunity' whilst management is concerned with efficiency. In some respects, DP's is a conservative book, for it seeks to ensure that these different motivations are recognised, the better to be able to reconcile them through uncovering their economic and social implications at every level. Accordingly, there is almost a personnel manager turned social commentator quality to their contribution. This is confirmed by the sympathetic view, adopted over a decade later, that internal labour market theory is concerned to understand the functions and functioning of those 'exchanges' that take place outside the market: 'The point of the term is that the pricing and allocational functions of the market take place within rather than outside of the establishment' (Osterman 1984: 2).

But DP's novelty lies in linking these necessary imperfections in the labour market to the creation of a definite dual labour market structure. On the one hand, there is the primary sector in which stable, preferential employment conditions are to be found with large-scale, capital-intensive and advanced production processes, an elaborate division of labour and hierarchy within the firm, and skilled and highly motivated and well-paid workers with promotion prospects. On the other hand, the secondary sector is the opposite with insecure employment in small-scale, backward firms and limited prospects for workers – jobs without internal labour markets.

How has this situation come about? Doeringer and Piore (1971) offer very little economic analysis as such, relying upon the institutional tradition in which they were trained. But in later work, an economic analysis is added. The most important factors are those concerning uncertainty for workers and managers alike, and how they can pursue the best strategy to minimise this. Thus for Berger and Piore:[6]

> Uncertainty . . . is central to the distinction between capital and labour . . . The distribution, or rather, redistribution of that uncertainty is the underlying issue in the labor market institutions which emerge in response to waves of worker unrest and which appear as the proximate cause of duality in the labor markets of advanced economies.
>
> (Berger and Piore 1980: 6)

The source of this uncertainty is twofold, corresponding to supply and demand – not in labor markets alone but also in product markets. For demand for commodities contains a stable component, around an upward trend for growth, together with a volatile and cyclical component. The stable demand is met by the workers in the primary sector and the residue by the secondary sector. Thus, the primary and secondary labour markets correspond to a dual economy, known as the 'core and periphery' in the literature more generally or as the 'monopoly and competitive sectors', respectively. Berger and Piore locate the:

> technical basis for duality in the product market: large scale enterprises with declining average cost curves catering to the predictable and largely stable segment of demand and much smaller firms with the traditional U-shaped average cost curves catering to the unpredictable and/or fluctuating portion of demand.
>
> (ibid.: 66)

On the supply-side then, stable demand is met by mass-produced, standardised goods within the core of the economy and the uncertainty is taken up by small-scale, flexible and precarious firms in the periphery. One uses a mass of tied down fixed capital (relative to variable costs) which reduces unit costs but requires high capacity utilisation; the other has higher unit costs with a higher proportion of variable costs in order to be able to respond to changes in demand.

This correspondence between industrial structure and market structure is carried over into the structure of labour markets. For Piore (1978: 29), workers within the core become part of the fixed capital of their firms, a 'quasi-fixed factor of production or quasi-capital'. This is the basis for DP's use of the notion of internal labour markets.

Suppose, to take an extreme example, that a worker once employed in the primary sector is guaranteed a job there for life. Then motivation will depend upon the internal organisation of the firm's labour and requires a hierarchy including openings and rewards along the promotion ladder. The exact form that this takes will depend upon market conditions faced for the product, the technology in use and its corresponding requirements for skills and on-the-job training (on which DP place much emphasis), and the respective strategies of trade unions and management. And, once in place, these internal labour markets become established as custom and practice.

Much of DP's analysis is concerned with how internal labour markets work and with what effects. They estimate that 80 per cent of the US work-force was in internal labour markets in 1965, and that the response of the economy to major unperceived changes, such as new technology, must be analysed against the internal labour market structures and relative wages which have developed in response to stable movements in technology and tastes (and which may, therefore, be inappropriate and inflexible to new conditions):[7]

> The utility of the internal labour market as an analytical construct depends upon the level at which the analysis is conducted . . . For macro-economic analysis, the administrative features of the internal labour market are treated, in effect, as random events which cancel out in the aggregate. But what is trivial on a macro level can turn out to be central on a micro level, where an understanding of the underlying market machinery is necessary.[8]

> (Doeringer and Piore 1971: 8)

This all, however, only applies to the primary sector. The secondary sector is perceived much more in terms of the *alter ego* of the primary sector, its negative image, without a structured labour market, with a poorly developed internal labour market and with some secondary employ-ment also being within the structures of the primary sector.[9] What becomes of key importance is the presumed immobility between the two sectors. This creates and reinforces existing worker characteristics, with the secondary sector denied skilled, stable jobs with the potential for training and promo-tion and, consequently, inducing negative attitudes to work.

The way then becomes opened for a terminological explosion as far as internal labour markets are concerned, with the creation of mobility chains, stations and seniority districts, for example.[10] The supply of labour to these different labour market positions is rooted in 'class subcultures' and the demand for labour in technology etc., as previously explained. For the supply, explanation now comes to rest on a sort of pop socio-psychology (Piore 1975: 145). For migrants are perceived to lead unstable lives because of their insecurity thereby confirming their secondary labour market participa-tion; and for youth:[11]

working- and middle-class *youth* . . . pass through a period of adventure and action-seeking in adolescence and early adulthood before settling down into the routine family life, stable employment, and, in the case of the middle class, professional career training.

(ibid.: 144; emphasis in original)

But let us leave aside these explanations of those who are disadvantaged within labour markets and which infuriatingly rely on images of their own inadequacies and examine the intellectual origins for the theory's division of the economy into two parts. This comes in part from the notion of dualism itself, with standard references being Boeke (1953) and Averitt (1968), for whom:

Contemporary American capitalism, then, is a composite of two distinct business systems. The new economy is composed of firms huge in size and influence . . . the 'center', . . . the firms in the small economy by the term 'periphery'.

(Averitt 1968: 6–7)

Whilst Boeke was concerned with part of the third world and the terminology of DLM is identical or close to much of that associated with dependency theory within development economics, references to such sources are rare.[12]

Analysis for the labour market is credited to Kerr (1954), who was first to conceptualise internal labour markets[13] and who referred to the balkanisation of labour. DP also refer to the DLM as a part of queuing theory, giving rise to ports of entry from the secondary market but with priority to those with primary sector characteristics, and this is associated with the work of Thurow (1975).

But clearly, these elements could have been put together at almost any time. What appears to have stimulated them is the desire to explain black urban (ghetto) poverty, this problem having been formulated in turn as a response to the inner city riots and black power movement of the 1960s. For Piore (1970: 60):[14] 'The dual labor market provides a convincing interpretation of the realities of labor markets in black urban ghettos'.

This was also the stimulus to REG's DLM theory. But it was equally motivated by the wish to break with human capital theory,[15] particularly in the light of the analysis of schooling being provided by Bowles and Gintis, ultimately leading to their classic work of 1976.[16] Here, it is shown that there is no systematic relationship between educational achievement and workers' rewards, and that the educational system serves to prepare workers and screen them for their generally limited roles under capitalist employment. Socioeconomic background proves more of an important indicator of labour market position than education (with the latter dependent itself upon social class).

Where REG also differ from DP is in a view of the labour market based on a fundamental conflict between capital and labour, not only over wages and conditions of work, but also over the control of the production process itself. Even into the 1980s, Berger and Piore (1980: x) take a 'balanced' view of dual labour markets when it comes to a class conflict scarcely recognised in DP: 'the expansion of dual labor markets – are, in fact, systematic and rational ways in which societies use the material and ideal resources that history and politics make available to resolve current conflicts'. And in Doeringer and Piore the break with neoclassical economics is, confessedly, extremely limited:[17]

> The contrast between the internal labour market and competitive neo-classical theory . . . should not be overemphasised. Many of the rigidities which impede market forces in the short run are eventually overcome, and there is probably a tendency for the economy to adjust, in time, in a direction consistent with the predictions of competitive theory. More-over, many of the short-term phenomena associated with internal labour markets could perhaps be incorporated into a suitably modified neoclassical model.
>
> (Doeringer and Piore 1971: 7)

By contrast, for REG, a divided work-force is part and parcel of a capitalist strategy to sustain profitability, and various forms of workplace control make up the management techniques for achieving this:[18] 'the social relations of the firm – particularly the 'system of control' – underlie the structure and operation of labor markets' (Edwards 1975: 21). Otherwise, there is little to distinguish REG from DP, although the former is marked by an explicit theory of *conflict* over production. Each is based to a greater or lesser extent on a distinction between a core and a periphery, internal labour markets, a segmented labour force (with education a major dividing instrument), variation in management strategies in pursuit of profitability, a significant role for stable as opposed to cyclical or seasonal demand, and particular emphasis on divisions by sex and by race (Edwards *et al.* 1975). And each is soon led to divide the primary sector into two tiers in recognition of higher and lower strata in conditions of work. This is the first modification of the theory in the light of empirical evidence. If this, then, is the starting-point for DLM, where has it ended up?

3 FROM DUAL TO SEGMENTED LABOUR MARKETS: THE CAMBRIDGE SCHOOL

The work of the Cambridge school of SLM is in some respects the most sophisticated in range and depth. None the less, it is most easily characterised as a supply and demand model of labour markets, although one that is much more complex and which also breaks with the neoclassical orthodoxy. Thus, Craig *et al.* (1985a) refer to the demand- and supply-side factors of the labour market. In particular, they criticise earlier work within the SLM tradition, Doeringer and Piore (1971) and Gordon *et al.* (1982), for having neglected the supply-side:[19]

> Important though these 'demand-side' explanations have been, our pre-
> vious research and analysis found them to be inadequate . . . they
> assumed that labour supply factors played no direct role in shaping the
> pattern of employment organisation and inequality. Labour supply was
> assumed to adapt to predetermined divisions in the labour market
> created by the demand for labour.
>
> (Craig *et al.* 1985a: 267–8)

This interaction of supply and demand, rather than reliance on demand alone, is one factor that indicates the advance of the Cambridge school over the previous literature – although its critical claims are slightly exagger-ated, as supply-side factors are not entirely absent from the earlier DLM literature nor from their institutional predecessors who stressed the role of trade unions and collective bargaining.

But what exactly is meant by the demand- and supply-sides? First, as already mentioned, there is a sharp break with conventional labour market theory (Craig *et al.* 1985b). Equally, there is a rejection of human capital theory in which workers are rewarded according to the well-defined skills that they bring to the market place whether these be inherited or acquired (Craig *et al.* 1982: 93–4).

Second, in place of this orthodoxy, the demand-side for labour is seen in terms of the personal (employer strategy) and impersonal forces of capitalist production, distribution and exchange, and this is very much within the existing DLM tradition. The demand for labour by employers depends on technology and work organisation, the extent and nature of product mar-kets, industrial organisation and the imperative of profitability:[20]

> segmentation requires multi-causal explanations, and that the various
> explanatory hypotheses – based on the structure of technology, product
> markets, control over the labour process and labour supply conditions –
> are complementary rather than competitive.
>
> (Rubery and Wilkinson 1981: 113)

This quotation has already mentioned the complementary supply-side fac-tors. These include the terms and conditions on which the labour force is willing and able to offer its services. This is not so much a question of its absolute size and skills as of its economic and social position, in which the existence or not and strength of trade unions and the social reproductive role of women are given greatest prominence.[21]

In short, the Cambridge SLM school differs from the neoclassical ortho-doxy in its supply and demand analysis by extending the scope of what con-stitutes factors forming supply and demand[22] and by rejecting equilibrium (Wilkinson 1981: ix). It differs from earlier SLM theory by emphasising the role that labour itself plays in the creation of labour market segments and the conditions within them, although such insights were standard for the earlier US institutionalists. But this is far from a complete description of the Cambridge school in so far as it takes no account of the way in which supply- and demand-side factors interact.

First, their interaction is seen in terms of a conflict between classes rather than as a more or less harmonious meeting of market forces. Capital and labour confront each other over wages and other conditions of work with, in the vein of the post-Braverman genre, special but not exclusive attention to control over the labour process.[23] Thus, for Rubery:

> If a more general approach to the analysis of labour market segmentation is to be developed . . . workers and workers' organisations must be assigned an active role in the development of labour market structure . . . This analysis must, we shall argue, be carried out within the context of a continuous struggle between capitalists and workers on the industrial front.
>
> (Rubery 1978: 18–19)

In other words, much more than equilibrium levels of labour quantities and wages are at stake when supply and demand confront each other. Apart from a range of conditions of and at work, there is the disequilibrium restructuring of the labour markets themselves.

A more ambiguous position is adopted on the role of intra-class conflict, especially with regard to labour, and more so in later writings. Thus, Rubery *et al.* recognise conflict between capitalists but are less strong-worded about labour:

> There is ample evidence of some firms existing and being successful at the expense of other firms and of some groups of labour enjoying high levels of pay and protected employment while others face low pay and vulnerable employment conditions.
>
> (Rubery *et al.* 1984: 100)

That is, until we confront distribution when one worker can gain at the expense of another:[24]

> The view put forward in this paper on the behaviour which underlies industrial relations is essentially based on a theory of conflict over the distribution of real national income, both between capital and labour and between different groups within capital and labour.
>
> (ibid.: 118)

The second way in which supply and demand interact is as the interpenetration and mutual conditioning of economic *and* social forces. The absence of this is seen as a major deficiency:

> The major weakness of (previous) segmentation theories is the failure to develop an adequate theory of worker organisation and collective bar-

gaining to be incorporated within an analysis of the social and economic determinants of segmentation.

(Craig *et al*. 1982: 79)

In principle, the social determinants concerned constitute a wide variety, for they encompass the social reproduction of the work-force. In practice, partly reflecting their significance and partly reflecting the empirical interests of the Cambridge school, particular attention is given to the role of the state and to the role of the family. Deakin (1986), for example, examines the role of labour law in structuring labour markets; Humphries and Rubery (1984) argue for the relative autonomy of social reproduction and against a functionalist/reductionist view of the family within the capitalist mode of production; and Craig *et al*. (1985b) range over trade unions, the welfare state and domestic and community organisation.

Third, then, the interaction of supply and demand as an interaction of economic and social factors mediated by conflict gives rise to definite structures, institutions and processes with definite links between them. This may be illustrated by a number of examples. In the case of economic forces, it is argued that the existence of a low paid work-force can enable the persistence within a sector of an impediment to rationalisation and progress even of the more advanced producers:[25] 'employment of workers at low wages can destabilise employment opportunities for other workers, destabilise product markets, retard innovation and reduce economic efficiency' (Craig *et al*. 1982: 95). For this reason, the state is called upon to implement policy 'restricting the ability of employers to exploit the disadvantaged labour market groups' (ibid.). At times, the state does do this so that 'one of the effects of extension of the welfare state has been to counteract effects of labour market segmentation' (Craig *et al*. 1985b: 109), although the state's role should not be exaggerated and is far from unambiguous as a protector of labour. Yet, there are pressures on the state to increase education expenditure and the quality of the work-force when there are labour shortages and conversely in a situation of labour surplus (when the pressures and potential for exploitation of disadvantaged labour are at their greatest). In so far as trade unions exist and organise on behalf of their own members alone, their efforts may be self-defeating, for the organised may undermine their bargaining power in the desperation for work (ibid.: 108). Similarly, 'in class terms, domestic and community organisation are sources of strength but at the same time they serve to sectionalise and fragment the working class' (ibid.). As a special instance of this, women's withdrawal from the labour force, or from certain jobs, may raise the value of (male) labour-power but at the expense of reducing women's wages.[26]

It is not the intention here to question either the validity or the significance of these theoretical arguments, and there are clearly many more that have not been included. Rather, it is to point to their wide range, their complex interaction to yield uncertain effects, and the resolution of

that uncertainty through class and other conflict whose outcome is historically contingent.

This leads then to a fourth aspect of the supply and demand interaction. It
depends upon a combination of factors whose presence and whose strength
and effects are to be discovered empirically. As Wilkinson (1981: ix) recognises, this allows for the significance and complexity of historical factors and
the interplay of the economic and the institutional (and much more besides).
But it is fraught with dangers. For whilst he frowns upon the notion of a
predetermined, possibly uni-causal, abstract theory, the alternative of an
ad hoc analysis in response to each historically contingent subject of investigation is equally unpalatable.[27]

Whilst it poses this problem, a resolution of it is not easily to be found in
the work of the Cambridge SLM school. Wilkinson, for example, does point
to clearly observable general tendencies, most notably the casualisation of
work in the metropolitan countries, but this does not lead to the implied
analysis of the general forces at work and how they interact to give rise
to more specific results. Instead, in line with the framework of sophisticated
supply and demand, a basic content of the Cambridge method is one of
simultaneous interplay of economic and social factors, much like that of
neoclassical general equilibrium theory, even with the significant difference
of incorporating structure, institutions, social reproduction, dynamics and
factors other than inputs, outputs and prices.[28]

This, of course, is to court for the Cambridge school, as Wilkinson fears,
the danger of *ad hoc*ery as the way of accommodating historical contingency. It is associated analytically with a strong and immediate identification of the theoretical categories and analysis with empirical observation.
This is, undoubtedly, an endemic feature of the Cambridge school. For it
has failed to build a theoretical structure moving from more abstract to
more concrete determinants, reflecting economic and social forces and corresponding to and incorporating the historically contingent developments.
This, as it were, is the traditional Marxist approach to the relationship
between theory and history, relying upon the study of contradictory social
forces and tendencies whose interaction gives rise to outcomes understood,
but not predetermined, at a more complex and concrete level of analysis.
This is to be contrasted with the simultaneity model in which the complexity
and concreteness is fully present but not in relation to any underlying theoretical structure of concepts and causation.[29]

But it would be a mistake to consider that the Cambridge school is without abstract theory, even if the concepts employed are closely related to an
immediate identification with the empirical. For abstract theory is possible
even for neoclassical economics, the most vulgar theory in this sense. The
latter uses the most abstract ahistorical categories, such as utility, inputs,
outputs, technology, etc., together with the unexplained historically specific
categories of wages, prices and profits, etc. How and why these are combined in the way that they are is a matter for the history of economic

thought. But this raises the question of what determines the theoretical content of Cambridge SLM theory.

One major component is derived from the existing tradition of SLM theory, even if the Cambridge school adopts a critical attitude towards it. Thus, there are frequent references to notions such as the primary and secondary sectors and to internal and external labour markets.[30] This is despite the rejection of much of the analysis on which these concepts are founded, for the Cambridge school's approach leads to a notion of segmentation as a set of structured and overlapping labour markets which tends to undermine the simple division of the economy and/or labour into two sectors (even with subsectors). This is made explicit in the criticism of those who treat the secondary sector as uniformly competitive and conforming to an ideal type.[31]

In addition, within the primary sector, the guarantee of primary sector working conditions is dependent upon trade union organisation and other factors and the presence of these is also possible within the secondary sector, potentially enhancing pay and conditions. Indeed, the significance of 'skilled' work in this context, for example, seems to depend upon bargaining power (Craig *et al.* 1982: 94) and not on primary or secondary sector membership as such, although these may be correlated. In short, the Cambridge school seems both to employ the abstract categories of existing SLM theory and simultaneously to undermine them.

This is brought out particularly by Kenrick (1981: 168), who points to 'the inherent sexism of the basic dual labour market model' for which the employment standard is defined primarily in terms of the stereotype of male worker in primary sector with women as a homogeneous cannon-fodder for the secondary sector. More generally, consideration of the position of women is carried furthest at the abstract level by Humphries and Rubery (1984). Their focus of differing gender roles for social reproduction contrasts with the limited development of an analysis of capital and its abstract tendencies. The latter is addressed mainly negatively by rejection of the neoclassical orthodoxy and, rarely explicitly, by Marxist theory which would presumably be seen as too deterministic.[32] There are occasional references to monopoly capital but the status of this remains obscure.

In short, the theoretical elements that go into the making of the Cambridge school are various and not entirely systematic. They are supplemented, however, by concepts which are considered appropriate to the particular studies being undertaken. In the case of those situated in Cambridge, much of their work has been concentrated on low pay, women and the Wage Council industries. This has had an effect on the factors considered and on the way in which they are considered, as discussed above in the context of the variety of theoretical arguments employed.

In this way, the Cambridge school has developed a theory of SLM which combines a number of abstract and a number of historically contingent influences to form what might be termed a 'middle-range' theory.[33] There are elements of structuralism and of underlying economic and social forces and relations, but they never depart far from an immediate identification with the most concrete phenomena. There is a temptation to associate this methodology with that of the better-known left-Keynesianism of Cambridge, for which there are some parallels – the insistence on aggregate macroeconomic and class relations that are independent of individualistic calculations or micro-foundations but which are more or less immediately empirically quantifiable. But this is little more than a shot in the dark over methodological influences, for the Cambridge SLM school rarely makes explicit its macro or aggregate economic theory.[34]

In the preceding discussion, the attempt has been made to bring out the rationale for the theoretical content of the Cambridge school. But this is only a complete exercise if we make explicit what is absent and might be considered to be of significance. We do not attempt to explain these absences completely. Indeed, it is fairly clear that many could be incorporated without much difficulty. But, as suggested, the theory is heavily dependent for its content upon the SLM tradition and upon the particular empirical studies undertaken; these dictate much of what is present *and* what is absent.

The SLM tradition has always been weak at the level of the economy as a whole, properly interpreted in its full complexity. This has had a number of effects. The first is the tendency to neglect the role of the world economy and international economic relations. Of course, it is possible to recognise that exports indicate a widening market and imports increasing competition; and that transnational corporations may have different management strategies and resources than indigenous firms. But SLM theory has rarely reached this level of understanding let alone taken a view of the movement of world capitalism as a system. For it to do so would widen the gulf to be straddled by the abstract/empirical concepts. This is not, however, to make demands upon SLM that are unreasonable in the light of the sorts of tasks that it sets itself. For, in the case of the casualised trades and services, for example, and the growth of married women's part-time employment within them, especially in the UK, surely some view must be taken of the nature of the British economy and its relative decline within the advanced capitalist countries.[35]

As a corollary of the absence of consideration of the global economy, SLM theory has little contact with what, within the Marxist problematic, would be termed the 'law of combined and uneven development'.[36] This is already implied by having pointed to the neglect of the international economy. But it also applies to the spatial distribution of economic activity more generally, normally the subject-matter of regional science and economic geography. This is not to deny the existence within the Cambridge school of a number of empirical studies which are confined to areas smaller than a country. But this predominantly serves to narrow down and define the labour market segments rather than to explain them in a spatial context.[37]

Yet another absence at the economic level is the role played by finance and financial management.[38] As a major lever in the restructuring of industry, and hence employment, at all levels of the economy, this is quite surprising, even though attention is given to two other sides of management: those concerning labour and product markets. On the other hand, finance and its associates of ownership and control are potential sources of difficulties for empirically minded studies. Take the case of small-scale component manufacture, for example, and whether this is done in-house or not. For own-manufacture, this might be part of a large-scale integrated plant or a fully owned but separate small plant. For subcontracting, the separately owned firm may be fully (market) dependent on the larger plant or, through a range of products and/or customers, be more independent.

The formal difference between these situations is sometimes significant, and sometimes not, as far as the likely influences on conditions of employment. In current circumstances of flexible technology and management and of high levels of unemployment, there is a presumption that this encourages dependent subcontracting. But whether this is so or not, the industrial restructuring and its labour market implications are clearly dependent on the availability and role of finance (and ownership) at different levels. Yet another problem at the empirical level for SLM analysis, of course, is that it merely takes a large firm to buy up a small one, and leave it otherwise unchanged, for the employees to have been transferred from the secondary to the primary sector (at least by definition by firm size) and, vice versa, should there be a change towards divestment and subcontracting.[39]

If, then, there are absences in the economic content of SLM theory, the same is true in considering the relationship between economy and society in which the focus is, the family apart, upon the role of the state. Certainly, the role the state plays is seen as significant in so far as it lays down legal and other conditions affecting labour markets. There has, however, been a curious neglect of the state as an *employer*. This reflects three serious deficiencies. The first is yet another corollary of the absence of global economics which makes impossible an assessment of the role of the state in (re)structuring economic activity and hence labour markets. The second is the priority granted to the private sector in economic life and the focus on the division between core and periphery industries, with the neglect of services and, *hence*, a presumption that these are passive in making the running in (re)structuring of labour markets. But, especially in the UK, for example, many of those segments of the secondary labour markets, i.e., women and blacks, were first and predominantly drawn into employment in the state (service) sector. Consequently, it cannot be presumed that such employment is a passive reproduction of the labour market (re)structuring to be found in the private sector.

The third neglect in considering the role of the state concerns the absence of political forces and the tendency to treat the state as the policies of government. But the conditions of labour depend upon the politics of the labour movement. This cannot be reduced to the effects this has on government policy or as transmitted through the other major institutions considered, the trade unions and the family. For otherwise, for example, the role of the feminist and anti-racist movements are wiped out. This absence of politics reflects the academic origins of SLM theory, for it has drawn predominantly upon economics and industrial relations (for labour market theory) and upon neo-Weberian sociology (for stratification theory). Political theory has only rarely been present and then as an output, rather than as an input, in the attempt to derive political consequences from labour market divisions.[40] Whilst the absence of politics might be perceived as an oversight to be rectified by adding it as one further determining factor, a deeper issue is involved. How is the role of the state to be incorporated in a more fundamental fashion, cutting across the traditional division between the economy and politics as well as their corresponding academic disciplines?

To a large extent, all of the absences (and also what is present) that have been observed within SLM theory correspond to a particular relationship to Marxism. The absence of a global economics is to view Marx's *Capital* as too deterministic. The simultaneity in the use of economic and social forces takes the same view of the relationship between economy and society. And the selective inclusion of certain economic and social factors, and the exclusion of others, reflects a notion of their relative autonomy and hence their contingent significance.

4 THE CHRONIC CRISIS OF THE SLM PARADIGM

The previous sections have examined the origins of SLM theory. From the urban ghettos of black America, a jump was made ahead to the Cambridge school through, as will be seen, a proliferation of complex and detailed studies of the incidence of differences at work. Throughout that journey, the theory has remained 'middle-range'. In this section, it is observed that SLM theory has been in a chronic state of crisis, not simply as a judgement in retrospect from an external vantage point, but from within the paradigm itself from the outset. First, this is established and then are considered the issues raised by the self-confessed theoretical crisis.

In an early and critical review of SLM theory, Cain argued that:

> Unfortunately, the SLM theories are sketchy, vague, and diverse if not internally conflicting. Description, narratives, and taxonomies crowd out model development. On the positive side the theories evolve from detailed data that are often richer in historical, institutional, and qualitative aspects than is customary among the econometrically oriented orthodox theories.

(Cain 1976: 1221)

The rich empirical side will be taken up later, but, having examined it, Wachter concludes that neoclassical economics has the answer:[41]

The data do suggest the existence of *segmented* markets with imperfect mobility, arising from human capital constraints as well as the barriers that the dualists emphasize. The segmented-market approach, however, has a long and established position in neoclassical economics.

(Wachter 1974: 678–9; emphasis in original)

In this light, we can view the chronic crisis of SLM theory as a continuing, but possibly unconscious, attempt to furnish both empirical evidence and an alternative theory to explain it which would leave neoclassical economics floundering. But it is the lack of well-founded SLM theory that has proved the difficulty, as yet another neoclassical critic notes: 'On the theoretical side labour market segmentation *analyses* are mainly descriptive in character and, therefore, do not qualify as alternative labour market *theories* (Psacharopoulos 1977: 34; emphases in original). And he confirms Wachter's view of the capacity of neoclassical theory to deal with these empirical analyses (and welcomes SLM's contribution to raising the emotive issue of poverty):

On the empirical side, I have found segmentation analyses demanding (wanting?) in the sense of not having gone beyond neoclassical explanations of the observed differential treatment of workers and mobility barriers.

(ibid.)

But these are all references to a hostile camp, more or less willing to recognise the empirical (and theoretical) limitations of its own position. Yet, the same attitude is to be found from within the SLM school. Osterman (1975: 509), for example, takes segmentation for granted:[42] 'The interesting question today is not whether the labor market is segmented, but rather along what lines'. A similar outlook seems to be adopted by Beck *et al.* (1980) in response to criticism of an original article (Beck *et al.* 1978) by Hauser. As it were, segmentation is a fundamental organising principle for understanding inequalities (and as such, becomes tautologous):

problems such as underemployment, poverty wages, job instability, race and gender inequalities, and regional or subregional disparities in wealth do not represent mere anomalies or market imperfections, in an otherwise orderly system, but rather, reflect an integral component of the economy of industrial capitalism.

(Hauser 1980: 718)

Of course, this fails to deal with the problem that, if these are integral components, then they should be readily explained and not merely described by segmentation and, secondly, that market imperfections performs the same theoretical job for neoclassical theory as segments do for the alternative. As it were, stick it in a black box marked 'SLM' or 'market imperfection' according to your ideological commitment.

Thus, when criticised by Kruse (1977) for improper testing of SLM theory,[43] Osterman (1977: 222) merely gives the name 'framework' to the black box: 'Dual labour market theory . . . is an alternative intellectual framework. (Actually, it is an invitation to an alternative framework because no complete and internally consistent model has as yet been advanced)'. The same invitation still seemed open some years later, as Lever-Tracy (1983: 354) asks: 'Is dualist labour market theory entering a period of paradigm crisis?'

Day *et al.* (1982) wonder where and by what criteria are the boundaries for labour market segmentation to be drawn. Baron and Bielby (1980) note the conceptual confusion in what they term the 'new structuralists'. Apostle *et al.* recognise:

> There is considerable debate concerning the level at which segmentation is to be operationalized, the defining criteria employed and the labels used for the segments themselves . . . Clearly, the segmentation perspective is in need of more theoretical development and perhaps more complex methodological treatment.
>
> (Apostle *et al.* 1985a: 254–5)

It is even claimed by Carter that:[44]

> the ideological force of the challenge to human capital orthodoxy that the segmentation theories present has been vitiated by the common perception that they lack a coherent, systemic theoretical foundation, despite their flashes of descriptive richness.
>
> (Carter 1982: 1063)

This, of course, is where Cain (1976) began, but the orthodoxy could hardly have hoped that the weight of SLM theory's own problems would remove the intellectual 'watershed'[45] of the 1970s, which, as even its own practitioners admit, saw off, at least temporarily, the relevance of the economics of education as a study of the internal rate of return on human capital.

Last, even the Cambridge school, within its own approach recognises the problem. For Rumberger and Carnoy (1980: 117): 'Labour market segmentation does not constitute a single, unified alternative to neoclassical theory.' For Rubery (1978: 18): 'This important new approach [REG] has so far progressed in an ad hoc fashion . . . Each new contribution adopted parts of the previous theories, with no one theory developing its arguments from first principles.'

But what exactly are the theoretical problems involved? Recall that SLM requires a *triple* analytical structure. First, there is the industrial structure, usually seen in terms of monopolised and competitive sectors (with the state as an all too occasional third participant). Second, there are the labour market structures (most obviously drawn between primary and secondary sectors). Third, there are the relationships between economy and society and these are variously characterised – by education, by racism and sexism, by pre- and in-market segmentation (Ryan 1981), by trade unionism and by migration and many, many other factors. What the theory must do is analyse each of these, where appropriate, in isolation and then explore their interrelationships. As has been seen, SLM theory has predominantly identified the industrial structure as the demand-side for labour, the relationship between economy and society as the supply-side, and the labour market structures as their interaction. Accept this for the purposes of exposition.

Beginning with the industrial sector, one is immediately confronted by the relative absence of any development or even presentation of economic theory. There is the notion of stable and volatile demand and its associated treatment of labour as a part or not of semi-fixed capital. This is totally inadequate as a theory of monopoly capital. What does appear to underlie the model is the monopoly stagnationist thesis of Baran and Sweezy (1966), with its antecedents in the work of Kalecki and its fuller theoretical development by Cowling (1982).[46] Elsewhere, Fine and Murfin (1984) have shown that this model depends upon setting aside both all of the competitive forces which would coerce large-scale corporations to invest and the potential for the macro-economy to be non-stagnationist.[47]

In particular, for example, the labour as fixed capital model, with lower unit cost than the competitive sector, would lead to competitive investment within the monopoly sector to obtain the lowest unit costs. These investments sustain the economy as a whole. For otherwise, as it is indeed motivated, this monopoly capital view of the world falsely generalises from the short-term constraints on individual sectors to the long-term development of the economy as a whole. This is certainly so for Piore, for whom, with explicit reference to the views of Adam Smith, the extent of the market is the major constraint on the continuing growth of mass production.[48] Recall that, for Smith, the limitation on the growing division of labour posed by the extent of the market would ultimately lead to falling profitability and a stationary state.[49]

Thus, SLM theory does not have an adequate understanding of monopoly capital. Nor does it present much of a theory for the competitive sector. By default, as in much other work on the duality between monopoly and competition within modern economies, the competitive portion would appear to correspond to the neoclassical model of perfect competition. The only difference is its existing under the shadow of the core sector, a relationship whose analytical content remains predominantly in the dark. The exception is the idea of the periphery relatively prospering during supply-constrained expansions and suffering during recession.

This lack of theory for the industrial structure would not be so much of a problem if SLM theory posed a simple correspondence between the industrial structure and the labour market structure. Then, primary sector workers could be identified with the core and secondary workers with the periphery. Where this did not occur, i.e., where employers did not get their way on the demand-side, this would be evidence of the intervention of labour on the supply-side. At an early stage, however, it was fairly clear that casual observation would not allow so simple a dual dichotomy of structures, and so theory would have to admit of primary and secondary workers in the periphery and core, respectively. Thus, Doeringer and Piore (1971) recognised from the outset that white-collar and craft workers would not be confined to the internal labour markets of single core firms as opposed to blue-collar workers.[50]

Thus, once it is recognised that the industrial structure develops in ways that do not directly structure labour markets in its own image, then an abstract formulation of the economic theory of advanced capitalism becomes essential. Similar considerations apply to the supply-side, although the empirical dissonances appear to be more limited, not only because the relationship between economy and society is more uniform across its more or less favoured segments but also since a primary or secondary sector cohort would not otherwise have been identified in the first place (women, ethnic minorities, migrants, immediately spring to mind).

How is this all resolved? As seen previously, use is made of middle-range theory. The supply- and demand-side determinants do make up, however little developed, a level of abstract determination. Their interaction with a waving of the wand of capital–labour conflict, historical contingency and empirical details leads to an overlapping complex of labour market segments. What is remarkable is the extent to which this has led to uniformity in the notion of the firm (or more often the industry or part of it in sampling from within the secondary sector) as the appropriate level at which to identify labour market segmentation. Thus, as Buchele (1983: 410) observes: 'Most writers on industrial dualism and labour market segmentation have emphasised that the firm is the appropriate unit of analysis.' For Baron and Bielby (1980: 742), firms mediate 'the links between social structure and processes at macro and micro levels' and Apostle *et al.* are persuaded of the virtues of the middle-range theory:[51]

> The anomalies cited by others . . . when examining segmentation at the industrial and occupational levels do not vanish when one turns to the firm or to the workplace. Nevertheless, for theoretical as well as for empirical reasons the latter seems the appropriate level for segmentation analysis. Industrial level specifications have been thoroughly criticized and now appear in an empirical bog.
>
> (Apostle *et al.* 1985b: 48)

Even where the firm as such is not the focus of analysis, it is some form of equivalent, whether it be behaviour (Tarling 1981), management and trade union strategy (Whalley 1984), or the micro-level:

> Our contention has been that the macro/aggregative approaches provided by Keynesians, Marxians and Dualists have insufficient regard for

the process by which bargaining for resources is conducted at micro-level and the manner in which minority groups evolve a collective identity and crystallize their objectives in the contest for scarce resources.

(Loveridge and Mok 1980: 407)

In this light, given the movement down to the micro-level, Tolbert's (1982: 474) praise for SLM seems slightly misplaced:[52] 'the new structuralism in social stratification underscores the inadequacies of wholly individualistic models of socioeconomic behaviour'. For the individualistic models are being restored, as will be discussed in the next chapter, with decreasing dependence on the macro-level, and with groups of one sort or another as the unit of analysis. As Lever-Tracy observes in a review of the Cambridge SLM theory of Wilkinson (1981):

not one of these writers describes a clear macro dualist system nor does any of them find an existing or developing system of segmentation that is adequate to or neatly fits the new situation of escalating uncertainty.

(Lever-Tracy 1983: 354)

She continues by pointing out that even in the case of outwork, where secondary employment should be well-established, multi-causal explanations continue to prove necessary. In this light, it is hard to envisage how fundamental propositions within SLM theory could have been satisfactorily clarified and justified.[53]

5 DOES THE THEORY FIT THE FACTS OR IS THE THEORY THE FACTS?

In characterising SLM analysis as middle-range, the focus has so far been upon its theoretical aspects. But, as one reason for its mixed theoretical character is for it to be able to confront complex and contingent segmentation of labour markets at the empirical level, it is hardly surprising that SLM theory should have stimulated a vast range of empirical studies. In this section, these empirical studies are considered, not so much to come to some definitive conclusions verifying SLM theory or not, as to follow how SLM analysis developed on the basis of its middle-range methodology.[54] Some of the statistical discussion may be beyond the reader, but more important is to recognise how the empirical studies not only reflect but consolidate theoretical weaknesses. For it should be borne in mind that these studies must also contain a theoretical element, for, leaving aside the problems of an empiricist methodology and of the operationalisation of SLM concepts statistically, the middle-range approach requires theory in order to specify particular relations between demand- and supply-side factors in the labour market.

SLM empirical work first requires the specification of an industrial structure of the economy – into core and periphery, for example. Second, it requires structures of the labour market to be identified – into primary and secondary, for example. Third, it requires the relations between the two to be specified – for example, that primary workers within the core economy have high wages, and beneficial prospects and working conditions, as compared to secondary workers within the periphery, who have restricted entry to the primary sector.

One hypothesis to be investigated, then, is whether there is a division of the economy into a distinct industrial structure, although this is necessary only for nation-wide segmentation theory. For the more complex view of segmentation at the level of the firm or industry, the industrial structure does not necessarily have to be identified and, for example, a study within the secondary sector can examine labour market structure independently of economy-wide industrial structure. Instead, the supposed core–periphery duality can be proxied by indicators such as firm size or capital-intensity within an industry.

At the economy-wide level, however, there is an embarrassment of riches in specifying the industrial structure. Oster (1979), for example, considers 25 different characteristics of US industry that might divide the core from the periphery – variables that involve size, investment, unionisation, race, sex and education of the work-force, profitability, etc. As these are all expected to be highly correlated with each other, the statistical technique of factor analysis can be used to sort out these correlations and see what are the principal features that industries do or do not have in common. He found that a combination of size and concentration, capital-intensity, unionisation and level of education of the work-force, and government and export sales dependence were of prime importance. Next in importance was a sex factor, followed by a race factor.

It should be understood that these factors, in order, are the best statistical way of identifying similarities and differences between industries. They do not, as such, suggest a dual economy. For this, we need to consider how the scores for these various factors are distributed across industries, whether there are clusters of scores which divide one set of industries from another. Oster does this for the first factor alone and finds evidence of duality. Kaufman *et al.* (1981) undertake a similar exercise with some change in the economic variables employed and in the sectors concerned (adding trade, service and financial industries) and conclude that there is a *sixteenfold* segmentation of the industrial structure. For Apostle *et al.* (1985a: 256), this problem of how many industrial segments is less one of statistical verification as such and more one of attempting to make the theory workable, 'the goal being to come up with a small number of clusters which adequately represents the theory'. They tend to favour three segments.

But at this point, statistical virtuosity seems to have blinded us to the analytical problems at hand. For factor and cluster analysis tell us nothing about causation, only about correlation. In drawing out the principal components of industrial structure, it is recognised that a variety of economic variables tend to be correlated with each other. The causes of that correlation are only weakly examined within SLM theory and it is not unique in explaining such correlations. At the same time, the SLM theory concerned would need to suggest that the economic processes that produce the industrial structure do their work and then the industrial structure starts on the labour market to produce wages and conditions, etc. So, unless there is a commitment to a rigid structure of causation (economic and social factors first yield the industrial structure and then this gives rise to the labour market structure), it becomes arbitrary to define industrial segmentation in a way that excludes labour market conditions at the outset.

In short, the correct empirical procedure would appear to be to include labour market variables within the factors affecting industrial structure, and obtain the latter with wages etc. included. Statistical or other inspection of the resulting principal combination of factors would yield both an industrial structure and the correlation of labour market characteristics with it.

Why has this not been done? One obvious reason is that this statistical procedure would diverge from the causal motivation of the SLM model. But, as has been argued here, the statistics merely sort out correlations and have no causal significance. None the less, to use labour market variables in defining the industrial segments is to court the charge of circularity.[55] And this is correct if the segments are identified with these variables included, and then, say, wages, for example, are argued to be high because they are in segments which employ labour with favourable labour market conditions. But this problem disappears[56] if labour market variables are included in the segmentation analysis and the two-stage statistical procedure – of identifying segments and then using them to explain labour markets – is reduced to the single procedure of identifying segments with labour market variables included. Conceptually, to do otherwise appears to presume that labour market determination is subsequent to each of the 25 or more factors that characterise industry, something which is both conceptually and chronologically implausible.

On the supply-side of the labour market, the statistical techniques, in principle at least, could be identical but reversed. Labour market characteristics could have been examined for principal factors, and then these set against industrial structure variables to reveal correlations. That this has not been done would appear to reflect two influences. The first, already mentioned above, is that, in running from labour market to industrial structure, the false notion that correlation is causation would devalue the notion in SLM theory of the significance of the core–periphery division. For this reason, there has been no attempt to segment the industrial structure on the basis of the labour market structure, although this would be the parallel step to the procedure on the demand-side. If our suggestion of determining the industrial and labour market structure simultaneously were taken up, then, of course, none of this would arise.[57]

The second influence on the supply-side has been its contact with human capital theory. SLM theory suggests that there are different determinants of labour market outcomes by segment and that human capital theory is less likely to apply, at least statistically, the lower down is the labour market segment.[58] So, with more or less sophistication, wages are explained by a combination of variables, including sex, race, education, experience, unionism, industrial structure, etc.

One of the problems with this has been truncation bias. As Kruse (1977: 219) points out, Osterman's results for the USA are weakened by the simple observation that a static picture of the labour market will always reveal 'skilled' workers in a secondary sector not requiring 'skills' prior to their elevation to the primary sector. As would be suggested by SLM theory in any case, this shows the need to examine worker mobility, and this has also been a favourite empirical theme. For the US, studies have been done by Buchele (1983) who emphasises the effects of duality on employment stability; Buchele (1981) finds for women that job segregation, tenure, recruitment, promotion and pay discrimination are important; Leigh (1976) reveals that race differences are more important for determining initial job than subsequent advancement but Alexander (1981) finds otherwise for non-college graduates; Rosenberg (1981) traces employment mobility over the business cycle for older men; Rumberger and Carnoy (1980) consider sex and race differences by employment in the public and different types of private sector; Schiller (1977), Snyder *et al.* (1978) and Tolbert (1982) look at mobility for blacks, for men and women between segments, and for men over their careers, respectively; Flanagan (1973) finds barriers to blacks for jobs leading to specific on-the-job training.

For the UK, Bosanquet and Doeringer (1973) accept human capital theory other than for race and sex (in the first European DLM study); Psacharopoulos (1977) and McNabb and Psacharopoulos (1981) find no evidence inconsistent with human capital theory, looking at male workers only; Barron and Norris (1976) identify the secondary sector with women; Mayhew and Rosewall (1979) investigate mobility for males between segments and question how distinct they are.

Other country studies include Jones (1983) and Lever-Tracy (1981) for Australia revealing a complex stratification by ethnic origin, immigration patterns and sex; for Canada, Meng (1985) rejects human capital theory for males and Apostle *et al.* (1985b) go for a three-segment industrial structure for the Maritimes; de Neubourg *et al.* (1982) and Valkenburg and Vissers (1980) investigate Holland with mixed results; House (1984) finds segmentation by sex, firm size and between the public and private sector for Cyprus; Sengenberger (1981) investigates the connection between SLM and business cycles for West Germany; McNabb (1980) examines female labour and poverty in Wales, where participation rates are low (but increasing as opposed to men); and Neuman and Ziderman (1986) test for duality in Israel on the basis of mobility.

These supply-side studies clearly cover many countries and many explanatory and proxy variables. But, as is or should be standard within econometrics, they are fundamentally flawed by estimating a supply-side equation when it is the interaction of supply and demand that is supposed to yield market structure and outcome within it. Formally, two equations and their simultaneous effects should be estimated as has already been suggested for the derivation of structures by factor analysis.

There is also the problem of reverse regression even for the simple one-sector econometric studies. Normally, studies within human capital theory will regress wages on labour market variables and, if supportive of segmentation, will find that women's wages, say, are lower for a given set of educational and other qualifications. But, even then, if the reverse regression were calculated, the opposite conclusion might result – that for a given level of wages, women require a lower level of qualifications than men. Such a conflict between the two regressions can only be resolved by a theory of how the errors in the data (preventing the two regressions being perfect inverses of each other) are generated.[59] As far as I know, these problems have never been broached by any empirical study in the SLM tradition.

But where supply and demand are considered simultaneously is in more specific case studies which are equally numerous by geographical region, industry and labour segment. Thus, we have Morgan and Hooper (1982) who show, for example, that wages are not lower where black workers are concentrated within the UK wool industry; Lawson (1981) discovers paternalism in a transnational corporation affiliate; fragmentation but not necessarily secondary workers are found in the Italian and UK construction industry by Villa (1981) and Moore (1981), respectively; small firms can do well for labour in Italian knitwear (Solinas 1982); engineers in the UK are selected for their loyalty as much as their skills (Whalley 1984); Deacon (1982) provides a history of the employment of women within the Commonwealth Service, starting with the marriage bar and the transfer of clerical work from the primary to the secondary sector as it became a female occupation; Roemer and Schnitz (1982) see non-tenure track academic posts in the US as a secondary labour market within university education; and Leon (1985) examines the implications of segmentation for retirement prospects.

Local labour markets are also studied in Danson (1982), who emphasises the role of virgin sites in overcoming inner city internal labour markets; in Lowell (1978) for the urban poor of Boston, Chicago and Detroit;[60] Horn (1980) for Manchester, New Hampshire, where primary and secondary factors are mixed; Wray (1984) for a comparison of the position of men and women in a small town and two industrial villages; and, for informal recruitment, Jenkins (1984) for women and ethnic minorities, and Ashton and Maguire (1984) for Sunderland, Leicester and St Albans.

Other topics include the success of training programmes, as entry tickets to the primary sector, by Fottler (1974) for Buffalo; how segmentation

affects racial prejudice (Cummings 1980); Cornfield (1985) finds worker pro-
test through quitting in the secondary sector but through striking in the
primary sector; and Mangum *et al.* (1984/5) studies the industry organising
temporary help as an outcome of DLMs.

The point of this long set of lists, with casually selected items from the
contributions concerned (and not necessarily the ones the authors or
others would consider the most important insights), is to illustrate that
SLM theory, with a relatively slim theoretical foundation, has been used
to justify a whole range of empirical studies whose common underlying
determinants from SLM theory must be open to question.

This is confirmed by LaMagdeleine's (1986) remarkable analysis, utilising
SLM theory, of employment in the US Catholic Church. The labour force is
divided along two cleavages, by gender and religious vocation. In principle,
this ought to lead to four categories of labour, but the division by gender
within the lay employees (non-vocational) is unexamined.[61] Within the
vocational, there is a sexual division between priests and sisters, embedded
in the monopoly of the former in presiding over the sacrament – hearing
confession, for example (LaMagdeleine 1986: 316):[62] 'Since only males
can be ordained, a fundamental ascriptive barrier keeps even the most
well-qualified female from the top organizational levels.' On the other
hand, sisters have an advantage over lay workers (implicitly of either sex)
in employment by the church:

> Much as mobility chains and educational credentials provide access in
> American society to the primary market, religious status seems to provide
> a ticket to jobs in the parish occupational sector . . . In other words, they
> are structurally determined.

> (ibid.: 322)

On the side of the 'industrial' structure, there are two sorts of sectors:
those involving vocation – including administering the sacrament which is
confined to males – and those involving pastoral duties, such as religious
education and campus youth work. The latter have been increasingly undertaken by lay workers and this is explained by liberalisation of the church,
following the Ecumenical, Vatican II.[63] Compared to 1950, there were in
1978, 8 per cent fewer priest and 29 per cent fewer sisters, although the
number of US Catholics had risen by 6 per cent. But, over the same
period, the proportion of teachers who were priests or sisters had fallen
from 84 per cent to 31 per cent. The corresponding rise in the proportion
of lay workers employed in a secondary employment role with limited security and, in 1979, an average salary of $7,000. For priests and sisters, how-
ever, employment in parish work is a temporary position from which to
gain the education, training and experience to move into higher administrative posts. In this upward movement, priests have an advantage, one not
necessarily corresponding to their abilities for the higher levels of pastoral

work, and there is a potential source of conflict with sisters over credential expertise and professional status.

LaMagdeleine appears to provide an exemplary instance of SLM theory, containing a dual economic structure, with sacrament a monopoly of the Church and pastoral work not, and a dual labour market with a two-tiered primary sector (priests and sisters) and a secondary sector (lay workers). Yet, whilst this study is motivated by SLM theory, it can have little correspondence with it, since the determining influences are far removed from the economic and social forces associated with SLM theory. This should shed light back upon our cursory review of the empirical literature. For there is found greater or lesser success in identifying labour market segments and the processes that produce them and, given the variety of explanatory factors employed, it is necessary to remain sceptical about the extent to which they contribute to a well-defined theoretical core as opposed to a system of empirical classification. Indeed, it is possible to draw the opposite conclusions to those of LaMagdeleine (ibid.: 315) whose clarity of hypothesis and verification is the exception that disproves her rule: 'Although dual market theory has been useful for generating hypotheses, it has not lent itself to empirical verification.' SLM theory has depended on ill-formed hypotheses that have been empirically investigated in a far from satisfactory way.

6 SEGMENTED LABOUR MARKETS AS A HISTORICAL CORE

In the previous section, it has been shown how SLM theory has led to a proliferation of empirical studies which collectively correspond to the approach to SLMs associated with the Cambridge school. However, this has not been the route taken by those who originated DLM theory, DP and REG. They have travelled in quite the opposite direction; far from narrowing down the scope of SLM theory and making it increasingly empirical, they have tended to generalise SLM theory into a fuller examination of economy and society.

For Piore, who has taken the lead for the DP school, this has involved a number of directions. First, though, he recognises that DLM theory needs to be generalised to segmentation:

> what is critical in these dualist theories is the notion of segmentation, and not the number of segments: two, three, or more are consistent with the structure of the argument. The number could not, however, be too large without tending to recreate the continuous array of variation of a unitary social model (liberal or Marxist). Equally, social segmentation does not rule out some mobility between sectors, so long as the volume and character of this mobility still permits the maintenance within each segment of different values, rules and institutions.
>
> (Berger and Piore 1980: 142)[64]

One wonders what Piore would make of the proliferation of segments implied by the empirical studies revealed in the previous section. But the search for common values, rules and institutions within segments is consistent with the way in which DP distinguished itself from neoclassical economics by its emphasis on the endogeneity of tastes of workers through feedback from the employment structure.[65] It has already been shown how this has led to a casual sociology, but more serious contributions have also been made.

However, DP's continuing basis is a dualism in which the secondary sector is increasingly seen as an economic and social unit that transcends national and historical boundaries, thus: 'Given any particular labour market, it is usually possible to identify a cleavage between stable and unstable (secure and insecure) employment which meets our definition of duality' (Berger and Piore 1980: 26). This not only applies across countries within the advanced capitalist world – Italy, France and the USA – but also to the third world. Despite rejecting a theory of convergence, it is argued that: 'the traditional sector in Italy and the informal sector in Colombia seem to have much in common, and in the former as in the latter case, they perform functions that are critical to the modern sector' (ibid.: 6).

What might these critical functions be? One example is given by the study of the effects of militancy in Italy and France in the 1960s (Piore 1978; Berger and Piore 1980). Here it is argued that employer strategy was to undermine primary sector bargaining strength by expanding a more flexible and compliant secondary sector, variously available in the form of women, youths and workers from rural areas. In other words, there is constructed a crude, almost market,[66] mechanism by which the balance between the primary and secondary sector is established according to the militancy of the primary sector (Berger and Piore 1980: 49), although the exact nature of that balance and its internal structures are open to sophisticated analysis and contingent determination:

> the category [of 'traditional'] is one created by an overlap of economic facts, social perceptions, political values, and state policy . . . Despite the heterogeneity . . . they owe their existence only in part to real, objective similarities in the economic interests of the members of the class but mainly to the members' common perception of having the same situation in society and to society's seeing them as the same and establishing rules that identify them as a political and social entity . . . It follows . . . that the groups and firms that belong to the traditional sector vary historically and across societies.

> (ibid.: 93)

Such historical and theoretical flexibility, however, should not blind us to the heavy (economic) determinism involved in the relations between the modern and traditional sectors, if not in their composition. Yet, Marxism is charged with this very sin:[67] 'the difficulty is that orthodox Marxists root social processes very tightly in the material conditions of production and assume that peoples' ideology and politics are a direct reflection of these conditions' (ibid.: 28).

Another area in which Piore (1979b, 1979c) seeks to widen the implications of SLM theory is in macroeconomics and, in particular, in the explanation of the Phillips curve, or the relation between unemployment and inflation. On the one hand, at full employment, secondary workers have unfulfilled aspirations pressing to a greater extent on wage costs (Piore 1979b: 16); otherwise, a customary wage structure within the primary sector translates pressure at any one point into general wage pressure (Piore 1979b: 142). This, however, is far from an 'alternative view', since it is simply cost push with institutional inflexibility. Piore, however, provides no theory for the mechanism by which this leads to levels of inflation and (un)employment and output.

There is, in addition, an irony in this casual relation between theory and empirical evidence. The Phillips curve itself was 'discovered' as an inverse empirical relationship between unemployment and inflation. Theory was developed to explain it and has persisted (with modification) long after the original empirical relationship had broken down into stagflation. As has been seen, SLM theory was developed to explain ghetto poverty and has since taken on a life of its own, including explanation of what the Phillips curve theory would seek to explain although its stylised facts have ceased to hold!

But, Piore's favoured sphere of application of SLM theory is in the analysis of migration and its relation to the secondary labour market, with his work being brought together in Piore (1979a). This cannot be examined in detail here, but it is worth observing the central role played by flux and uncertainty, the stereotypes of migrants (and of women and youth), the ambiguous relation to orthodox theory and the role of historical contingency in the context of a dual economy model.

For REG, Gordon *et al.* (1982) expand the sphere of application of SLM theory to the history of US labour, by offering an economic history of US capitalism. They confine SLM to the current period (from the 1920s) of three overlapping periods of capitalism, its having been preceded by a period of labour homogenisation (1873 to the Second World War) and initial proletarianisation (1790 to late 1890s). Periods themselves are explained in terms of long-wave cycles of 'exploration, consolidation and decay', in which structures of accumulation with definite institutions, and associated methods of organising labour, emerge and grow prior to being displaced.

This complex combination of concepts – periodisation, social structures, long waves and the organisation of labour – has limited connections to any theoretical analysis.[68] Consequently, it comprises a crude structuralism[69] which circumstantial evidence suggests is a response to the particular empirical history it seeks to explain.[70] It is married to a crude functionalism in which the social structures, for example, respond to capitalism's needs, except when they break down, only to re-emerge transformed.[71] Taken together, all of these features of REG confine it also to the status of a middle-range theory, in which intermediate categories of analysis serve equally for the most immediate empirical evidence as well as to reveal underlying trends.[72]

This leads to a number of problems. First, predominance in causality is heavily skewed towards labour at the expense of other factors, both within the economy and society, see Bronfenbrenner (1982), for example. Second, segmentation within the labour force is overlooked prior to the modern period for which, as has been seen, there are too many exceptions to the core–periphery rule (see Lever-Tracy 1983: 354; Conk 1984). Thus, Brody (1984) notes that craft work was at the heart of nineteenth-century production and then immigrants were a source of skilled labour and not necessarily forced into unskilled work. Hirsch (1983: 467) argues that: 'Ethnic, race, and sex fragmentation within the working class continued unabated in the early part of the twentieth century, reinforced by employer divide-and-rule tactics.' Third, then, more generally, there is a wider set of anomalies between the theory and the evidence which leads Gallie (1985: 507) to suggest REG are 'skating at times on pretty thin historical ice' and Brody (1984: 703) to observe of them that, 'if the facts do not square with the theory, so much the worse for the facts'.[73]

In a separate but supporting paper to the book, Reich (1984) attempts to verify the segmentation and periodisation hypotheses over the last 60 years. He does so by the sort of nation-wide study that has been discussed in the previous section. He begins by giving a concise definition of the segmentation 'approach':

> Constructed explicitly as an alternative to traditional competitive labour market theories, segmentation analysis posits the existence of bounded submarkets distinguished both by industry (an oligopolistic core and competitive periphery, or primary and secondary sectors) and by occupation within the core or primary submarket. The labour segments markets behave differently and mobility between them is somewhat but not totally circumscribed.

> (Reich 1984: 63)

He then observes that there have been two generations both of theoretical and of empirical work. The first generation of theory, DP and early REG, has given way to the second, later REG and the Cambridge school. This has the 'refinement' of institutional, historical, qualitative and dynamic materials, often at a case study level and 'more able to incorporate formerly dissonant anomalies' (ibid.: 65).

The first generation of empirical studies is criticised for focus on males alone, presuming a test for SLM by absolute immobility or mobility over

too short a period, and for truncation bias (ibid.: 63–4). The second generation of empirical studies is rebuked for static concentration on the industrial
structure (factor and cluster analysis) and its relation to labour market variables. To some extent, these statistical deficiencies are excused, particularly
for the first generation, because the theory they were attempting to test was
made far from clear.

Clearly, Reich's SLM retrospect has resonances with our assessment
made in the previous section. In this light, he might have been expected
to have developed a clear set of theoretical propositions for empirical testing. He does not. He simply puts down five hypotheses, with no further
theoretical justification than is to be found in Gordon *et al.* (1982), and considers that the test of them over a long period, from 1914 to 1979, is the
appropriate way to proceed (Reich 1984: 67).

The five hypotheses for the period of segmented labour markets are that
value added per worker, wages, employment, ratio of non-production to
production workers, and employment stability should grow faster in the
core than in the periphery. He also looks at cyclical behaviour of wages
and the level of unionisation, expecting the former to be pro-periphery in
the boom and the latter to grow faster in the core.

Before considering the statistical results, it is important to emphasise that
it is far from clear how these propositions, if empirically verified, would support SLM rather than any other theory. In many ways, these would be the
stylised facts of an economic orthodoxy. As to the results themselves, they
involve considerable problems unnoticed by Reich. He uses Oster's (1979)
segmentation to divide industry into core and periphery, correctly observing
that truncation bias for labour market segmentation is minimised by the
division of the sectors through exclusion of labour market variables. But
because this is done through the use of industrial variables, these will be
highly correlated with the movement of the variables specified in Reich's
hypotheses.

To be specific, for example, Oster's significant factors for the core include
investment per worker in 1965, a measure of education of male workers,
level of unionisation in 1960 and a variety of size and concentration variables over the period 1953–66. These factors are almost self-selecting in supporting the hypotheses that Reich puts forwards once we realise simple
connections such as that the largest firms over a period are liable to have
grown the most, etc. Ironically, Oster tests for the factor of increase in
value added per worker-hour over the period 1953–63 and finds it an insig-
nificant element in the definition of the core, even though increase in value
added per worker is a verified hypothesis for the core for Reich (except for
1963–7 when it grew faster in the periphery)! This is statistics through the
looking glass.[74]

But what of the finding that the hypotheses work for the post-war period
but not for the 1920s, leading Reich to suggest a different stage of capitalism
for the earlier period? This is unproven. Even if we had defined industrial

structure perfectly by Oster's methods, we would have done so on variables relating to the period 1953–66. Differential performance across sectors in output and investment levels would tend to yield a more even movement of the test variables in the 1920s when examining them by use of the industrial structure of 30 years later.

There are many other such problems, with just two more highlighted here. Reich observes that manufacturing contains less than half of employment but that mining, transport and construction would by Oster's method be assigned to the periphery:

> Yet workers in these industries have been able to form relatively strong unions and are paid relatively high wages. Hence to maintain consistency with the theory, which views unionisation as a potential shifter of industries from periphery to the core, the above industries should be classified in the core. In order to avoid these conflicts, which cannot be resolved here, I concluded that the present study would best be served by excluding such industries altogether. Therefore, I have included in the periphery only those non-manufacturing sectors that meet both the industrial structure and non-unionisation result.
>
> (ibid.: 74)

Here, then, we have the exclusion of the sectors that do not fit, a reduction of SLM theory to the idea that unions cause higher wages and a consolidation of self-supporting hypotheses by selection of sectors for the periphery.

This all concerns industrial variables, but Reich also deals with occupational segmentation, focusing on sex and race differences. In the case of unemployment rates, he finds that between 1954 and 1974, changes were as shown in Table 1. Clearly, the relative changes are very small, but with females doing worse. But whether this is sufficient to support SLM theory against some alternative explanation, Reich thinks it so by constructing a segmentation index from these figures that moves from 4.85 to 8.78! He comments that 'the index increased substantially over the postwar period' (ibid.: 76). Such an index clearly obscures what is going on.[75]

In short, a critical assessment of Reich's contribution confirms the view presented here of the way in which SLM theory has developed. It is an 'approach' with mixed empirical support for hypotheses ill-defined absolutely and in their capacity to be distinguished from other theories. It fails

Table 1 Male and female unemployment rates for whites and non-whites, 1954 and 1974

Year	White males	Non-white males	White females	Non-white females
1954	4.8	10.3	5.6	9.3
1974	4.3	9.1	6.1	10.7

at the national level and is perceived as best proceeding at the micro level. Thus:

> A quantitative study based primarily on industry rather than workplace data cannot capture adequately the patterns suggested by the theory, and the work presented here must be complemented by qualitative, detailed case studies.

(ibid.: 77)

Last, but not least, it commands a loyalty that allows Reich to conclude on the basis of his and other work that: 'We now have systematic evidence that segmentation has been operating to produce divergent trends in the postwar period' (ibid.). We would suggest otherwise – case not clearly stated and certainly not proven.

7 CONCLUDING REMARKS

In this chapter, a number of central features of the SLM approach have been highlighted. First, and methodologically foremost, is what even its own sympathetic practitioners have described as a middle-range theory. As such, it has occupied an ill-defined theoretical terrain, at times relying on abstract explanatory variables, like the industrial structure or social reproduction and, at other times, forging an immediate correspondence between the theory and empirical evidence, most notably in rejecting human capital theory, for example. As a result, SLM theory has been in a chronic state of disarray and one that has remained irresolvable on its own terms.

A second feature of SLM theory is that its analytical content is drawn from a wide range of disciplines and most especially from economics, sociology and industrial relations. The contribution from each of these has often been deficient; for economics, there has been an undue reliance on the core–periphery view of capitalism, but necessarily modified in an *ad hoc* way in the empirical light of proliferating segments; for sociology, neo-Weberian concepts of stratification have been significant but which tend to involve a tautologous identification between theory and evidence; and for industrial relations, there has been a more satisfactory use of labour process theory but also a continuing attachment to simplistic notions of internal labour markets. Trade unionism has been reduced to sectional pursuit of self-interest (usually against those in disadvantaged segments). And the articulation of the politics of production with the economy has been weak both in detail (as in how productivity is or is not generated, since primary concern is with access to jobs and the rewards attached to them) and in historical sweep (as in how the post-war period, for example, is to be understood as a phase in the development of capitalism and how particular economies fit into this context).

SLM theory has very much become an approach based on looking out upon the world from within small, usually disadvantaged, sections of the work-force. Not surprisingly, grander questions have suffered as a consequence despite the intentions of REG in the first instance. Taken together, these analytical and descriptive components have led to a number of weaknesses: of politics in general and even of the role of the state, especially as employer rather than as presumed determinant of the labour market environment; of finance and its role in restructuring the economy; and of the international economy as a determining factor. There has also been a failure to forge an interdisciplinary approach to SLM analysis, except at the empirical level in throwing together a variety of explanatory factors.

These features may be summed up in terms of the absence of a theory of periodisation and, associated with this, lack of an understanding of the current stage of capitalism as an abstract determinant of the labour market structure. The obvious exception is the work of REG. But here, it is possible to see their periodisation as theoretically unfounded in principle and as an *ex post* support for their empirical analysis in practice.[76] In short, whilst SLM theory prides itself on its lack of theoretical dogma and on the role played by historical contingency, its analytical content is profoundly ahistorical. For it ends up as a series of contingent factors bound by a series of equally contingent institutions (or forms of institutions in the case of the family, the state or trade unions).

The theoretical problems are to some extent concealed by resort to empirical evidence. SLM theory gives rise to ambiguous hypotheses, and these have been tested against the 'facts', often in a far from satisfactory manner. Consequently, from the heady, early days when SLM theory commanded the field in the absence of competitors if not opponents, it has now experienced a decline in influence and prominence. At best, it has become a point of reference for eclectic analyses that need to draw upon some understanding of particular segments of the labour market. At worst, as will be seen in the next chapter, it has been eclipsed by the challenge of the alternative offered by neoclassical economics.

NOTES

1 See also Dunlop (1958) and Reynolds (1956), for example.
2 See Cain (1976) for some discussion of segmented labour market in the history of economic thought, including neo-institutionalists. See also Loveridge and Mok (1979).
3 For a more general discussion of Smith's theory of wage determination and its relation to his theories of the division of labour, growth and value, see Fine (1982).
4 See also p. 67.
5 For possibly the shortest and most convenient presentation of DLM theory, see de Neubourg *et al.* (1982).

6 The reference to 'unrest' is not typical of the original work and reflects a response to developments in France and Italy in the late sixties.

7 For a view contesting the lack of inefficiency, despite these structures, see Wachter (1974: 678).

8 With true bravado, it is then claimed that internal labour markets may be the micro-foundations on which to explain the macroeconomic Phillips curve – presumably through labour market rigidities pushing up money wages in the primary sector, with core firms increasing prices correspondingly. See section 6.

9 Doeringer and Piore (1971) confine consideration of the secondary market to their Chapter 8 other than a separate chapter on racial discrimination.

10 See Doeringer and Piore (1971) and Piore (1975). Such terminology has now become standard in explanations of labour management and hierarchies.

11 Piore (1983) also adopts a pop sociology of knowledge to explain why dual labour market theory, along with the human capital theory of Becker, have been rejected by the orthodoxy.

12 But see Berger and Piore (1980: 1–2), who refer to the parallel dualism of underdevelopment. See also Cornwall (1977) and Carnoy (1980), for example.

13 As claimed by Loveridge and Mok (1979: 6).

14 See also Piore (1979d: xiii) for a confirmation of this motivation in retrospect.

15 See Harrison (1971), who explains an emerging DLM theory in terms of a dual attack on the problems posed by black poverty and human capital theory.

16 Gordon (1972) sees orthodox (human capital) theory, DLM theory and radical economic theory as the three competing paradigms in explaining poverty and unemployment.

17 See also Piore, where a reconciliation is sought between himself, radical DLM, first referred to below as the Marxist tradition, and new classical economics (!):

> Postwar developments within the Marxist tradition . . . focussed on the independent role of the systems of ideology and belief . . . These are essentially the same analytical issues that . . . are entrained by the hypothesis of rational expectations now preoccupying conventional economics, and by the notions of cognitive structure in which we have attempted to root the dual labor market hypothesis. If these analytical ideas were to be pursued, this suggests, these three apparently different understandings of economic activity would begin to converge.
>
> (Piore 1979d: xxviii)

The cognitive structure 'tries to build into the economic model a process that generates technology and tastes, one (which) goes beyond neoclassical theory' (Piore 1974: 685). In other words, some form of socio-psychology as outlined above.

18 For a fuller account, see Edwards (1979). It is not our intention to assess the post-Braverman literature on the labour process, management strategies and workplace conflict, only to point that this is the main element distinguishing REG and DP in the first instance.

19 Supply- and demand-side are initially placed in inverted commas, although it is not clear whether this is because of an intended total break with supply and demand analysis or because of the intended distancing from the version of the neoclassical orthodoxy. See also Rubery (1978: 18), Humphries and Rubery (1984: 336) and Craig *et al.* (1982: 79) for similar criticisms of neglect of the supply-side within SLM theory. REG have accepted this criticism, see Reich (1984).

20 The imperative of profitability comes through the consideration of unit labour costs. See also Tarling (1981: 287) for a diagrammatic exposition of the relevant

factors. Over time, however, there is a discernible trend in the Cambridge SLM school to de-emphasise the importance of labour and production, and to emphasise other sources of profitability such as marketing and market structure.

21 See, for example, Craig *et al.* (1985a) and Humphries and Rubery (1984), respectively. See also Garnsey *et al.* (1985) and Rubery et al (1984).

22 Thus, Villa (1981: 148) concludes for the Italian construction industry that the 'cumulative changes in market, technology, skills, labour market environment and trade union organisation have interacted to continuously restructure the labour market'.

23 Some of the Cambridge SLM school have been associated with the Braverman critique in which the tendency to deskilling is tempered by continuing struggle over control at the workplace with labour exerting a greater or lesser but persistent effect. See the Elbaum *et al.* (1979) symposium in the *Cambridge Journal of Economics*, and Wood (1982) and Thompson (1983), for example. This is also true of the radical tradition within SLM theory for which the Cambridge school would, to that extent, be incorrect in suggesting that it has no supply-side component.

24 This ambiguity over the centrality or not of class conflict is carried over into policy, with growth depending on whether, Rubery *et al.* (1984: 137), 'management and labour . . . find the successful compromise at industry level'. In Garnsey *et al.* (1985), Cambridge SLM broach this issue in the most sociological form of presentation of their views (although in apparent ignorance of the substantial sociological literature). Reference is made to 'sheltered' and 'unsheltered' employment, following Freedman (1976), which has interesting resonances with Keynes's analysis of industry when studying the 1925 return to gold.

25 For a similar view, see the sectoral analyses of the casualised trades in London presented in GLC (1985b, 1986). See also Chapter 4.

26 Rubery and Wilkinson (1981: 128) and following the controversial article by Humphries (1977) on the family.

27 See also Wilkinson (1983: 425) for posing but not resolving this problem. Thus, the underlying 'forces which can be identified as modifying productive systems include changes in the pattern of demand, economic conditions, technology, power relations between organised labour and capital and state policy'. But, 'there are and can be *no* universal pre-determined, 'true' systems to which underlying economic forces are tending' (ibid.: 413; emphasis in original).

28 See Tarling (1981: 285–9) for what appears to be a confirmation of this sort of modelling as underlying the Cambridge school.

29 This view of the Marxist method is illustrated, for example, in the interpretation of the tendency of the rate of profit given in Fine and Harris (1979) in contrast to the simultaneity method of Sraffians. See also Fine (1982). These issues are taken up in detail in Chapter 7.

30 See especially Garnsey *et al.* (1985).

31 See Humphries and Rubery (1984: 336–7) and the withering criticism by Craig *et al.* (1982: 155) of Piore for downgrading the work capacities of those employed in the secondary sector. The same would apply to Blaug's view that:

> No wonder, then, that employers resort to stereotypes like sex, colour, ethnic background, educational credentials, marital status, age and previous work experience, indicators which experience has shown to be good predictors of job performance, at least on average.
>
> (Blaug 1985: 22)

It is difficult to imagine anyone managing to be guilty of so many '. . . isms' with any fewer words!

32 See Wilkinson (1981: ix), for example.

33 The term 'middle-range' derives from Merton (1957), who proposed it positively as an intermediate level of analysis between grand theory and more immediate empirical outcomes. A critique was made by Wright Mills (1959). For an assessment, from the perspective of sociology, of segmentation theory as a 'new structuralism' and as a 'middle-range' theory for similarly bridging the abstract and empirical in this way, see Baron and Bielby (1980). For them, firms are the unit of analysis to mediate 'the links between social structure and processes at macro and micro levels' (Baron and Bielby 1980: 742). See also Tolbert (1982) for a further reference to the middle-range new structuralism. For him, however, 'the new structuralism in social stratification underscores the inadequacies of wholly individualistic models of microeconomic behaviour' (Tolbert 1982: 474). There is some tension here once these observations are translated to the plane of economic theory. For here, the theory of the firm tends to be rooted in 'individualistic models of microeconomic behaviour'. But it is interesting to note that the method of being middle-range in this way appears to require the choice of some economic agent or institution lying between the level of the individual and an entire class.

34 But see Rubery *et al.* (1984) for an explicit reliance on Keynesian macro-economics as the context in which to analyse labour markets.

35 In Fine and Harris (1985), for example, the UK is characterised as a low-wage, low-productivity, low-investment economy within the advanced capitalist world, and this is explained by the relations between (transnational) capital, labour finance and the state. This might be extended to explain the increasing reliance on part-time female labour on which, in this vein, see Fine (1992). But those who explain Britain's problems in terms of too high wages and trade union power would have to put forward a different explanation. The point is, however, that some overall assessment appears essential.

36 For a partial exception, see Vietorisz and Harrison (1973), who discuss the reinforcing feedback of productivity increase upon itself.

37 See, for example, Solinas (1982) for the knitwear industry in Carpi; Lawson (1981) for Pye in Cambridge; Brusco (1982) for the Emilian model; and the studies of Craig *et al.* (1982, 1985a) for a number of areas and industries.

38 This despite the emergence of a stream of radical accountants who link financial calculation with control of the labour process. For a start, see Berry *et al.* (1985).

39 Thus, Bluestone and Stevenson ask:

> Why is it that, while some 'core' firms . . . find it desirable to structure all their jobs to fall within the primary market, other 'core' firms . . . find it desirable to locate some of the jobs within the secondary market while maintaining a primary market for the rest?
>
> (Bluestone and Stevenson 1981: 41)

40 REG have a very simple approach to politics, with lack of revolutionary consciousness following on from labour market divisions. See Rozen (1983), for example, who comments on the neglect of trade unions and their significance for political strategy. Penn goes further in criticising Edwards (1979):

> Is Edwards' notion of working class fractions useful sociologically? Does Edwards capture the real relations between labour market structuration and control? Finally, can one explain political phenomena – rhythms of socialist politics – in the way suggested?
>
> (Penn 1982: 95)

For Apostle *et al.* (1986: 905), labour market segmentation is a source of political heterogeneity so that: 'As many segmentation proponents are aware, conventional liberal and Marxist theories have systematically underestimated the persistence of heterogeneous structures and processes in advanced capitalist societies.'

41 Wachter presumably relies upon the work of Williamson, for whom imperfect information gives rise to efficient hierarchies and structures across a wide range of economic phenomena. See Williamson (1975) and Williamson *et al.* (1975), which includes Wachter as an author. Whatever the validity of this in explaining segmentation, the problem remains of not arbitrarily explaining who is assigned to which segment.

42 In a study showing that human capital theory is relevant at most for the upper tier of the primary sector.

43 For truncation bias, the use of cross-section rather than longitudinal data and the proxy of age for experience within work, on the first two of which, see later. See also Langley (1978) and Osterman (1978).

44 See also Wallace and Kalleberg (1981) and, interestingly given their responsibility for its neoclassical resurgence, Dickens and Lang (1985) for further doubts about the valid status of SLM theory.

45 The phrase and assessment is due to Blaug (1985). See Chapter 3.

46 For a spirited defence of Baran and Sweezy, see Foster (1986).

47 For Baran and Sweezy, the forces and economic phenomena undermining monopoly-stagnation, as they understand it, are usually explained in terms of an attempt to moderate its effects.

48 See Berger and Piore (1980: 59 ff). Appeal is also made to the theory of managerial capitalism to explain the monopoly sector.

49 As opposed to the notion within (Ricardian) classical political economy that declining productivity in agriculture was the source of declining profitability. For an assessment of the links between Sweezy and Smith in the context of the transition to capitalism, see Brenner (1977). See also Fine (1988, 1990) which explore the origins of Sweezy's notion of monopoly. All of this points to the market-oriented notions involved in much of Sweezy's work and the same applies to Piore.

50 See also Humphries and Rubery (1984: 336–7) and Craig *et al.* (1985a: 268) for criticism of the secondary labour market as competitive and unstructured.

51 See also Jones (1983: 27).

52 An alternative to going micro within the sociology of stratification theory is to move into the realm of abstract and ideal determinants. Thus, Kreckel (1980) begins with the primary asymmetry between capital and labour, moves onto five processes – demarcation, exclusion, solidarism, inclusion and exposure – and finally ends up with eight labour submarkets. For the use of SLM for stratification from a more down to earth point of view, see Bibb and Form (1976/7) who stress firm, occupation and gender together with consequent income rather than status variables as such, education and inter-generational mobility.

53 Morrissey (1982) is also concerned that the labour market position of women cannot be determined by dual economy structure, since they straddle that structure and make up much of state employment. For this, he is dismissed by Lord and Falk (1982) for dogmatic Marxism, with the lesson that the dual economy and the dual labour markets are not mirror images of each other but are overlapping. In their original article, on the basis of a sample of 415 males and 348 females, Lord and Falk (1980: 376) concluded that 'the structural model worked better for men; the human capital model worked better for women'.

54 For early surveys of empirical work, see Wachter (1974), Cain (1976), Carnoy (1980), Ryan (1981), Zucker and Rosenstein (1981) and Dickens and Lang (1985).

55 See also the debate between Hodson and Kaufman (1981) and Horan *et al.* (1980), following Tolbert *et al.* (1980).
56 The problem of circularity is diminished to the extent that labour market variables do not appear in the principal factors used to segment industrial structure, as is the case with Oster (1979).
57 Dickens and Lang (1985) overcome these problems simply by testing whether the distribution of earnings comes from one or more frequency distributions. This, however, carries no causal significance in terms of its simply explaining labour as segmented by wages being drawn from a number of separate frequency distributions.
58 This is because education is less significant both in work and as a screening device for access to jobs.
59 For a comprehensive discussion of the issues involved, see Goldberger (1983).
60 Affectionate observers of New York will not be surprised to learn from Lowell (1978: 102) that it exhibits two job markets but not in accordance with DLM theory. For unionisation and establishment size are not so important as compared to 'personal' characteristics and the degree of labour turnover.
61 It would, of course, also be desirable to have an analysis of the employees by race within the categories of employment.
62 Put another way (ibid.: 316): 'Either one is ordained or one cannot become a pope. Without being a bishop one cannot be pope, nor have a say in deciding who becomes pope.' In other words, to parody the stating of the obvious, one might as well ask whether the pope is male. The same does not apply to the bear in the woods on gender grounds.
63 The liberalization is, of course, not independent of material economic pressures, possibly reflecting the church's decline, although it did not presumably arise from a wish to exploit a secondary labour market in the USA.
64 See also Piore (1979: xii–xiii).
65 See Wachter (1974) and Piore (1974) in 'Discussion'.
66 It is very Malthusian, as it were, with demand for primary sector population declining with its wage and other conditions of supply.
67 Piore continues: 'Thus, for example, revolution is brought about by changes in the mode of production . . . economic reality is automatically reflected in a unique and essentially complete and correct way in the understanding of actors' (ibid.). This false view of the Marxist theory of revolutionary consciousness is then identified with 'precisely the assumption made in conventional economics in the theory of rational expectations'!
68 Staples comments:

> Within an emerging perspective, empirical research has often a tendency to outspace [outpace?] theoretical development. Such has been the case with the 'dual economy' or 'dual labor market' literature . . . This new book . . . attempts to provide a theoretical foundation of what is becoming an empirically popular, but theoretically disorderly, perspective.
>
> (Staples 1984: 281)

69 Shergold (1983) points to the lack of integration of market forces with capitalist strategy in Gordon *et al.* (1982).
70 Thus, two periods (competitive and monopoly, the latter emerging between 1890 and 1920, as in Edwards *et al.* (1975)) can be replaced by three with no apparent theoretical perturbations.
71 Thus, Blackburn and Mann (1979: 30–1) point to the problems of functionalism for radical segmented labour market theory particularly since there can no presumption that segmentation reduces the overall average level of wages.

72 This is particularly emphasised across a wide range of issues taken up by Nolan and Edwards (1984). See also Schatz (1985: 98), who observes the gap between the analysis of social structures and the detailed determination of labour supply, wage rates, etc.

73 See also Montgomery (1983: 117), who observes that REG's period of labour homogenisation is consolidated by worker quiescence between 1898 and 1920 but that 1916–22 is a peak period of working class unrest.

74 There appears to be a misprint in Oster (1979: 36) with 'KINTEN' in place of 'INVEST' in line 19.

75 For this reason and others, it is not worthwhile taking Reich's statistics as something to be explained by reasons others than his own – the statistics obscure what is going on.

76 A more bizarre stance on periodisation has ultimately been taken by Piore who has championed flec-spec analysis which can in part be interpreted as a simple reversal of the primacy of the core Fordist sector over the secondary flexible sector. See Chapter 4.

6 Neoclassical colonisation

Process, structure and methodological individualism

1 INTRODUCTION

In the mid-1980s, SLM theory was perceived to be radical, to lie outside the mainstream neoclassical and, when not totally overlooked, to be subject to hostile critique by the latter. Within a few years, however, this situation had been noted to have changed dramatically. Morrison (1990: 492), for example, quotes from Dickens and Lang (1988a: 132): 'At one time, segmentation theory may have suffered from a lack of theoretical foundations . . . Now the problem is choosing among the many competing explanations.' Similarly for Hayter and Barnes (1992: 335):[1] 'The problem now, though, is choosing among a swathe of recently developed competing segmentation theories.'

What had brought about this change? The answer is to be found in more general developments in the neoclassical microeconomic theory of market imperfections. Particularly, but not exclusively, informational problems were perceived as the basis upon which individual optimisation could be used to explain the endogenous creation of market structures. Such considerations could apply equally well to the labour market, and some of the analytical innovation derived from within labour market economics itself. For the orthodoxy, it became a matter of explaining how workers with the same attributes could be remunerated differently. Why would employers or employees create structures that could persist and across which there would be limited mobility evening out conditions and rewards? McNabb and Ryan (1990) perceive this as a neoclassical 'fightback', a significant shift from hostility and dismissal characteristic of the earlier years of SLM analysis. Bulow and Summers (1986) are often credited with having legitimised SLM theory because of their model of efficiency-wages. More broadly, Lang and Leonard (1987) offered an overview of a variety of models that are designed to explain labour market structures, particularly in the context of inter-industry differences in wages. The latter might depend upon unions which can influence recruitment (insider–outsider models) and share in any surplus profits ('monopoly rents') accruing to the sector (through product market and capital-intensity effects). Efficiency-wages, in which workers are paid above the market-clearing level, are reckoned to induce harder work and loyalty and to reduce turnover costs. Implicit contracts, tacitly insuring workers against the risk of unemployment, also mean that labour markets do not clear. Each of these effects is hypothesised to be uneven across different sectors of the economy. Conveniently, the variables used to test for such segmentation and its effects do not differ significantly from those associated with the erstwhile radical tradition – unionisation, product concentration ratios, plant and firm size, and capital-intensity – although the models and econometrics involved tend to be more sophisticated for being based upon optimising models in which agents sort or are sorted across (labour) markets.

Elsewhere, Fine (1997a) has argued that neoclassical economics is currently going through a resurgence in which it is reversing its traditional retreat and separation from the subject-matter of the other social sciences with which its integration had always been difficult, if not impossible, in view of its methodological individualism. In particular, social structures and institutions, previously shunned by the economics orthodoxy in deference to the isolated optimising agent, have been taken as endogenous products of such optimising behaviour. Consequently, economics has begun to occupy analytical territory that previously lay outside its preserve.[2]

Exactly this process can be observed in the case of SLM theory. As will be shown in what follows, the neoclassical assault on political economy and social sciences more generally has far from totally displaced the radical tradition within labour market theory which has continued to persist, albeit in the chronic form of an agglomeration of analytically and empirically fragmented studies. Even these, however, have been influenced by the newly emerged orthodoxy – with factors such as human capital becoming far more prominent and the search for greater depth in grand theory fading away. This assessment is confirmed by reference to the sympathetic review of radical political economy (RPE) and labour markets provided by Rebitzer (1993), whose honest account is most revealing and is worthy of discussion.

He characterises the literature as exhibiting three fundamental underlying features: that power is exercised through institutions, that the latter can be a source of inefficiency and inequity, and that outcomes are historically contingent upon the form and content taken by these institutions. It is worth noting that this general appeal to institutions and power moves seamlessly between economics and politics – as if the politics and power of the shop-floor, other than in the institutional forms involved, were similar to those attached to the state.[3] Consequently, there is limited attention to socio-economic processes and structures and the relationship between them. This is a serious, but unnoticed, breach with more traditional propositions from within Marxism (and other social theory). The conceptual collapse of the social into a few institutionalised power relations stands alongside, and is related to, the breach between RPE and neoclassical economics. But that breach or distance has now been accompanied by a compromise, even marriage with, orthodox neoclassical economics:

> The RPE conception of economic processes as political, remediable, and historically contingent clearly derives from the Marxian approach to economic analysis . . . However, RPE has adopted neoclassical economics' concern with the careful analysis of the behavior of individual economic agents. Therefore RPE makes extensive use of theoretical ideas and statistical techniques developed for neoclassical economics. As a result of this attention to microeconomics, the RPE literature has been highly critical of such fundamental Marxian constructions as the labour theory of value, and the tendency of technical change to depress the aggregate profit rate.
>
> (Rebitzer 1993: 1395)

Consequently, with the eschewal of Marxian analysis and its replacement by general and unstructured concepts such as power and institutions, the specific content of the theory is wide open in principle. In practice, it has proved more or less indistinguishable from the orthodoxy (ibid.: 1397): 'Although they were independently developed, the formal structure of the dismissal based incentive models in the RPE literature is no different from those found in the mainstream literature on "efficiency-wage" or "effort regulation".' As in the work of Bowles (1985) or Green (1988), for example, there is an extreme affinity in theory, and even in empirical methods, between neoclassical economics and RPE, although one might be interpreted in terms of informational asymmetries rather than power relations. This is all made explicit in terms of absorption of RPE into the mainstream (which we might interpret as a voluntary acceptance of 'colonisation' of its territory by neoclassical orthodoxy):[4]

> On many microeconomic issues, the clear line that once distinguished RPE accounts of labor market segmentation has been blurred. Indeed so many of the microeconomic issues raised by the RPE literature have been absorbed so thoroughly into (and often improved by) the mainstream of the economics profession that it is often impossible to distinguish one body of work from the other . . . Here the difficulty is not one of *identifying* the contribution of RPE so much as *translating* the RPE ideas into a language accessible to other economists.
>
> (ibid.: 1411; emphases in original)

In this chapter, then, against a background of increasing synthesis between the previously opposed camps of RPE and the mainstream, more recent SLM studies will be categorised according to four criteria: is a particular variable, such as race or gender, used to explain labour market structures; or is it by reference to another parallel structure such as that of industry and product markets; is it the consequence of particular processes such as recruitment or career paths; or is it some hybrid combination of all of these. In other words, whilst the previous chapter was more concerned with the evolution of SLM theory, this addresses the relationship between variables, structures and processes in the more recent literature. It does so with some potential rough justice to the various contributions since there is ambiguity in the meaning of factors such as race – does it, for example, constitute a socioeconomic variable, a systemic structure reflecting the outcome of racism more generally, or the processes whereby racial inequality is established in the labour market. However carefully such distinctions are addressed in the literature, the latter is currently evolving in the context of a resurgence of neoclassical economics in which it will be shown that the problems raised by deploying middle-range concepts and theory are not so much addressed and resolved as completely side-stepped.

2 CATEGORICISM

In its simplest form labour market segmentation is examined as an empirical outcome. If labour market conditions exhibit sufficiently extreme inequalities – typically wage differentials, for example – this is taken as evidence of structuring of the labour force. Analytically, in the much more general context of other forms of socioeconomic inequality, this has been dubbed 'categoricism'.[5] Inequality between identified groups on some aspect, whether by race or gender for instance, is associated with an outcome determined by what is presumed to be a corresponding socioeconomic structure. This clearly runs the danger of tautologous reasoning. For, wage differences between men and women, for example, are then explained by patriarchy or some other expression of gender inequality. In short, inequality is taken as evidence of a social structure which is itself used to 'explain' that inequality. Racism explains why black workers are paid less, etc.

The weakness of categoricism lies in its failing to distinguish what constitutes a socioeconomic structure, how it is reproduced and how it functions to create the differentials with which it is coupled. It is primarily guilt by association with the presumption that (labour market) inequality is synonymous with the presence of a corresponding structure. To some extent, this can be taken as dependent upon the tacit assumption that the explanatory structures are self-evident or are the consequence of factors pitched at a higher-level theory. Racism, sexism or institutions are social structures which influence labour markets outcomes in ways which are presumed to be covered elsewhere – an ideal illustration of the SLM approach as middle-range theory.

Whilst categoricism neatly side-steps the need to specify the exact character and functioning of social structure at the theoretical level, the focus upon identifying segmentation through empirical outcomes leaves two unresolved problems for such analysis. The first is to distinguish between 'legitimate' and 'illegitimate' sources of inequality, with segmentation only associated with the latter. The second is to ascribe differences in labour market outcomes to these two sources in order to be able to assess whether segmentation or genuinely legitimate differences are primarily responsible. Of course, genuine differences in one instance, such as differences in wages in view of differences in qualifications, may be considered illegitimate from an alternative perspective – if there is differential access to education and training. More generally, there is the issue of whether segmentation is associated with pre- or post-entry factors.

The standard technique for resolving these problems is through statistical estimation based on human capital theory. A critical assessment of this and its empirical application has been made in Chapter 3. Here, it suffices to observe that segmentation is most readily identified with differences in the estimated human capital equations across various sections of the workforce. This suggests that the process of wage-setting is different in one segment as opposed to another. Typically, for example, quite apart from human capital being lower in secondary than primary segments, it is also not so well-rewarded where it does arise. As Dickens and Lang (1988a) make explicit, the test of dual labour market theory is on whether a single labour market equation performs statistically better than two different equations, one for each segment. Potentially, this can be generalised beyond duality to investigate an ideal number of separate labour market segments, each with its own estimated wage equation. Implicit, of course, is the idea that education or other forms of human capital contribute well-defined increases to productivity, and hence wages, a conclusion contested by Hunter and Leiper (1993), who measure education, credentials and workers' skills separately and find independent effects on earnings of years of schooling and credentials – in short, evidence of segmentation for them.

Within the human capital vein, McNabb (1987) finds there are a few clearly distinct segments in the UK labour market, with occupational segmentation being more important than by sector. Not surprisingly, Baffoebonnie (1989) finds that household labour supply is different for males and females from within the same household but in ways which vary with the segment of employment. Similar studies are undertaken for The Netherlands by Vanhophem (1987) and for Canada by Osberg *et al.* (1987). The latter suggests that human capital estimates work well for some but not for all labour market segments, with the implication that segmentation can be by differences in the rates of return for human capital, even to the extent that there are no such rewards for some at all in accumulating human capital:

> Although quite ordinary HK [human capital] results can be obtained for wage equations when the sample is all male in all segments, when separate regressions are run for separate segments, the HK model fits the data quite well in some segments and quite poorly in some others. When alternative hypotheses are tested against the most popular operationalization of the human capital hypothesis, the conclusion for roughly

half the labour force . . . is that those alternative hypotheses should be
preferred to a HK specification of the wage equation.

(Osberg et al. 1987: 1616)

Morrison (1990) finds that there are different earnings functions for different
labour market segments, with human capital rewarded differently including
the impact of on-the-job training. Graham and Shakow (1990) investigate
whether inferior jobs, as far as the risk of death, injury and disease are concerned, receive compensating differentials in pay. They conclude that these
labour markets function differently, with compensation arising only in the
presence of trade unions. Both Torres (1991) and Waddoups (1991) conclude that human capital wage equations differ by race. Wilson *et al.*
(1995) suggest that the racial gap is particularly strongly associated with
unemployment for college-educated men. Segmentation within the female
labour market is observed by Waddoups and Assane (1993) and through
the lower rewards paid to part-time workers once allowing for their lower
levels of human capital on average, as in Harris (1993). England *et al.*
(1994) explore the existence of labour market segments according to the proportion of men and women in each occupation, with both men and women
earning less where women are predominant, especially in nurturing occupations. For lawyers, Kay and Hagan (1995) and Dixon and Seron (1995)
observe persistent differences in the earnings of men and women, even
after taking account of credentials, specialisation, and type of employment.
Fichtenbaum *et al.* (1994) find that workers' characteristics do divide into
separate segments which interact with gender and race to yield different
returns to human capital. Boston (1990) corrects for race, gender and occupational segmentation and still finds that human capital returns are greater
in the primary than in the secondary sectors (with a 15 per cent unexplained
residual difference in wage levels). In Brazil, Telles (1993) also suggests that
human capital, as well as race and gender, are important determinants of
wages in the formal, but not in the informal, sectors of the economy. In
addition, however, an ethnic Asian economy provides preferential self-
employment for some males within the informal sectors.[6] For Martin
(1994) rewards for workers are differently determined than for experts and
managers, with education explaining more earnings variation for the latter.

Zagorski (1992) examines the role of education at two different levels.
Those occupations for which more education is the norm pay more on average irrespective of the individual level of education of the workers involved.
But, within such more highly educated sectors, human capital is of less
importance in explaining wage differentials compared to other sectors
with lower human capital. It seems that all workers' wages are dragged
up by average educational requirements but at the expense of individual
rewards. It is also found that the role of such variables as gender, race
and unionisation have different effects depending upon whether they are
studied by occupation or by industry. Quite clearly, this sheds doubt on

any simple notion of segmentation even if it remains understood as derived from a range of overlapping categorical variables. Blackaby *et al.* (1995) consider their study of the unemployed supports the presence of labour market segmentation, for they find that correcting for differences in characteristics by comparison with the employed, the unemployed suffer a 30 per cent penalty in terms of their potential earnings, even after correcting for differences in worker characteristics.

A further variable deployed as a potential proxy for segmentation is in whether the state or the private sector is the employer. Hinrichs and Lyson (1995) investigate the proposition that women and minorities gain through state employment. Distinguishing between sectors in which there is or is not both private and public sector employment, they discover differences in outcomes but that these are modified by the sector involved and by an interactive effect. It does matter whether the state is the sole employer or not.[7]

It has already been suggested that there is limited explanatory, as opposed to exploratory, power in associating labour market structures with the inequalities in labour market outcomes attached to particular variables. This remains so where statistical techniques are used to identify the categorical variables rather than for them to be posited a priori, as in gender, race, etc. Cluster or factor analysis, for example, can be employed across a range of variables to infer the presence of labour market segments. In this case, it is a mix of factors that constitutes a single, but compound, categorical variable. Whilst a single variable is no longer used and privileged in advance as a potential determinant of labour market structure, such statistical techniques are even more deeply entrenched within the framework of simply associating inequality with socioeconomic structure. This particular mixture of disadvantage differentiates one labour market outcome from another. Statistical techniques are used to identify the mix as well as to measure its effects. Notably absent, at best implicit, is a discussion of the mechanisms by which this inequality is generated by the structure (and/or vice versa) and what exactly is meant by a structure in this hybrid categoricism. In short, the apparent empirical openness in determining labour market structures in cluster or factor analysis has its counterpart in the neglect of causal and conceptual content. Analysis is reduced to identifying the statistically most important bundle of correlates of labour market inequality.

Sloane *et al.* (1993), for example, test for segmentation in local labour markets by using four different techniques, including cluster and factor analysis. Theirs is one of the few studies tending to reject segmentation. Sakamoto and Chen (1991) estimate attainment across and within sectors simultaneously, with different wage functions for the latter. Flatau and Lewis (1993) use principal components analysis to identify three labour market segments in Australia. Gittleman and Howell (1995) cluster jobs into six categories by using 17 different measures of job quality, and then examine how the numbers of jobs in each category have changed over time and in their distribution by gender and race. Black and Hispanic men are found to have a worsening mix of jobs relative to whites and a sharp drop in job quality. By using cluster analysis on the characteristics of jobs, as for Anderson *et al.* (1987), explanatory circularity can be avoided as would occur if gender inequality in wage outcomes were identified, for example, by using gender to define the labour segments in the first instance. None the less, the specification of labour market structures remains under-developed other than at the descriptive level of inequality in outcomes and extent of membership by socioeconomic characteristics.

In referring to studies of segmentation based on human capital effects, no account yet has been taken of those which adopt more sophisticated estimation techniques. In particular, it is not simply a matter of comparing earnings of those in one segment with those in another. There is the prior question of whether the assignment of workers across the segments reflects a choice by either employees themselves or by employers of attributes that may or may not have been measured. Consequently, wage differentials may reflect genuine but unmeasured worker characteristics. As Dickens and Lang (1988a) observe, however, it is difficult to distinguish between the effects of segmentation and of market-clearing. Are workers, for example, failing to gain access to preferable jobs because they do not have the appropriate characteristics or is it because of structural barriers? Further, Dickens and Lang (1988b) also recognise that it is necessary to determine whether trade unions mark up wages and create a union/non-union differential/segmentation or whether the causation runs in the opposite direction, and unionisation is more likely around better and better paid jobs. Scott *et al.* (1989) suggest how legislation to enforce uniform fringe benefits at the same place of employment might lead to unintended effects on labour market segmentation through the sorting of workers through differential benefit provision. Demekas (1987) constructs a model in which there is unemployment in the secondary sector, as this leaves open greater opportunities of higher paid employment in the primary sector. This can be rationalised on a number of grounds – availability to be employed as well as secondary employment not being used as a negative screening device for primary jobs, although one might expect unemployment itself to be an even worse signal. A more sophisticated version of such a model, in which firms offer training to workers from the primary sector only if they are unemployed, is provided by Gottfries and McCormick (1995). Both Sloane *et al.* (1993) and Theodossiou (1995) model the choice of career and non-career job paths, together with earnings functions within the separate segments.

In short, models as well as statistical estimates have to take account both of the allocation of workers to jobs and of the outcomes for those jobs. Otherwise, segmentation will be unreasonably inferred simply because workers are being sorted, or sorting themselves, on the basis of factors that might genuinely reflect differences in productivity or preference. Thus,

Magnac (1991) examines how workers decide whether to work or not and in which sector of the economy and attempts to distinguish between genuine choice and barriers to entry. Boston (1990) allows unobserved characteristics to allocate workers between segments but still finds wage differentials by race and gender. Gindling (1991) also draws a positive conclusion concerning the presence of segmentation between public and private sector employment and between the private formal and informal sectors. Schuld *et al.* (1994) investigate segmentation between men and women, modelling allocation to job level, and find that women are caught in a vicious circle of high turnover, limited on-the-job training and inferior jobs and careers.

3 STRUCTURAL CORRESPONDENCES

Use of cluster or factor analysis to identify labour market structures can be considered to provide a bridge between categoricism and a more developed understanding of the source of segmentation, one based on a correspondence between structures rather than between variables and structures. Cluster and factor analyses implicitly presume that the cumulative interaction of socioeconomic variables grinds out labour market structures which are statistically identified. Instead of relying upon one or more variables to stand as a proxy for structure or structural determinant, much of the literature presumes that labour market structures are the more or less passive reflex of other structures that need to be identified, whether statistically or a priori. This is most notable in the modern origins of SLM theory, in which dual labour markets are the consequence of the dual industrial structure. Such an approach can be adopted at the grandest level of theory or in the most concrete detail. For Tokman (1989), for example, labour market segmentation arises out of the structures of dependency between centre and periphery. Wallace *et al.* (1993) argue that wage differentials arise out of the structure of power that workers can exert over the system of production through disruption, either directly in their own employment or indirectly through potential impact on upstream sectors. In a more conventional vein, Smit (1995, 1996) suggests that different theories of differential wages reflect differences within industrial economics, whether industrial structure is taken as exogenous (as in the structure-conduct-performance paradigm) or not (more recent game-theoretic approaches to industrial structure). Residential structure and travel to work areas (TTWA), especially for women, are often taken as determinants of labour market structures, as in Scott (1992), McLafferty and Preston (1992) and Hanson and Pratt (1992), although there is considerable interaction with race, gender, technological factors and managerial strategies (especially where home working is concerned).

At the micro-level, Cobas *et al.* (1993) identify an ethnic economy, alongside core and periphery, within the United States, which modifies the process of labour market segmentation. Complementing LaMagdeleine's

(1986) work on the segmentation of work within the Catholic Church, Chaves (1991) finds shifting segmentation within the Protestant labour market depending on the separation between congregational and non-congregational duties. Belzer (1995) argues that deregulation led to a restructuring of the US road freight industry into one of full and less than full loads, only over the last of which was the Teamsters' Union able to retain bargaining power. Beggs (1995), correcting for human capital, hours worked and establishment size, investigates how the institutional environment around equal opportunities by gender and race affect wage inequality. Bagchisen (1995) examines the impact on occupational segmentation of the shifting sectoral composition of output between manufacturing and services, concluding that men continue to hold the better jobs in services whilst women are concentrated in low-level occupations within sectors with volatile product markets.

4 FROM PROCESS TO STRUCTURE

If factor and cluster analyses provide a link between categoricism and structural correspondences, sorting models can be interpreted as leading to an understanding of labour market structures as based upon the outcomes derived from associated socioeconomic *processes*, that is, activity through time. Thus, at the most elementary level, segmentation through endogenous sorting involves the assignation of workers to one segment or another. In this, there is a clear correspondence to the origins of SLM theory in ideas of *mobility* across primary and secondary sectors, and career paths within the primary sector. In other words, labour market structures are now a reflection of the processes that create them rather than simply the reflection of a corresponding structure.

This is one way of interpreting the rise of SLM theory within orthodox neoclassical economics. Efficiency-wages, higher than those at which the labour market would clear, are paid in order to attract higher-quality workers, to induce higher work effort and to worsen the consequences of being fired for poor work when it is occasionally monitored successfully. Internal labour markets arise out of the consequences of otherwise unduly expensive transactions costs. These all represent, somewhat weakly through the notions of asymmetric and imperfect information and problems of contract enforcement, the imperative of exercising control over the labour force in the process of production. As the factors involved will differ across industries, segmentation will occur, and wage differences will not merely reflect differences in human capital. Thus, Demekas (1990) views segmentation as arising out of any process that creates a primary sector of employment with above equilibrium wage and queuing for the rationed jobs. In addition, Dickens and Lang (1988a) also point to the potential for wages to benefit from 'rent-sharing' – anything that increases profitability over time unevenly is open to gains to the work-force, particularly in the presence of trade unions.[8] Consequently, high levels of capital-intensity, market concentration and unionisation are postulated to be correlated with higher levels of wages, not exclusively because of their structural influence but through the processes by which rewards from the process of productivity increase are distributed. Further, insider–outsider models reflect union power over the process of recruitment, and implicit contract theory anticipates wage bargaining over the process of the business cycle.[9]

An important characteristic of this new orthodoxy within SLM theory is that, whilst motivated by processes that recur and which are modelled, it leads to *equilibrium* outcomes which can be tested empirically in terms of wage differentials. Less formal models are, however, more open-ended. Morrison (1990) has drawn attention to the way in which attention to socioeconomic processes have become prominent in SLM theory. It is seen as a weakness, in diluting the focus on what are considered to be the two key concepts: barriers to career development and opposition to human capital theory. Thus, for segmentation:

> The most important distinction . . . is between the term used to describe the set of *all* processes which somehow lead to differentiation of the labour force and the more precise meanings present in the original theoretical formulation of the segmentation concept itself. This descriptive use of the term segmentation as a synonym for differentiation is an unfortunate development for it serves to blunt the potential analytical power of the concept.
>
> (Morrison 1990: 489; emphasis in original)

This is, however, to bemoan a much more general trend within SLM analysis in which description has displaced explanation.

Studies of career paths and recruitment, for example, tend to look for empirical evidence to support the processes of segmentation that they favour for attention. Anleu (1992) finds that women lawyers are differentially recruited to the less prestigious and worse-paid jobs, even correcting for a range of individual characteristics, and this in part reflects the type of employer and the type of legal work involved. For financial services tend to be located at a single place of employment which can be used to exploit the lesser labour market mobility of women. Rosenblum and Rosenblum (1990) highlight the division of the academic labour market into one which is internal and based on a firm career in research. This is to be contrasted to the casualised external market for temporary teachers, 'the gypsy scholars' who have been neglected in most research on academic labour markets and who have very limited chances to cross the divide and join their more 'cosmopolitan' colleagues. The latter set the criteria of entry and progress, often on a localised basis, putting them beyond the reach of the vast majority of those without permanent jobs – particularly in view of the increasing emphasis on research criteria over the years, as revealed by Finnegan (1993), for whom there have been a succession of academic cohorts over the post-war period.[10] Langton and Pfeffer (1994) have found, correcting for human capital, that the variation in academic salaries across various disciplines is greater the more there is mobility between jobs. The latter is also associated with greater wage differentials between men and women.

In commercial markets, management strategy in the light of technology, product and the work process have been prominent. For Natti (1990), part-time workers are more liable to be used in retailing in cut-price stores as opposed to those selling quality goods with a high level of service. Peck and Stone (1993), in the context of Japanese direct investment in the UK, demonstrate that the nature of the production process, whether a sophisticated engineering product or electronic assembly, has a major impact on the structuring, skilling and gendering of the work-force – there is no single form of Japanisation.[11] Keltner (1995) discovers differences in (internal) labour market segmentation in the US and the German banking systems because of the match between product mix, training and labour turnover, with Germany more committed to training its employees for longer-term employment and the provision of business services. Dymski (1995) sees banking as playing a different role – how redlining in the housing market structures access to finance, thereby influencing house prices and location of bank branches, as a source of economic activity perpetuates disadvantage where they are absent which spills over into the labour market.

Segmentation has also been linked to childbirth. McRae (1994) has examined how employers' policies on maternity leave affect the extent of return to work and the hours of work and whether return is to the same employer. Whilst enhanced benefits do have some effect, segmentation through other variables are considered to be more important, such as the availability of work, especially in close proximity. McCrate (1990) discovers a link between fertility and labour market participation in the opposite direction, with young black teenagers having a child in face of limited primary job opportunities and low wages and job security. On the other hand, Lehrer (1992) finds that the greater negative impact of fertility on female labour market participation for white as opposed to black women is less pronounced at higher levels of education.

One important process within the SLM literature has been migration and immigration, for it focuses upon the absorbtion of new workers into particular segments of the labour market. Not surprisingly, outcomes are dependent upon origins of migrants as well as the broader conditions that they confront and create in terms of sector of employment, ethnicity and residential location, a matter revisited below.[12] Consequently, Campbell *et al.* (1991), whilst observing the descriptive nature of much of the literature, argue that it is necessary to understand the specific and varied segmentation processes through which migrants are assigned to job structures, although common channelling into low-paying jobs with little exit mobility can be the experience of immigrants from very different backgrounds. For agricultural labour, Collins (1993) finds that which labour is used – seasonal migrant or local, male, female or child – depends upon the quality of the product to be harvested as well as the form of contracting by farmers to international markets.

For internal labour markets, emphasis can be placed upon management strategies as well as organisational or institutional factors (Bernard and Smith 1991). Miller (1992) provides a detailed discussion of how different factors affect the way in which workers are supervised, and hence internal labour markets structured, arguing that social factors, such as occupational status, as opposed to economic factors, such as skill and responsibility, are much more prominent in the supervision of women than of men. For external labour markets, Claussen *et al.* (1993) find that the unemployed are more likely to be sick and to take longer to recover from illness, thereby consolidating their disadvantage within labour markets.

5 HYBRID THEORY

So far, the more recent literature on segmentation has been examined separately for categoricism, for structural correspondences and for structures as the consequence of socioeconomic processes. Much of the literature combines these separate analytical components together to give rise to hybrid accounts. As Desmidt (1986: 399) puts it, 'labour market processes mirror the structural changes taking place at a certain time and at a certain place'. It is not clear whether structures and processes are being distinguished, for reference is made to a range of factors such as globalisation, mobility, recruiting, flexibility, etc. in order to examine internal, external and craft segments. Gimble (1991) argues that cultural processes have to be added to the role of institutions and technological forces. Pietrykowski (1995) studies the relationship between labour market segmentation and industrial location in the context of Henry Ford's own Fordist production, which, he argues, embodied both centralising and decentralising tendencies before post-Fordism had ever been invented. Inui (1993) postulates a correspondence between the education and labour market systems in the UK and Japan. For the UK, the lack of job opportunities in the youth labour market undermines the incentive for competitive achievement in school, whereas the reverse is the case in Japan, where 70 per cent–80 per cent of school-leavers obtain secure jobs, with recruitment based on school performance.[13] Rich (1995) posits a gender queuing theory (GQT) in which human capital theory provides the framework for individual choice (of workers and employers) but without the socio-historical context, DLM theory the socio-historical context but without the choice framework, and these are supplemented by power relations sex-typing. A particularly wide-ranging example of hybrid theory is provided by Rosenfeld (1992), who examines

how structures interact with resources to provide job 'opportunity structures', including consideration of internal labour markets, credentialism,
occupational segregation, work histories, etc.

One of the most common applications of hybrid SLM theory is by
geographers in focusing upon the interaction between spatial and residential
processes and structures and their correspondence to labour market structuring. Schreuder (1989) argues that labourers are conscious beings, not
just oriented around work resistance, so that labour markets are structured
by migration, the formation of cities, residential location and ethnicity.
Similarly, Peck (1989) argues that the labour market is not like any other
market, so that segmentation should be seen as the consequence of historical
tendencies which work themselves out in locally specific ways which cannot
be reduced to the simple parameters of TTWAs, for which women and
professionals tend to lie at the opposite extremes in terms of the distance
from work that they are prepared to accept. Peck (1992a) argues that the
(re)location of firms is dependent upon labour control strategies which
need to be addressed in the broad context of the political dynamics underlying local labour markets. Gentrification and social provision of housing
are studied for their impact upon labour market opportunities by Cameron
and Doling (1994). Hiebert (1995) establishes the connection between evolving occupational, residential and ethnic ties in Toronto in the 1930s.
Similar conclusions are drawn by Lee (1995) for the current Korean community in Los Angeles. Gilbert (1994) links the complexity of the restructuring
of third world cities to the segmentation of labour markets. Law *et al.* (1993)
examine how defence industries, now in decline, have interacted with their
location. For Bosman and Desmidt (1993), the formation of international
management centres for multinational corporation headquarters gives rise
to joint segmentation of both labour and housing markets.

From hybrid theory, it is but a short step to acknowledge that segmentation is not only the consequence of categorical variables, corresponding
structures and socioeconomic processes, but that it too has a feedback
effect. For Peck for example:[14]

> Local labor markets need not be assumed all to work in the same way. In
> particular, they may be segmented in locally specific ways in different
> places and as institutional structures evolve around (and subsequently
> change as well as being changed by) these locally specific structures.
>
> (Peck 1989: 53)

Similarly, in the context of homeworking, Peck (1992b: 676) suggests,
'industries and their labour processes both shape and are shaped by urban
labour markets'. For Hernes (1991), increasing segmentation of labour
markets has had political repercussions in terms of the representation of
labour's interests which in turn has affected labour market policy and,
hence, the processes of labour market segmentation.

6 CONCLUDING REMARKS

Reviewing the recent literature on radical SLM analysis demonstrates how it has relied upon categorical variables and correspondences between structures and processes to posit differentiation of labour market outcomes. In this respect, it has not moved far beyond its intellectual origins in DLM theory. In addition, there is a notable trend towards abandoning the grander theory previously associated with REG and DP and accepting the tenets of the orthodoxy in terms of concepts like human capital and efficiency-wages. DLM, with its internal labour markets, its dual industrial structure and its disadvantaged inner city black unemployed, already incorporated a hybrid account across variables, structures and processes. None the less, as with the earlier evolution to the Cambridge SLM school, a wider variety of theoretical elements and of empirical case studies has been accumulated. The preceding pages are, then, a testimony to one aspect of continuity in SLM analysis – the ever-expanding range of case studies, employing an equally broad set of explanatory factors and empirical applications. The scope runs over gender and race, from services to manufacturing, part-time and full-time work, management strategy and product market conditions, location and residence, technology and work organisation, fertility and migration, etc. Whatever change there has been, considerable analytical chaos persists, reflecting the diversity of approaches, variables and empirical material.

Most of the empirical work has been concerned with identifying and explaining segmentation in labour market outcomes. In this respect, orthodox neoclassical theory has claimed an advance over the past decade, as discussed in the introduction to this chapter. Labour market structures are taken as endogenous to the system and are explained on the basis of individual optimisation in the context of market imperfections. For labour market theory, the latter involve efficiency-wage, insider–outsider, implicit contract and more general screening models. These are also complemented by increasingly sophisticated econometrics in which human capital and other variables can be used not only to estimate differences in wage determination between the different labour market segments but also the boundaries between the segments themselves are open to estimation as a consequence of optimising choice by self-sorting agents, whether employers or employees.

As suggested earlier, irrespective of the validity of methodological individualism, such models can be considered to fall into the hybrid category. For they involve a complex interaction between variables (e.g. human capital), structures (between products and labour markets) and processes (recruitment and work effort). What is distinctive, however, about the orthodox approach – and it is a more general property of the vast majority of neoclassical and other orthodox economics – is that the various factors involved effectively neutralise one another, grinding out an equilibrium structure of labour markets and conditions within and between them.

In this light, the only potential for change is through an externally imposed shift in one or more exogenous parameters, as in comparative statics. Another way of interpreting this outcome of the theory is in terms of the excessively static nature of the understanding of reproduction that is involved. Essentially, although there is deviation from the idealised model of perfect competition, there is much in common with it methodologically, and not only in terms of individualistic optimisation. For in equilibrium, the forces or processes of competition, for example, are deemed to exhaust themselves by bringing about an efficient allocation and use of resources in production and, ultimately, to consumption across an economy whose structure has been reduced to the level of the individuals. This creates the analytical space for a theory of imperfect competition, as deviation from perfect competition for whatever reason, in which labour is inefficiently allocated and even unemployed, across an economy whose structures are no longer trivial. But the notion of the reproduction of those structures, and the understanding of the conditions that create and might transform them, remains highly underdeveloped. For all that happens is that a range of variables reflecting market imperfections are thrown together, whether unionisation, market concentration, access to finance, gender, race, etc., all serving as proxies for structures and/or market imperfections.

In other words, the new orthodoxy asks a particular question: Why might ('illegitimate') wage differentials or labour market structures persist *in equilibrium*? Quite apart from the question presupposing a particular answer – because of one or more ingenious notions of deviation from perfect competition – it necessarily precludes the rather more demanding question of why and how labour market structures and inequalities are created during the processes of socioeconomic change and development. For example, if we view competition as based upon the imperative to enhance profitability through productivity increase, this involving raising capital-intensity and the forging of productivity deals with organised workers, then a theory of wage differentials emerges which denies equilibrium as an outcome and in which structures and processes have a systemic relationship to one another. It is a relationship that can readily shift over time, be mediated by other (socioeconomic) factors, and which may or may not be reproduced depending upon commercial outcomes as well as managerial and trade union strategies, for example.

Such is the point of departure for SLM theory in the other social sciences, an approach that is illustrated admirably by the work of Kalleberg and Berg (1987). They posit the importance of six 'work structures' (Kalleberg and Berg 1987: 2): nation-states, industries, business organisations, occupations, classes and unions. These are, then, counterposed to four specific markets, those for finance, for different products, for labour, and for resources – although these are later complemented by a fifth market, that for political influence. They review earlier literature in which they argue that there has been inadequate treatment of none, one or more of the analytical structures that they have identified. Theoretically, they put forward three hypotheses: that there are structural forces that mutually interact; that the results give rise to socially and historically specific outcomes across the four markets; and that the structures generate processes which feed back upon them through the formation and intervention of interest groups.

There are certain problems with this account. Why are these six structures and four (or is it five?) markets privileged, especially as there is an admission that there are other structures and markets and that they are open to further disaggregation? Second, there is some ambiguity in the use of the terms since structural forces imply processes and, presumably, the pursuit of economic or other interests? Third, why are structures privileged causally, especially as they are reproduced, and possibly transformed, by the processes through which they interact with one another.

This last point is the one that is crucial to the further analysis that follows in the next chapter. Kalleberg and Berg can be considered to have established a dialectic between structures and processes, and between interest groups and socially and historically contingent outcomes. But have they done so in the most appropriate way? The answer can only be in the affirmative by accident. For, as suggested above, there are two arbitrary elements to their framework – the particular structures and other elements that they choose to highlight and the causal structure they attach to them. Why should structures take precedence over processes and interest groups? Significantly, the three central hypotheses are scarcely open to refutation and reflect more a way of organising an understanding of empirical material. In short, Kalleberg and Berg can be considered to have posed the right question – 'How do these various theoretical elements fit together?' – but not to have provided a correct or justified solution.

NOTES

1 See also Blackaby *et al.*:

> Dual labour market theory has recently been integrated into the mainstream of labour market theory and is no longer regarded as a fringe idea . . . Efficiency wage theory and insider-outsider theory are two recent theoretical innovations . . . They stand comfortably within the older more anecdotal tradition of a dual segmented labour market.
>
> (Blackaby *et al.* 1995: 37)

2 See also Chapter 4.
3 Thus:

> The radical analysis of labor markets begins with the 'political structure' of the enterprise. It may seem odd to think of firms as having a political structure. However, in the RPE analysis, social relationships are political if they involve conflicts of interests between parties that are resolved by the exercise of power.
>
> (Rebitzer 1993: 1396)

4 See also Rebitzer's conclusion:

> Moreover, as this review makes clear, the RPE conception of economic rela-
> tionships as political, remedial, and historically contingent has increasingly
> been incorporated into the mainstream of economic research. Over time, this
> process is likely to erode much of the distinction between RPE and the rest
> of the economics profession – *to the benefit of both.*
>
> (Rebitzer 1993: 1429–30; emphasis added)

For a defence, and mirror-image interpretation, of these developments in RPE,
see Reich (1993, 1995). He judges it to have influenced the orthodoxy rather
than vice versa, and to be valid in view of its influence over the current policy process in the United States. For a critique of Reich on methodological grounds, see
Hands (1995), and on political grounds, see McIntyre and Hillard (1995). For
another account of the silent revolution in labour economics as it embraces institutional factors, see Humphries and Rubery (1995b, 1995c).

5 See Connell (1987) for a critique of categoricism in the context of patriarchy. See
also Fine (1992) for a discussion.
6 For some caution over the use of the term ethnic (enclave) economy in the
context of labour market segmentation, see Light *et al.* (1994).
7 For emphasis on the importance of the role of the state in segmenting labour
markets, see Brosnan *et al.* (1995).
8 Although Morrison (1994) finds for Ecuador that inter-industry wage differentials are more explained by institutional differences, such as minimum wage
laws, than by availability of shared 'rents' within sectors.
9 See Smith *et al.* (1995) for a discussion of how labour market 'external flexibility'
(shifts in employment levels) has different implications for labour market segmentation in Sweden as opposed to Canada.
10 See also Fairweather (1995). Rosenblum and Rosenblum (1996) find that the
'external' market for non-tenured academics is prevalent and expanding, especially for women but that it does form the most common entry point for the
'internal', tenure track jobs for which 20 per cent or so of the external market
eventually succeed even if at an older age over time.
11 See also Patchell and Hayter (1995).
12 See Schreuder (1989). See also Massey *et al.* (1994) for international and Gordon
(1995) for internal migration.
13 See also Sakamoto and Powers (1995).
14 See also Kubin and Steiner (1992: 295), for whom: 'Labour market performance
is not an isolated circumstance but is firmly embedded in a regional feedback process between structure, conduct, and performance.'

7 Towards a Marxist alternative

1 INTRODUCTION

From a Marxist perspective, the fundamental division within the economy is between capital and labour. In particular, the class relations of production are such that the ownership of capital is 'monopolised' by the capitalist class and labour can only gain access to a livelihood through the sale of the capacity to work, through entering the labour market. In these bald terms, such propositions are clearly empirically false. Many non-capitalists own means of production. Workers, and their family members, can survive, however pitifully, without working, quite apart from the self-employed, who appear to fall neither into the category of capital nor labour.

Consequently, the division between capital and labour as the central relationship or structure should not be understood as an exhaustive statement. Rather, it lies at the core of the capitalist economy in two different senses. First, it is causally of the highest priority. Second, as a corollary, those economic relations and structures that fall outside the simple capital–labour dichotomy will, none the less, be heavily conditioned by it in ways which have to be examined. This point will be taken up later in greater detail in the context of what will be termed 'marooning'. But it can only be done once the implications of the core capital–labour relationship have been explored. Here, a number of key features need to be examined, together with their implications for labour market segmentation. In later sections, this is taken further by drawing on a critical discussion of two different approaches to the more detailed determination of the value of labour-power. As is usual, this is more positively interpreted in terms of two different aspects, both as a norm of consumption and as a mode of social reproduction of the class of labour, with the impact of the first of these differentiated by the items of consumption involved, and the second understood as something much more than an economic effect (such as merely the payment of a wage within the labour market). This is, then, followed by a discussion of 'marooning' – how to account for those labour market structures that fall outside those directly defined by the 'standard' capital–labour relations.

Finally, these separate elements of analysis are brought together to suggest how labour market structuring should be understood.

The argument is that labour market structures are differentiated from one another by the complex interaction of the underlying processes and structures that have previously been identified. This is, however, not a simple division of the labour market in terms of occupation of jobs and wages and conditions. Different labour market segments are not only separated from one another but are structured differently from one another. As such, structuring cannot be determined in advance, since it is contingent upon how the various causal factors interact with one another. Labour market segments have to be identified analytically in terms of an integral structure across these factors rather than directly in terms of empirical outcomes. For otherwise, as seen in the earlier account of the SLM literature, the account of labour market segmentation tends to become both descriptive and, where it is not, analytically and tautologously self-supporting as middle-range concepts directly mirror select descriptive material.

2 CAPITALIST CLASS RELATIONS AND ECONOMIC STRUCTURES AND PROCESSES[1]

The discussion commences with three fundamental arguments. First, consider that, whilst the capitalist economy depends upon a complex set of exchange relations, a diverse set of buyers and sellers across a multitude of markets, the key exchange is that between capital as a whole and labour as a whole. Second, within the capitalist economy, there is a fundamental structural distinction between the sphere of production, where commodities are created, and the sphere of exchange through which they are bought and sold and distributed either for further use in production or for final consumption. Third, and Marx considered this to be one of his most important insights, labour as such is not bought and sold in this exchange across the labour market. Rather, capital purchases the capacity to work, or 'labour-power', as Marx termed it. Irrespective of how this labour-power is purchased (by salaries, time or piece rates, etc.) and when it is paid in practice, the exchange between capital and labour must *precede* production. The production process itself generates surplus value, a defining characteristic of capitalism, through the extent to which labour contributes a quantity of labour-time over and above the value that has been paid for the sale of the commodity labour-power.

It follows that the value of labour-power, as the terms of exchange between capital and labour taken as a whole is a crucially important analytical category. It will be examined below in greater detail. Indeed, one way of looking at Volume I of *Capital* is that it is completely uninterested in the world of exchange once the bargain has been struck between capital and labour as a whole. Its focus is upon the world of production, explaining how it is that capitalism sets about generating the surplus value upon which it depends for its profits, interest and rents.

It is as if we have been transported to Mars and, looking down on capitalist Earth, the multiplicity of exchange relations are indistinct even though the broad outlines of the capital–labour relationship are sharply defined and reveal how capital is able to generate and appropriate a surplus. Such are the simple economic structures and relations through which capital and labour confront one another. But they do not remain static, since capital seeks to expand the surplus value that it creates. How is this done and with what implications for differentiation within the work-force and hence the potential to create labour market structures?

First, since capitalist production is not simply a technical relationship between inputs and outputs but requires command over the labourers to ensure that capacity to work is realised in practice, there is a requirement for the 'labour' of supervision. Although a task of the functioning capitalist, supervision might become the specialised duty or part of the duties of a paid employee. The same applies to other capitalist functions such as marketing, accounting, etc.

Second, the allocation of work depends upon the allocation of workers across the various sectors of the economy. Workers are differentiated by the distinction between the sectors in which they work as well as by the distinctions within their sector or work. The overall division of labour, that is, the allocation of tasks to workers, is made up of two broad components. One is the *social* division of labour demarcated by the market as workers belong to different sectors which can only interact with one another through exchange relations. The other might be termed the *internal* division of labour, how tasks are allocated within the production process.

Marx argues that the interaction between these two forms of the division of labour is both complex and indeterminate and not reducible by a technological imperative alone to the nature of the tasks themselves. Either previously separate sectors of the economy might be brought together into a single sector so that the social division of labour is internalised (as in the classic Ford automobile factory) or an integral production process is fragmented into a number of constituent but separate trades (as in dependence on bought-out components previously provided in-house). Whilst orthodox neoclassical economic theory considers these issues in terms of economies of scale and scope and the relative transactions costs through the market or internally, Marx situated the tensions between the internal and social divisions of labour in the much broader context of the competitive struggle between accumulating capitals. Thus, for example, vertical as well as horizontal integration can be pursued in order to guarantee markets either up or down stream, quite apart from any technical advantages that may or may not accrue through such integration. Similarly, vertical disintegration, as in contracting-out, as has been frequently emphasised recently in the context of flexibility, can reduce a firm's capital requirements and exert competitive pressure on fragmented suppliers.

Third, closely related to, but distinct from the division of labour within and between firms, is the division of labour between workers within the firm. Again, two opposing tendencies can be observed. On the one hand, the production process can be divided into an ever-finer set of distinct tasks to which individual workers are assigned. They become specialised in a single task or so, as a consequence of which they are generally thought of as deskilled, certainly relative to the production process as a whole. On the other hand, workers may be required to undertake a variety of tasks simultaneously or in sequence, thereby increasing the intensity of labour and the range of skills involved. This might be thought of, then, as skill-enhancing. The two processes together differentiate the place of workers within the production process.

So far, the discussion has primarily ranged over the consequences of viewing the capitalist production process as one requiring the production of surplus value, although some attention has been given to how this involves competition between capitals and the attempt to expand the surplus value generated. For the latter, Marx focused upon two broad analytical categories, absolute and relative surplus value, although he examined how they were realised in practice in considerable empirical detail. By absolute surplus value is meant increasing the amount of work that is done in return for the exchange for the value of labour-power. The classic form taken by the production of absolute surplus value is the lengthening of the working day, but it can also involve greater intensity of work within a given length of working day or reducing in the work process. In addition, given that the value of labour-power constitutes the means by which the class of labour reproduces itself, absolute surplus value can also be considered to arise when working time is extended to other household members. The issue is how much labour-time is provided by labour as a whole in return for the means of livelihood, irrespective of who may be contributing that labour – male or female adults or even children.[2]

The production of relative surplus value depends upon increasing productivity, either directly or indirectly (through the inputs they use), in the wage goods industries. By this means, the same material goods that make up the means of working-class consumption can be supplied at a lower level of expenditure of labour-time so that the value of labour-power can be reduced and surplus value increased, to the extent that the levels of working-class consumption remain the same. What is crucial in Marx's theory is the focus upon the systematic sources of productivity increase that can be realised through the accumulation of capital. In particular, as commodities are the consequence of the working up of raw materials into output, productivity increase is associated with the transformation of an increasing mass of raw materials into output by a given amount of labour. One of the most important means through which this can be achieved is through the introduction of ever more sophisticated machinery – displacing the power and tasks of the labourer by a mechanical process which itself breaks production down into its separate constituent parts, only to recombine them into a smooth and fast system for generating output.

A fourth differentiation between workers, then, that follows from how capitalist production itself is organised and developed, corresponds to the different ways and pace with which machinery is adopted both within and across sectors. As is apparent, this factor modifies and interacts with others. The pace of machinery, for example, does potentially serve as a supervisor of the pace of work, reducing the need for the labour of supervision. Machinery has the potential to enhance both the economies of scale and the economies of scope, although the two can also conflict with one another. In any case, the result is a further intensifying of the indeterminacy in the tension between the social and internal divisions of labour. Machinery also intensifies the division and integration of the production process, deskilling some to the status of machine-minders, but equally reskilling those who are responsible for the machines, 'minding' their increasingly complex functioning.

Fifth, a consequence of large-scale production is the increasingly cooperative nature of work in which the coordination and common effort of different workers becomes essential. This is a further source of differentiation through the formation of what Marx terms the 'collective labourer'. Workers belong to more or less closely and permanently linked groups rather than serving as free-floating individuals.

The preceding five factors all derive from considering the impact of capitalist production upon differentiation of the work-force. There are, however, further implications from how capital accumulation proceeds as a whole. In particular, Marx argued that this both creates and depends upon a reserve army of labour, a shifting pool of unemployed. On the one hand, as capital is reorganised with larger-scale, more productive capitals displacing their less effective rivals and, as the economy goes through cyclical movements, workers are added to the reserve army. On the other hand, those capitals that do succeed and expand need to draw upon the reserve army for their work-force to grow. Further, for those in unemployment, there is the potential for them to be used as a source of cheap wage labour, prolonging the viability of less efficient producers. In other words, the same processes that promote employment in large-scale efficient capital also support its antithesis in small-scale, sweated labour, even where the two do compete in the same markets for output.

The earlier discussion examines how differentiation amongst the work-force can be generated by the development of capitalist production. What it does not address, with the exception of analysis around the reserve army of labour, is whether this leads to differences in labour market outcomes in terms of wages and conditions and whether particular sections of the population are confined to particular sorts of jobs – nor how such differences might be determined. In short, there is a distinct parallel to the notion of the demand-side in radical SLM theory in terms of the creation of a hierarchy of jobs, although the various explanatory factors are not jumbled together simultaneously to generate, along with the supply-side, labour market segmentation and corresponding wages and conditions.

The reason why the supply-side, as it were, is missing here is because the exchange between capital and labour has remained confined to the aggregate level for which differentiation of the work-force, other than in production alone, is set aside. The value of labour-power, however, can be examined at a more developed level of complexity in two different aspects, each of which can be associated with differentiation of the work-force.

3 THE VALUE OF LABOUR POWER AS A NORM OF CONSUMPTION

It has been standard to understand the value of labour-power as a customary or average standard of living which is, in turn, often associated, especially in formal models, with a vector of consumer goods. Consequently, the value of labour-power can be interpreted as the labour-time required to produce this fixed bundle of goods. This, however, leaves open a number of questions. First, how is this normal consumption bundle determined? Second, outside a world of equilibrium and comparative statics, how does the consumption bundle change in response to changing socioeconomic conditions – and how quickly? This is, in part, a question of timing, but also one of analytical structure. Relative to the movement of other variables, how long can we keep the consumption bundle constant, especially whilst other, possibly influential, factors are changing?[3] Third, then, as a particular combination of the first two questions, given the productivity increase associated with the production of relative surplus value, is it simply the bundle of consumption goods that remains the same and the labour-time required to produce it that decreases (to the benefit of surplus value) or, at the other extreme, do the benefits of the increase in productivity accrue entirely to workers in the form of an expanded level of consumption?

Previously, interest in these questions has primarily been implicit and indirect through concern with Marx's theory of the law of the tendency of the rate of profit to fall. Those wishing to deny the law[4] argue that the rate of profit cannot fall for a fixed consumption bundle and, consequently, it does so only in response to the prior and exogenous redistribution that follows from wage increases that outstrip productivity increases. Others argue that this is an overmechanical interpretation of the law that overlooks its focus upon the tensions or contradictions that derive from the accumulation of capital.[5]

These differences over Marx's theory of crisis are not of concern here except in so far as they provide a point of departure for understanding the role of consumption in determining the value of labour-power. This is so in two different respects. First, the consumption aspect of the value of labour-power has been perceived simply as an average level of consumption across the working class. This is exceptionally simplistic, even relative to the oft-repeated phrase in which reference is made to the 'moral and historical' elements in consumption. Instead, in advanced capitalist countries, the standard of consumption varies, often systematically, across different sections of the population. For some items of consumption, such as a TV set or a washing machine, more or less every household is liable to be able to include them as typical items of consumption; for other items, incidence of consumption rises more frequently with income; for others, generally considered inferior, consumption can even decline with income. Accordingly, the role of consumption within the value of labour-power needs to be interpreted in a much more sophisticated way than as an average across the working population. Rather, it constitutes *systematic* patterns of consumption, those which may vary not only with income but also with a range of other socioeconomic variables such as age, region, household composition, etc.[6]

The second consumption aspect concerning the value of labour-power follows on immediately from the first. It is that the patterns of consumption, or consumption norms, suggested in the previous paragraph will be established and evolve differently from one commodity to the another. This is so for a number of different reasons. The pace of productivity increase across commodities will differ, as will the respective shares of the benefits taken by labour as opposed to capital. More important, such economic changes alone do not determine consumption norms. Rather, as has been argued elsewhere,[7] consumption norms are not only determined differently for each commodity but are dependent upon what has been termed the system of provision for these commodities – the separate but integral chain of activities that unites production to consumption, including the reproduction of the material culture or ideology attached to commodities. For example, the ways in which housing and food are provided and enter into (working-class) consumption are very different from one another.

Thus, the approach adopted here to the consumption aspect of the value of labour-power differs from those taken previously, even relative to what is otherwise a range of very different theoretical stances. The value of labour-power is distributed differentially but systematically across the work-force. The nature of that distribution, and how it is determined, varies from one commodity or group of commodities to another. Finally, the determinants of the value of labour-power in the consumption aspect are not reducible to economic factors alone, and certainly not to a simplistic trade-off between workers and capitalists of the benefits of productivity increase – although this is necessarily an *ex post* outcome in the form of the newly established value of labour-power from which the accumulation process is renewed.

Methodologically, the approach to consumption suggested here has been dubbed 'vertical', since it emphasises distinctions between the various

separate items of consumption in and of themselves and how they are determined by the structure of activities and socioeconomic relations to which
they are attached. The notion of vertical contrasts to the more common
'horizontal' approach to consumption in which, usually drawn from
within the confines of a particular social science discipline, one or more
factors are employed to determine consumption across a wide range of commodities – as in neoclassical economics and utility-maximisation or differentiation and emulation in stratification theory, for example. In many ways,
traditional treatments[8] of the (consumption aspect of the) value of
labour-power have conformed to the horizontal approach, reducing the
issue to the quantity of labour-time, undifferentiated across commodity
and consumer, that is required to produce a given wage bundle.

What are the implications of these considerations for labour market differentiation? The standard approach, even within Marxist economics and its
value theory, is to view differences in consumption as the simple outcome of
differences in money rewards as previously determined by labour market
outcomes. Workers go for as much cash as they can get and, having got
it, spend it in ways that do not have to be examined. In contrast, the argument here is that different items of consumption will enter to a greater or
lesser extent into the consumption patterns of the various sections of the
work-force, and this will be reflected in pay and other differentials in conditions of work. Such considerations can be perceived to have their analogue
in 'supply-side' of radical SLM theory. For, in less abstract terms than those
just employed, consumption norms are, for different sections of the
work-force, closely associated with race, gender and other socioeconomic
characteristics.

It would be of the greatest convenience, analytically and illustratively, if
these relatively abstract propositions concerning the relationship between
the consumption aspect of the value of labour-power and labour market
segmentation could be understood as an immediate translation from differentiation in consumption, however explained, to labour market differentiation and even structures or segments. This can, however, only occur by way
of exception, although these can be significant and telling. The mode of
payment of agricultural and occasionally other workers can be linked to
consumption in kind or other conditions such as housing provision. The
same can apply to other sorts of workers much more generally in the
form of fringe benefits in which, for example, car provision might have
originated as a necessary item for work itself for some occupations, only
to be extended to other workers, for whom it is not a job pre-requisite,
simply by virtue of their being classified as belonging to a similar grade or
strata.

In general, however, the relationship between the socioeconomic construction of consumption norms and labour market structuring is not so
direct. This is so for a number of reasons, already covered above, but
which warrant being made explicit and which form the basis for adequately

incorporating this aspect into any labour market analysis. First, the way in which consumption norms enter into labour market structuring will vary from one commodity or commodity group to another – the level and mode of formation of the 'moral and historical element' in the value of labour-power differs across the constituent consumption goods as well as across the different sections of the work-force. Second, the role of consumption in forming the value of labour-power cannot be reduced to economic factors alone – as if it were simply a matter of the sharing of productivity increases between capital and labour. Certainly, how productivity is generated is an important determinant of broader economic outcomes but even these are conditioned, especially in the context of consumption norms, by the material culture or ideology and non-economic practices attached to consumption itself. Third, these factors in the determination of consumption norms and in the structuring of labour markets do not act in isolation from the other determinants but interact with them in a complex and not a predetermined fashion. As is apparent, for example, from the review of the SLM literature in Chapters 5 and 6, transport, housing and education can have a significant impact on the workings and structuring of labour markets, quite apart from their role in the provision of items of consumption themselves. The same is true, if less apparent, of privately provided consumption goods – as wage levels need to accommodate norms of consumption with complex connections between such differentiation in consumption and across labour markets.

The distinctive position being offered here can be clarified by reference to the more common methods of dealing with the issues involved. In economics, for example, it is usual to discuss wages and wage differentials by reference to the real wage, often denominated as w/p where w denotes the money wage and p a composite of the prices of consumption goods. For analytical convenience, this glosses over a number of important aspects. First, the wage bargain is much more than the payment of a money wage, although this may be central. It also involves a range of other conditions of work, some involving fringe benefits (such as holiday pay), which can be easily translated into their monetary equivalent, and others which cannot be so readily monetarised (conditions governing sick or compassionate leave).

Rightly or wrongly, treating the real wage as w/p in this way has the effect of treating these conditions, other than payments themselves, as peripheral. However, casual observation suggests that variations in such conditions, as well as money wages themselves, are indicative and even constructive of differences between labour market segments. The part-time and casualised do not have pension schemes and maternity leave. Nor, significantly, did the majority even of the most privileged work-force before the most recent period of welfare capitalism. It follows that the processes that determine the 'w' component of the real wage are historical, range across socio-economic variables (as in pensions, holiday entitlements, etc.), and differentiate the work-force. These factors are significant over and above the differentiation that arises out of and through the purer effects associated with shifting and uneven monetary rewards within the wage or salary packet itself.[9]

Nor is this simply a matter of the collection together of a number of independent factors determining the ingredients of consumption with the latter becoming much like a dog's dinner which is represented by the monetary and other components of the real wage. For the separate aspects interact with one another as is transparent over long periods or rapid periods of change. Consider, for example, the emergence in the UK of privatised schemes in what were primarily areas of public provision as in pensions and health-care. The effect has not simply been for the private to substitute for public provision but for wages of professionals to incorporate the cost of private provision whereas this has not been so for those at the lower ends of the labour market. As a result, the UK has witnessed a widening dispersion of wages over the past 20 years, although the uneven privatisation of various payments does not constitute the sole explanatory factor.[10] In short, if labour market differentiation is simply seen in terms of differences in w as the sources of differences in w/p, then both the substance and the source or the processes of differentiation will be neglected.

Second, by the same token but possibly even more easily and frequently overlooked, the treatment of p as composite in the real wage, w/p, necessarily obliterates the distinct role played by different wage goods in the formation of real wages. Two different aspects are involved, in parallel with the previous discussion of the 'w' aspect. On the one hand, every wage good is reduced to a monetary equivalent. All that matters is how much it costs, thereby setting aside how it enters into working-class consumption. On the other hand, and by way of corollary, each wage good apparently enters into consumption in exactly the same way as any other.

Recall that this discussion, in the context of the value of labour-power, is concerned initially with the way in which the moral and historical content of consumption is determined and, then, with the corresponding relationship with labour market segmentation. Although such considerations have been marginalised in the literature, they have not been neglected altogether. For example, it is commonplace to argue that increased productivity leads to the sharing of a firm's additional profits between capital and labour. Further, the implied wage increases can be passed on to workers in other firms or sectors by comparability whether to maintain differentials or not. Such processes can even be institutionalised in productivity deals.

The examples given here are all at one extreme in which, as is usual in the literature, the process of wage determination is understood in monetary terms alone as a central feature of the wage system. However, as is implicit in the notion of a given vector of consumption goods making up the wage, the latter can be treated as if it were a payment in kind. Those who work in a chocolate factory might be expected to incorporate an element of chocolate consumption in their wage, which might even expand with productivity. The chocolates might be for own consumption or for sale, as in more realistic payments in kind, such as coal allowances or agricultural goods. Traditionally, professionals in the financial services are the beneficiaries of cheap loans for house purchases. At a more general level, the notion of a family wage is geared towards the monetary equivalent required to satisfy the consumption norms of a working father with dependent wife and children.

Now each of the preceding examples can only reveal the sorts of processes by which differentiation in consumption might be attached to the labour market. Consider the home loans in more detail. The potential for privilege does not tell us which sections of the work-force will be included as beneficiaries and which will be excluded. We cannot infer the level of subsidy, its proportion of the wage nor how it varies with the commercial fortunes of the individual firm or the financial sector as a whole. Nor can we determine in abstract whether this from of reward will establish standards for consumption norms in housing, reflect those established by others or some combination of the two. More generally, wages can be differentiated leading to distinct but shifting patterns of consumption, for different as well as for the same levels of remuneration since those with the same money do not have to consume the same. Further, the shifting differentiation in consumption can lead to differentiation in wages as these are consolidated within the labour market. As previously emphasised, the processes of establishing consumption norms will differ across both consumption goods and sections of the work-force, and the source of such differences will not be confined to narrowly defined economic processes alone. The last point follows from the consumption aspect of the value of labour-power being tied to social reproduction, as is taken up in the next section.

Paradoxically, the form in which these arguments have been most readily accepted is one in which the required attention to detail, in labour market or consumption goods, has been set aside. The notion of Fordism as a phase of capitalism is readily associated with a link between high-productivity, low-cost, mass production and consumption. The idea is that, as factory techniques produce cheap, uniform commodities, so workers are sufficiently well-rewarded to be able to purchase them (with the added systemic function of sustaining aggregate demand for ever-growing capitalist production). The general theoretical and empirical veracity of this account (see Chapter 4) is not of concern so much as the issue of the uniformity of the argument for which the term Fordism is a particularly apt cliché. Is the argument that, as mass production hits the car industry, all workers suddenly become car owners in parallel to the chocolate factory example suggested earlier? The answer is in the negative even if, over a period of time, car ownership becomes a standard item of consumption. Rather the process by which cars enter as part of a consumption norm – the moral and historical element – differs across the work-force and will itself differentiate the work-force in a way that is potentially distinct from other commodities.

Some care needs to be taken in situating these arguments appropriately. The point is not to set aside the economic considerations underlying segmentation that were presented in earlier sections, nor those processes that tend to even out or eliminate differentials, through labour market competition or mobility, once they are established. Only in an equilibrium approach, and its corresponding methodology, are such tendencies seen not only as primary but also as exclusive of other influences over time.

Further, putting the same point in a different way, the capitalist mode of production does incorporate at its core the differentiation of labour market segments through the expression of wages in monetary equivalent. For to pursue a *reductio ad absurdum*, for example, in which wages are entirely paid in kind or surplus was divided in physical terms, as in sharecropping, this would essentially preclude the presence of capitalism altogether. However, the presence of mixed forms of payments, especially where in kind not readily convertible to money, is only a direct if relatively rare example of the processes of wage differentiation through consumption. As argued, how goods enter into consumption as much as the economic processes by which their values are determined – the two separate aspects determining the value of labour-power – is a central, if at times indirect, determinant of labour market structures.

4 SOCIAL REPRODUCTION AND THE VALUE OF LABOUR POWER: FALSE BEGINNINGS

In the previous section, it has been argued that the value of labour-power from its consumption aspect needs to be disaggregated into its constituent components that make up the standard of living. By doing so, a further link can be forged with the differentiation of the work-force as consumption norms are systematically, if unevenly, distributed across the population. Such an approach moves beyond the simple treatment of the value of labour-power as a quantum of labour-time corresponding to the value of a fixed, or even shifting, bundle of consumption goods. However, whilst a more complex understanding of what constitutes the consumption aspect of the value of labour-power is adopted, it does remain wedded to the idea of the value of labour-power as the labour-time of production of differentiated consumption. In this respect, it does not break with the traditional, if simpler, concept of the consumption aspect of the value of labour-power. In short, the focus is upon value as labour-time and, as such, it does not set labour-power as a commodity apart from other commodities. We might, for example, consider the determinants of the value of constant capital, of the raw materials and wear and tear of fixed capital in the production process. This will also vary across and within sectors in more or less systematic ways.

There is, however, a difference between labour-power and other commodities, in that it is not labour-power itself which is produced or reproduced by the labour-time required to provide consumption norms. This is only the case from the direct perspective of the capitalist paying-out value, 'variable capital', in Marx's terminology, to hire the labourer. But the value of labour-power, as such, only provides one necessary condition for the reproduction of the labourer – the payment of the wage. In principle, this secures, at least in part, the material reproduction of the work-force through the consumption that it allows. But even this primarily takes place outside the direct control of the capitalist employer in social relations which are separate, if not detached, from the accumulation and circulation of capital. In short, even if the value of labour-power does support the reproduction of the labourer, there are other social relations which are essential for this to occur which are not directly or primarily economic – those through civil society, the state and the household. In a common terminology, the value of labour-power is attached to the *social reproduction* of the work-force.

Further, there is an immediate connection between social reproduction and segmented labour markets once it is acknowledged that social reproduction can itself differentiate the work-force or the population more generally. One way in which labour has been rendered heterogeneous, and hence segmented, is to differentiate it by the skills with which it is reproduced. In this, there has been a Marxist literature treating skilled labour as something that is produced by the allocation to it of teaching or training labour, which itself may well be exploited.[11]

The standard method has been to modify the Sraffian or input–output theory of inputs, outputs and prices to incorporate a separate skill-creating sector. As Fine and Harris (1979) have observed, this involves a substantial degree of theoretical anarchy in so far as the production of skills is falsely understood as a form of commodity production that is identical in all but its specific type of output to other (capitalist) commodity production. It is simply a question of relating inputs to outputs with the appropriate prices attached. But, certainly as part of the state welfare system, it is immediately transparent that the conditions under which skills are produced diverge dramatically from those of the factory. It is as if the distinction between economic reproduction (by capital) and social reproduction (by capitalism) are all but formally equivalent.

This understanding of skill derives from the imposition of a Sraffian analysis of commodity production onto economic and social relations which are not commodity production, except in the sense of creating the special commodity labour-power.[12] Such a procedure leads to a close parallel with the analysis of skill associated with neoclassical economics, namely, human capital theory. This is hardly surprising, for Fine (1980) has argued that the Sraffian model can be interpreted as a reconstruction of neoclassical production theory[13] – the supply-side, with the demand theory of neoclassical economics to close the model replaced by distributional conflict.[14]

In this light, as will be seen below, the Sraffian model becomes one of determining prices according to a discounted stream of labour costs. If the latter also include training costs, so we have yielded the analytical basis for orthodox human capital theory, in which individual educational investment takes place according to whether it accrues a rate of return greater than the rate of interest or not. Whilst the Sraffian version, with its emphasis on class-based distributional struggle, might doubt the validity of equal and uniform access to (human) capital markets, this is itself a key empirical focus for the orthodoxy – to see whether there are equal rates of return to the investment of human capital and, where there are not because of market imperfections, whether there is a basis for segmented and inequitable and inefficient labour markets.

In short, this approach to skill as a factor in SLM theory depends upon a false extrapolation of the market to non-market relations as the basis for segmentation. It cannot otherwise provide an explanation for segmentation in the separate and distinct nature of social reproduction. The mirror image to this approach to skilled labour is to deny the importance of social reproduction in generating skills and to locate the source of labour market segmentation purely within the processes of social reproduction. Thus, in the work of Bowles and Gintis, the analysis of heterogeneous labour involves a complete rejection of human capital theory. Based on their work, *Schooling in Capitalist America* (1976), it is argued not only that returns to skills are unequally compensated according to socioeconomic background, but also that skill differences and education's contribution to them are exaggerated. Rather, skill differences are socially constructed, or *reproduced*, in conformity with such social relations as sexism and racism, underpinning and rationalising the inferior position that certain sections of the working class occupy in heterogeneous labour markets.

Before examining their theory of heterogeneous labour markets in detail, it is worth considering their views on the labour theory of value more generally. For, ironically in view of its use in the previous account of skilled labour, they first of all fully embrace the Sraffian system for its logical consistency but consider that it is too economistic. Accordingly, they seek a synthesis with the outlook of E.P. Thompson (1979) that *Capital* is unable to comprehend capitalism because it isolates the science of the economy as a separate region for study:

> The Sraffian school has thrown down the gauntlet: justify the need for a concept of 'value as distinct from' price in understanding the dynamics of price and profit. Thompson, by contrast, queries how *any* analysis of price and profit abstracting from class practices can comprehend the dynamics of the capitalist system.
>
> (Bowles and Gintis 1981a: 2; emphasis in original)

There then follows a rejection of the notion of labour-power as a commodity – although, relative to Marx's own work, this is repetitive in part of his recognition of the special nature of labour-power and the wage system. Drawing from the Sraffian tradition, a *labour* theory of value is seen as no more justified than a peanut or energy theory of value. Drawing from Thompson, the labour theory of value is perceived to strip away the social character of production by neglecting the role of the family and the state (ibid.). In addition, it is seen as necessary to open up analysis of production itself for the labour theory of value 'presents the capitalist production process as a technologically determined black box, the companion formulation labor-power as a commodity – presents the family as a black box' (ibid.: 17).

Bowles and Gintis's contribution raises two issues initially. First, to what extent do they adequately represent Marx's theory of value, rather than construct a false opponent, and, second, how valid are their criticisms? It is not the intention here to deal with the latter at length,[15] for they are already in value theory the subject of extensive and continuing debate, although we do observe, again with some irony, that the insistence on the social and non-technical nature of production relations has always been the basis on which the Sraffian system has been criticised by supporters of value theory. Hence the need for Sraffa with a human face or, more exactly, the benefits of E.P. Thompson's critique so that in place of Marx's 'infatuated' and 'grand dialectical reason', we are offered the following suggestion by way of conclusion that:[16] 'Our representation of labor as an ensemble of appropriative, political, cultural and distributive practices better captures the essence of the labor theory of value' (ibid.: 17).

These insights are built upon in practice in Bowles and Gintis' (1977) theory of heterogeneous (segmented) labour markets. Here it is argued that a theory of value must go beyond technical and market structures to confront other social structures that recognise the *unequal* exploitation of the labour force in its separate segments. In formal terms, these grand intentions are reduced to a simple generalisation of the Sraffian model in which different sections of the work-force are paid a different wage. Algebraically, where p is the vector of prices, A the input matrix for unit outputs, r is the rate of profit, l_1 and l_2 the labour inputs in two labour segments with corresponding wage rates, w_1 and w_2, respectively, this is equivalent for two labour segments to a price equation of the form:

$$pA(1 + r) + w_1 l_1 + w_2 l_2 = p$$

The Sraffian formulation of their theory, as we have seen, is derived from two sources. One is direct in so far as Marx's treatment of prices and profits 'is a theoretical casualty of modern treatments of the traditional "transformation problem"' (Bowles and Gintis 1977: 183).[17] The other follows from the social content of their analysis, for which it is claimed by Bowles and Gintis in response to Morishima (1978) that:

In fact, an input-output matrix embodies the totality of social relationships – including class struggle inside and outside the firm, as well as the forces relating to market dynamics and the accumulation process – in terms of which the gross translation of economic inputs to outputs is determined.

(Bowles and Gintis 1978: 313)

This is, of course, an enormous burden for a simple matrix, A in the equation above, to carry. It is remarkable that from a critique of value theory for economism and lack of dynamics, Bowles and Gintis should have proposed an alternative that is the epitome both of static equilibrium theory and of an ahistorical, asocial notion of production, namely, the fixed coefficients of an input–output matrix.

Indeed, the only concession made to the totality of social relationships is the insistence on labour market segmentation and unequal rates of exploitation, whereby the totality and complexity of the economy, and society more generally, are collapsed into a matrix of coefficients and a set of wage differentials. Also necessarily involved are the arbitrary divisions to be made between and within segments of the labour force. Whilst sex and race might appear to be model divisions of the work-force, what is to prevent a much finer division into many more or any number of segments, including nations and regions, for example, (and sex and race themselves overlap)? Clearly, even within the model of heterogeneous labour markets, an assumption of homogeneity must be made *within* the labour segments, and no justification is given for this.

This absence is closely related to the collapse of economy and society into the input–output matrix described earlier. For within Bowles and Gintis's model, prices become a sum of discounted wage costs, as in the less general Sraffian model of homogeneous labour, incurred across the labour segments:

$$p = (w_1 l_1 + w_2 l_2)(I - \{1 + r\}A)^{-1}$$

Hence:

$$p = (w_1 l_1 + w_2 l_2)(I + \{1 + r\}A + \{1 + r\}^2 A^2 + \ldots)$$

What this also involves is the expenditure of labour of both segments to produce wage goods for each set of workers. Without establishing some equivalence, then, between these different types of labour, it becomes impossible to establish rates of exploitation for the different segments, for whilst workers only perform labour within their own segment, they consume from the products of others. Bowles and Gintis (1981b: 286) freely confess both the absence of such conversion ratios and the lack of necessity for them. This is despite the claim that their model reveals that 'while all types of labour are exploited *vis-à-vis* the capitalist, some workers are in effect "exploiters" *vis-à-vis* others' (Bowles and Gintis 1977: 185). With two (or potentially more) wage rates and the rate of profit all in inverse relation to each other, this presumably occurs once the higher-level wage rate becomes too high.

But Bowles and Gintis do not allow so simple a solution. For them to do so would admit to commensuration between different types of segmented labour, so that each could count against another (if not equally) and labour would be homogenised. Instead, they insist that conversion ratios are not necessary for their purposes and that their determination is a political issue, presumably concerning the totality of social relationships:

> We are convinced that the assumption of equal rates of exploitation represents a serious obstacle to understanding the internal structure of the working class and the possibilities for alliances between it and other segments of the population . . . The issue of the ratios of conversion of different types of labour is relevant only when discussing the distribution of labor times among the types of labor . . . To arrive at quantitative estimates, however (of rates of exploitation), some conversion ratios must be assumed. How these conversion ratios are determined is a political question which we have no interest in pursuing.
>
> (Bowles and Gintis 1978: 313)

To conclude, whilst the intentions of Bowles and Gintis emerge quite clearly, they result in analytical chaos – homogeneity within heterogeneous labour markets, the critique of economism leading to its perfection, and a lack of clarity in the status of exploitation so that, consequently, the distinction between wages and profits becomes obscured (if one set of workers can exploit another through higher wages). The only clarity is the commitment to the generalised Sraffian model of distributional conflict between profits and various wage rates (and over the economic and social totality that makes up the coefficients of the input–output table).

One interesting attempt to resolve these difficulties has been made by Himmelweit (1984). She argues that the rate of exploitation is a common experience of the working class as a whole (although it is not always clear whether this is because the rate of exploitation for a segment of workers is considered a theoretically invalid concept or because exploitation is equalised).[18] Consequently, she comes to the conclusion that workers contribute value in proportion to the value of their labour-powers irrespective of the reasons for differentials within these (e.g. genuine skills or not). In other words, workers produce more value the more they are paid.

This approach is erroneous, for it depends upon the idea that the market (in this case for labour-power) determines value relations rather than vice versa. This is made explicit by Himmelweit for commodities in general:

> It is only through its sale that the quantity of 'socially necessary' labor that went into a product can be evaluated. Abstract labor is therefore measurable, as a quantity of socially necessary labor, only when it is turned into a measurable quantity of money on the sale of its product.
>
> (Himmelweit 1984: 327)

For Marx, by contrast, quantitative value relations exist prior to commodities entering exchange even if exchange relations affect whether those values are realised. Otherwise we move, in principle at least, as far along the route to the orthodox theory of value, as determined by supply and demand, as we care to go, including value being determined by the contribution of differential wages to differences in prices.

Paradoxically, then, Himmelweit's treatment of the problem of heterogeneous labour has a close parallel with that of Bowles and Gintis in so far as the structure and processes of the capitalist economy (and society) are collapsed into a simple formula relating value creation to wage levels. Where she does make an advance over Bowles and Gintis, however, is in the attempt to justify her resolution of the problems by a materialist account of the way in which different labours are 'homogenised'. Through the exchange mechanism, different concrete labours are brought into equivalence with each other, and generalised commodity production ensures the validity of the concept of abstract labour.[19] Just as different types of labour are brought into equivalence, weaving and sowing for example, so different skills of labour are brought into equivalence, however they might have been created. As Itoh argues:

> Traditionally, the twin problems of how to deal with concrete and abstract labour and how to reduce skilled to simple labour are regarded as theoretically distinct, and to be handled separately. However, the solution of these two problems must now be linked.

> (Itoh 1987: 49–50)

Not surprisingly, Bowles and Gintis utilise the concept of abstract labour in a random way without justification and without recognising the inconsistency with a dependence otherwise on heterogeneous labour. For Marx, in contrast to Himmelweit, the issue of the value of labour-power is quite distinct from that of the value contributed by the labourer (Marx 1976: 305–6). Her appeal to Marx, however, does little more than defend him against the charge that his value theory is incompatible with a comprehension of labour market segmentation in which the rate of surplus value is equalised across segments.

What each of the approaches previously covered has in common is the treatment of the social reproduction aspect of the value of labour-power as counterposed to its economic reproduction. For skilled labour, it is by way of extension of the economic to the non-economic sphere; for Bowles and Gintis, it is a projection in the opposite direction – from the externally given socioeconomic characteristics of the work-force (and for Himmelweit, there is imposed an accounting identity between wages and skills to guarantee an equal rate of exploitation across a heterogeneous work-force). In addition, the content of the interaction between economic and social reproduction is underdeveloped in three different ways. First, social reproduction encompasses a wide range of factors, as many and more than have been recognised in the traditional radical SLM theory, such as sexism, racism, trade unionism, etc. There is no reason to believe that each of these will interact with economic reproduction in the same way to generate labour market differentiation.

Second, the role of each of these factors will vary historically and according to different periods of capitalism – both the state and the household, for example, have witnessed significant changes in their contribution to social reproduction and its interaction with economic reproduction (with the growth of the welfare state, the demographic transition to smaller family sizes, increasing female labour market participation, and the commercial displacement of much household production).[20] Third, it follows that the differentiation of the work-force through social reproduction will itself arise in different ways – how women are reproduced as members of the work-force is very different from how men are reproduced (and there are, of course, intra-group differences as well). These cannot be simplistically captured by an abstract or, more exactly, formalistic quantification of the labour-time required to produce skills and differences in rates of exploitation and/or remuneration.

5 MAROONING AND SEGMENTATION

In the discussion so far, attention has been focused exclusively upon segmentation in the context of wage labour employed by (industrial) capital. This does not, of course, exhaust either the whole labour market or even the market for wage labour alone. The self-employed might be construed to constitute one or more labour market segments, and there are wage labourers who are not employed by capital – those who provide personal services and, more significant over the recent period, those employed by the state especially for services or products that do not involve a sale. How are we to understand segmentation for such workers?

To do so the concept of 'marooning' will be employed.[21] Whilst wage labour employed by capital for a profit is taken as the central determining category of analysis, it does not preclude those other forms of labour that differ from it and that are, indeed, defined by it. Wage labour that does not create surplus value, unproductive labour for Marx, is defined by what it is not. Similarly, the self-employed,[22] possibly simple commodity producers, are neither workers nor capitalists but combine attributes of both and are defined as such within capitalist society. And professionals can be considered as that special category of worker who, by virtue of the functions that they perform for capital or as a consequence of their levels of remuneration, fall outside the boundaries defined for the productive worker.

These workers are marooned in the sense that they are potentially open to rescue, if this is the appropriate term, by capitalist penetration of their activity. Why has wage labour not displaced these other forms of labour through its superior commercial viability? There are a whole variety of answers, each form of marooned labour depending upon a socially or historically specific structural barrier to capitalist incorporation (as in the state's command of law and order and its personnel, for example, the political and economic imperatives of the welfare state, or the guild-like protection of the professions – none of which creates an absolutely impenetrable barrier, especially in the age of privatisation).

In the context of segmentation through marooning, it is worth emphasising three points. First, the labour market segments will in part be defined by their not being incorporated into capitalist production, for reasons that do need to be uncovered in order to understand how the structures involved are reproduced. Second, this will vary from segment to segment. Third, the functioning of such labour market segments will not be independent of the broader labour markets but they will experience structures and dynamics of their own which will be distinct from those previously outlined as derived from capitalist production directly. It is precisely for this reason that the state, as a significant employer of marooned labour, can have a profound impact on the structuring of labour markets through its own employment practices, quite apart from the general labour market conditions for which it legislates or makes policy.

6 TOWARDS AN ALTERNATIVE BY WAY OF CONCLUSION

In the previous sections, a number of theoretical propositions have been advanced and their potential significance for labour market segmentation has been highlighted. The commentary has been organised around three themes: developments derived from capitalist production, marooning, and the determinants of the value of labour-power (which has itself been considered from both its consumption and its social reproduction aspects). It would be tempting at this stage to throw all these insights together, add a few extra explanatory variables at lower levels of abstraction, pay lip-service to historical contingency and, abracadabra, a theoretical account of labour market segmentation is specified.

Before such claims can even be contemplated, some further implications of the analysis need to be reiterated or emphasised. First, the focus has been upon those socioeconomic processes that positively generate labour market differentiation. By default, pushed into the background, are those processes which undermine differentiation, especially in so far as the latter is attached to the stronger notion of more or less permanent labour market structures. Thus, workers are differentiated by abilities, job requirements, as well as by pay and conditions – without their necessarily belonging to different labour market structures. Such a proposition can be allowed without necessarily degenerating into the ideal world of labour markets in which all differentiation is an efficient, harmonious and fair reflection of individual differences subject to the absence of market imperfections.

In particular, the emphasis here has been upon how labour market differentiation is a systematic consequence of the accumulation of capital, not an abnormality or aberration, especially from equilibrium, as in orthodox theory.[23] This has some advantage over neoclassical approaches, even those of more recent vintage which are able to explain labour market structures on the basis of an imperfect market and individual optimisation. For, the latter grind out labour market segmentation as an equilibrium outcome, something which is alien to everyday experience of labour markets as well as incapable of addressing labour market restructuring except by way of comparative statics. Even radical segmented labour market theory, although not necessarily tied to equilibrium notions, tends to take labour market structures as given, whether through categoricism or otherwise, and such outcomes are only loosely tied to underlying socioeconomic processes and structures.

None the less, even if within a different analytical framework, it is essential to recognise that labour is mobile across sectors and occupations – that is the market process by which orthodox theory would suggest that differences in pay and conditions are matched to individual attributes. Consequently, labour market *structures* do not arise simply because there is *differentiation* of the work-force. A productivity increase in one sector or firm might be induced through higher wages, but these can also be eroded by a subsequent influx of labour. Such is the logic of the neoclassical orthodoxy, subject to the prevalence of market imperfections. However, the alternative offered here suggests that structures can be created out of differentiation, since, other or the same renewed socioeconomic processes can intervene and have an effect prior to the labour market having trundled its way to equilibrium. In short, in some ways extending the critique of categoricism, differentiation of the work-force has to be distinguished from labour market structuring.

Consider unionisation, for example. Are those workers in a union in a different labour market segment or structure than those who are not? This is one way of interpreting the implications of the trade union mark-up on wages. But even if it is found to be significant, it does not follow that the labour market is structured rather than simply differentiated along these lines. You might be paid more simply because you belong to a union just as you might be paid more simply because you have a degree or years of service. Labour market segmentation as a theory of socioeconomic structures requires the latter to be more deeply rooted within an understanding of the accumulation of capital and social reproduction more generally.

As another example, consider the pay differentials experienced by women. Do these alone imply labour market segmentation? Whilst the answer might be in the affirmative for those socioeconomic processes that structure women into sectoral or occupational segregation, other aspects of women's labour market disadvantage might be better construed as due to differences rather than structure. If they did not work part-time, if they did belong to trade unions, if they did not have primary responsibility for child-care (or it was publicly provided), if there were effective comparable worth legisla-tion, then much of the apparent 'structural' differentiation between men and women would be eroded, as it can be for individual women. As such progressive changes have been realised to some extent with some significant effect, it suggests that the labour market outcomes are not necessarily as deeply embedded in structures as the degree of differentiation in outcomes might suggest.

Thus, inequality in labour market outcomes is not evidence, as such, of the presence of labour market segments interpreted as structures. Consider the comparison between those marooned employees, doctors and lawyers, as a further illustration. It is a moot point, all things taken into account, which of these is more handsomely rewarded. Such an issue is much less important than the differences in the separate labour market structures to which they belong – how they are trained, how their careers are structured, etc. Out-comes can be comparable, with our aspiring professional finding it hard to choose between them on financial grounds, without this implying absence of structures.

The point can be put in another way. Typically, in orthodox and radical labour market empirical analysis, wages are empirically estimated by human capital equations in which the independent variables range over unionisa-tion, gender, market concentration, capital-intensity, etc. A significant co-efficient for any of these would be taken as indicative of the presence of labour market structure. But this does not follow, except in the trivial sense that differentiation and structure are taken to be the same. In contrast, the presence of such differentials can only be taken as evidence of labour market structuring once the way in which the labour market structures are shown to function and to be reproduced.

The first conclusion, then, is that considerable analytical care needs to be taken in identifying and explaining labour market structures, especially in distinguishing them from differentiation as inequality in outcomes. Second, a remarkably simple proposition follows – but one that tends to be overlooked in general SLM theory which sees all labour markets as being (re)structured simultaneously and in micro-studies which focus upon one segment alone – that each labour market segment is structured dif-ferently. The means vary by which each is created, reproduced and has effects. It is a matter not only of differentiated labour market structures, but also of differentiated labour market structuring. In particular, how the value of labour-power is determined across sectors (in each of its aspects) and how marooning materialises are dependent upon specific inter-actions between underlying socioeconomic processes and structures. More-over, these factors also interact with the potential for labour mobility across sectors and occupations

A contrast with orthodox theory might prove helpful. For it has an ideal competitive equilibrium from which a portfolio of potential (labour) market imperfections can create a further portfolio of potential labour market structures and outcomes. Only in this sense is there the possibility of (equilibrium) differences between labour market structures – one is due to implicit contracts, another to efficiency-wages, etc. The view adopted here is that theory merely identifies underlying structures and processes in the structuring of labour markets. How these interact and give rise to labour market segments differs and is not predetermined in an axiomatic way. Rather, it depends upon the outcome of conflicts over, around and within the labour markets themselves. Further, in contrast to radical SLM theory, for which dynamic, shifting and overlapping segmentation is simultaneously realised across the labour markets as a whole, labour market structures need to be understood as different from one another and differently, not simultaneously, reproduced or transformed except in some tautologous sense. Perhaps the strongest evidence for this conclusion is the weakness of the various SLM theories, previously reviewed – in which grand, overarching theory is found to be arbitrary and refuted by the empirical evidence and in which, otherwise, there is an agglomeration of heterogeneous microeconomic studies.

To some extent, this stance can be understood, and has been motivated by, an analogy with the earlier discussion of systems of provision in the determination of the consumption aspect of the value of labour-power. There, it was argued that consumption norms are a consequence of vertically delineated structures around specific commodities or groups of commodities, as in the food, energy or housing systems, for example, each of which is distinct and differently structured. Now, it is possible that labour markets will be structured in conformity with such commodity systems; that, for example, particular sectors of the economy, such as mining, incorporate their own labour market structure. But, it is equally possible, and here there is a contrast with the stance taken on consumption,[24] that labour markets are structured horizontally if, for example, mobility across sectors predominates over structuring within them, as may be the case for highly skilled as well as for unskilled workers.

A third conclusion, then, is that labour markets can be structured either horizontally or vertically or through some combination of the two. In effect, there is a potential lattice of labour market structures, combining both intra- and intersectoral content. This, then, raises a fourth issue of how it is that the labour market structures are demarcated from one another (and when is differentiation sufficiently entrenched to warrant designation as a structure). Where does one labour market segment begin and another one end, quite apart from the ambiguity already highlighted between labour market differentiation and structures? In the work on consumption (Fine *et al.* 1996), it has been argued that the boundaries of a system of provision cannot be determined abstractly, by theory alone. Rather, which commodities are sufficiently linked to one another and integrated to create a structure around socioeconomic processes and structures (is there a single meat system or different ones for each meat or meat product, for example?) can only be determined empirically. Similarly, whilst an attempt has been made to identify some of the factors involved in labour market structuring, what constitutes the nature and scope of particular structures is necessarily socially and empirically contingent. Labour market structures are not pre-determined. Analytically, it is essential to uncover how they are structurally differentiated from one another and reproduced or transformed in practice.

These are disarmingly simple but important conclusions – labour markets are structured both horizontally and vertically, creating structures that are distinct from one another, that function differently from one another, and such structures are contingent upon the more complex outcome of underlying socioeconomic processes and structures. In other words, labour market structures are actively created out of the economic and social reproduction of capitalism. Analysis of the latter has informed and been the route through which these conclusions about labour market structures have been reached. Even if this analysis remains controversial in total or in detail, the particular stance adopted here to SLM structuring may be found to be compelling to those working within various alternative theoretical frameworks.

NOTES

1 This section contains a drastic summary of selected aspects of Marxist political economy, which is itself complex and highly controversial. For a more extended and elementary account, see Fine (1989).
2 With capitalist development, child labour tends to be withdrawn but, as in the most recent period in advanced capitalist countries, female labour market participation has increased. This raises the question of how the value of labour power is to be understood in terms of the labour contribution of different household members, given that men and women tend to hold unrelated jobs and careers. This contrasts with Marx's discussion of the issue in the nineteenth century, especially where family labour worked as a unit. For the moment, however, concern here is only with labour contributed as a whole, even if recognising that it is structured in the ways in which it is provided.
3 Green (1991), for example, discusses the relationship between the longer-term value of labour power and the shorter-term value of wages, in which the latter moves around but in part determines the former along with other factors. However, although his model extends time indefinitely, it is peculiar in not allowing for any technological change and productivity increase, something that is taken central here as a determinant of the value of labour power and, by implication, the value of wages. Ong (1980) stresses that the value of labour power is bounded by the need to guarantee subsistence reproduction at the lower end and profitability at the upper end, with class struggle determining the outcome within these logically determined bounds. Of course, the movement of these bounds by the accumulation process itself is bound to render this framework of analysis redundant.
4 As in Sraffian versions of the Okishian theorem.
5 See Fine and Harris (1979) for an overview of the literature, but also Fine (1982, 1989).
6 Harvey (1983) provides a sophisticated account of the value of labour power in which there are six determinants – own subsistence, family subsistence, costs of

education, length of working day, intensity of labour and the productivity around each of these. However, these factors are not systematically related to one another analytically other than to view them all as mediated by class struggle. In any case, no progress is made along the lines of differentiation of consumption as suggested here.

7 See Fine and Leopold (1993) and, specifically for food, Fine *et al.* (1996).

8 As in *all* sides in the Sraffian debate over Marx's value theory.

9 Note that in its full version, neoclassical economics would distinguish between the different items that make up the pay settlement as well as the consumption goods that they can purchase through reference to maximisation of utility. This, however, is obsessive around a single principle and overlooks the particular and varying ways in which consumption norms come to be determined.

10 For an account of the relationship between access to private health insurance, the labour market and other socioeconomic factors, see Muntaner and Parsons (1996).

11 See Rowthorn (1980), for example.

12 Gough (1975, 1979) extends such Sraffian analysis to other areas of the welfare state. See Fine and Harris (1976) for a critique.

13 See also Bliss (1975) and Hahn (1982) for a similar assessment from a neoclassical point of view.

14 Or by a monetary theory of interest with the latter related to the rate of profit. For the most advanced development of this closure, see Panico (1988) and, for a critique, see Fine (1985/6).

15 Nor how well made is the interpretation of Thompson and its projection to value theory – a long journey from its origins in social history.

16 This conclusion is most obviously entirely eclectic and chaotic but is equally matched by the most immediate leap from the ensemble of practices to the court of political judgement: 'The representation of labor-power as a commodity and of labor as its use value supports a political perspective which we believe to be antithetical to the creation of a democratic mass socialist movement' (ibid.).

17 Again, this view of the transformation problem is controversial and the subject of a long and continuing debate. See Fine (1986) for an assessment.

18 Thus, 'exploitation is not an individual relation between a worker and his or her own capitalist employer. It is a class relation, between the class of those who sell their labour-power and the class of capitalists' (Himmelweit 1984: 330). On the other hand, 'capitalist competition in the labor and product markets ensures that the rate of exploitation does not vary across different groups of workers' (ibid.: 342), suggesting that such lack of variation is contingent upon the extent of competition. For an alternative account along the same lines, see Harvey (1985). Whilst recognising correctly that skilled labour is not a depository of previously exercised labour, like constant capital, but is itself value-creating, he argues incorrectly for differing rates of exploitation across skilled and unskilled labour, thereby correctly suggesting that irresolvable problems are posed for the labour theory of value (since relative wages will affect values). For both Himmelweit and Harvey, the problem lies in collapsing wage and value determination to the same level of abstraction, even if in different ways.

19 This is the subject matter of Marx's opening chapters of *Capital* and is essential to the debate over value theory.

20 These issues are discussed at length in Fine (1992) and thus the discussion of social reproduction and its relationship to the family system and the welfare state are not covered at length here. See Siltanen (1994) for a penetrating analysis

in the context of a particular labour market – telephone and postal workers – and also Humphries (1995).

21 The idea comes from Cannadine (1983) in terms of the anachronism presented by the monarchy. The same concept is used in the context of food in Fine *et al.* (1996).

22 Leaving aside subcontracting where self-employment is merely a way of evading taxation or whatever.

23 Botwinick (1993) argues for this approach with great sophistication and has informed the position adopted here, even if there are differences in the way in which the argument is structured.

24 Glennie and Thrift (1992, 1993) dispute with Fine (1993) that consumption should be understood vertically and not as a lattice, the position taken here for labour markets. See also Fine *et al.* (1996).

Part IV
From theory to policy

Part IV is concerned with the application of theory to policy issues. Chapter 8 addresses equal pay, and minimum wage legislation is the subject of Chapter 9. Each of these chapters was inspired by specific policy concerns, an equal pay claim by the NUM canteen workers and cleaners, and recommending minimum wage legislation for South Africa in the post-apartheid era.[1]

The rationale for a minimum wage in South Africa and the context of labour market disadvantage in which it has been assessed does not warrant further motivating discussion.[2] From a theoretical point of view, the issue is one of whether labour markets work sufficiently closely to the parable of supply and demand, in which a minimum wage has the effect of decreasing employment through a backward shift along the demand curve for labour. The theoretical and empirical evidence has swung towards a negative answer, even for those continuing to rely upon mainstream neoclassical economics.

Interestingly, the minimum wage debate has led to an increasingly sophisticated modelling and estimation of labour markets. For, in order to deduce the impact of minimum wage legislation, it is necessary to net out the impact of other variables that affect the functioning of the labour markets. Paradoxically, the same analytical developments have not been experienced in the equal pay literature, where relatively simple human capital models to measure discrimination have persisted. Given that equal pay legislation can be interpreted as a partial form of targeted minimum wage legislation, applicable to women, this is surprising. Possibly it is explained by the general persistence and recognition of pay discrimination against women – although, as will be seen, this does not always lead to universal support for equal pay legislation – whereas there has been a much more tenacious hold on the idea that minimum wages will force down employment substantially despite current evidence to the contrary. In such circumstances, mainstream theory has to be made more sophisticated to maintain propositions that are no longer empirically well-founded.

The background to the NUM equal pay claim will be entirely unfamiliar to most readers, and it is worth presenting in some detail as a motivation for the more theoretical discussion to follow. The account also illustrates how labour markets are differentially segmented, along the lines of the lattice structuring suggested in the Part III. There are interesting aspects to the case, reflecting the interaction between underlying socioeconomic tendencies and historically contingent factors. Here is a predominantly male union, under assault from a hostile Tory government following the year-long national strike of 1984/5, pursuing a claim at enormous expense on behalf of a tiny minority of women workers with little or no industrial muscle of their own. A state-owned corporation, ultimately heading for privatisation, is equally embattled in a struggle whose litigation and costs far exceed the disadvantages, if any, of not simply conceding to the spirit of equal pay legislation. British Coal was determined that equal pay should not be effectively applied to its canteen workers (and cleaners). This is true of its response to an initial claim in 1985 for equal pay for work of equal value[3] – arising out of legislation forced on the British government by the European Community. But it has a longer history, as will be seen, going back to the response to earlier legislation of 1970 which required the same pay for the same work whether done by men or women.

One of the grounds used by British Coal to avoid equal pay has essentially been to argue that its canteen workers belong to a separate bargaining unit and hence are not subject to the legislation.The formal allocation of British Coal's canteen workers into separate grading structures has allowed avoidance of what has been the most effective mechanism by which a move towards equal pay has been implemented in other sectors of the economy. Even placing women workers on the lowest grade of the joint scale with male workers has proved in other industries to be of significant benefit to women. British Coal's refusal to do this must be considered a deliberate policy for minimising the impact of equal pay legislation. Separate pay scales have been a device for preventing the harmonisation of minimum pay scales for men and women.

Such a conclusion can be strengthened by turning the issue around. Subject to a job evaluation exercise, suppose the canteen workers had been placed on a combined scale with male workers, would they have benefited from equal pay legislation? With a few minor exceptions, the characteristics of employment in the coal industry are such that women are most likely to have been granted equal pay on a minimum grade with men. This is for the following reasons.[4]

First, British Coal has had a most highly developed grading structure which has been modified over time to take account both of piecework and daywage forms of payment, as well as complex gradings within these two broad categories. There seems no reason why the evolving wage structure could not have been successfully extended to cover canteen workers too rather than assigning them to a separate bargaining structure. The NUM first put forward a proposed uniform grading structure for mineworkers in 1950. This ultimately led through negotiation to the first Daywagemen's

Agreement of 1955. To arrive at this, 6,000 separate local job names were assigned to 300 group names. These were, in turn, arranged into five underground grades, five surface grades and three grades for craftsmen. Subsequently, the 1966 National Power Loading Agreement assimilated, following a whole series of District Agreements, most of those miners who had previously been on piecework. Finally, the 1971 Third National Daywage Structure Agreement encompassed other coalface workers, eliminating all remaining piece and task work. Subsequently, the 1980 Revision of the Wage Structure brought into operation the wages structure operating in the industry at the time of the equal pay claim. From then until 1987, a National Grading and New Technology Committee was set up to look at the (re)grading issues raised by implementation of new technology. This has meant that grading structures have been under constant revision, review and negotiation to take account of new tasks as they arise (and to compare them with old ones).

It is worth observing that the complexity of the wages structure inherited upon nationalisation was so great that rationalising it was both delayed for a decade and staggered over a 15-year period to reach completion for the vast bulk of the workforce. As Sales and Davies (1957) observed, the day-wagemen and pieceworkers could not be handled simultaneously because of the enormity of the task involved. Consequently, the formal exclusion of the few grades of canteen workers from this evolving wage structure is a deliberate bargaining policy by the employer, consistently held over a long period. It is not a matter of administrative convenience nor of economic logic. It is also worth recalling that the Union asked as early as 1953 that the lowest canteen rate be based on the surface worker minimum, with corresponding rates for other canteen grades.

Second, then, supposing that British Coal had extended its grading scheme to canteen workers, conditions are highly favourable for such a grading scheme to have been relatively free of gender bias. British Coal is highly practised in job evaluation, for which there has been employee participation, and it has also involved a sophisticated and experienced personnel department (with a special division for industrial relations). All of these factors in other employments have been associated with successful pursuit of equal pay.

Third, the evaluation would concern manual workers, a situation which, experience from other industries suggests, has proved more favourable to moving towards equal pay. Fourth, the establishments concerned do include some large-scale mines, as far as number of employees is concerned, even if all are not large-scale workplaces by industrial standards. Fifth, there is an extremely high level of trade unionism. Sixth, bonus schemes and overtime are an important component of male earnings, so that it would have been possible to have retained a male earnings differential even with the introduction of equal pay. These factors have all proved favourable to women occupying a position, even if the lowest, on a common pay structure with men.

On the other hand, there are some factors that would have limited the chances of a relative rise in women's pay. First, there is an extreme imbalance in the proportion of men and women employed. Second, there is limited representation of the interests of women workers through the trade union as officials, in negotiations and in attending meetings. There has only rarely been a female branch committee member, and women have never negotiated their own pay and conditions. This has been done as an appendage to the main negotiations. Third, there is the presence of part-time workers. Fourth, as previously discussed, there is the apparent adoption of the employer of an avoidance or minimisation strategy as far as equal pay is concerned.

Certainly, given the union's stance in support of equal pay, of these negative factors only the latter is of importance in the sense that it would render the others irrelevant if it were otherwise. Had the employer been committed to equal pay policy and, as part of this, a more unified bargaining structure, experience from elsewhere suggests that men and women workers would have shared at least a common minimum grade. It must be concluded that the formal rejection of a common bargaining structure by the employer was a deliberate policy to nullify conditions that have otherwise been shown to be of considerable advantage to women in other industries when seeking equal pay.

This is confirmed by the historical experience of the industry in a number of ways. First, formal separation of bargaining structures has meant that job evaluation across the entire work-force (including canteen workers) has been avoided. Yet, such schemes appear to require frequent reassessment, especially where rapid technical change is involved – which is certainly so for coal mining and arguably also applicable to canteen workers, given the new technology in food preparation. And it is generally the case that, for women, job evaluation exercises do positively affect job hierarchies, especially with joint commitment to eliminate gender bias.

Second, there has been a history of unequal pay in the industry. In the account given earlier of the evolution of the grading structure, an important point to add is that this was done in the absence of gender differentiation. Although there were no women workers underground, there were women surface workers. They were assimilated to the same grades as men. Unequal pay was cemented into the wage, not the grade, structure by the simple expedient of paying women doing the same job a wage set initially at a level of 80 per cent or so of the male rate.

Before 1969, then, there were separate scales for men and women doing the same jobs, with women receiving substantially lower levels of pay when on the same grades. For example, the 1968 wage agreement included the pay levels for surface workers after a 2/6 weekly flat rate increase per shift, subject to a limit not being exceeded as shown in Table 2.[5]

Table 2 Male and female pay levels after the 1968 wage agreement

Surface grade	Male	Female	Male	Female
	Standard		Limit	
I	47/4	42/5	56/-	42/5
II	46/1	41/2	55/9	41/2
III	45/5	40/6	55/9	40/6

In the specific case of canteen workers, the ingrained inequality of pay for those men and women doing the same jobs was combined with a formal exclusion of canteen workers from the main body of grading and bargaining. As a result, in the 1955 pay agreement, for example, there was contained the following 'spiral' of unequal pay. A canteen manager controlling between 31 and 40 workers (the highest grade) earned a rate of 203/9 compared to a manageress' rate of 157/6. This compares with the rate for a male cook of 156/3. A female cook earned 104/5. The latter was equivalent to the wage of the lowest paid 20-year-old male.

After failing to persuade the employer to assimilate canteen workers with the minimum for surface workers, the Union proposed in 1953 that a national agreement for canteen staff be set at a rate of 50 per cent above the Wage Council rate for the Industrial and Staff Canteen workers.[6] The Board refused and offered a range up to 25 per cent above the Wage Council rates, which was eventually accepted. Subsequently, in 1956, the NUM did press for equal pay for canteen workers. It was met with the following response:

> The Industrial Relations Member of the Board stated that the conditions of service of colliery canteen and snack bar staffs were, by agreement with the Union, governed by the Orders made from time to time by the Industrial and Staff Canteen Undertakings Wages Board. These Orders did not at present provide for equal pay, and unless and until such an Order was made, the Board could not concede the Union's claim.

This is of some importance, since it shows that the Wage Council comparability was used, in part, to negate claims for equal pay. In practice, however, it did not even serve as a basis for determining canteen workers' pay. Over the period from 1963 to 1976, the differential varied from as little as 15.4 per cent (1967/8) to as much as 99.2 per cent (1974/5), having been set at 25 per cent in 1955. The Wage Council rates seem to have served as a number you first think of before coming up with another number by which to multiply it! The tracking of the timing and the level of pay awards to mineworkers and, paradoxically, comparability with the minimum rates for surface workers remains the strongest explanation of canteen workers rates of pay. This is despite the Board's view that agreements covering canteen workers are 'designed to dissociate the wages and conditions of service of male and female employees from Agreements relating to the coalmining industry'.

In short, historically, with union compliance, the Board has discriminated against women by paying them 20 per cent or so less than men in the same grades but also, against the union's wishes, it has formally disassociated canteen workers from the mineworkers' pay structure and refused equal pay for canteen workers.

This situation changed in 1969 when, presumably in anticipation of the 1970 equal pay legislation, there was the simplest of responses to the problem of discrimination – the abolition of the distinction between male and female grades, where the two were doing the same jobs, with women taking the male wage rate. The way in which this was done, as evidenced by the limited scope of the change in the Agreement concerned, can only be interpreted as satisfying the minimum as far as the first round of equal pay legislation was concerned.[7] Since then, the ratio of female canteen workers' pay to that of, predominantly male, surface workers has remained remarkably close to the 80 per cent differential that had effectively been previously proposed by the union (in assimilating male canteen workers to the lowest surface worker grade and female wages to 80 per cent of the male). Since 1969, however, the union has increasingly changed its own position and has pressed not only for a unified grading structure for all workers on the surface but also for the *de facto* linking of the pay and conditions of canteen workers to those of surface workers to be acknowledged in considering equal pay. It has argued that British Coal has refused to recognise this latter point formally in order to avoid equal pay claims, as appears to be consistent with the evidence presented here.

Third, the pay discrimination against women has been a consequence of the choice of a Wages Council as an external reference point for wage determination (in so far as this has, in fact, been the case). The Wages Council system has its origins in the 1909 Trade Boards. They were designed to fix legally enforceable minimum rates of pay for workers in the absence of sufficiently evolved employers associations and trade unions – to protect workers against the absence of the conditions necessary for the existence of, and balance in, collective bargaining. It has generally been envisaged that a Council would be abolished once voluntary negotiating machinery became available. Trade unions, in particular, feel that the minimum can operate as a downward pressure on wage levels:

> Wages Councils do not set earnings, their function is to set statutory minimum rates of wages and it is on this basis that they must be judged. Rates set by Councils may influence earnings but a primary function of the Wages Council system is to set reasonable minimum time rates for the workers covered by Wages Council legislation. The system has been regarded for most of its history as a temporary substitute for main-

taining wage levels until organisation of trade unions and employers associations reached sufficient levels for voluntary maintenance and there has been an implicit desire on the part of legislators, commentators and interested parties for the statutory system to be gradually replaced by voluntary means for setting minimum rates.

(Steele 1979: 225)

It immediately follows that Wage Council workers are liable to be low paid and low in trade union density of membership. This seems to have been especially true of the Industrial and Staff Canteen Undertakings Wages Board (ISCUWB), as was revealed in a study by Craig *et al.* (1982) of the effects of the abolition of Wages Councils. The ISCUWB was included in their study having been abolished in 1976. The sector is different from others in that it does not produce a commodity for sale outside the enterprise (and hence was not subject to downward wage pressure from the competition between firms in the product market) and in that the workers were inevitably a small proportion of those employed. In other words, canteen workers are scattered across many different places of employment in relatively small numbers:

Catering workers are particularly vulnerable because they are separate from the main labour force, work in small units, and are peripheral to the main interests of the employers and unions in their workplaces.

(Craig *et al.* 1980: 105)

Craig *et al.* (1982: 45) found that trade unionism was highest in the medium and large-scale and in the public sector establishments. In 45 per cent of the establishments run by the private sector, there was no union present at all (Craig *et al.* 1980: 36). Given the high level of trade union membership amongst canteen workers in the coal industry, it follows that its wage levels would be dragged down by comparison with canteen workers as a whole. It is also the case that collective bargaining arrangements are liable to have been less favourable in the sector as a whole, with these often being absent altogether or conducted exclusively at a local level. The low levels of pay associated with subcontractors is also liable to have been a downward pressure on wage levels. Thus, British Coal has sought, through not formally recognising that canteen workers belong to the same bargaining structure as mineworkers, to neutralise the bargaining advantages that its canteen workers might be thought to have by virtue of their high levels of unionism.

This is all confirmed by more recent evidence of wage settlements over the past few years – long since the ISCUWB has been abolished. A study has been made by the Labour Research Department of the levels of wage settlements for canteen workers over the period 1986 to 1989. First, it found that of 33 basic wage rates examined, the level ranged from £187.08 to £87.75 per week (with the median at £113.13). Second, the review concludes that separate bargaining for canteen workers has meant lower levels of pay:

> For canteen assistants covered by agreements which have separate grades for canteen workers or lowest grades which do not apply to non-canteen staff, the weekly basic average rate is £97.00. However, canteen workers who share a lowest paid grade with non-canteen staff have an average basic of £117.46 a week . . . The technique of abolishing lowest grades is increasingly being used by bargainers to improve the position of the lowest paid workers, and if this were used to apply to canteen workers otherwise covered by separate grades a major area of pay discrimination would be removed.

It follows that British Coal has nominally chosen, as its standard for fixing its own canteen workers wages, the wages of those employees in a considerably worse bargaining position, and it has attempted to neutralise the impact of the union's strength in pressing for higher wages, especially for equal pay, through the device of formally separating bargaining structures. The first point is well-illustrated by the results of the post-abolition survey of Craig *et al.* (1984: 53). They found that as many as one-third of establishments paid hourly rates of less than the minimum set by comparison with continuing Wages Councils covering other catering and related staff. Underpayment was highest where the majority of women worked part-time, illustrating the implicit linking, in principle, of this source of low pay to corresponding wages in the coal industry.

It is what might be termed the 'tea-lady' principle. These workers are in the weakest of labour market conditions confined, for example, given their child-care responsibilities, to limited job opportunities within local labour markets.[8] Often working part-time, with few alternative job opportunities, they are poorly unionised and have few colleagues with which to organise collectively. The job is itself precarious, squeezed between the threats of staff making their own tea arrangements, on the one hand, and of displacement by a drink-dispensing machine, on the other. Clearly, such workers require the protection designed to be given by the Wage Council system. But it must be doubted whether they are the relevant standard for comparison for canteen workers in the mining industry! The minimum weekly rate for the ISCUWB in 1974 was £12.25, at a time when the TUC was recommending a minimum wage target of £30 per week (Craig *et al.* 1980: 69).

In practice, British Coal has always paid above Wage Council Rates. This is not unusual in industries covered by Wages Councils in those establishments where trade unions and collective bargaining are present. Nor is this surprising for such conditions are the ones for which the Council's function has been rendered redundant. This begs the question of why British Coal should have insisted upon token indexation to Wage Council rates up to 1976 and to have fixed wages subsequently, 'dissociated from Agreements relating to the coal industry'. Indeed, if it were serious in this regard, and wished to be consistent with its stated policy of the past, it would have continued to link pay, at least nominally, to the continuing Wages Councils covering canteen and related workers.

It has, however, insisted upon a bargaining structure that effectively divides men from women and pays the latter less. Craig *et al.* (ibid.: 100) report: 'that rates of pay were likely to be highest in the large highly unionised establishments following collective bargaining agreements which related canteen workers' pay to that of the main workforce'. Although this was less common in the private sector and not a guarantee of reasonable rates of pay in the public sector, 'the most successful results of integrating catering workers with the main pay structure were in the public sector' (ibid.: 106). In short:

> The ideal arrangement for the canteen workers is for them to be integrated into scales applicable to other manual workers, so that they automatically receive the same increases as other workers; they are also more likely to have benefitted from the introduction of equal pay.
>
> (ibid.: 40)

The formal avoidance of such an arrangement by British Coal seems to reflect a deliberate strategy of separate bargaining structures in order to disadvantage the position of occupationally segregated women workers. There are extremely strong links in this policy with the overt discrimination against women in the period prior to 1969. Nor is this apparently motivated by the extra wage costs involved. For it has been estimated that if the wage of a canteen attendant were made equal to that of the lowest-grade surface worker, and other differentials were maintained, then the increased cost would be as little as 0.1 per cent of the annual wage bill. Surely a very small price to pay for a non-discriminatory wage policy?[9] The following chapter explains why equal pay claims are at times resisted as a matter of principle even at the expense of great costs in practice, and why legislation has proved to be impracticable often, it would appear, by design.

NOTES

1 The author served as an adviser to the British NUM and to the South African Presidential Labour Market Commission, respectively. The research on the equal pay claim for the NUM was undertaken jointly with Kathy O'Donnell.
2 See ILO (1996) and LMC (1996).
3 Equal does not mean identical work in this context but with the same or compensating demands or characteristics as revealed by job evaluation.
4 See the next chapter for the general evidence for these propositions.
5 In old English money, prior to decimalisation, 'x/y' denotes x shillings and y pence – with 20 shillings to a pound and 12 pence to a shilling. Conventionally, x/- rather than x/0 stands for x shillings and no pence.
6 On Wage Councils, see below.

7 Essentially, the agreement of 25 February 1969 simply read as follows: 'Delete – the columns headed 'Female' and the word 'Male' from the column headings.'

8 An index of British Coal's wish to tie canteen workers to local labour market conditions has been the denial to them of the transferred workers scheme, even though they have been eligible for the Redundant Mineworkers Scheme.

9 Less information is available on the conditions governing the (relative) pay of cleaners. But similar conditions appear to have applied. British Coal has categorically refused to include ancillary workers (such as cleaners) within the mineworkers' terms and conditions and have held the view that this group of workers is best covered by wage determination by comparison with local authority terms and conditions – as determined by the National Joint Council for local authority manual workers. This serves to disassociate cleaners bargaining from colleagues within the coal industry and to link them to other workers who are liable to be less well-placed in the labour market. Again, separate bargaining structures seem to have been deliberately adopted and maintained in order to pay women a lower rate of pay, this representing a practice continued since the earliest days of nationalisation – following the Increases in Wages Agreement of 18 December 1947 and the Ancillary Workers Agreement of 5 August 1948. A further anomaly is the difference in treatment of male and female office cleaners. The former were assimilated into the mineworkers' grading system (at a level of Grade S6).

8 Comparable worth
Lessons from the UK experience

1 INTRODUCTION

The purpose of this chapter is to draw lessons from the UK experience of equal pay legislation. The lessons are primarily negative in the sense of a general recognition of how ineffective has been the UK example – in other words, it shows how not to proceed. The first section reviews some of the literature on comparable worth in order to bring out the analytical issues involved. This is followed by a section on the relationship between collective bargaining and equal pay. The final section draws some general conclusions from the experience of the legislation, making some suggestions on how legislation might be introduced to be as effective as possible.

2 ANALYTICAL CONSIDERATIONS

Comparable worth, or equal pay for work of equal value, is concerned with pay equity where men and women are engaged in work which is neither identical nor necessarily even similar. Rather, there is a presumption that the content of women's different work is liable to be undervalued in some objective sense and, consequently, unfairly rewarded relative to men's work. It is a form of discrimination against women which comparable worth or equal pay legislation is designed to rectify. It has, for example, been adopted in the EC and, hence, in the UK in January 1984 (by compulsion of the European Court of Justice) but also, effectively, from 1975 in Australia. Progress has been mixed in the USA, depending upon shifting precedents set by case law and upon state legislation, often confined to public sector employees alone.

There is now a significant literature on the issue equal pay or comparable worth for women. It has encompassed a distinctive analytical content and has addressed specific empirical and policy issues. Why do wage rates differ between men and women? To what extent are these differences due to discrimination? How much can comparable worth rectify wage differentials? How might legislation be made more effective? What has been the impact of equal pay legislation in practice? The literature has primarily been concerned with the USA and the UK,[1] but it has also included other countries and international comparisons.[2]

Central to much of the literature has been a particular model about how labour markets function – the model derived from human capital theory. It is based upon the idea that an appropriately working labour market without discrimination will reward individual workers according to their personal attributes – each will have acquired skills and preferences for particular types of work with corresponding rewards according to the demand for the products of their labour. In other words, competition within and between labour markets, more usually designated as the market or market forces, will grind out non-discriminatory wage rates if allowed to do so. There is, then, a presumption that labour markets could operate in this fashion in principle. Further, comparable worth is designed to measure divergence from this ideal and to amend women's wages accordingly.

In empirical work, as discussed in earlier chapters, there is a standard procedure for measuring the degree of discrimination.[3] Wages are regressed against a range of variables supposedly reflecting productivity, such as qualifications and experience. To the extent that male/female wage differentials remain unexplained by the multiple regression, the residual difference signifies wage discrimination. Thus, Rubinstein explains the matter informally. To measure employer discrimination, other (legitimate) sources of wage differentials have to be identified:

> Women, on average, have less productivity-enhancing characteristics than men. This results in part from free choice, in part from 'socialisation' about women's role, in part from the division of labour within the family and in part from discrimination in education and pre-employment training.
>
> (Rubenstein 1984: 2)

More formally, in explaining differences in male–female relativities between Australia, Great Britain and the United States of America, Gregory *et al.* put it that:

> There are many reasons why men and women are paid at different rates within a country. These reasons may include differences in the quality of workers, the distribution of workers across industries and occupations, the degree of pay discrimination against women, and the relative demand and supplies of labor. The usual way to measure the contributions of these factors is to fit earnings equations to the data for each sex. The most common earnings equations adopt a human capital framework and hypothesize that the differences in the earnings of men and women can be explained primarily in terms of differences in human capital, as measured by years of schooling, work experience, marital status, and so on.
>
> (Gregory *et al.* 1989: 223)

Whilst the techniques for doing this are simple enough in principle, it has led to a number of competing models and assessments (Dex 1988). For Ghobadian and White (1986: 6): 'It appears that econometric analysis can lead to widely different conclusions regarding the effects of legislation, depending on the model specification adopted.' The problems leading to these differences are that, first, some judgement has to be made about what factors constitute the normally functioning labour market. The more factors taken into account, the more likely it is that the empirical measure of discrimination will be reduced, since what are considered positive labour market attributes are generally more characteristic of men, and can serve as a statistical proxy for discrimination. At the extreme, and given the heavy segregation of men and women into separate jobs, discrimination could be analytically chipped away almost to nought by identifying the labour market characteristics that distinguish low-paying (female) jobs from higher-paying (male) jobs whether by occupation or by industry. None the less, most studies stop short of what is tantamount to a tautology and, consequently, establish empirically the existence of a degree of residual discrimination inexplicable in terms of labour market characteristics alone and, thus, due by default to gender differences alone. Figure 1 (see p. 65), drawn from Paci *et al.* (1995), shows one way in which wage differentials might be explained in terms of discriminatory and non-discriminatory factors, including those that occur inside and outside the labour market.

Second, even if there were agreement over what factors to include in modelling discrimination, some judgement has to be made about how they have an impact upon discrimination directly, indirectly and through their interaction with each other. In other words, the model ought to be structured, as is recognised, for example, in the analytical scheme offered by Chiplin and Sloane (1976) and reproduced in Figure 2. This is not generally recognised within the human capital literature. Rather, the labour market is treated as an uneven playing field, whose surface irregularities are a simple reflection of discrimination. In contrast, for example, it is well known that large-scale firms usually pay higher wages than small-scale firms. Equally, those with a higher density of trade union membership tend to pay more. A triangular relationship between these factors, however, is a consequence of the strong correlation between trade union membership and large-scale firms. So, in deciding to what extent trade unions raise wages (or relativities against non-unionists), account has to be taken of direct effects, through trade union membership itself, and indirect effects due to the presence of large-scale firms in raising trade union membership (quite apart from the direct effect of the large firm on wages). Many other factors than these are potentially involved.

The example given in the previous paragraph makes no reference to the relative position of male and female workers. But exactly the same sorts of considerations apply. Women tend to work for smaller firms and in industries that are less unionised. This is a structured source of lower

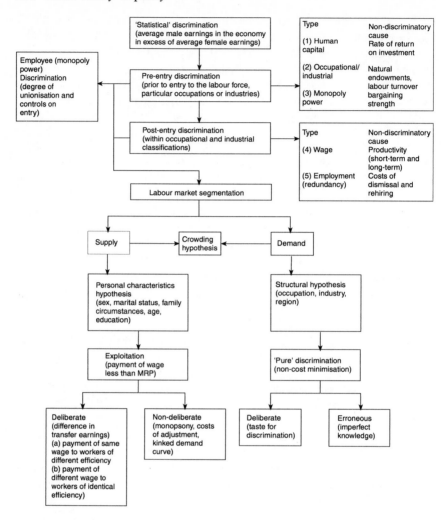

Figure 2   Components of discrimination

Source: Chiplin and Sloane (1976: 50)

wages in conjunction with any direct discrimination involved. Again, how these other and more complex structures of causation are modelled has an effect on how the level of discrimination is understood and measured. Such measures inevitably differ across occupations and characteristics within the female work-force itself.[4] In short, in measuring discrimination in order to make a case for equal pay, a view has to be taken of what counts as a legitimate reason for differentials. This, in turn, depends upon a full understanding of how labour markets function so that direct and indirect sources of discrimination can be identified and measured.

This absence of a clear analytical structure in the extant literature on the measurement of wage discrimination has a number of aspects. First, in standard statistical terms, it implies that the model is improperly specified. Even on its own terms, there seems to be a presumption that the estimated equation represents a demand function for human capital (what the employer is prepared to pay for worker characteristics). But this would take no account of supply-side factors which are, in principle, of equal importance to labour market outcomes – do women choose job characteristics or are they constrained from so choosing by employers, for example?

Thus, labour markets ought at least to be structured by supply and demand. Second, more generally, as implied by the example previously given, labour market structures are considerably more complex than the interaction of supply and demand. In line with much empirical investigation in economic and social theory, the latter is used by human capital analysis to identify what are presumed to be relevant causal factors, and these are simply thrown into a multiple regression. As Winship and Mare (1992) observe, this involves sample selection bias; they explicitly refer to the relationship between women's labour market rewards and socioeconomic achievement (if women are paid too little, those entering the labour market may be biased towards the less able, and there is less incentive to obtain the characteristics that the labour market values).

Diprete (1993) focuses upon this problem in the context of differences in human capital 'endowments' and their 'rates of return'. He eloquently argues for 'a proper *substantive* understanding of the process that generates inequality', recognising that this poses theoretical as well as statistical problems: 'If the *theory* for why groups have unequal levels of structurally generated resources is inadequate, then the statistical differences generated by our lack of understanding will contaminate our decomposition estimates' (Diprete 1993: 437; emphases in original). In lay language, this implies no proper estimate of direct discrimination without estimates both of indirect discrimination *and*, potentially, any other source of labour market inequality.

Third, as has emerged in more recent labour market analysis, labour market differentiation can be explained for reasons other than human capital differences and gender discrimination. England (1992) points to models based on implicit contracts, transactions costs and six different forms of efficiency-wages.[5] Manning (1996) sees the UK's Equal Pay Act of 1970 as an ideal opportunity to test traditional notions of how labour markets function. Given rising wages and employment for women over the subsequent period, it is hardly surprising that he should find that the theory fails the test, and he suggests that women are better seen as belonging to monopsonistic labour markets. Consequently, the degree of monopsony can be reduced, and women's wages and employment increased simultaneously by equal pay or minimum wage legislation. However, the notion of monopsony can be understood as a proxy for a range of factors that potentially drive the labour market away from equilibrium – or undermine the relevance of equilibrium as an organising notion at all – at the expense of women's wages and employment. How such factors interact with gender would need to be examined, in particular whether their effects be direct or indirect.

Fourth, each of these aspects is a reflection of the projection of relatively poor, standard labour market models upon female labour markets, even though the models were originally developed for the stereotypical male worker. The result is that the theory and conditions of men's employment are taken as the norm from which female employment is explained as a deviation (Kenrick 1981). Thus, female employment is understood by reference to its differences from male employment. This means that some of the enduring features of male work – full-time and without breaks for parenthood, for example – are taken as natural and not deserving of analytical attention. Women, on the other hand, are observed not to share all of these features which then become the focus for explaining (some of) their inferior position, whether by pre- or post-entry labour market factors.

This has the previously observed effects of limiting the analytical structure of the models developed, the range of variables incorporated and, as a further point, the methodology of causation employed. However complex and structured the model might be, outcomes are determined axiomatically with no role for conflict with contingent consequences, historical context, nor impact of economic and social movements, etc. For the models imply that comparable worth is an exogenously imposed policy that shifts supply and demand curves with corresponding effects on wages and employment. In contrast, it is necessary for comparable worth to be understood both as a cause and as an *effect* of the distinctive socioeconomic circumstances under which women have entered the labour market over the post-war period, these in turn needing to be differentiated from one country to another (and, equally, from one sector and occupation to another).[6]

In short, whilst it might be thought that labour market analysis appropriate to the study of comparable worth should be more sophisticated in content and approach than less specialised studies dealing with levels of (un)employment or wages, for example, exactly the opposite has materialised.[7] Not surprisingly, this has led to alternative approaches which have been broadly categorised as institutionalist. This can be illustrated by reference to international comparisons. These show that male/female wage relativities are significantly different between different countries and also that the pattern of change for each over time is not uniform. Thus, in Australia and the UK, wage relativities changed quite dramatically around equal pay legislation in the 1970s whereas, in the USA, much earlier legislation had no such effect. Gregory et al. (1989) explain this in terms of institutional differences between the countries in pay determination. They conclude that, 'an application of the usual human capital model cannot explain pay gaps across countries' (Gray et al. 1989: 238), and suggest an 'increased emphasis on institutions and the impact of the law' (ibid.: 239).[8] Whilst an acceptable conclusion, it reveals a paradox in so far as an unexplained residual from human capital calculations is then associated with causal factors that have previously been excluded from the model. So it seems appropriate to begin with 'institutions' as explanatory factors rather than to end with them to deal with the unexplained residual.

This can be done by taking a very broad view of what constitutes the institutional environment in which women are disadvantaged in the labour market. Thus, the general oppression of, or discrimination against, women is taken for granted – partly for ideological reasons which is what the earlier models primarily sought to estimate as a residual – but equally, and more fundamentally, as a result of women's material position in society in taking primary responsibility for domestic labour and child-care, for example. However, the level of discrimination is not simply read off from this broadly identified factor on the labour 'supply-side'. Other supply-side factors must be taken into account, such as the role of the state and the stance and strength of trade unions. On the demand-side for labour, it is important to recognise the imperatives derived from the nature and degree of competition in product markets – secure markets with low competition might induce a more secure (male) labour force – as well as the organisation and skill requirements of the production processes involved. Equally, the size distribution of industry, in terms of its level of concentration, is an important determinant of the types of jobs available and the types of workers that fill them.

These factors are all potentially a part of any theory of wage determination, but they are given a distinct approach when wedded to the idea that they create definite labour market structures with associated segments of better- and worse-off employees. As discussed in Part III, the leading exponents of (radical) segmented labour market (SLM) theory have been a group of Cambridge economists, although the literature is now vast, covering a wide range of countries, industrial sectors and different strata of employees. The Cambridge school have been particularly concerned with microeconomic case studies, and especially with the sources of low pay. They have found in the context of small firms that:

> the most important dividing line in pay and employment practices to be that between men and women, a distinction which was not always clearly related to job characteristics. The gender of the worker appeared to affect not only the allocation of workers to jobs, but also the grading and pay of jobs and the organisation of work and working-time arrangements.
>
> (Craig *et al.* 1984: 1)

In short, SLM theory sees the male/female wage differential to be part and parcel of contemporary labour markets which structure pay and conditions of work alike. In contrast to the human capital theory approach, SLM theory does not understand residual wage differentials as a deviation from an otherwise harmonious interaction of supply and demand. Rather, economic and social relations are the systematic source of labour market segments which are particularly disadvantageous to women.

Whilst SLM analysis has the merit of shifting the focus in comparable worth away from the methodological individualism attached to human capital theory, it simultaneously incurs a cost. For, especially in the UK, comparable worth legislation is based upon the comparison between *individual* workers. Thus, paradoxically, whilst our social theory, informs us that wage determination is a social process, equal pay legislation is primarily designed to correct isolated distortions. This is even so for 'class actions', where permitted, for these are simply a conglomeration of a number of individual cases.

More generally, much of the ambiguity in equal pay legislation can be understood as an uneasy resolution of the tension between underlying social determinants and individual outcomes.[9] One way of seeing this is in terms of the displacement of the tension on to the distinction between market and non-market forces or factors. There is often a presumption that the market would even out pay differences and reward according to comparable worth. But a moment's reflection reveals that the distinction between market and non-market does not stand up to close examination for it presumes that the economy is confined to acts of exchange. Are trade unions, employer organisations, the organisation of production, the system of industrial relations, etc. part of market forces or not?[10] In fact, the distinction in this context simply poses the issue of what is allowable and what is not in a different, and more obfuscating, form. Indeed, reliance upon market forces to justify wage differentials is more a pseudonym for what employers do, and the wider the scope of definition of the market, the more with which they get away.[11]

An alternative resolution of the tension between social determinants and individual outcomes is the removal of comparable worth away from the realm of the 'market' altogether by appeal to an intrinsic or objective assessment of worth through a job evaluation system (JES). As is apparent, however, a JES is itself socially constructed – especially where it overlooks or weights gendered job characteristics.[12] Even though JES is logically distinct from human capital theory in intellectual origin by discipline and in analytical content, it inevitably tends to incorporate some commercial evaluation in its criteria and weightings so that it forges a compromise with the 'market' in practice.[13]

The tension between the social and the individual is also explicit in UK equal pay legislation through the need to choose a comparator of the opposite sex. Who should count as potential candidates? Two important issues have arisen in practice. The first, covered by Section 1.3 of the Equal Pay Act, 1984 concerns whether two employees belong to the same place of work or not. In deference to the market, comparison with an employee of a different employer is not permitted. But otherwise does this entail the same premises and, if not, what criteria are to be used? The second issue, covered by Section 1.6 of the Act, is whether separate collective bargaining structures constitute a sufficient material difference to allow for pay inequality between men and women. Similar questions can be raised in deciding what makes up one bargaining structure as opposed to another. Significantly, neither JES nor human capital theory have much to tell us about either of these factors. However, as will be seen, they have been crucial in equal pay, having been manipulated by the employers to evade 'fair' settlement.

3 THE ROLE OF COLLECTIVE BARGAINING

Paradoxically, whilst human capital theory is prepared to go to some lengths to detail workers' attributes and, thereby, to assess the impact of comparable worth as institutional change on pay and employment, it has neglected the role of collective bargaining in determining pay (since it is a social and not a personal attribute). Collective bargaining is often the most important proximate cause of pay levels and operates through a small number of agreements covering large numbers of workers. As Zabalza and Tzannatos report:[14]

> The system of pay determination in Britain is highly centralised. A relatively small number of collective agreements determine the rates of pay of a very large number of workers. In the early seventies, the 15 largest national agreements covered around five and a half million workers, which represents around one-quarter of the total working population. A total of three million workers were covered by only four agreements. If in addition one considers wage orders, then the total number of covered workers is 14 million (63 per cent of the working population), of which 9 million are men (64 per cent of the male working population) and 5 million are women (61 per cent of the female working population).
> (Zabalza and Tzannatos 1985: 38)

Although there has been a continuing trend towards greater decentralisation in collective bargaining, 71 per cent of workers still remained covered by it in 1984 (Millward and Stevens 1986: 312–13).

Second, the level of bargaining and how bargaining takes place do change and are a matter of choice, or conflict, between employers and employees, subject to the economic and political environment within which they negotiate. Decentralisation of collective bargaining is illustrative of this and of the choice of bargaining at the levels of industry, company or plant – or not at all.

Consequently, there is a theoretical literature on the likely contours of collective bargaining structures. Some, such as Fulcher (1988), attempt to explain why structures and the scope of issues covered vary between countries. On the other hand, Booth (1989) constructs an analytical scheme which attempts to relate the choice of bargaining structure to economic variables and employer and trade union characteristics although, in the case of Britain, bargaining structures seem to have been determined primarily by management.[15] Significantly, in this theory and in the empirical testing of it, no reference is made directly to gender effects in the labour market. Once again, there is an implicit notion that the male labour market is the standard.

This means that collective bargaining has not been studied as much as it might have been in the context of discrimination. As Dickens *et al.* (1988: 35) observe: 'The extensive literature on the reasons why women are paid less than men focuses more on theoretical debates in economics and sociology than on the ways in which collective bargaining currently influences income distribution.' This is unfortunate for the EOC (1989: 3–4) has argued that:[16] 'Collective bargaining [is] by male-dominated trade unions [and] allied to women's traditional reluctance to use industrial action . . . [with] employers perceptions of men as breadwinners and women as working only for pin-money.'

Moreover, over the past two decades, collective bargaining has become influenced by the presence of anti-discrimination legislation. This has led employers to respond in one of two ways. Either they have embraced the legislation or they have attempted to avoid it altogether. Thus, Snell *et al.* (1981: 18) report from a survey of twenty-six firms: 'Twelve organizations implemented equal pay by removing discrimination from collective agreements and, in many cases, by bringing women up to at least the lowest male rate in the agreement.' But they summarise their results as a whole somewhat differently:

> In over half the organizations, action was taken which reduced employers' obligations under the Equal Pay Act and resulted in women receiving less benefit than they would otherwise have done. Such actions included: the tightening of women's piecework rates to offset increases in basic rates; the introduction or restructuring of grading systems such that women ended up on lower rates or grades regardless of their skill level; increased job segregation to prevent equal pay comparisons and the comparative under-grading of women in job evaluation exercises.
>
> (ibid.)

Similar sorts of conclusions can be drawn from Ghobadian and White's (1986) study of job evaluation and equal pay. They find that there is liable to be less sex bias in job evaluation in the following circumstances – in manufacturing, the more full-time employees there are, the more formal (analytical) the job evaluation scheme, the more there is (female and trade union) employee participation, the more organised are personnel functions, the larger the establishment and the greater the proportion of female workers.

From these studies, a clear picture is obtained of the sorts of circumstances in which sex discrimination in pay is more likely, although this is, in part, a product of employer and, to a lesser extent, trade union strategy as well. In particular, the structure of collective bargaining in allocating different groups of employees to different job evaluation schemes is important as well as the evaluations themselves across the sexes within a particular group of workers. To put it sharply, if job segregation is extremely pronounced, then men and women can *either* be allocated to different grades within a single job evaluation scheme (with women occupying the lower grades) *or* they can be evaluated in two separate schemes in which there is no possibility of sex discrimination as such since there are no gender comparisons to be made within each scheme.

For an employer wishing to minimise the impact of equal pay legislation, the second of these options is to be preferred. For it creates a double obstacle to equal pay – job and pay comparisons have to be made across the separate bargaining structures *and* female grades in the one have to be placed as high or higher than some male grades in the other (assuming this to be appropriate). Only the latter is necessary in case of a single bargaining structure covering both male and females. It should be emphasised that which of these outcomes actually occurs is the consequence, not of undertaking a logical exercise, but of collective bargaining itself and subject to the range of influences already discussed.

In practice, an important way of responding to equal pay legislation has been to combine male and female workers into a single set of grades and to place women on the lowest rungs of the grading. For Snell *et al.* (1981: 64): 'The level of pay determination was also found to be an important factor . . . As a result women's rates in many organizations were raised to the lowest male rate in the agreement.' This is confirmed by the analysis of Gregory *et al.* who argue:

> It was the adoption of the simple rule that the lowest pay in any agreement must be shared by men and women that was the crucial consideration. It was this clause that extended the British Equal Pay Act, somewhat loosely, into the domain of comparable worth. As in Australia, the large pay increase for women was not the result of detailed analysis of appropriate pay rates for women but the result of the adoption of a simple, across-the-board rule.
>
> (Gregory *et al.* 1989: 233)

They continue:

> The experience of Britain and Australia suggest . . . in each country, and before the official interventions, the labor market institutions – trade unions and national pay agreements – explicitly recognized pay discrimination and built it into the pay structure. As a result, it was relatively easy

to identify where pay discrimination occurred. In addition, given the desire, it was relatively easy to remove that which was identified as pay discrimination and, as a result, to affect dramatically the pay relativities between the sexes. The mechanism with the largest quantitative impact was the adoption of a simple rule that extended across firms and stated that within each pay agreement there should be a common rate of minimum pay for men and women.

(ibid.)

The findings of Zabalza and Tzannatos (1985) are not quite so specific. They conclude, following the Equal Pay Act of 1970,[17] that the system of collective bargaining did lead to a substantial narrowing of the relativity between male and female wages over the mid-1970s by the process of creating common grades and raising female wages rather than by lowering male wages.[18] The relativity was decreased by about one-fifth. This is certainly consistent with the idea that the major mechanism by which this was done was through paying women what was previously the minimum for male workers. Using a human capital model, to take account of differences in labour market characteristics of men and women, they then estimate that this had reduced sex discrimination in pay by between 30 and 50 per cent.

In this respect, Snell *et al.* (1981: 65) adopt an ambivalent attitude towards the impact of paying women at the men's lowest rate. For, whilst millions of women benefited by this, it has also been the means by which discrimination has been retained within bargaining structures. Dickens *et al.* argue that this need not be so, reporting on the results of the new regrading scheme covering local authority manual workers:

> The results of the job evaluation exercise produced very significant changes in the rank order of jobs covered by the manual workers' national agreement. This can be explained partly by the length of time that had elapsed since the previous major review in 1969, but more importantly, by the joint commitment to incorporate equal value principles into the new scheme, and wherever possible, remove sex-bias from the gradings.

(Dickens *et al.* 1988: 38)

To some extent, however, the local authority scheme may give a false impression of what has happened more generally. For job evaluation schemes tend to be changed more often than once in every 20 years. Ghobadian and White (1986: 24) report that, 'between 1980 and 1982 11 per cent of establishments discarded their job evaluation schemes without replacing them'. Presumably a number did replace those discarded. Dickens *et al.* recognise the need for a much faster rate of replacement of job evaluation schemes:

It is usually argued that any scheme has an effective life of little more than five, or at most, ten years, and that in sectors characterised by a rapid introduction of new technology (for example, banking), salary structures should be frequently revised.

(Dickens *et al.* 1988: 37)

Along with Ghobadian and White (1986: 70), it is suggested that the effect of job evaluation is to change the existing job hierarchy and that, where evaluation has not been changed recently, it is liable to have been rendered redundant by the equal value legislation of 1984: 'It can also be assumed that few schemes introduced before 1984 were informed by an awareness of 'equal value'; they should, therefore, be reviewed in the light of the Amendment' (ibid.).

To sum up, bargaining structures have been important in the implementation of equal pay legislation. They have been most common in circumstances where men and women have been brought into a single evaluation structure, with women's pay being raised to the level of the lowest male. This has left, however, two factors in continuing discrimination; one where women have been retained in separate bargaining structures and the other where their grading has been too low. In the first case, both grading and the necessarily frequent regrading of men and women together will have been avoided.

The motives for such an avoidance strategy can only be guessed at. One might be fear of heavy increases in the wages bill. Another might be management inertia in face of the administration involved. The negative implications may well be and have been exaggerated. For Snell *et al.*:

The most striking finding about the costs of equal pay legislation was that the majority of organisations did not feel, after implementation, that it was important to know how much equal pay had cost, although most expressed grave doubts about the effects of the extra costs when the Act was passed . . . information from an outside source (Incomes Data Services) suggested that worry over the effects of costs had dictated an implementation strategy leading to almost total job segregation.

(Snell *et al.* 1981: 60–1)

They also conclude: 'Our analysis suggests that, given a well-constructed jointly agreed job evaluation scheme, minimization [of equal pay impact] was unlikely as well as difficult, (ibid.: 65). Ghobadian and White (1986: 53–4) recognise that the management of an analytical job evaluation scheme carries some difficulties with it but that there are liable to be net benefits overall in personnel management and labour relations. It is functional in giving care and attention to effective labour utilisation. Thus, whether taking into account wage costs or management resources, the avoidance of equal pay legislation through separate bargaining structures for men and women seems to have little to recommend it.

4 SOME LESSONS

What lessons can be drawn from this analysis? First, as has already been widely recognised, the UK equal pay legislation is totally unsatisfactory. Reform has proceeded at a snail's pace, usually against the government's own wishes, often by appeal to the European Court of Justice (ECJ).[19] In the first 10 years since the 1984 Act, 7,837 equal pay applications have been made to industrial tribunals involving 565 employers. Only 119, covering almost 1,000 individuals, have been referred to independent experts, with 18 per cent having been upheld (and 57 per cent otherwise settled or withdrawn). On average, cases referred to independent experts have taken 18 months to complete; this average, however, only takes account of this one stage in the process (and is subject to appeal) and does not include cases still in the pipeline for which delay has been even longer.[20] More generally, four cases were still outstanding almost 10 years after applications were originally made.

There has, however, been progress in undermining a defence against equal pay based on separate collective bargaining structures. Whilst one judgment did accept separate non-discriminatory collective bargaining structures as a material defence for differences in pay, another ruled otherwise on the grounds that it is the outcome of the processes, rather than their structure, that counts. On appeal, the former judgment was overruled by the ECJ, effectively sounding 'the death knell for the collective bargaining defence' (*EOR*, 58: 11). On the other hand, progress on what constitutes same employment has been limited. Separate establishments can be used for purposes of comparison but only as long as *no* differences in locally negotiated conditions apply.[21]

In short, progress in equal pay legislation and dealing with claims has been so limited that the Equal Opportunities Commission (EOC), as well as the TUC, has taken the unprecedented step of appealing to the EC to take legal action against the UK government. This follows the EOC's submission of proposed reforms to the government in March 1988, and a response only five years later with minimal concessions:[22] 'In the EOC's view the equal pay legislation is 'uniquely unworkable within the framework of British labour laws and continues to fail to meet' the UK's Community obligations' (*EOR*, 52: 20).

If the first lesson of this chapter is to confirm the inadequacy of the UK equal pay legislation, the second lesson is to reinforce the conclusion that the human capital approach to comparable worth is totally inappropriate. Apart from its limited merits as a theory of how (female) labour markets operate in general, it has no purchase whatsoever on the necessary contradictions (between social determinants and individual outcomes) that characterise comparable worth claims in practice even if it were to include factors such as collective bargaining in its wage equations. Of course, human capital type calculations might be used as evidence in comparable worth claims but they cannot adequately capture analytically the way in which labour markets function.

This leads to a third, more general lesson concerning the status and worth of equal pay legislation. As previously observed, the human capital approach makes judgement on the basis of an exogenous shift in the wage equation. Some have interpreted this as equivalent to minimum wage legislation and, for Killingsworth (1990: 47), to a tax on female labour: 'In sum, requiring comparable worth wage increases for predominantly female jobs is akin to putting a tax on employment in such jobs: it makes it more expensive to employ predominantly female labor.' This has led some to reject comparable worth on the grounds that it cannot redress much of the male/female wage differential, it differentially favours women better placed in the labour market,[23] and that it only functions successfully at the expense of employment.[24]

Each of these objections is open to dispute for the narrow and erroneous foundations upon which they are constructed. Most important, comparable worth is more appropriately examined as an *effect* as well as a causal factor in the functioning of labour markets. Thus, Kessler-Harris (1992) observes how the meaning of equal pay has shifted over the last century, from seeking to stifle competition between male and female workers to a commitment to comparable worth as a source of justice in the form of a 'just price'.[25] Further, comparable worth must be situated in its appropriate social and historical setting, one in which women have rapidly approached labour market participation rates comparable to those of men – despite continuing child-care and other domestic responsibilities and other forms of inequality in and out of the labour market.

The view of the tensions between market and non-market principles in the determination of a just price for labour are implicitly seized upon by Brenner (1987). She emphasises the limitations of comparable worth due to its dependence upon liberal values, meritocracy and the principle of market evaluation.[26] This is undoubtedly correct (but, presumably, any process of wage bargaining must accept bourgeois principles), although too precipitous in disparaging comparable worth by overlooking the contradictory tensions at work. As Acker observes:

> In the short term, better wages for low-wage women will ease the poverty problem. In the longer term, its most important consequence may be that it will draw women into labor union activity and push unions into realizing that women's issues are important labor issues. Comparable worth also has the radical potential to question what our society really values and who has the power to set those values.
>
> (Acker 1989: 26–7)

But she is acutely conscious, as an unintended effect of an alliance between women workers and management, that there is a potential for comparable worth to displace control of wage setting to management through JES (ibid.: 202). Similarly, comparable worth can maintain and reproduce the internal hierarchies of organisations, together with their class and gender relations (ibid.: 212). Evans and Nelson (1989) also argue that comparable worth can challenge received notions of the value of women's labour in and out of the home, but recognise that it may become dependent upon the creation of female elites and be more successful and rapidly implemented to the extent that it is imposed top-down by management rather than through active worker participation. Blum (1991: 168) acknowledges the potential conflict of interests amongst women, and how this might obstruct labour–feminist alliances. More generally, she points to:

> four contradictory tendencies in the politics of comparable worth, each of which poses problems for the issue's radical or transformative potential. These tendencies arise from the complex intertwining of the class and gender interests of low-paid women, as well as from the movement's need to operate and gain legitimacy within bureaucratic organizational settings.
>
> (ibid.: 182)

In short, comparable worth is both an expression of, and a terrain of conflict over, the conditions under which both men and women enter the labour market, necessarily incorporating the divisions and complexities that this involves and which cannot be avoided by exclusive reliance upon supposed access to unfettered market forces or purer forms of gender and/or class conflict. On balance, comparable worth is to be supported for promoting the interests of women and of labour, despite the attendant tensions and limitations.

This assessment is confirmed in a perverse way by reference to the stance at the opposite extreme, that attached to the neo-Austrian right. Moens and Ratnapala recognise that comparable worth is part of a broader set of socio-economic processes, ones that they seek to prevent:

> The implementation of the comparable-worth method involves a 'fundamental change in the way our society operates' . . . It involves replacing the impersonal forces of the market with the discretions and determinations of officials exercising subjective judgement. To the extent that it seeks to remove wage-setting from the influence of the market, the method also undermines the fundamental tenet of a liberal society, namely, that individuals are primarily responsible for their own well-being.
>
> (Moens and Ratnapala 1992: 97)

Despite the ideological extremity revealed by this quote, the stance adopted readily recognises that what is at stake is whether women shall have the opportunity to pursue their self-interest *collectively*, whether this should be recognised institutionally and legally within the system of industrial relations, together with what this might all imply for further economic and social change.

Comparable worth legislation is designed to deal with post-entry labour market discrimination – that is, given workers are in employment, are they being paid the appropriate wage by comparison with one another? It is not directly concerned with why female workers enter the labour market from a disadvantaged position as a result of inherited disadvantage in education, health, welfare, transport, etc. Consequently, as observed, critical responses to comparable worth legislation have fallen at two extremes. One occupies a *laissez-faire* stance and perceives it as undue interference in the (objective) workings of the market, thereby allowing public servants to make subjective judgements about levels of wages. Such ideology is totally out of touch with the realities of how (labour) markets function in general. It is, however, complemented by a critique that sees comparable worth as incapable of redressing labour market inequality satisfactorily and as unduly favouring those workers best able (often already the better-off) to make use of the legislation and, thereby, undermining the pressure for more fundamental change. Equal pay legislation becomes hi-jacked, as it were, by professionals or others well-placed in the labour market, at the expense of a broader scope incorporating the lower paid. It is also possible that equal pay can occupy undue attention relative to other, possibly more fundamental, aspects of labour market inequality – such as unemployment and pre-entry labour market conditions.

These are serious points but they can be positively embraced in the design of comparable worth legislation and in its practice. It must be recognised that comparable worth can only have a limited, if significant, impact, contingent upon other aspects of labour market functioning – as observed, equal pay is more effective in the presence of trade unions, collective bargaining, and the active participation of women negotiators. Thus, equal pay will inevitably favour those who are in secure, organised employment. Whilst this has to be accepted, comparable worth strategy can still be oriented as far as possible to support as many as possible in lower-paying occupations. There is no reason to believe that this must prejudice those who do not benefit directly from equal pay legislation. There may be off-setting deterioration in their working conditions, but it is more reasonable to assume that there will be a positive trickle-down or demonstration effect. Even if not, the indirect effect of equal pay on one set of workers is only liable to disadvantage others in conjunction with, and through, a range of other factors that will not remain the same and which will be open to other forms of government support – from minimum wage legislation to employment creation schemes.

From the UK experience, and elsewhere, it is apparent that the more comparable worth is tied to a formal legal system, the more ineffective it can prove to be both in speed and in cost of deliberation. Excessive legality also tends to favour employers with their greater access to funds and legal advice. In addition, formal legal systems, however well-intentioned, because of their necessary precision whether by statute or case law, inevitably open up the potential for abuse through evasion. Consequently, informal rather than strictly legal procedures should be adopted for the implementation of comparable worth policy. It is necessary to rely upon informed and guided judgement rather than a court of law although, inevitably, outcomes are highly contingent on the balance of power within industrial relations and the stances adopted on gender issues.

In promoting comparable worth, however, an important starting-point would be within the public sector itself, where government can be prevailed upon to fund and implement the necessary wage adjustments without undue opposition for commercial or other reasons (such as ideological resistance to equal pay). This would then potentially create a model and precedents for adjustments within the private sector. These, in turn, could be reinforced by sanctions against private companies tendering for public contracts if they had not met equal pay requirements.

NOTES

1 Most recently, see Killingsworth (1990), Sorenson (1994), Rhoads (1993), England (1992), Gregory (1992), Jarman (1994), and Kahn and Meehan (1992).
2 See Eyraud (1993), Eyraud *et al.* (1993), Perlman and Pike (1994), Gunderson (1989, 1994), and Moens and Ratnapala (1992).
3 See Humphries and Rubery (1995a) for an account.
4 Thus, Joshi (1990), for example, employs a model in which the effects of gender are analysed, together with motherhood, part- and full-time work and other, more traditional, labour market variables such as education and experience. This disentangles the effects on relative pay over time, distinguishing the impact of motherhood (as such and through lost work experience) and gender. It is found that the latter was smaller than the level of pure discrimination but has also varied both for mothers and for non-mothers through the passage of time. Levels of discrimination have been much more severe for part-time as opposed to full-time women workers. See also Ermisch *et al.* (1990) and Wright and Ermisch (1990), but especially Davies and Joshi (1995).
5 Higher wages paid for greater effort, lesser turnover, adverse selection, to discourage unionisation, to reduce recruitment costs, and to solicit group morale. See Chapter 2.
6 Fine (1992), for example, argues that women's labour market position in the UK is unique for the extent of its dependence upon part-time work because of the economy's low wage, low investment, and low productivity de-industrialisation, the separation between welfare and labour policy, and the lack and form of support in government policy for each of the latter.
7 Thus, to give a formal example, Killingsworth (1990: 85) estimates an equation of the type:

$$W = bX + kC$$

where W is wage level, X is a vector of worker characteristics, and C signifies presence or not of comparable worth policy. This is complemented by an employment equation (ibid.: 90):

$$\log N = cX + gW$$

Substituting between the two equations implies that employment, N, is purely a function of C and X. In this way, nearly all the historically and socially variable factors determining the ways in which labour markets operate and generate different levels of employment are simply set aside.

8 For evidence of the importance of institutions in explaining relativities between male and female wages in cross-country comparisons, see Blau and Kahn (1996), who emphasise wage dispersion across the labour force as a whole as particularly disadvantageous to women in particular – in the USA as opposed to Sweden and Australia, for example; for Australia, the presence of centralised collective bargaining is seen to be important for favouring women, as in Hunter and Rimmer (1995) but also Eyraud *et al.* (1993) which also examines the impact of comparable worth across a selection of countries as does Dex and Sewell (1995); CEVEP (1994) makes the same point for New Zealand.

9 Gunderson (1994: 2) argues that 'discrimination is socially and culturally determined', whilst also suggesting that, 'The average pay gap between men and women is *obviously* a *result* of the pay received by *individual* men and women and hence it reflects all determinants of individual compensation' (ibid.: 5; emphases added).

10 For an emphasis on the neglected importance of wage differentials that arise out of predominantly male as opposed to female occupations as opposed to a union/non-union differential, see Millward and Woodland (1995).

11 Rubinstein's position is that market forces should not be accepted as a criterion for unequal pay:

> [if] women can be induced to work for lower pay than men on jobs of equivalent value [this] cannot be accepted as a valid justification except by making a mockery of the law . . . [yet] . . . market forces are one possible justification for unequal pay for work of equal value.
>
> (Rubenstein 1984: 146–7)

Our position differs from his in logic and is stronger; it rejects market forces as the basis on which to be able to formulate a well-defined criterion for equal pay.

12 See especially Burton *et al.* (1987) and Steinberg (1992). England (1992) analyses the effect on wages of percentage of women employed in a sector (intended to reflect occupational segregation through crowding effects by denial of access to male jobs) and the extent of nurturance in work (the caring professions) and finds the latter to be significantly negative (reflecting low valuation of women's skills).

13 England (1992) suggests that JES is neither purely intrinsic nor does it internalise market criteria alone in practice, but lies somewhere in-between. Note that, in rejecting comparable worth, Rhoads (1993) considers the market to be objective but JES to be subjective!

14 Over the subsequent period, much centralised bargaining and many national agreements have collapsed.

15 See Deaton and Beaumont (1980).

16 On the other hand, the decline of collective bargaining in the UK over the most recent period has not been marked by a substantial improvement in women's pay relative to men's.

17 This merely ruled out unequal pay for men and women when doing the same job.

18 The common attempt to distinguish the impact on male/female wage differentials in the 1970s between equal pay legislation, collective bargaining, and incomes

policy is futile since each factor is itself dependent upon the others (and the growth of trade unionism and its influence at that time).

19 See various issues of *Equal Opportunities Review (EOR)*. Legislation for compara- tive worth was forced upon the UK Government in 1984 by the EC.

20 For an overview of the process of making an equal pay claim, see Gregory (1992).

21 Just as this manuscript was receiving its final touches, following a judgement in the House of Lords in June 1996 against employers, equal pay was granted to a speech therapist more than 11 years after the claim was first made (*EOR* 1996a). The case had been fought at a cost of over £1 million to the employers although the cost of the judgement, if extended to other employees, could amount to £30 million in backpay. The case of the NUM canteen workers still remains to be settled although just as longlasting.

22 *EOR* (1996b) reports that the average time for a case to be resolved after a tri- bunal's appointment of an independent expert to assess a claim has increased to 20 months. However, from July 1996, a tribunal can choose to deliberate itself without reference to an independent expert.

23 See Smith (1988).

24 For an overview of these arguments, see Perlman and Pike (1994).

25 For the earlier period, see Henderson (1992).

26 For a response, see Steinberg (1987).

9   Minimum wages
Some analytical considerations

1 INTRODUCTION

Over the past decade, and with growing momentum, the minimum wage has become an increasingly prominent topic in labour market economics. In part, this is a response to its rise in political importance. This is itself a consequence of the association of higher levels of unemployment with a widening dispersion of wages, especially in the United States and the United Kingdom. Those at the bottom end of the labour market seem to have been hit hard both by lower wages and lower levels of employment. Not surprisingly, there has been concern with whether a minimum wage would improve the well-being of those in or potentially in low-paid employment. Not surprisingly, the very same *laissez-faire* ideology and politics that have contributed, through a range of policies, to the marginalisation of those already badly off in the labour market, have also been associated with strenuous support for the abolition let alone the extension of minimum wages. In short, deteriorating labour market conditions for the low paid, and higher unemployment, jointly have the effect of intensifying debate over the minimum wage – some determined to support those apparently suffering from the consequences of market forces, others determined to alleviate that suffering through the supposed fuller reliance upon the market.

Academic interest in the debate has also been fuelled by the emergence of a body of empirical evidence, as discussed below, that raising the minimum wage has very little effect on employment and can even be favourable. This goes against the grain of academic wisdom. As Whaples (1996) reports from a survey of 193 US labour economists, 87 per cent accepted the conclusion that an increase in the minimum wage would have a negative impact upon employment among young and unskilled workers. This is despite the extensive publicity that has been attached to the empirical evidence to the contrary.[1]

The purpose of this chapter is to assess some of the arguments for and against a minimum wage, particularly drawing upon the most recent economics literature. In section 2, conventional arguments against are considered, and whilst they are found to be wanting in section 3 by those more favourably inclined towards minimum wage legislation, the more important conclusion, drawn from consideration of both sets of literature, is that assessing the impact of minimum wage legislation depends upon sophisticated and disaggregated studies of a wide range of factors and the interaction between them. This is so even though the empirical and theoretical balance in the debate, covered in section 4, has shifted considerably against the orthodox position that minimum wage legislation is a source of economic inefficiency and lower levels of employment. In the final section, some implications and concluding remarks are presented.

It is worth observing initially, however, that the recent standard economic debate around minimum wage legislation, whatever the scope of factors considered and the conclusions drawn, is extremely limited in content. Essentially, it is concerned with the mechanical effects, often formally modelled mathematically and statistically, of introducing minimum wage legislation. It is a matter of whether the levers of economic policy are best pulled in one or another direction or not at all. Historically, however, minimum wage legislation was first introduced in the state of Victoria, Australia in 1896 and was later promoted in Britain in 1909 by Winston Churchill on behalf of the reforming Liberal government. The concerns at that time were in part very different from those currently engaging the developed economies, involving then the protection of sweated labour from wage levels that would not even allow for subsistence.[2] The position of women was central to the debate, not only as workers particularly poorly placed in the labour market but also in view of what was often perceived to be their more traditional roles as wives and mothers. In addition, the struggle for minimum wage legislation has been intimately related to other measures of social reform and to the emancipation of women and other sections of the work-force and populace, whose unequal position in society more generally inevitably reflects and is reflected by labour disadvantages.

Consequently, as has been equally argued in the chapter on comparable worth, minimum wage legislation is not simply an economic policy but the reflection and consolidation of much broader socioeconomic processes. In this light, it is more readily seen as a measure that potentially shifts the balance of power in favour of the weaker bargaining sections of the labour force. What it achieves in practice is much less certain given the other factors that influence labour market outcomes. But, it is important to establish the legislative and ideological context within which minimum wage legislation is set. At one extreme, it is just an economic policy with more or less favourable effects and open to effective implementation or abandonment according to the economic and political pressures of the time. At the other extreme, it can become an issue of constitutional rights in which society more securely recognises its obligations to its work-force.[3] Should minimum wage legislation be a matter of principle and the rights of labour to a living wage or should it be left more as a matter of pragmatism under the control of powerful vested interests, both capitalists jealous of their profitability and other workers jealous of their differentials?

At the beginning of the 1990s, only 10 per cent of workers were covered by minimum wage legislation in the UK, and the minimum wage was abolished in 1993. By contrast, in the USA, 90 per cent of workers, however effectively, were covered by minimum wage legislation, set in 1992 at $4.25 per hour or approximately 40 per cent of the average industrial wage. If comparative history is to be our guide and a minimum wage our goal, the deeper minimum wage legislation is embedded the better.

2 THE ORTHODOXY

It is crucial to recognise that the traditional theoretical arguments against a minimum wage are extremely crude for a number of different reasons. First, the labour market is treated like any other market with the presumption that a restriction on the capacity of the market to clear at a low enough price will lead to excess supply or, in this case, unemployment. But it is inappropriate to analyse the labour market as if it were identical to other markets, not least because of the roles played by institutions and, within them, the impact of industrial relations in determining the shifting content of what is bought and sold. It is necessary to take account of the skills, initiative, cooperation and goals of the work-force, none of which applies individually nor collectively in the case of other markets.

Second, in the context of partial equilibrium at the microeconomic level, the labour market is treated in isolation from other markets and as a single market. This is inappropriate since minimum wage legislation will have an impact upon other non-labour markets and across different segments of the labour market. These spill-over effects, even within an orthodox economic analysis, do not necessarily lead to outcomes which correspond to the intuitive reasoning associated with conventional one-market partial equilibrium models.

Third, at the macroeconomic level, a minimum wage tends to be fed into a model through its positive impact upon the average level of real wages. As such, models are generally, but not necessarily, designed to incorporate an inverse relationship between real wages and employment, there is inevitably a negative employment effect associated with a minimum wage – and, potentially, an inflationary impact to the extent that wage increases are passed on in the form of price increases. This implies that such macroeconomic models are insufficiently sensitive to the specific impact of minimum wages which are designed to target particular sections of the work-force and particular sectors of the economy. These will not necessarily be characterised by the general features of the labour market, as employed in conventional macroeconomic modelling, however appropriately these may have been modelled in the first instance.

Fourth, traditional analysis is based upon comparative statics in which a minimum wage is considered for its impact in shifting the economy from one equilibrium to another. This is deficient in failing to address the dynamic processes in economic development which cannot be accommodated within an equilibrium approach.

Fifth, and closely related, standard arguments tend to set aside, possibly as exogenous and long-term, a whole series of relevant factors. Some of these could, in principle, be included in a comparative statics, such as market imperfections associated with monopolisation and externalities. But others, especially those which give rise to industrial restructuring, productivity increase and growth and to which the level of real wages is ultimately linked, cannot be readily included within standard economic analysis.

Sixth, the role of anything other than a narrow range of economic factors is excluded. The socio-political impact of minimum wage legislation is ignored. With the exception of trading off distributional goals (higher pay for some of the lower paid) against efficiency and employment, the significance of minimum wages for more general socioeconomic progress and stability is totally ignored.

Finally, and in part encapsulating the other weaknesses, the standard analysis of minimum wage legislation is a deceit in the sense that it does not specifically address the issue, but rather treats it as a particular application of a more general stance towards labour market regulation. In short, minimum wage legislation is opposed on the spurious grounds that all market interventions are disadvantageous, especially those that move prices away from their presumed natural, equilibrium level.

In other words, the case against minimum wage legislation has primarily been made on the grounds that high levels of unemployment, especially amongst the low-paid, must reflect too high a level of real wages. Consequently, a minimum wage can only worsen the problem and, as a separate point, the distributional or equity goals attached to minimum wage legislation might be better achieved and targeted through other mechanisms such as the tax/benefit system.[4]

Before considering these issues in greater depth and genuinely within the context of minimum wage legislation, it is worth cursorily reviewing them in the more general context of the experience of stabilisation and structural adjustment policy in developing countries, especially as these are perceived to suffer from labour surplus or excessively higher levels of unemployment for which a reduction in real wages would appear to offer a solution. However, the World Bank, as in Horton *et al.* (1994c), for example, has explicitly rejected oversimplified accounts of labour market functioning, despite its general and increasing antipathy to state intervention:

> In this framework, therefore, the test for whether the labor market was working really well would focus on whether the real wage fell sufficiently

to maintain employment and output in the face of a reduction in total national expenditure.

(Horton *et al.* 1996c: 3)

Instead, there is an explicit recognition that:

With persistent unemployment, therefore, the finger can point to *at least one of three factors*: imperfectly competitive product markets, aggregate demand feedback from real wages, or labor markets not working well [by which is meant downward real wage rigidity.]

(ibid.; emphasis added)

This concession to factors other than wages being too high is a consequence of the empirical observation that unemployment has not necessarily been eliminated, even in those countries where downward wage flexibility has not been a problem, as Riveros (1994) suggests for Chile. It can even be argued that real wages have been forced down too far with detrimental effects on employment and output because of reduced aggregate demand. Even so, the emphasis of the study is on the reasons why wages may exceed their market-clearing level – as a consequence of trade union power, insider-outsider factors, efficiency-wages and implicit contracts. Notably absent is the role of monopsony power of employers in potentially forcing wages down *below* ideal levels.

What is important in such studies is the recognition of the variety of linkages to the labour market of structural adjustment policies. Export-orientation, for example, has an impact dependent upon the relative labour intensities and levels of wages of the encouraged primary sector and the discouraged industrial sector. The notion that the outcome allevi-ates poverty in rural areas amongst those for whom wages and employment are worst, is contested (Jamal 1995). Labour market adjustments, whether around minimum wages or not, have complex effects which can be counter-intuitive, even within orthodox thinking, both in terms of distribu-tion and upon employment. This is because of shifts in levels and com-position of expenditure, in the composition and levels of production, and potentially in the capital-intensity and productivity of employment.

To recognise, however, that standard arguments against minimum wages have been unacceptably crude in scope and depth does not in itself imply that more sophisticated arguments would support the opposite conclusion. This, for example, is the thrust of Saintpaul's (1994) contribution which, however, also conforms to many of the critical propositions previously out-lined. He employs a one-sector model but in which there are two sorts of labour, skilled and unskilled. He argues against the introduction of a mini-mum wage for the unskilled for four separate reasons. It increases un-employment amongst the unskilled and, hence, lowers output. To the extent that unskilled and skilled workers are complementary in production, it lowers the productive contribution of skilled workers. A minimum wage makes the impact of tax incidence on employment more dramatic. Finally, inequality may even be harmed by a minimum wage because of the higher incidence of unemployment which either has to be shared amongst the unskilled work-force with a high turnover of labour or concentrated for low turnover on a pool of long-term unemployed. Accordingly, redistributional goals could be best met through other policies involving taxes and transfers without suffering the efficiency losses associated with a minimum wage.

Further, he dismisses other arguments in favour of the minimum wage, for example the possible dynamic effects on productivity, although these are added as an afterthought without being incorporated within the formal model. He considers that the adverse effect on human capital of greater long-run unemployment will outweigh the efficiency gains of paying higher wages to those in higher paid secure employment. If, he argues, greater security of employment were the outcome, it could be disadvantageous. For it could impede a shift in the composition of output as labour mobility is required for economic restructuring to be realised. Even if this were not the case, he suggests that firms would themselves be able to internalise the efficiency gains arising out of more secure employment within their own decision-making.

Saintpaul's analysis is remarkable in combining a continuing faith in market forces with a recognition of the scope of factors that need to be addressed in considering minimum wage legislation. In particular, it is necessary to deal with the interaction between labour markets, labour market turnover, the tax/benefit system, and dynamic effects attached to security of employment, quite apart from the putative inverse relationship between wages and employment. Even these additional considerations only begin to scratch the surface of what is involved, as will emerge later. His approach is also a clear illustration of the failure of the orthodoxy to address the issue of minimum wages specifically. For, as he observes himself:

> The above discussion has focused on a peculiar type of rigidity, namely the minimum wage. More generally, it is applicable to *any* institution [such as unemployment benefits] that allows unskilled workers to raise their compensation beyond the market-clearing level.
>
> (Saintpaul 1994: 639; emphasis added)

Other contributions emphasising the negative impact of minimum wages have also been compelled to incorporate a range of further factors. For Neumark and Wascher (1995),[5] other studies more favourable to minimum wages have neglected the interaction between schooling, employment and the minimum wage. Examining US inter-state data between 1977 and 1989, they suggest that an effective minimum wage discourages teenagers from staying on at school and encourages employers to substitute more highly skilled for less-skilled teenager employees. This substitution by employers on the demand-side for labour is reinforced on the supply-side with pupils leaving school earlier because of the lower rewards for skills resulting from reduced employment opportunities. Paradoxically, higher minimum wages increase the skill level of those employed at the minimum, but with falling overall employment and skills in aggregate. Irrespective of the virtues of such arguments, it constitutes a recognition that the issue of the minimum wage is intimately related to skills, and the segmentation of the labour market by age, although segmentation by race and gender is also undoubtedly of extreme importance in this context.

Although not necessarily suggesting opposition to minimum wage legislation, Schiller (1994a) raises the issues of training and career paths in the US context, finding that youths who start out at minimum wages usually receive less initial training than those on lower wages, but they do subsequently progress more in wage gains than those who did not enter on a minimum wage. It may, of course, be that those who survive the experience of minimum wage sectors without training and who remain in employment for future comparison are unrepresentative of all of those who start in minimum wage sectors. Many of the latter may have dropped into long-term unemployment. Schiller (1994b, 1994c) also argues that it is necessary to take account in empirical studies of the uneven application of minimum wage legislation, as affected by differences in federal and state legislation, strength of enforcement and extent of coverage by economic sector and labour market segment. He finds that state minimum wages as such have had limited impact upon youth employment and entry wages but exemptions encourage both higher employment and, perversely, wages.

The issue of enforcement has been explicitly modelled by Chang (1992) in which law evasion following the introduction of minimum wage legislation has the effect not only of adverse disemployment from the higher wage but also a positive employment effect from lower wage non-compliance. The higher wages but lower employment in the covered sectors tends to bring down the wages for those taking residual employment in the same sectors with firms that breach the law. This may lower wages there below the level prevailing in the absence of the minimum wage legislation, although the extent depends upon the degree of risk aversion of firms and the level of fines imposed for non-compliance along with the chances of being successfully prosecuted.

Koning *et al.* (1995) treat workers as heterogeneous in their skills, inducing the better endowed to remain frictionally unemployed until they discover better-paying jobs consonant with their abilities. They contrast with the lesser skilled who are voluntarily and structurally unemployed as a result of too high levels of benefit or minimum wage. Koning *et al.* (1995) estimate, for Dutch teenagers, that an increase of 10 per cent in the minimum wage would increase structural unemployment from 5.2 per cent to 10.1 per cent A search model is also the focus for Fershtman and Fishman (1994).[6] They argue that workers spend time looking for a better wage so that employers will generally pay different wages, with those paying more enjoying a more secure work-force, providing an incentive for them to do so. With the introduction of a minimum wage, workers may reduce their search time satisfying themselves with the minimum wage itself. Consequently, there is a reduced incentive to pay wages above the minimum with the possible effect of reducing the average overall wage. Paradoxically, then, raising the minimum wage may be counterproductive in lowering wages that were previously paid above this level – and the same argument is employed in discussing the effects of price ceilings, with lower prices to promote sales being potentially undermined.[7] Wimmer (1996) points to a different set of factors, arguing that an increased minimum wage will not lead to a fall in employment in the short run in fast-food restaurants since a given level of service will need to be maintained in order to retain brand-loyal customers. Employment will, however, fall in the longer term.

Another issue in assessing the impact of minimum wage legislation is the interaction with other forms of remuneration and working conditions. The latter have tended to be neglected but it presumably ought to be investigated in the same way as non-wage remuneration with the conventional analysis suggesting that compulsory higher wages will lead to a compensating worsening of other employment conditions such as fringe benefits. Ressler *et al.* (1996) suggest that a minimum wage will lead to a substitute of part-time for full-time workers in order to avoid the fringe benefits paid to the latter. In an extremely crude empirical exercise, Gallaway and Vedder (1993) argue that a series of public policy measures, including minimum wage legislation, have all contributed to the decline of employment in US restaurant employment. One of the measures they cite is the taxation of tip income; Wessels (1993) estimates that if tip income were allowed to contribute towards satisfying minimum wage requirements, at least 360,000 new high paying jobs would be created in restaurants with total income of tipped workers rising by 8 per cent!

3 THEORETICAL REASONS TO BE SCEPTICAL

The cursory survey of the literature already mentioned suggests that the conventional view of minimum wage legislation as decreasing employment can be sustained in a more sophisticated way than has been common but only at the expense of introducing a whole range of arguably important considerations. However, doing so has opened the conventional conclusions to an even greater degree of doubt. In formal modelling employing comparative statics, Fields (1994), for example, shows how an economy with just two sectors, one covered by a minimum wage and one uncovered, does not necessarily reproduce conventional results for the employment effects of a minimum wage. Informal reasons why this might be so are easily understandable. Minimum wage legislation is necessarily redistributive towards the lower-paid, even if employment decreases.[8] If the demand for goods by the lower-paid is highly labour-intensive, either directly through their own purchases or indirectly through multiplier effects, then the net effect on employment for the whole economy could well be positive. In short, even with conventional economic analysis, general equilibrium considerations of interactions between markets means that it is impossible to be certain about the overall impact of shifts, such as minimum wage legislation, within particular markets and upon employment in aggregate.

Marceau and Boadway (1994) consider an economy with two types of individuals, each group differing in ability and, hence, wage-earning capacity. Although a minimum wage for those of lower ability creates involuntary unemployment, redistributive social welfare can be improved especially if it can be combined with an optimal income tax and unemployment insurance.[9] Swinnerton (1996) considers that two empirical questions are relevant to the study of minimum wages in the context of a search model. First, is an existing minimum wage binding in the sense that none is paying above? If not, this can be taken as evidence of excessive job search since some workers are finding real wages above the minimum, corresponding to their abilities. Others, with the same ability, would have to or choose to search for less time if guaranteed a higher minimum wage. Second, are employers paying below the minimum wage ever subject to labour shortages? If they are, this would suggest that workers are being paid too little, and going elsewhere for higher wages when the opportunity arises.

Another general rationale for minimum wage legislation arises where the social productivity of labour is greater than the private productivity. This can occur for a variety of reasons associated with "market failure" apart from search costs. If firms have monopoly power in product or labour markets, they will seek to restrict output, and hence employment, in pursuit of higher profitability. An enforced minimum wage has the effect of increasing both wages and employment. McClure (1994) shows that if employers have monopoly power in the labour market, minimum wage legislation can increase employment even with a compensating curtailment of fringe benefits. Further, Rebitzer and Taylor (1995) use a conventional efficiency-wage model to create similar effects even though there are large numbers of employers.

More generally, efficiency-wage effects can be broadly interpreted to include gains from lower turnover and greater commitment to gaining and using on- and off-the-job skills. Carter (1993) uses a model of inefficient labour market turnover to show that productivity and welfare can be increased by wage-rate subsidies, hiring taxes or minimum wage legislation, although these lead to higher unemployment. Freeman (1989) argues that trade unions (and, by the same token, minimum wage legislation) can serve as a collective voice, rather than individualised quitting, to signal to otherwise ill-informed employers what are acceptable working conditions. This may reduce inefficient turnover and enhance training and wages.

4 THE SHIFTING BALANCE IN FAVOUR OF MINIMUM WAGES

In the cut and thrust of debate, then, there are theoretical arguments that have been made on both sides. To recognise this, however, is insufficient in weighing up the balance of debate which has shifted considerably over the last decade. Previously, the conventional view has been accepted more or less by default:

> In view of the prominence that issues of low pay and minimum wages have had in Europe – both at the national and Community level – it is striking that, until recently, relatively little research has been undertaken for many countries.
>
> (Bazen and Benhayoun 1994: 5)

As mentioned, recent research has been prompted by the increasing importance of minimum wage legislation as a policy issue, with the persistence of high levels of unemployment in the 1990s raising the role of protecting those who are vulnerable in the labour market. Would they be protected by a minimum wage? If so, would it be at the expense of employment? Would a social charter of minimum standards decreases overall employment or pre-empt international competition based on a downward spiral in wages and working conditions (Bazen 1994).[10]

Debate, though, has also been heavily influenced by two other factors. The first is empirical. Studies of the effect of minimum wage legislation have increasingly questioned the quantitative significance of the conventional view and even found it to be seriously misleading. Minimum wages have been found to be positively correlated with levels of employment. Thus, as Freeman (1994) suggests in his survey of empirical studies, the issue in the 1980s was how great was the negative impact of minimum wage legislation upon employment. At the end of the decade, the balance had shifted, first, towards finding small effects and, secondly, towards rejecting a negative effect altogether. Raising minimum wages appeared to have increased employment! As Ehrenberg summarises the conclusions of a symposium:[11]

> *It is significant that none of the studies suggests that at current relative values of the minimum wage, large disemployment effects would result from modest future increases in the minimum wage – increases up to, say, 10 per cent.* In this sense all the findings are very consistent.
>
> (Ehrenberg 1992: 5; emphasis in original)

Just a few years later, particularly in the light of cross-section micro-studies as opposed to aggregate time-series, Machin and Manning detect a further change in the balance of debate towards denying the conventional effect altogether:

> It is clear that these results have . . . shifted the focus of the debate: in the past studies divided between those estimating large employment losses and those estimating small losses, whereas the focus now is on whether minimum wage legislations have negative effects or no effects on employment.
>
> (Machin and Manning 1994: 320)

This stance has been supported by a series of recent empirical studies over and above those summarised by Freeman (1994),[12] together with those of Dickens *et al.* (1993, 1994, 1995a, 1995b), Card and Krueger (1994),[13] and Gregg *et al.* (1994). In tune with the literature opposing a minimum wage, the favourable revisionists have addressed the issue with increasingly sophisticated techniques and an ever widening range of explanatory variables.

Leaving aside its increasing prominence in policy and the supposedly perverse results from empirical studies, a further factor providing impetus to a reassessment and rejection of the conventional view on minimum wage legislation has been developments within labour market economics itself. As a subdiscipline, it has increasingly focused upon the microeconomic sources and consequences of labour market imperfections. The result has been to allow theory to be constructed, and hence empirically tested, in which the conventional view is contested rather than simply verified or not. As Dickens *et al.* observe:[14]

> It is important, when constructing a theoretical model of the labour market to use as a basis for empirical work, to start from a framework in which the effect of minimum wages on employment can be positive or negative. The conventional approach often fails to satisfy this criterion as it generally works from the assumption that (in the absence of minimum wages) the labour market is perfectly competitive.
>
> (Dickens *et al.* 1995b: 3)

The thrust of the revisionist position on minimum wage legislation is, then, to emphasise labour market imperfections.[15] Of particular importance is the monopsony power exercised by employers over workers. Taking on more workers often requires all of them, including those already working at a lower wage, to be offered higher wages. Consequently, employers hold down both wages and levels of employment. This may be so even in the presence of high levels of unemployment. Local labour market monopsonies can result from lack of mobility of workers as well as limited alternative employment opportunities given the constraints imposed by housing, transport, and family responsibilities. It is hardly surprising that the issue of minimum wage legislation arises for those most poorly situated within the labour market in these respects, often dependent upon casualised employment, especially characteristic of women and youth and those suffering from discrimination whether by age, race or gender.

Further, to the extent that there is a monopsony effect in labour markets, it has knock-on effects although these can, as market imperfections, provide a rationale for minimum wage legislation in their own right. Thus, too low wages discourage labour market participation and promote casualised employment, high turnover costs and limited incentives within work and to gain skills. These factors can encourage the entry or persistence of low productivity firms and industrial fragmentation, with low levels of both capital intensity and productivity increase.

The latter effect is emphasised by a number of writers; Gregg *et al.* (1994: 107), Bazen (1991) – as shock effects of minimum wage legislation hitting managerial inertia, Bazen (1994: 22–3) and Dickens *et al.* (1994: 42). For Wilkinson:

> A floor to wages plays an important role in obliging firms to become more efficient or to transfer workers to more productive and hence more socially useful purposes. When this discipline is relaxed as unemployment rises, the more disadvantaged in the labour market become increasingly vulnerable. The ease with which their wages and conditions of work can be depressed, and their labour further devalued, forms the basis for the competitive survival of inefficient producers . . . The consequent intensification of competition adds to the increased uncertainty and risk induced by economic depression, further reduces the incentive to invest and innovate, and builds up reliance on forms of low pay as the only means of survival.
>
> (Wilkinson 1992: 35)

These considerations involve dynamic issues of how economic development proceeds over time rather than static inefficiencies. In the context of minimum wage legislation, they have hardly been addressed at all, and certainly not in formal models nor in empirical investigation. This is hardly surprising as these dynamic issues are difficult to accommodate within conventional economic analysis, the vast majority of which is organised around equilibrium, steady state growth paths and comparative statics.

However, some progress has been made in recent endogenous growth models, although these have only recently been applied to labour market imperfections and minimum wage legislation. These models argue that there are positive externalities in investment. The more investment that is made, the more productive are subsequent investments, as markets, technologies and skills are mutually developed and shared. These models have been important in explaining why growth rates might differ and why convergence between them and levels of development across countries might not be realised. If they were to be applied to the labour market, it could be argued that minimum wage legislation would encourage higher capital-intensity, productivity increase and economies of scale. Whilst the net direct effect on employment might be ambiguous – with output and productivity both increasing – the higher growth rate would provide for compensating benefits or subsidised employment creation schemes.[16]

It is possible to address the impact of the labour market and minimum wages on the growth rate, rather than static inefficiencies, in another way – one with a long, if neglected, lineage. This is through Domar's contribution to the Harrod–Domar model. For him, the rate of growth was not only dependent upon s/v (the saving rate divided by the capital–output ratio, or the amount of investment and the rate at which it is turned into output), but also upon the level of capacity utilisation, σ, so that the growth rate becomes $\sigma s/v$. As investment proceeds, market demand and corresponding input resources must be shifted from capital of older and/or lower productivity to the newer, higher productivity capital stock. This involves the scrapping of the less technically efficient equipment and plant.[17]

There is no reason to presume that this will be achieved smoothly or at all. The perfect market would function by bidding up the prices of scarce inputs, including labour, rendering the less productive equipment uneconomic. Owners of the scrapped machines would, however, inevitably seek to remain in business by resisting the pressure to raise wages. To the extent that they succeed, this would deprive the new investments of markets for output, and depress capacity utilisation and the growth rate across the economy as a whole. Nor is there necessarily an unambiguous incentive for the owners of the new, higher productivity investments to bid up the wage, for example, and induce labour to quit from the old investments and take employment on the new. This would depend upon whether the higher market demand and capacity utilisation for them proved a more profitable avenue than working at less than full capacity but paying at lower levels of wages.

Essentially, this model depends upon labour market imperfections in which labour market mobility is imperfect and/or employers have monopsony power. In this respect, it is very similar to the static models previously considered, although it is important for suggesting how minimum wage legislation can have a positive impact upon the growth rate, productivity, and capacity utilisation. Moreover, it can also be connected to knock-on effects. Should new investments fail to realise full capacity, then this creates a disincentive to make such investments. In addition, those that are made and which embody increased labour productivity will, for given levels of demand, have the effect of increasing the level of unemployment, thereby supporting the very labour market from which competing, but less efficient, employers can draw.[18] As Wilkinson (1992: 22) observes: 'Rather than low pay being an answer to unemployment, high levels of joblessness are a precondition for many accepting low pay, which they very soon quit when job prospects improve.' Many sweated, crowded-in, labour markets are characterised by industrial fragmentation, low competitiveness, and low levels of productivity and innovation. Failing to protect workers consolidates these features in the long term without necessarily even preserving jobs in the short term.[19]

5 IMPLICATIONS AND CONCLUDING REMARKS

Although the unambiguous conclusion of this chapter is that the literature, both theoretical and empirical, has swung in favour of minimum wage legislation, this is not the most important conclusion. Rather, it should be emphasised that the impact of minimum wage legislation is highly complex and dependent upon a range of factors which are liable to be sector specific in their presence and interaction. This does, however, reinforce the conclusion that the conventional inference of an inverse relationship between minimum wage legislation and employment is totally inappropriate as a way of proceeding either in policy or in analytical terms.

For the workings of labour markets do not comply with this simple conventional economic logic and, to the extent that such mechanisms of supply and demand are in place, they are often dominated by other socioeconomic factors and interaction with them. Not surprisingly, as soon as labour markets are empirically examined in detail, they do not conform to such traditional thinking. It is well known, as discussed in Chapter 3, that more sophisticated human capital models than those that have been employed for examining minimum wage legislation have failed to explain a residual of discrimination in labour markets involving age, race and gender. Many of the revisionists in the minimum wage debate have pointed this out – Wilkinson (1992: 22) and Gregg *et al.* (1994: 104), for example – notwithstanding other more longstanding arguments in favour of minimum wages such as the macroeconomic effect on aggregate demand and considerations of efficiency and equity in case of fragmented and sweated employment. Moreover, at a macroeconomic level, especially over the longer term, major increases for the low paid, as in equal pay legislation for women, have not had the effect of preventing growth in their employment which has proceeded apace.

By the same token, the further studies of the labour market are disaggregated, the more they are found to flout the conventional wisdom. Reproducing the earlier results of US labour economists in the 1950s, Krueger and Summers (1988) find that wages for workers with the same characteristics are significantly different from one industry to another, suggesting other, industry-specific factors are important in wage determination. Other studies have confirmed this for other countries.[20]

In this light, it is important that minimum wage legislation be designed to take account of the specific workers and sectors upon which it has an impact, although this does not rule out an absolute minimum for the work-force as a whole or for the low-paid in general. Freeman (1994) points to the following advantages of minimum wage legislation: it is directly redistributive without direct budgetary consequences (as compared to wage subsidies and a negative income tax); it increases the incentive to work (as opposed to income-related benefits); it is administratively simple and easily targeted; and it has the potential to charge low-wage employers the full social cost of labour. In addition, in practice, it is necessary to take account of the extent of coverage, the extent of enforcement, and the relationship to other, potentially off-setting, labour costs – quite apart, as has been emphasised here, the dynamic and sectorally specific interactions with a range of other factors.

Although the employment effects of a minimum wage continue to command substantial attention, the more general welfare effects have become more prominent, as is evidenced by the recent compendium in the *Economic Journal*. Freeman (1996) views a minimum wage as primarily redistributing income, although account needs to be taken of those earning below a proposed minimum not necessarily belonging to the poorest households (in case of multiple or no earner households) and that the already better-off may be induced to take jobs at the higher wage at the expense of the worse-off.[21] Sloane and Theodossiou (1996) argue that *only* 44.4 per cent on low pay in 1991 were still so in 1993 (although three-quarters of these are women) and *only* 30 per cent in low pay are in low-income households, suggesting that low pay is a temporary fate for those who remain in the work-force without necessarily confining them to poverty even for that period.[22] Bell and Wright (1996) deduce a limited impact of a minimum wage in view of the weakness of implementation – 47 per cent of part-time workers and 25 per cent of full-time workers in licensed residential establishments, for example, were found to have been paid below the statutory minimum in the UK in 1991.[23] Machin and Manning (1996) also consider that a minimum wage will have limited employment effects but be of particular benefit to women workers on very low pay.

Finally, to return to one of the opening themes. Far from setting wages, minimum wage legislation is an intervention in the wage-setting process and all that this entails for labour markets and for socioeconomic progress more generally. Whilst, like any other legislation or policy, it can be reversed, care should be taken to scrutinise arguments that suggest other policies with the same goals are more effective, such as income support or wage subsidies to address poverty, possibly because of avoiding market distortions and questionable disemployment incentives. This is because some policies are more secure and harder to reverse than others. Once in place, minimum wage legislation can become a source of trade union recruitment and mobilisation both to ensure compliance and to negotiate the level of the living wage. Other policies are liable to be less secure, irrespective of their overall efficacy in meeting socioeconomic objectives, because of the way in which they are formulated and implemented within central government and by whom. In any case, and this is why the minimum wage assumes such a symbolic as well as a real importance beyond its immediate and direct impact, it tends to move forward, or back, with other measures favourable to the labour movement. Minimum wage legislation appears to swing in popularity with the strength of the trade union and labour movements. It is less vigorously pursued when labour market objectives can be achieved by other means. Yet, when trade unions are weak, minimum wage legislation potentially secures both higher wages and an object for mobilisation.

NOTES

1 Note that 89 per cent of labour economists also felt that comparable worth would decrease labour market efficiency.
2 As was observed by the New York activist Pauline Newman in 1915, 'while the theoretical debate rolls on, "in the meantime the girls are absolutely starved"' (Hart 1994: xii).
3 This substantially reflects, respectively, UK and US developments in minimum wage legislation, see Hart (1994).
4 This means that the theory of the second best is also usually set aside by those who object to minimum wages.
5 See also Neumark and Wascher (1992).
6 See also Williams (1993) who finds a significant reduction in employment for US teenagers, taking account both of the 'queuing' for jobs in sectors covered by minimum wage legislation, and a 'discouraged' worker effect and fall in labour market participation by those unprepared to wait for a minimum wage job and unwilling to work for the lower wages that result in the residual uncovered sector.
7 This argument supports a potential trade union view that a minimum wage may lower the wages of those who are previously paid more than the level at which it is set.
8 For the low paid as a whole, this depends on employment decreasing by less than wages are increased.
9 Husby (1993) argues that a combination of minimum wage legislation and a wage subsidy is superior than either by itself in minimising the adverse disemployment effects of augmenting the lowest wages.
10 For discussion of the recent context of minimum wage legislation, also see Shaheed (1994) and Bazen and Benhayoun (1992).
11 See also Freeman (1996: p. 642): 'The debate over the employment effects of a minimum is a debate about values around zero.'
12 See also the other contributions in the special issue of *International Journal of Manpower*, vol. 15, no. 2-3, 1994, and the special issue of *Industrial and Labor Relations Review*, vol. 46, no. 1, 1992. In a preliminary paper, Dickens *et al.* (1995b) find that wage rates were clustered around the minimum level set by Wages Councils prior to their abolition at the end of August, 1993. Subsequently, wages fell below the minimum without corresponding effects increasing employment. Dolado *et al.* (1996), surveying the impact of minimum wages across Europe, conclude that it is extremely hard to find evidence of an inverse relationship between minimum wages and employment, despite the conviction with which such a belief is held by many commentators. For continuing defence of the conventional position, see the special issues mentioned above as well Kim and Taylor (1995).
13 This study takes account of new store openings as well as other factors such as tips, the distinction between full- and part-time working, prices charged, and non-wage employee benefits. See also Card and Krueger (1995) for the bringing together of their various contributions. Their work has by far been the most

important in promoting the revisionist position on the minimum wage and in generating subsequent debate.

14 See also Dickens *et al.* (1994: 26–7).

15 Gregg *et al.* (1994) lay out clearly the issues involved in what follows.

16 Since this was first drafted, Cahuc and Michel (1996) have argued that a minimum wage may induce higher welfare for all agents in the economy since lower levels of employment will be associated with the unemployed accumulating higher levels of human capital and generating higher long-run endogenous growth.

17 For Prasch (1996), a minimum wage can induce productivity increase through the attempts to sustain competitiveness. He also stresses the enhanced bargaining power of labour and the positive impact on aggregate demand.

18 See Fine (1990) for this argument in the context of the British interwar coal industry – with the result that the industry remained highly fragmented, insufficiently mechanised and based on low wages and poor working conditions.

19 For a similar view of the way in which low wages can sustain a vicious circle of low productivity, in the context of women's pay, see Breugel and Perrons (1995).

20 See discussion in Gregg *et al.* (1994) and, for Ecuador, Morrison (1994). For an earlier account, see Krueger and Summers (1987) and Dickens and Katz (1987).

21 But see Burkhauser *et al.* (1996) for a contrary view, that minimum wages will not necessarily unduly benefit those who are worse-off since many are not earners, are not in low income households, and are already paid wages above the proposed minimum.

22 However, this seems to be an unusual use of the term 'only' as the percentages are large if not a majority.

23 This is not unrelated to the limited penalties for underpayment. For example, Bell and Wright (1996) report that, between 1979 and 1991, over 100,000 establishments were caught underpaying but only 82 were prosecuted, with a maximum possible fine of £400.

Part V

The forward march of labour market theory halted?

10 The specificity of labour

1 INTRODUCTION

From the arguments already presented in this book, simplifying enormously, the following conclusions can be drawn. First, it is inappropriate to examine labour markets in terms of equilibrium outcomes. There is absolutely no reason to presume that the forces that operate within labour markets interact more or less harmoniously and efficiently to grind out equilibrium levels of employment and associated working conditions, irrespective of whether such equilibrium notions are used as points of departure for what actually happens.

Second, labour markets are differentiated from one another, giving rise to empirically recognisable labour market segments or structures. However, labour market segmentation theory, even in its most sophisticated forms, has tended at most to proceed in terms of divisions across the labour market as a whole, even if these divisions are perceived potentially to be shifting and overlapping. This has given rise to a wealth of empirical case studies with limited, chaotic or mutually inconsistent theoretical content. In contrast, emphasis here has been placed upon recognising that labour markets are not only structurally differentiated from one another in the limited sense of being separate or divided, but that they are internally structured in different ways. In other words, underlying socioeconomic determinants endow particular labour markets with particular labour market structures, relations and processes attached to their reproduction and/or transformation.

Third, in broad terms, these labour market structures can be derived from what have been termed 'horizontal' and 'vertical' factors. The former refers to determinants that potentially prevail across all sectors of the economy, such as differentiation by gender and skill – the latter refers to the structuring within particular sectors of the economy. This approach allows for the analytical incorporation of direct factors operating from within labour markets and the economy, as well as the broader factors associated with social reproduction, with specific attention having been paid here to the value of labour-power in its two separate aspects – the productivity with which wage goods are produced (and how workers are rewarded) and the way in which consumption patterns are differentiated from one another across the work-force and society more generally.

Fourth, on the basis of this analytical framework, and with the rejection of equilibrium, it becomes necessary to demonstrate how labour market structures are socially reproduced, or transformed, and how they have arisen historically. To accept that labour market structures are historically contingent is not necessarily to degenerate into an empiricism, in which structure becomes categorically identified with sufficiently large differences, as long as the structures are shown to incorporate underlying socioeconomic factors in an integral fashion.

Fifth, then, labour market structures are to be derived from more fundamental determinants and, in particular, from the socioeconomic relations and forces that arise out of the division between capital and labour and out of the profit imperative. This, in turn, implies a particular analytical and causal structure to labour market analysis, in which labour market structures are the reproduced and complex outcomes of the capital–labour relation and its associated tendencies, such as productivity increase, deskilling, monopolisation, etc.

Each of these propositions has been justified at many different points throughout the book by reference to methodological, theoretical and empirical arguments. At times, this has been done by drawing upon the existing literature whether it consciously supports the arguments offered here or not. At other times, the support is gained through critical re-evaluation of the literature or through bringing together what are often compartmentalised contributions from across the social sciences. Consequently, the student of the labour market is liable to accept some of these conclusions more readily than others, such as the need to differentiate the functioning of labour markets as well as the labour markets themselves. This acceptance will also tend to vary by the discipline with which the labour market is addressed. Equilibrium is less attractive to sociologists just as social relations and forces are anathema to mainstream economics.

Whether the reader is willing initially to buy into the whole analytical package or just bits and pieces, in what follows, the issues concerned will be examined from a slightly different perspective – what is different about, or specific to, labour as opposed to other markets. An answer will be given in terms of the inseparability of labour-power from the labourer and the need for social reproduction of the latter. Examining carefully the answers given to this question will reinforce the individual and collective cases for the propositions outlined above. But it will, in turn, lead to an even less popular conclusion relative to the bulk of the literature on labour markets and economic theory more generally – namely, that labour market theory should be based on the labour theory of value properly understood. As Marx observed in his famous letter to Kugelmann of 11 July 1868, drawing together a child's common sense with sophisticated theory:

Every child knows that a nation which ceased to work, I will not say for a year, but even for a few weeks, would perish. Every child knows, too, that the volume of products corresponding to the different needs require different and quantitatively determined amounts of the total labour of society . . . And the form in which this proportional distribution of labour asserts itself, in a social system where the interconnection of social labour manifests itself through the *private exchange* of individual products of labour, is precisely the *exchange value* of these products . . . Science consists precisely in demonstrating *how* the law of value asserts itself.

(Marx and Engels 1975: 196; emphases in original)

In short, it is how value relations assert themselves that holds the key to the understanding of the labour market.

2 FRUIT, FISH AND LABOUR

Within orthodox economics, the core starting-point for labour market analysis is essentially that labour is just like any other commodity. In the simplest terms, it is subject to the laws of supply and demand or deviations from them in case of market imperfections, especially with the intervention of trade unions, for example. But monopsonies are not unique to the labour market, so suggesting that they have an impact does not in itself set labour apart from other commodities. In more technical analysis, supply and demand can themselves be derived from the marginal productivity of labour and from the marginal utility of leisure (or disutility of work), and in conjunction with optimisation over other decisions such as how much to save.[1] In these respects, however, labour is no different in principle, since exactly the same analysis would be used for other factor inputs and consumption goods, although few of these act on both supply and demand simultaneously – apart from the simplest one sector models in which a capital good, such as corn, can be used both for immediate consumption and for investment.

For some, moving forward slightly, but with labour still similar to any other asset, it is merely a matter of who buys and sells it and the conditions under which they do so. This does not represent a major disagreement with those who do proceed on the basis of labour being no different since the uniqueness of labour tends to be specified in terms of its conditions of supply and demand alone. Thus, Sapsford and Tzannatos (1990), for example, do see labour markets as special and theory as having enjoyed considerable analytical progress over the most recent period of time. They suggest that analytical innovation has revolved around a focus upon the allocation of time and the notion of human capital. These, however, merely serve to set up an appropriate optimisation problem over time in which labour has some special properties as an asset.

Slightly less superficial in addressing the specificity of labour are those theoretical innovations that have occurred around the micro-foundations of macroeconomics. These essentially deal with issues of imperfect and asymmetric information, as well as with the problem of the setting and monitoring of contracts. It is crucial to recognise, however, that it is only the application of these models or ideas to labour that appears to set it aside as something special. Exactly the same principles can be applied to other commodities. Indeed, the intellectual origin of many of the ideas involved are to be found in the study of non-labour markets. Informational problems have been associated with the market for 'lemons' (second-hand cars), with insurance (moral hazard and adverse selection also), and with credit markets. Price-setting in the context of uncertainty is not specific to the labour market, and insider–outsider models can be interpreted in terms of entry problems for oligopolies (see p. 258 on Solow), whilst implicit contracts can, in principle, combine two markets together without either of them being for labour.

More progress is made when it is acknowledged that, unlike other physical goods, labour plays an active role in its own sale and has feelings about the terms and conditions that are realised. If the price of lemons goes up relative to the price of oranges, for example, the oranges do not feel aggrieved because they are being paid relatively less than before.[2] The same may not be true of labour, where one section of the labour force may wish to preserve its differential over another section. For the moment, set aside two different aspects of this argument. First, it draws upon a particular factor in the labourer's motivation, whether it be to maintain status by pay relativities or through some notion of fairness. Clearly, there might be a range of other attitudes, objectives and modes of behaviour that are carried into the labour market both by workers and employers (and other agents that are a party to bargaining, such as the state and its institutions for industrial relations). Such is the subject matter of the industrial relations discipline. Oranges and lemons do not and cannot enter their markets with such fanciful notions of their own. Second, there are the issues of how, from the orthodox standpoint, do these rogue motivations arise and how do they persist given, for example, the presence of competition which would eliminate those firms that paid wages that were too high or workers that demanded too high a wage in face of underbidding by the unemployed.

Consider, though, to what extent labour has been specifically differentiated by such insights. Truly, oranges and lemons and all physical objects and services do not *themselves* engage in purposeful activity *directly*. On the other hand, once they are entered into the world of exchange, they are subject to the whims of economic agents. Those agents that wish to buy and sell commodities can and do engage in a variety of motivations indirectly and, as it were, on their behalf. Fairness, relativities, etc. are not simply confined to the labour market. If orange growers were taxed but not their lemon counterparts, there would be an outcry on the grounds of fairness. And, at least in the short run, if conditions moved favourably for one and not the other, economic support would be sought for the loser with good chances of success. Similar considerations apply in other markets where, for example, subsidies to food, housing, health and education are often to be found – not just as a corrective to the imperfections and inequity of the market but also as a consequence of notions of fairness and custom.

The difference, then, between labour and other markets is not that one contains human or subjective factors and the others do not. Exactly the same considerations can arise in both sets of markets. The difference, and there is one in this context, is more subtle. It is that the commodities outside the labour market can only and must be represented by human agents as they cannot represent themselves. This means that such commodities are represented indirectly. Labour can also be represented indirectly as conditions for workers, for example, are negotiated formally by trade unions or informally through other types of worker solidarity. In addition, however much this occurs and whatever the relative importance of each form of representation, the labourer is also necessarily involved directly since it is the activity of working that is the subject of exchange and this is attached to the worker. The fruit wholesaler or retailer does not, in general, continue to accompany his or her wares once a sale has been made!

In short, this line of enquiry leads to the differentiation of labour from other commodities by recognising that the human agency involved in sale and purchase is inseparable from the worker. In this respect, there is an affinity with the notion of human capital in which the productive skills of the worker are necessarily attached to the worker. But there is one important difference. For human capital theory, the worker is otherwise treated like a physical asset or, at least, a stream of potential productive services contingent upon work experience and (investment in) education, etc. Whilst complicating or specifying informational and contracting issues, this does not capture analytically the idea of *social* difference in the operation of labour markets. It is simply a matter of technical difference in the physical properties of the goods that are for exchange and what can be known about them. In contrast, the earlier discussion of relativities and fairness as sources of labour market difference, although in the event only serving as a catalyst in the argument, does serve to demonstrate that *all* markets incorporate a social content around the participation of labour (and capital) whether directly or indirectly (or both).

There are, then, two separate conclusions to be drawn. One concerns the properties that all commodities have in common – that they incorporate not only their physical properties, as in the production functions and utility functions of neoclassical orthodoxy, but also they are the indirect 'representatives' of the agents, customs and motivations of those engaging in exchange. One way of seeing this, which is set aside by neoclassical orthodoxy, is by recognising that 'goods' which are not exchanged incorporate a different set of social properties – whether this be the love or other emotions and activities, that cannot be readily bought in an exchange society, or the totally different social mores that govern societies in which market exchange is altogether absent. The second conclusion is that for the commodity purchased by the wage, the difference with other commodities is not in the incorporation of a social content to the exchange but in its direct nature. The seller accompanies what is sold in the delivery of the commodity.

Crucially, this distinguishes labour, not in a general way in all circumstances but only in the specific content of a labour market as we know it today, under a capitalist market. For, in the case of slavery, it is not a labour market as such that is involved but the sale of human beings themselves. This does not necessarily guarantee the delivery of work in the most orderly and efficient fashion but, significantly in this case, the seller or slave trader does not accompany the worker after the exchange has taken place. And, of course, the customs and mores that are represented in such exchanges are themselves totally different from the economic freedoms, not least in the labour market, that accompany capitalism. Similarly, the self-employed sell what they produce and do not accompany their wares after the exchange (except in certain personal services).

For Marx, the general *social* property of markets is that they bring into equivalence with one another the different types of labour that are used in the production of commodities. Whatever labour is contributed to the production of commodities, and no matter how much it is rewarded in the form of wages or otherwise, is guaranteed a return in the sale of product from which, in principle, a corresponding amount of any other commodity can be purchased. This is a property that does not originate from individual motivation, although individuals are governed by the need to produce for the market, but is a consequence of the way in which the economy is organised, one in which the products of labour take the form of commodities for exchange. All labours do not necessarily count equally when contributing to the ultimate price of commodities but they are measured against one another, not directly, but indirectly through the commodities in which they are embodied.[3]

Now, in many analyses both sympathetic and antagonistic to Marx, it is possible to interpret such labour embodied in commodities as a physical property, like its weight or some other quantitative aspect. As such, this would be to deny the social aspect that it is involved since such physical properties are characteristic of all things that are produced. What is special about labour, if not labour markets, is that the value of a commodity in terms of the labour-time of production represents a social property specific to an exchange society. Value, as interpreted by Marx, can only be legitimately understood as a social property of a commodity-producing society. It expresses the notion that different labours are brought into equivalence with one another through exchange. Paradoxically, from this perspective, those who seek to differentiate the labour market by virtue of the social properties that it brings to the market are mistaken. For, as has been argued above, social properties of one type or another are characteristic of all markets and, in so far as they concern the labour market, the difference is only in whether they enter directly or indirectly into influencing the processes of exchange. The question is what is the different social property that sets the labour market apart.

The property specific to the labour market has to be found elsewhere. To do this, Marx distinguishes between labour and labour-power, the latter being the capacity to work from which the former follows. For Marx, unlike all orthodox economics in which the labour market is synonymous with the market for labour, labour itself cannot be bought and sold. Rather, this only applies to labour-power, and how much work is actually delivered, and its quality, depend upon conflict within the production process itself. None the less, the capacity to work and the work itself always accompany one another, both being inseparable from the worker. But the value of labour-power, the equivalent in labour-time which is paid for the capacity to work, is different from the actual amount of work that is delivered and must exceed the value of labour-power if capital is to make a profit. Thus, what differentiates the labour market from other markets is that it contains a commodity that has the potential to create more value than it does itself command in exchange. This, to be more accurate in Marxist terminology, is the source of surplus value from which all forms of exploitative revenue – profit, interest and rent – are derived.

Later, the issue of value theory will be revisited. For the moment, it is worth reviewing a valiant, but ultimately futile, attempt by a top-notch neoclassical economist to draw out the specificity of labour. Solow (1990) recognises that common sense tells us that the labour market is different even if this has rarely been recognised by macroeconomists as opposed to specialists in labour economics and industrial relations. Indeed, he implicitly suggests that economists lack a healthy pinch of common sense:

> A non-trivial part of the history of economics during the past 60 years could be written in terms of the profession's attempts to find a believable story that can account for the facts with minimal damage to the structure of economic theory.
>
> (Solow 1990: 23)

Solow seeks to rectify this undue commitment to prevailing theory by bringing in sociology and social norms as constraints, and by acknowledging that factors such as fairness and social status enter into the labour market. It is a remarkable commentary on economic theory, but not inappropriate, that Solow consider it necessary to be innovative in order to incorporate such factors into his study of labour markets even though the basis on which he does so is relatively superficial. Indeed, he advises that his contribution is not necessarily radically subversive of mainstream economic theory.

Solow begins by observing that the notion of fairness is extremely important in labour markets, as is recognised in manuals of industrial relations and human resource development and the extent to which social status is tied to income and occupation. He is, however, honest enough to acknowledge that fairness is not unique to the labour market since it has a long history in terms of the notion of a 'just price'. This is simply set aside for being less common for unstated but 'obvious reasons' (ibid.: 7). Irrespective of the empirical validity of this view of the distribution of concern over fairness – and it implies some form of money illusion from an orthodox perspective if, *ceteris paribus*, fairness is not applied equally across all goods – this means that the difference in the labour market has not been specified from a theoretical point of view since, in principle, it has been accepted that it is not a difference. None the less, Solow does locate the notion of fairness in the labour market – workers feel they deserve earnings and are underpaid – in the broader context of social relations in which the labour market represents something more than a simple exchange between the two sides of the bargain: 'Employment and the income it brings are not simply *equivalent* to a set of bundles of consumer goods' (ibid.; emphasis in original).

The way in which this insight is explored is confined to a particular issue – how is it that wages can persist at a level at which there is unemployment without the unemployed underbidding those in employment at the prevailing wage rate. From within efficiency-wage theory, Solow correctly draws the conclusion that the wage is playing two different roles, as a cost and as an index of quality. It cannot perform both functions efficiently at the same time. As an index of quality, Solow perceives the labour market as a social institution, presumably as an informal and unofficial authenticator of quality. But, significantly, exactly the same considerations can apply in other markets, not least that for fish, although Solow appears to see this as a parody, confirming rather than undermining his specification of the uniqueness of the labour market:[4]

> By the way, if it should happen that consumers of fish come to judge quality by price – so that salmon tastes better the more you pay for it, *just because* you pay more for it – then the market for fish will begin to behave unclassically too.
>
> (ibid.: 34; emphasis in original)

For insider–outsider models, Solow observes that it 'starts from a different elementary observation' (ibid.), those in unemployment are not necessarily costlessly interchangeable with those in employment. This is because insiders have powers to impose costs on employers, either deliberately as in disruption of production or unwittingly as a consequence of hiring costs, etc. As Solow concludes:

> The economist would say that the insiders generate a rent jointly with the rest of the apparatus of the firm. They are therefore in a position

to bargain with the firm over the division of the rent. The rent may arise initially simply because the insiders are more productive in this firm than outsiders would be. It will be enlarged if the insiders can jointly threaten to resist the hiring of outsiders by refusing to train them or to co-operate with them. That may require a certain amount of solidarity.

(ibid.)

'Solidarity' now appears to be the social institution involved. Observe, however, that the labour market is now no longer fish-like as in the previous example of efficiency-wages. Rather, it has become land-like, since labour is now commanding an extra wage in the form of a rent. Again, it follows that, irrespective of the extent to which landed property and rent are themselves properly understood, the labour market has not been uniquely specified. On the contrary, and explicitly in terms of the terminology employed, labour has simply adopted the features characteristic of a general economic circumstance in which, within the limits of external conditions (the wage offered by outsiders or, by analogy, the availability of alternative land), those insiders (in employment or sitting tenants) can extract a rent.[5]

For Solow, these examples serve to show how markets might not clear in the Walrasian sense, thereby, even on the basis of individualistic optimisation, inducing customs, notions of fairness and social institutions which consolidate the patterns of behaviour involved. In this vein, Solow adds an example of his own.[6] An unemployed worker considers offering a lower wage than that currently being enjoyed by those in employment but, in doing so, knows the wage rate in general will permanently fall to a lower level. It is necessary for the unemployed worker to trade off the benefits of a definite job at the lower wage against the higher wages of not undercutting but with a much reduced possibility of getting a job. It is relatively easy to show that there is a range of wages for which the unemployed worker will not undercut, preferring to hold out for the lower chances of a higher wage. Consequently, it can become customary not to undercut.

This model is readily formalised within a game-theoretic context and Solow refers to the prisoners' dilemma as an example of the way in which labour markets might not clear.[7] Significantly, as the name suggests, the prisoners' dilemma has nothing as such to do with labour markets. It has been used in a very wide range of applications, not least nuclear deterrence, for example, where engaging in the arms race is the best strategy for each side, whatever the other side does (to gain an advantage by war or threat of war if the other side does not arm and to provide protection if the other side does arm), even though both sides neutralise one another and would be better off without the burden of defence costs. Indeed, this use of game theory is not even unique within economics. There is an exact parallel with the theory of oligopoly in which different firms are considering whether to break a cartel or not. The initial advantage of undercutting by a lower price and sweeping the market has to be set against the loss of a share in oligopoly profits that result from breaking the cartel. Again, there will be a range of prices at which firms would be unwilling to break the cartel.[8] This potential range of outcomes or equilibria, as in the case of unemployment, is considered to allow not only for the presence of social institutions but also for the impact of history in determining which of the equilibria along the range actually materialises.[9] In short, Solow has not developed a specific insight into labour markets – he has simply extrapolated from general non-Walrasian models of the market, possibly with the presumption that their incidence is empirically more likely in the case of labour.

A much more promising start is made by Purdy (1988), not least because, methodologically, he begins with the social relations that Solow attempts to construct on the basis of methodological individualism (thereby restricting the nature and the content of the social relations that will be addressed). He recognises the distinction between labour and labour-power and that they are inextricably attached to one another:

> Labour power is not separable from its owner and bearer, an individual endowed with consciousness and will. This fact makes human labour-power simultaneously the most versatile and the most problematic of all agents of production.
>
> (Purdy 1988: 16)

In addition, he emphasises the need for the labourer to be socially reproduced; of necessity, the worker does not simply belong to the economy or even to the production process alone (a veiled criticism of the crudest forms of Marxist reductionism). Consequently, Purdy points to five separate characteristics of workers which render ambiguity in the formation of their interests with corresponding implications for the functioning of labour markets. Workers act as traders in the commodity labour-power, are active within the production process, engage in the economy as consumers, organise their lives within households, and undertake a range of activities in society more generally (strangely dubbed 'demi-urges' by Purdy).

For Purdy, these all constitute separate but interconnected areas of struggle on the basis of social and, at times, individual power. Wages and prices might be higher or lower, work conditions improve or deteriorate, households be more or less sexually oppressive, and the grievances of workers represented to a greater or lesser extent, with or without success, in the realm of politics. As a result, despite differentiating the uniqueness of the labour market correctly in terms of the inseparability of labour from labour-power and the need for the labourer to be socially reproduced, there is a singular lack of theory for taking the analysis forward. In part, this reflects the absence of a causal and analytical structure since other characteristics could simply be added to the five suggested – such as racism and nationalism, for example. It is also due to a marked reluctance to draw out the implications of the economic forces that are generated by capitalism as a system of accumulation.

Thus, despite recognising that economic and social reproduction requires social relations and structures that may themselves be reproduced or transformed, core consideration of the labour market is dependent upon a balance of power that is even attached to the notion of equilibrium:

> Strictly speaking, the 'value of labour-power' is the vector product of the various physical elements of the equilibrium real wage and the labour time required, directly and indirectly, to produce each one of these elements. Since I am not concerned with the labour theory of value, the labour time component can be ignored. The term 'value of labour power' can then be used to refer to the equilibrium real wage.
>
> (ibid.: 83)

That Purdy should not be concerned with the labour theory of value (as labour-time embodied in physical objects), and that the value of labour-power is otherwise simply seen as a fixed vector of consumption goods, are connected with one another and with the heavy orientation around equilibrium. Further, in Chapter 7, it has been argued that the value of labour-power is a crucial concept in the understanding of the workings and structuring of labour markets, but it has to be understood in terms of its different aspects, especially with respect to the *changing* and *differentiated* conditions of production and consumption, for which notions of equilibrium are totally inappropriate. The final section seeks to show how the labour theory of value addresses these issues.

3 THE VALUE THEORY OF LABOUR MARKETS[10]

The debate over value theory, interpreted as the labour theory of value, has been fought hard and long with no sign of its abating.[11] The debate can be broadly characterised as splitting into two parts. The first is one which accepts the ground rules laid out by orthodox economics which, not surprisingly, rejects the labour theory of value for being an inadequate theory of equilibrium price both in its neglect of the conditions of demand and for its dependence upon a limited set of production conditions for it to be valid (or for Marx's putative theory of prices to be correct). Those who are sympathetic to Marx's theory but who, like the mainstream critics, see the labour theory of value simply in terms of a physical definition of value as the labour-time required to produce commodities, have argued that the labour theory of value, often ingeniously modified and interpreted, is consistent with an appropriate theory of equilibrium prices. This is, however, a futile exercise and can only correctly serve to consolidate the orthodoxy's rejection of the labour theory of value as understood.

The second part of the debate, one which is in tune with Marx's own treatment and yet is totally overlooked by the orthodoxy, rejects the notion of the labour theory of value both as the basis for an equilibrium theory of price and as simply defined by labour embodied in production.

Rather, it emphasises value as a social relationship as briefly discussed earlier in this chapter – value exists in commodity producing societies, not as a physical property, but because different types and quantities of labour are brought into equivalence with each other through the process of exchange.

This is one way in which labour is different in a commodity-producing society, since we do not need a commodity-producing society to tell us about the energy, iron or other physical inputs embodied in a product whether it be a commodity or not. But, again as argued above, this does not distinguish the labour market from other commodity markets, since the presence of social relationships in commodity exchange is general across commodities and not unique to the labour market. What is unique to the labour market is the direct association of the seller with what is sold. The two are inseparable but they are not identical. Consequently, the labour market is distinct in that it is labour-power, not labour that is sold, and the value of labour-power is a key concept for the understanding of the capitalist labour market.

Otherwise, as has been eloquently argued by Rowthorn (1980), the exchange between capitalist and labour can be understood in terms of the labourer hiring the services of the capitalist rather than vice versa.[12] To be more direct, value theory, as applied to the distinction between labour and labour-power, extracts the key aspect of capitalist society in a way that is impossible for theory based on methodological individualism. For it focuses on the exchange between capital and labour as a whole, in which capital monopolises the means of production whilst labour's access to a livelihood is contingent upon selling labour-power which, of course, it is free to do.

Value theory, then, incorporates two important properties, central to the specification of the labour market – it specifies social relations unique to a commodity producing society and the class relations unique to a capitalist society. Fine (1997c) has argued that value theory is characterised by three other fundamental and interrelated features. First, methodologically, it is dependent upon a process of abstraction in which more complex concepts reproduce and do not displace the simpler concepts during the course of the analysis. Price, for example, represents a more developed outcome for value, once account is taken of differences in composition of capitals across sectors. It is a more complex understanding of the way in which different labours are brought into equivalence with one another. In contrast, a more orthodox methodology simply adds one factor after another or, alternatively, views the simple assumptions as an unrealistic but necessary virtue.

Second, value theory involves an understanding of socioeconomic structuring – between classes, between production and exchange, and between the economy and society more generally. However, it is recognised that these structures need to be reproduced, possibly even transformed. This renders equilibrium totally inappropriate as an organising concept.

Third, capitalism is subject to systematic economic forces, particularly those attached to accumulation, and these do not interact harmoniously with one another to grind out an equilibrium, Walrasian and efficient or otherwise. Rather, value theory is concerned with how different labours are brought into equivalence with one another as levels of productivity are themselves in the process of being changed. The repercussions of such developments are not so much to be seen as leading to higher or lower prices (or profits and wages) as reverberating throughout the entire socio-economic system, involving continuing restructuring and, from time to time, economic crises and recessions.

Finally, there is a historical component to value theory. Whilst it does have an abstract component, as laid out above, which is independent of historical circumstances, how the economy is structured and how economic forces are currently integrated is dependent upon how outcomes have materialised in the past. In particular, it is possible for distinct stages of capitalism to emerge – ones in which monopolies, finance and/or the state play decisive roles in ways which are themselves variable across time and place.

In some respects, the preceding discussion is a more abstract return to the analysis presented in Chapter 7, where the dynamic of labour markets was addressed more directly in the light of structures, processes and tendencies. This final chapter has had a slightly different purpose. It has pointed to the merits of value theory in its own right, and it has attempted to show how the issues which we know, as a matter of common sense, to echo Solow, do arise in labour markets, are only liable to be confronted adequately on the basis of value theory. For, otherwise, how are we satisfactorily to incorporate method, class, structure, processes, tendencies and history?

The alternative, certainly that offered by a colonising economic orthodoxy armed with the weapon of social structures formed on the basis of methodological individualism and equilibrium, is highly unsatisfactory. It does not offer a specific theory of labour, except on a contingent empirical basis. In this respect, there is an appealing irony in the work, taken together, of Samuelson and Solow, both leading and longstanding neoclassical economists and Nobel laureates. In rejecting the labour theory of value, in construing it simply as labour embodied, and in viewing it as an unnecessary detour in the derivation of equilibrium prices, Samuelson (1971) has argued that there is *nothing special* about labour. It might just as well be replaced by iron or energy as an irrelevant element that is embodied to a greater or lesser extent in products. Yet, as has been seen above, for Solow (1990), it is merely common sense that there is *something special* about labour, although he has not himself been able to identify it despite claims to the contrary. Twist and turn and contradict itself, neoclassical economics cannot decide whether labour is special or not and, if it is, what makes it so. Despite all their newnesses, the new political economy, the New Institutional Economics, the new microfoundations of macroeconomics or new

Keynesianism all have one thing in common. They do not treat the labour market as different in any qualitative sense, as is apparent for example in appeal to market or informational imperfections or the incidence of trans-action costs whether before or after contracting.

Other social science disciplines, or schools of economic thought, eschew-ing methodological individualism, do offer much more insight into the social relations that set labour markets apart. But they tend to do so on the basis of contingent and often arbitrary empirical foundations. If coherent and rigorous theory is to inform these invaluable studies, value theory, properly understood, provides the only systematic option. In short, this book has traversed two parallel routes simultaneously which have now arrived at a common destination. One, the high road and visible, has been to argue for the differentiated structuring and functioning of labour markets. The other, the low road, underpinning the structure and content of the argu-ments, has been to press the case for an appropriated constructed labour theory of value that incorporates a full understanding of the complexities of the dynamics of the capitalist economy and its constituent labour markets.

NOTES

1 Fine (1980) argues that the marginalist revolution was based on the notion that distribution in all factor markets – specifically, profit, wages and rent from capi-tal, labour and land, respectively – is determined in exactly the same way (and rent-like from a Ricardian perspective) and that this prompted a resistance from those schooled in the classical tradition for which these factors and classes are different from one another and not subject to the same law of distribution (class revenues simply as factor prices).

2 This insight was suggested by Derek Robinson in discussions during the South African Labour Market Commission.

3 In this and later arguments, only a brief overview of the qualitative arguments involved in Marx's value theory will be offered in order to demonstrate that they do seriously address the issue of the specificity of labour. For an elementary beginning, see Fine (1989). See also Fine (1997c) for an account with applications and references to the literature.

4 Of course, in efficiency-wage theory, and asymmetric informational models more generally, the price is not only believed to serve as an indicator of quality, it does do so endogenously – driving out or drawing in quality on average as the equi-librium price is above or below that otherwise needed for market clearing. Efficiency-wage theory is not Veblenesque conspicuous consumption applied to the labour market. Pay higher wages and you do get better work or workers even if in what is induced to come to the market – in contrast, the physical qualities of luxury items such as diamond, or even the commonplace like fish, do not vary with the price paid.

5 As Solow himself perceptively observes:

One of the advantages of family life is that my wife, in reading a draft . . . was able to remind me that she had come to similar conclusions when studying the market for long-term tenancy agreements in nineteenth century Irish agricul-ture. That is not surprising, when you come to think of it. In agricultural communities, the occupation of land is likely to be encrusted with as many and as intense non-Walrasian characteristics as the occupation of a job in industrial communities.

(Solow 1990: 58–9)

This makes clear that the argument is not about the specificity of labour but about any circumstance in which markets do not clear, whether for labour or otherwise. The reason why rent so often appears in neoclassical accounts of deviation from equilibrium is because a more or less permanent revenue persists and has to be explained – hence such factors are liable to be thought of as land-like and give rise to Solow, Marshall's quasi-rents for temporary profits, and the notion of rent-seeking in the new political economy.

6 See also Hahn and Solow (1995).

7 In more detail, the game is a repeated prisoners' dilemma in which the lower wage in the event of undercutting serves as a punishment for undercutting. Note that there is an inconsistency in Solow's argument or, at least, a refinement of the concept of involuntary unemployment that some might consider had rendered it voluntary once more. For, whilst the unemployed want to work at the going wage if offered a job, they choose not to offer themselves for work at a lower wage.

8 Refer to the previous footnote and consider whether a firm in an oligopoly is *involuntarily* holding up its price because it would prefer to sell more output at a slightly lower price but does not do so because of the impact of retaliation from its competitors.

9 Admittedly, Solow (1990: 59) does not consider this to incorporate history 'in any deep sense, in which institutions themselves are to be regarded as the outcome of a particular evolution'. As discussed in Chapter 4, this is not just a matter of how we play the game but what is the game that we are playing and why.

10 The expression 'value theory of labour' is taken from Elson (1979).

11 For reviews of the debate, see Elson (1979), Steedman *et al.* (1981), Fine (1986) and Fine (1997c).

12 Apart from Marx, Marglin (1974) is the classic reference for the role played by the labour market as an exchange between capital and labour, specifically for control over the production process.

References

Acker, J. (1989) *Doing Comparable Worth: Gender, Class, and Pay Equity*, Philadelphia: Templeton University Press.

Agbodza, C. and B. Fine (1996) 'The Genealogy of Human Capital Theory – One Step Forward, Two Steps Back', mimeo.

Aglietta, M. (1979) *A Theory of Capitalist Regulation, the US Experience*, London: New Left Books.

Akerlof, G. (1984) *An Economic Theorist's Book of Tales*, Cambridge: Cambridge University Press.

Alexander, K. (1981) 'Determinants of Early Labor Market Entry and Attainment: A Study of Labor Market Segmentation, *Sociology of Education*, vol. 54, no. 3, pp. 206–21.

Amin, A. (1991) 'Flexible Specialisation and Small Firms in Italy: Myths and Reality', in A. Pollert (ed.) *Farewell to Flexibility*, Oxford: Blackwell.

Anderson, K. *et al.* (1987) 'Labor Market Segmentation – A Cluster Analysis of Job Groupings and Barriers to Entry', *Southern Economic Journal*, vol. 53, no. 3, pp. 571–90.

Anderson, M. *et al.* (eds) (1994) *The Social and Political Economy of the Household*, Oxford: Oxford University Press.

Anderton, B. and K. Mayhew (1994) 'A Comparative Analysis of the UK Labour Market', in R. Barrell (ed.) *The UK Labour Market: Comparative Aspects and Institutional Developments*, Cambridge: Cambridge University Press.

Anleu, S. (1992) 'Recruitment Practice and Women Lawyers Employment – An Examination of In-House Legal Departments in the United States', *Sociology*, vol. 26, no. 4, pp. 651–72.

Anthias, F. (1980) 'Women and the Reserve Army of Labour: A Critique of Veronica Beechey', *Capital and Class*, no. 10, pp. 50–63.

Apostle R. *et al.* (1985a) 'Segmentation and Labour Force Strategies', *Canadian Journal of Sociology*, vol. 10, no. 3, pp. 253–75.

Apostle, R. *et al.* (1985b) 'Segmentation and Wage Determination', *Canadian Review of Sociology and Anthropology*, vol. 22, no. 1, pp. 30–56.

Apostle, R. *et al.* (1986) 'Economic Segmentation and Politics', *American Journal of Economics*, vol. 91, no. 4, pp. 905–31.

Ashton, D. and M. Maguire (1984) 'Dual Labour Market Theory and the Organisation of Local Labour Markets', *International Journal of Social Economics*, vol. 11, no. 7, pp. 106–20.

Atkinson, J. (1984) 'Manpower Strategies for Flexible Organisations', *Personnel Management*, August, pp. 28–31.

Atkinson, J. (1987) 'Flexibility or Fragmentation: The United Kingdom Labour Market in the Eighties', in D. Meulders and L. Wilkin (eds) *Labour Market Flexibility*, special edition of *Labour and Society*, vol. 12, no. 1, January, pp. 87–105.

Averitt, R. (1968) *The Dual Economy*, New York: Norton.

Baffoebonnie, J. (1989) 'Family Labor Supply and Labor Market Segmentation', *Applied Economics*, vol. 21, no. 1, pp. 69–83.

Bagchisen, S. (1995) 'Structural Determinants of Occupational Shifts for Male and Females in the US Labor Market', *Professional Geographer*, vol. 47, no. 3, pp. 268–79.

Bain, G. and H. Clegg (1974) 'A Strategy for Industrial Relations Research in Great Britain', *British Journal of Industrial Relations*, vol. 12, no. 1, pp. 91–113.

Bakke, E. *et al.* (eds) (1954) *Labor Mobility and Economic Opportunity*, Cambridge, MA: MIT Press.

Baran, P. and P. Sweezy (1966) *Monopoly Capital*, New York: Monthly Review Press.

Barker, D. and S. Allen (eds) (1976) *Dependence and Exploitation in Work and Marriage*, London: Longman.

Baron, J. and W. Bielby (1980) 'Bringing the Firms Back in: Stratification, Segmentation, and the Organisation of Work', *American Sociological Review*, vol. 45, no. 5, October, pp. 737–65.

Barrell, R. (ed.) (1994) *The UK Labour Market: Comparative Aspects and Institutional Developments*, Cambridge: Cambridge University Press.

Barron, R. and G. Norris (1976) 'Sexual Divisions and the Dual Labour Market', in D. Barker and S. Allen (eds) *Dependence and Exploitation Work and Marriage*, London: Longman.

Bartholomew, D. *et al.* (1995) 'The Measurement of Unemployment in the UK', *Journal of the Royal Statistical Society*, Series A, vol. 158, Part 3, pp. 363–417.

Bates, R. (1996) 'Social Dilemmas and Rational Individuals: An Assessment of the New Institutionalism', in J. Harriss *et al.* (eds) *The New Institutional Economics and Third World Development*, London: Routledge.

Bazen, S. (1991) 'The Economic Effects of Introducing a Minimum Wage', in IPM *Minimum Wage: An Analysis of the Issues*, London: Institute of Personnel Management.

Bazen, S. (1994) 'Minimum-Wage Protection in Industrialized Countries – Recent Experience and Issues for the Future', *International Journal of Manpower*, vol. 15, no. 2–3, pp. 62–73.

Bazen, S. and G. Benhayoun (1992) 'Low Pay and Wage Regulation in the European Community', *British Journal of Industrial Relations*, vol. 30, no. 4, pp. 623–38.

Bazen, S. and G. Benhayoun (1994) 'Introduction', *International Journal of Manpower*, vol. 15, no. 2–3, pp. 1–7.

Bean, C. *et al.* (eds) (1987) *The Rise in Unemployment*, Oxford: Blackwell.

Beardwell, I. (ed.) (1996) *Contemporary Industrial Relations*, Oxford: Oxford University Press.

Beatson, M. (1995) *Labour Market Flexibility*, Employment Market Research Unit, Employment Department, Research Series, no. 48, Sheffield.

Beck, E. *et al.* (1978) 'On Stratification in a Dual Economy: A Sectoral Model of Earnings Determination', *American Sociological Review*, vol. 43, no. 4, pp. 704–20.

Beck, E. *et al.* (1980) 'Reply to Hauser, Social Stratification in Industrial Society: Further Evidence for a Structural Alternative', *American Sociological Review*, vol. 45, no. 4, pp. 712–19.

Becker, G. (1992) 'Habits, Addictions, and Traditions', *Kyklos*, vol. 45, no. 3, pp. 327–46.

Becker, G. (1993) *Human Capital: A Theoretical and Empirical Analysis, with Special Reference to Education*, London: University of Chicago Press, third edition.

Beer, S. and R. Barringer (eds) (1970) *The State and the Poor*, Cambridge, MA: Winthorp.

Beggs, J. (1995) 'The Institutional Environment – Implications for Race and Gender Inequality in the US Labor Market', *American Sociological Review*, vol. 60, no. 4, pp. 612–33.

Bell, D. and R. Wright (1996) 'The Impact of Minimum Wages on the Wages of the Low Paid: Evidence from the Wage Boards and Councils', *Economic Journal*, vol. 106, no. 436, pp. 650–6.

Belzer, M. (1995) 'Collective Bargaining after Deregulation – Do the Teamsters Still Count?', *Industrial and Labor Relations Review*, vol. 48, no. 4, pp. 636–55.

Benhayoun, G. (1994) 'The Impact of Minimum-Wages on Youth Employment in France Revisited – A Note on the Robustness of the Relationship', *International Journal of Manpower*, vol. 15, no. 2–3, pp. 82–5.

Bennell, P. (1996a) 'Rates of Return to Education: Does the Conventional Pattern Prevail in sub-Saharan Africa?', *World Development*, vol. 24, no. 1, pp. 183–99.

Bennell, P. (1996b) 'Using and Abusing Rates of Return: A Critique of the World Bank's 1995 Education Sector Review', *International Journal of Educational Development*, vol. 16, no. 3, pp. 235–48.

Berg, I. (ed.) (1981) *Sociological Perspectives on Labor Markets*, New York: Academic Press.

Berger, S. and M. Piore (1980) *Dualism and Discontinuity in Industrial Societies*, Cambridge: Cambridge University Press.

Bernard, R. and M. Smith (1991) 'Hiring, Promotion, and Pay in a Corporate Head Office – An Internal Labour Market in Action', *Canadian Journal of Sociology*, vol. 16, no. 4, pp. 353–74.

Berry, A. *et al.* (1985) 'Management Control in an Area of the NCB: Rationales of Accounting Practices in a Public Enterprise', *Accounting, Organizations and Society*, vol. 1, no. 1, pp. 3–28.

Besley, T. and S. Coate (1995) 'The Design of Income Maintenance Programmes', *Review of Economic Studies*, vol. 62, no. 2, pp. 187–221.

Bibb, R. and W. Form (1976/7) 'The Effects of Industrial, Occupational and Sex Stratification on Wages in Blue-Collar Markets', *Social Forces*, vol. 55, no. 4, June, pp. 974–96.

Blackaby, D. *et al.* (1995) 'Dual Labour Markets and the Potential Earnings of the Unemployed', *Scottish Journal of Political Economy*, vol. 42, no. 1, pp. 37–52.

Blackburn, R. and M. Mann (1979) *The Working Class in the Labour Market*, London: Macmillan.

Blanchflower, D. and A. Oswald (1994) *The Wage Curve*, Cambridge, MA: MIT Press.

Blanchflower, D. and A. Oswald (1995) 'An Introduction to the Wage Curve', *Journal of Economic Perspectives*, vol. 9, no. 3, Summer, pp. 153–67.

Blau, F. and L. Kahn (1996) 'Wage Structure and Gender Earnings Differentials – An International Comparison', *Economica*, vol. 63, no. 250, pp. S29–S62.

Blaug, M. (1985) 'Where Are We Now in the Economics of Education?', *Economics of Education Review*, vol. 4, no. 1, pp. 17–28.

Blaug, M. (1987) *The Economics of Education and the Education of an Economist*, New York: New York University Press.

Bliss, C. (1975) *Capital Theory and the Distribution of Income*, Amsterdam: North Holland.

Bluestone, B. and M. Stevenson (1981) 'Industrial Transformation and the Evolution of Dual Labour Markets', in F. Wilkinson (ed.) *The Dynamics of Labour Market Segmentation*, London: Athlone Press.

Blum, L. (1991) *Between Feminism and Labor: The Significance of the Comparable Worth Movement*, Berkeley: University of California Press.

Boeke, J. (1953) *Economics and Economic Policy of Dual Societies as Exemplified by Indonesia*, New York: Institute of Pacific Relations.

Booth, A. (1989) 'The Bargaining Structure of British Establishments', *British Journal of Industrial Relations*, vol. 27, no. 2, July, pp. 225–34.

Bosanquet, N. and P. Doeringer (1973) 'Is There a Dual Labour Market in Great Britain?', *Economic Journal*, vol. 83, June, pp. 421–35.

Bosman, J. and M. Desmidt (1993) 'The Geographical Formation of International Management Centers', *Urban Studies*, vol. 30, no. 6, pp. 967–80.

Boston, T. (1990) 'Segmented Labor Markets – New Evidence from a Study of Race-Gender Groups', *Industrial and Labor Relations Review*, vol. 44, no. 1, pp. 99–115.

Botwinick, H. (1993) *Persistent Inequalities: Wage Disparity under Capitalist Competition*, Princeton: Princeton University Press.

Bowles, S. (1985) 'The Production Process in a Competitive Economy: Walrasian, Neo-Hobbesian, and Marxian Models', *American Economic Review*, vol. 75, no. 1, pp. 16–36.

Bowles, S. and H. Gintis (1976) *Schooling in Capitalist America: Educational Reform and the Contradictions of Economic Life*, London: Routledge & Kegan Paul.

Bowles, S. and H. Gintis (1977) 'The Marxian Theory of Value and Heterogeneous Labour: A Critique and Reformulation', *Cambridge Journal of Economics*, vol. 1, no. 2, pp. 173–92.

Bowles, S. and H. Gintis (1978) 'Professor Morishima on Heterogeneous Labour and Marxian Value Theory', *Cambridge Journal of Economics*, vol. 2, no. 3, pp. 311–14.

Bowles, S. and H. Gintis (1981a) 'Structure and Practice in the Labor Theory of Value', *Review of Radical Political Economy*, vol. 12, no. 4, pp. 1–26.

Bowles, S. and H. Gintis (1981b) 'Labour Heterogeneity and the Labour Theory of Value: A Reply', *Cambridge Journal of Economics*, vol. 5, no. 3, pp. 285–88.

Bowles, S. and H. Gintis (1993) 'The Revenge of Homo Economicus: Contested Exchange and the Revival of Political Economy', *Journal of Economic Perspectives*, vol. 7, no. 1, pp. 83–102.

Boyer, R. (1987) 'Labour Flexibilities: Many Forms, Uncertain Effects', in D. Meulders and L. Wilkin (eds) *Labour Market Flexibility*, special edition of *Labour and Society*, vol. 12, no. 1, January, pp. 107–29.

Brenner, J. (1987) 'Feminist Political Discourses: Radical Versus Liberal Approaches to the Feminization of Poverty and Comparable Worth', *Gender and Society*, vol. 4, December, pp. 447–65.

Brenner, R. (1977) 'The Origins of Capitalist Development', *New Left Review*, 104, pp. 25–93.

Brenner, R. and M. Glick (1991) 'The Regulation School and the West's Economic Impasse', *New Left Review*, no. 188, July/August, pp. 45–119.

Breugel, I. and D. Perrons (1995) 'Where Do the Costs of Unequal Treatment for Women Fall? An Analysis of the Incidence of the Costs of Unequal Pay and Sex Discrimination in the UK', in J. Humphries and J. Rubery (eds) *The Economics of Equal Opportunities*, Manchester: Equal Opportunities Commission.

Brodsky, M. (1994) 'Labor Market Flexibility: A Changing International Perspective', *Monthly Labor Review*, vol. 117, no. 11, November, pp. 53–60.

Brody, D. (1984) 'Review of Gordon *et al.* (1982)', *Journal of Interdisciplinary History*, vol. 14, no. 3, pp. 701–5.

Bronfenbrenner, M. (1982) 'Review of Gordon *et al.* (1982), *Journal of Economic History*, vol. XLII, no. 4, pp. 958–59.

Brosnan, P. *et al.* (1995) 'Labour Market Segmentation and the State – The New Zealand Experience', *Cambridge Journal of Economics*, vol. 19, no. 5, pp. 667–96.

Bruno, S. (1979) 'The Industrial Reserve Army, Segregation and the Italian Labour Market', *Cambridge Journal of Economics*, vol. 3, no. 2, pp. 131–51.

Brusco, S. (1982) 'The Emilian Model: Productive Decentralisation and Social Integration', *Cambridge Journal of Economics*, vol. 6, no. 2, pp. 167–84.

Brusco, S. and C. Sabel (1981) 'Artisan Production and Economic Growth', in F. Wilkinson (ed.) *The Dynamics of Labour Market Segmentation*, London: Athlone Press.

Buchele, R. (1981) 'Sex Discrimination and the US Labour Market', in F. Wilkinson (ed.) *The Dynamics of Labour Market Segmentation*, London: Athlone Press.

Buchele, R. (1983) 'Economic Dualism and Employment Stability', *Industrial Relations*, vol. 22, no. 3, pp. 410–18.

Bulow, J. and L. Summers (1986) 'A Theory of Dual Labor Markets with Application to Industrial Policy, Discrimination, and Keynesian Unemployment', *Journal of Labour Economics*, vol. 4, no. 3, part I, pp. 376–414.

Burkhauser, R. *et al.* (1996) 'Who Gets What from Minimum-Wage Hikes – A Re-estimation of Card and Krueger's "Myth and Measurement: The New Economics of the Minimum Wage"', *Industrial and Labor Relations Review*, vol. 49, no. 3, pp. 547–52.

Burton, C. *et al.* (1987) *Women's Worth: Pay Equity and Job Evaluation in Australia*, Canberra: Australian Government Publishing Service.

Cahuc, P. and P. Michel (1996) 'Minimum Wage Unemployment and Growth', *European Economic Review*, vol. 40, no. 7, pp. 1463–82.

Cain, G. (1976) 'The Challenge of Segmented Labor Market Theories to Orthodox Theory: A Survey', *Journal of Economic Literature*, vol. XIV, no. 4, pp. 1215–57.

Cairnes, J.E. (1967) *Some Leading Principles of Political Economy Newly Expounded*, New York: Kelley Reprints, original of 1874.

Calmfors, L. (1993) 'Centralisation of Wage Bargaining and Macroeconomic Performance – A Survey', *OECD Economic Studies*, no. 21, Winter, pp. 161–91.

Cambridge Women's Studies Group (1981) *Women in Society*, London: Virago.

Cameron, S. and J. Doling (1994) 'Housing Neighbourhoods and Urban Regeneration', *Urban Studies*, vol. 31, no. 7, pp. 1211–223.

Campbell, I. *et al.* (1991) 'Occupational Mobility in Segmented Labour Markets – The Experience of Immigrant Workers in Melbourne', *Australian and New Zealand Journal of Sociology*, vol. 27, no. 2, pp. 172–94.

Cannadine, D. (1983) 'The Context, Performance and Meaning of Ritual: The British Monarchy and the "Invention of Tradition"', in E. Hobsbawm and T. Ranger (eds) *The Invention of Tradition*, Cambridge: Cambridge University Press.

Card, D. (1992a) 'Using Regional Variation in Wages to Measure the Effects of the Federal Minimum-Wage', *Industrial and Labor Relations Review*, vol. 46, no. 1, pp. 22–37.

Card, D. (1992b) 'Do Minimum-Wages Reduce Employment – A Case-Study of California, 1987–89', *Industrial and Labor Relations Review*, vol. 46, no. 1, pp. 38–54.

Card, D. (1995) '*The Wage Curve*: A Review', *Journal of Economic Literature*, vol. XXXIII, June, pp. 785–99.

Card, D. and A. Krueger (1994) 'Minimum-Wages and Employment – A Case-Study of the Fast-Food Industry in New Jersey and Pennsylvania', *American Economic Review* vol. 84, no. 4, pp. 772–93.

Card, D. and A. Krueger (1995) *Myth and Measurement: The New Economics of the Minimum Wage*, Princeton: Princeton University Press.

Carlin, W. and D. Soskice (1990) *Macroeconomics and the Wage Bargain: A Modern Approach to Employment, Inflation, and the Exchange Rate*, Oxford: Oxford University Press.

Carnoy, M. (1980) *Segmented Labour Markets in Education, Work and Employment*, Paris: UNESCO.

Carnoy, M. (1995a) 'Economics of Education: Then and Now', in M. Carnoy (ed.) *International Encyclopedia of Economics of Education*, Oxford: Elsevier Science.

Carnoy, M. (ed.) (1995b) *International Encyclopedia of Economics of Education*, Oxford: Elsevier Science.

Carnoy, M. (1995c) 'Introduction to Production of Education', in M. Carnoy (ed.) *International Encyclopedia of Economics of Education*, Oxford: Elsevier Science.

Carnoy, M. (1995d) 'Political Economy of Educational Production', in M. Carnoy (ed.) *International Encyclopedia of Economics of Education*, Oxford: Elsevier Science.

Carnoy, M. (1996a) 'Race, Gender, and the Role of Education in Earnings Inequality: An Introduction', *Economics of Education Review*, vol. 15, no. 3, pp. 207–12.

Carnoy, M. (1996b) 'Education and Racial Inequality: The Human Capital Explanation Revisited', *Economics of Education Review*, vol. 15, no. 3, pp. 259–72.

Carter, M. (1982) 'Competition and Segmentation in Internal Labour Markets', *Journal of Economic Issues*, vol. XVI, no. 4, pp. 1063–77.

Carter, T. (1993) 'Distortions and Policies when Labor Turnover is Costly', *Zeitschrift Für Die Gesamte Staatswissenschaft*, vol. 149, no. 3, pp. 547–58.

Cassim, F. (1982) 'Labour Market Segmentation: The Theoretical Case', *South African Journal of Economics*, vol. 50, no. 4, pp. 362–74.

Cassim, F. (1983a) 'Reply to Truu', *South African Journal of Economics*, vol. 51, no. 4, pp. 574–78.

Cassim, F. (1983b) 'Rejoinder to Truu', *South African Journal of Economics*, vol. 51, no. 4, p. 580.

Catephores, G. (1981) 'On Heterogeneous Labour and the Labour Theory of Value', *Cambridge Journal of Economics*, vol. 5, no. 3, pp. 273–80.

CEVEP (1994) *Just Wages: History of the Campaign for Pay Equity, 1984–1993*, Wellington: Coalition for Equal Value Equal Pay.

Chadha, B. (1995) 'Disequilibrium in the Labor Market in South Africa', *IMF Staff Papers*, vol. 42, no. 3, pp. 642–69.

Chang, H. (1994) *The Political Economy of Industrial Policy*, London: Macmillan.

Chang, Y. (1992) 'Noncompliance Behavior of Risk-Averse Firms under the Minimum-Wage Law', *Public Finance Quarterly*, vol. 20, no. 3, pp. 390–401.

Chaves, M. (1991) 'Segmentation in a Religious Labor Market', *Sociological Analysis*, vol. 52, no. 2, pp. 143–58.

Chiplin, B. and P. Sloane (1976) *Sex Discrimination in the Labour Market*, London: Macmillan.

Chrystal, K. and S. Price (1994) *Controversies in Macroeconomics*, Hemel Hempstead: Harvester Wheatsheaf, third edition.

Clairmont, D. *et al.* (1983) 'The Segmentation Perspective as a Middle-Range Conceptualization in Sociology', *Canadian Journal of Sociology*, vol. 8, no. 4, pp. 245–71.

Clark, N. (1994) *Manufacturing Apartheid: State Corporations in South Africa*, New Haven: Yale University Press.

Claussen, B. *et al.* (1993) 'Health and Re-Employment in a Two Year Follow-Up of Long-Term Unemployed', *Journal of Epidemiology and Community Health*, vol. 47, no. 1, pp. 14–18.

Coase, R. (1993) 'Concluding Comment', *Journal of Institutional and Theoretical Economics*, vol. 149, no. 1, pp. 360–1.

Cobas, J. *et al.* (1993) 'Industrial Segmentation, the Ethnic Economy, and Job Mobility – The Case of Cuban Exiles in Florida', *Quality and Quantity*, vol. 27, no. 3, pp. 249–70.

Cock, J. (1980) *Maids and Madams: A Study in the Politics of Exploitation*, Johannesburg: Ravan Press.

Coddington, A. (1983) *Keynesian Economics*, London: Allen & Unwin.

Collins, J. (1993) 'Gender, Contracts and Wage Work – Agricultural Restructuring in Brazil's Sao Francisco Valley', *Development and Change*, vol. 24, no. 1, pp. 53–82.

Conk, M. (1984) 'Review of Gordon *et al.* (1982)', *Journal of Social History*, vol. 17, Spring, pp. 520–2.

Connell, R. (1987) *Gender and Power: Society, the Person and Sexual Politics*, London: Polity.

Cooke, P. (1983) 'Review of Gordon *et al.* (1982)', *Environment and Planning*, Series A, vol. 15, pp. 1414–17.

Cornfield, D. (1985) 'Economic Segmentation and Expression of Labour Unrest: Striking versus Quitting in the Manufacturing Sector', *Social Science Quarterly*, vol. 66, no. 2, pp. 248–65.

Cornwall, J. (1977) *Modern Capitalism*, London: Martin Robertson.

Corry, B. (1995) 'Politics and the Natural Rate Hypothesis: A Historical Perspective', in T. Cross (ed.) *The Natural Rate of Unemployment: Reflections on 25 Years of the Hypothesis*, Cambridge: Cambridge University Press.

Costabile, L. (1995) 'Institutions, Social Custom and Efficiency Wage Models: Alternative Approaches', *Cambridge Journal of Economics*, vol. 19, no. 5, October, pp. 605–23.

Cowling, K. (1982) *Monopoly Capitalism*, London: Macmillan.

Craig, C. *et al.* (1980) *After the Wages Council: Industrial and Staff Canteens*, mimeo, Cambridge.

Craig, C. *et al.* (1982) *Labour Market Structure, Industrial Organisation and Low Pay*, Cambridge: Cambridge University Press.

Craig, C. *et al.* (1984) *Payment Structures and Smaller Firms: Women's Employment in Segmented Labour Markets*, Department of Employment, Research Paper no. 48.

Craig, C. *et al.* (1985a) 'Labour Market Segmentation and Women's Employment: A Case Study from the United Kingdom', *International Labour Review*, vol. 124, no. 3, May/June, pp. 267–80.

Craig, C. *et al.* (1985b) 'Economic, Social and Political Factors in the Operation of the Labour Market', in B. Roberts *et al.* (eds) *New Approaches to Economic Life*, Manchester: Manchester University Press.

Crankshaw, O. (1996) *Race, Class and the Changing Division of Labour under Apartheid*, New York: Routledge.

Crompton, R. and K. Sanderson (1994) 'The Gendered Restructuring of Employment in the Finance Sector', in A. Scott (ed.) *Gender Segregation and Social Change: Men and Women in Changing Labour Markets*, Oxford: Oxford University Press.

Cross, R. (1995a) 'Introduction', in B. Corry *The Natural Rate of Unemployment: Reflections on 25 Years of the Hypothesis*, T. Cross (ed.), Cambridge: Cambridge University Press.

Cross, R. (ed.) (1995b) *The Natural Rate of Unemployment: Reflections on 25 Years of the Hypothesis*, Cambridge: Cambridge University Press.

Cross, T. (1993) 'The Political Economy of a Public Enterprise: The South African Iron and Steel Corporation, 1928–1989', unpublished D.Phil. thesis, University of Oxford.

Crush, J. (1989) 'Migrancy and Militance: The Case of the National Union of Mineworkers of South Africa', *African Affairs*, vol. 88, no. 1, pp. 5–23.

Crush, J. (1993) '"The Long-Averted Clash": Farm Labour Competition in the South African Countryside', *Canadian Journal of African Studies*, vol. 27, no. 3, pp. 404–23.

Crush, J. *et al.* (1991) *South Africa's Labor Empire: A History of Black Migrancy to the Gold Mines*, Cape Town: David Philip.

Cummings, S. (1980) 'White Ethnics, Racial Prejudice, and Labour Market Segmentation', *American Journal of Sociology*, vol. 85, no. 4, pp. 938–50.

Damania, D. and J. Madsen (1995) 'Monetary Policy and Macroeconomic Equilibrium in an Oligopolistic Economy', *Journal of Macroeconomics*, vol. 17, no. 4, pp. 651–65.

Danson, M. (1982) 'The Industrial Structure and Labour Market Segmentation: Urban and Regional Implications', *Regional Studies*, vol. 16, no. 4, pp. 255–65.

Darity, W. (ed.) (1993) *Labor Economics: Problems in Analyzing Labor Markets*, Boston: Kluwer.

Davies, H. and H. Joshi (1995) 'Social and Family Security in the Redress of Unequal Opportunities', in J. Humphries and J. Rubery (eds) *The Economics of Equal Opportunities*, Manchester: Equal Opportunities Commission.

Day, G. *et al.* (eds) (1982) *Diversity and Decomposition in the Labour Market*, Aldershot: Gower.

Deacon, D. (1982) 'The Employment of Women in the Commonwealth Public Service: The Creation and Reproduction of a Dual Labour Market', *Australian Journal of Public Administration*, vol. XLI, no. 3, pp. 232–50.

Deakin, S. (1986) 'Labour Law and the Developing Employment Relationship in the UK', *Cambridge Journal of Economics*, vol. 10, no. 3, pp. 225–46.

Deaton, D. and P. Beaumont (1980) 'The Determinants of Bargaining Structure: Some Large Scale Survey Evidence for Britain', *British Journal of Industrial Relations*, vol. 18, no. 2, pp. 202–16.

Deem, R. and G. Salaman (eds) (1985) *Work, Culture and Society*, Milton Keynes: Open University Press.

Demekas, D. (1987) 'The Nature of Unemployment in Segmented Labor Markets', *Economic Letters*, vol. 25, no. 1, pp. 91–94.

Demekas, D. (1990) 'Labor Market Segmentation in a Two-Sector Model of an Open Economy', *International Monetary Fund Staff Papers*, vol. 37, no. 4, pp. 849–64.

Desmidt, M. (1986) 'Labor Market Segmentation and Mobility Patterns', *Tijdschrift voor Economische en Sociale Geografie*, vol. 77, no. 5, pp. 399–407.

Dex, S. (1988) 'Gender and the Labour Market' in D. Gallie (ed.) *Employment in Britain*, Oxford: Blackwell.

Dex, S. and R. Sewell (1995) 'Equal Opportunities Policies and Women's Labour Market Status in Industrialised Countries', in J. Humphries and J. Rubery (eds) *The Economics of Equal Opportunities*, Manchester: Equal Opportunities Commission.

Dex, S. *et al.* (1994) *Women and Low Pay: Identifying the Issues*, Research Discussion Series no. 9, Manchester: Equal Opportunities Commission.

Dickens, L. *et al.* (1988) *Tackling Sex Discrimination Through Collective Bargaining: The Impact of Section 6 of the Sex Discrimination Act 1986*, London: HMSO.

Dickens, R. *et al.* (1993) 'Wages Councils – Was There a Case for Abolition', *British Journal of Industrial Relations*, vol. 31, no. 4, pp. 515–29.

Dickens, R. *et al.* (1994) 'Minimum-Wages and Employment – A Theoretical Framework with an Application to the UK Wages Councils', *International Journal of Manpower*, vol. 15, no. 2–3, pp. 26–48.

Dickens, R. *et al.* (1995a) 'The Effect of Minimum-Wages on UK Agriculture', *Journal of Agricultural Economics*, vol. 46, no. 1, pp. 1–19.

Dickens, R. *et al.* (1995b) 'What Happened to Wages and Employment after the Abolition of Minimum Wages in Britain?', mimeo.

Dickens, W. and L. Katz (1987) 'Inter-Industry Wage Differences and Industry Characteristics', in K. Lang and J. Leonard (eds) *Unemployment and the Structure of Labor Markets*, Oxford: Blackwell.

Dickens, W. and K. Lang (1985) 'A Test of Dual Labor Market Theory', *American Economic Review*, vol. 74, September, pp. 792–805.

Dickens, W. and K. Lang (1988a) 'The Re-Emergence of Segmented Labour Market Theory', *American Economic Review*, vol. 78, no. 2, pp. 129–34.

Dickens, W. and K. Lang (1988b) 'Labor Market Segmentation and the Union Wage Premium', *Review of Economics and Statistics*, vol. 70, no. 3, pp. 527–30.

Diprete, T. (1993) 'Discrimination, Choice, and Group Inequality – A Discussion of How Allocative and Choice-Based Processes Complicate the Standard Decomposition', *Social Science Research*, vol. 22, no. 4, December, pp. 415–40.

Dixon, H. (1991) 'Macroeconomic Policy in a Large Unionised Economy', *European Economic Review*, vol. 35, pp. 1427–48.

Dixon, H. (1995) 'Of Coconuts, Decomposition, and a Jackass: The Genealogy of the Natural Rate', in T. Cross (ed.) *The Natural Rate of Unemployment: Reflections on 25 Years of the Hypothesis*, Cambridge: Cambridge University Press.

Dixon, H. and N. Rankin (1994) 'Imperfect Competition and Macroeconomics: A Survey', *Oxford Economic Papers*, vol. 46, no. 2, April, pp. 171–99.

Dixon, J. and C. Seron (1995) 'Stratification in the Legal Profession – Sex, Sector, and Salary', *Law and Society Review*, vol. 29, no. 3, pp. 381–42.

Doeringer, P. and M. Piore (1971) *Internal Labor Markets and Manpower Analysis*, Lexington: Heath Lexington Books.

Dolado, J. *et al.* (1996) 'The Economic Impact of Minimum Wages in Europe', with discussion, *Economic Policy*, no. 23, October, pp. 317–72.

Domar, E. (1946) 'Capital Accumulation, Rate of Growth and Employment', *Econometrica*, vol. 14, no. 1, pp. 137–47.

Dow, S. (1985) *Macroeconomic Thought: A Methodological Approach*, Oxford: Blackwell.

Dow, S. (1996) *The Methodology of Macroeconomic Thought: A Conceptual Analysis of Schools of Thought in Economics*, Oxford: Blackwell.

Dunlop, J. (1958) *Industrial Relations Systems*, New York: Holt.

Dymski, G. (1995) 'The Theory of Bank Redlining and Discrimination – An Exploration', *Review of Black Political Economy*, vol. 23, no. 3, pp. 37–74.

Edwards, P. (ed.) (1995) *Industrial Relations: Theory and Practice in Britain*, Oxford: Blackwell.

Edwards, R. (1975) 'The Social Relations of Production in the Firm and Labor Market Structure', in R. Edwards *et al.* (eds) *Labor Market Segmentation*, Lexington: Heath & Co.

Edwards, R. (1979) *Contested Terrain*, New York: Basic Books.

Edwards, R. *et al.* (eds) (1975) *Labor Market Segmentation*, Lexington: Heath & Co.

Ehrenberg, R. (1992) 'New Minimum-Wage Research – Symposium Introduction', *Industrial and Labor Relations Review*, vol. 46, no. 1, pp. 3–5.

Elbaum, B. *et al.* (1979) 'Symposium: The Labour Process, Market Structure, and Marxist Theory', *Cambridge Journal of Economics*, vol. 3, no. 3, pp. 229–304.

Elson, D. (ed.) (1979) *Value: The Representation of Labour in Capitalism*, London: CSE Books.

England, P. (1992) *Comparable Worth: Theories and Evidence*, New York: Aldine de Gruyter.

England, P. *et al.* (1994) 'The Gendered Valuation of Occupations and Skills – Earnings in 1980 Census Occupations', *Social Forces*, vol. 73, no. 1, pp. 65–99.

EOC (1989) *Equal Pay . . . Making It Work*, Consultative Document, London: Equal Opportunities Commission.

EOC (1995) *Flexibility in Practice: Women's Employment and Pay in Retail and Finance*, Industrial Relations Services, Research Discussion Series no. 16, Manchester: Equal Opportunities Commission.

EOR (1996a) 'Common Terms and Conditions Test', no. 68, July/August, pp. 46–48.

EOR (1996b) 'Equal Value Update', no. 70, November/December, pp. 13–27.

Equal Opportunities Review, various issues.

Ermisch, J. *et al.* (1990) 'Women's Wages in Great Britain', Birkbeck Discussion Paper in Economics, no. 8/90.

Evans, S. and B. Nelson (1989) *Wage Justice: Comparable Worth and the Paradox of Technocratic Reform*, Chicago: Chicago University Press.

Eyraud, F. (1993) 'Equal Pay and the Value of Work in Industrialized Countries', *International Labour Review*, vol. 132, no. 1, pp. 33–48.

Eyraud, F. *et al.* (1993) *Equal Pay Protection in Industrialised Market Economies: In Search of Greater Effectiveness*, Geneva: ILO.

Fairweather, J. (1995) 'Myths and Realities of Academic Labor Markets', *Economics of Education Review*, vol. 14, no. 2, pp. 179–92.

Fallon, P. (1992) 'An Analysis of Employment and Wage Behaviour in South Africa', Washington DC: World Bank.

Fershtman, C. and A. Fishman (1994) 'The Perverse Effects of Wage and Price Controls in Search Markets', *European Economic Review*, vol. 38, no. 5, pp. 1099–112.

Fichtenbaum, R. *et al.* (1994) 'New Evidence on the Labor Market Segmentation Hypothesis', *Review of Social Economy*, vol. 52, no. 1, pp. 20–39.

Fields, G. (1994) 'The Unemployment Effects of Minimum Wages', *International Journal of Manpower*, vol. 15, no. 2–3, pp. 74–81.

Fine, B. (1980) *Economic Theory and Ideology*, London: Edward Arnold.

Fine, B. (1982) *Theories of the Capitalist Economy*, London: Edward Arnold.

Fine, B. (1985/6) 'Banking Capital and the Theory of Interest', *Science and Society*, vol. XLIX, no. 4, pp. 387–414.

Fine, B. (ed.) (1986) *The Value Dimension: Marx versus Ricardo and Sraffa*, London: Routledge & Kegan Paul.

Fine, B. (1987) 'Segmented Labour Market Theory: A Critical Assessment', Birkbeck Discussion Paper in Economics no. 87/12, reproduced in shortened form as Thames Papers in Political Economy, Spring 1990.

Fine, B. (1988) 'The British Coal Industry's Contribution to the Political Economy of Paul Sweezy', *History of Political Economy*, vol. 20, no. 2, pp. 235–50.

Fine, B. (1989) *Marx's 'Capital'*, London: Macmillan, third edition.

Fine, B. (1990) *The Coal Question: Political Economy and Industrial Change from the Nineteenth Century to the Present Day*, London: Routledge.

Fine, B. (1992) *Women's Employment and the Capitalist Family*, London: Routledge.

Fine, B. (1993) 'Modernity, Urbanism, and Modern Consumption – A Comment', *Environment and Planning D, Society and Space*, vol. 11, pp. 599–601.

Fine, B. (1994a) '"The Rise in South African Wages" – A Dissenting and Wide-Ranging Commentary', mimeo.

Fine, B. (1994b) 'Towards a Political Economy of Food', *Review of International Political Economy*, vol. 1, no. 3, pp. 519–45.

Fine, B. (1995) 'Flexible Production and Flexible Theory: The Case of South Africa', *Geoforum*, vol. 26, no. 2, pp. 107–19.

Fine, B. (1997a) 'The New Revolution in Economics', *Capital and Class*, no. 61, Spring, pp. 143–8.

Fine, B. (1997b) 'Playing the Consumption Game', *Consumption, Markets, Culture*, forthcoming.

Fine, B. (1997c) 'The Continuing Imperative of Value Theory: A Personal Account', *Outopia*, forthcoming.

Fine, B. and L. Harris (1976) 'State Expenditure in Advanced Capitalism: A Critique', *New Left Review*, 98, pp. 97–112.

Fine, B. and L. Harris (1979) *Rereading 'Capital'*, London: Macmillan.

Fine, B. and L. Harris (1985) *The Peculiarities of the British Economy*, London: Lawrence & Wishart.

Fine B. and L. Harris (1987) 'Ideology and Markets: Economic Theory and the "New Right"', in R. Miliband *et al.* (eds) *Socialist Register*, London: Merlin.

Fine, B. and M. Heasman (1997) *Consumption in the Age of Affluence: Diet, Health, Information and Policy*, London: Routledge, forthcoming.

Fine, B. and E. Leopold (1993) *The World of Consumption*, London: Routledge.

Fine, B. and A. Murfin (1984) *Macroeconomics and Monopoly Capitalism*, Brighton: Harvester Wheatsheaf.

Fine, B. and Z. Rustomjee (1997) *South Africa's Political Economy: From Minerals-Energy Complex to Industrialisation*, Johannesburg: Wits University Press.

Fine, B. and C. Stoneman (1996) 'Introduction: State and Development', *Journal of Southern African Studies*, vol. 22, no. 1, March, pp. 5–26.

Fine, B. *et al.* (1996) *Consumption in the Age of Affluence: The World of Food*, London: Routledge.

Finnegan, D. (1993) 'Segmentation in the Academic Labor Market – Hiring Cohorts in Comprehensive Universities', *Journal of Higher Education*, vol. 64, no. 6, pp. 621–56.

Fischer, S. (1988) 'Recent Developments in Macroeconomics', *Economic Journal*, vol. 98, no. 391, pp. 294–339.

Flanagan, R. (1973) 'Segmented Market Theories and Racial Discrimination', *Industrial Relations*, vol. 12, no. 3, pp. 253–73.

Flatau, P. and P. Lewis (1993) 'Segmented Labor Markets in Australia', *Applied Economics*, vol. 25, no. 3, pp. 285–94.

Foster, J. (1986) *The Theory of Monopoly Capitalism*, New York: Monthly Review Press.

Fottler, M. (1974) 'Employer Size and Success in Manpower Training for the Disadvantaged', *Relations Industrielle*, vol. 29, no. 4, pp. 685–708.

Freedman, M. (1976) *Labor Markets: Segments and Shelters*, New York: Allanheld Osman.

Freeman, R. (1989) *Labor Markets in Action*, New York: Harvester/Wheatsheaf.

Freeman, R. (1994) 'Minimum-Wages – Again', *International Journal of Manpower*, vol. 15, no. 2–3, pp. 8–25.

Freeman, R. (1995) 'The Limits of Wage Flexibility to Curing Unemployment', *Oxford Review of Economic Policy*, vol. 11, no. 1, Spring, pp. 63–72.

Freeman, R. (1996) 'The Minimum Wage as a Redistributive Tool', *Economic Journal*, vol. 106, no. 436, pp. 639–49.

Freeman, R. and H. Medoff (1984) *What Do Unions Do?*, New York: Basic Books.

Freund, B. (1991) 'South African Gold Mining in Transformation', in S. Gelb (ed.) *South Africa's Economic Crisis*, Cape Town: David Philips.

Fulcher, J. (1988) 'On the Explanation of Industrial Relations Diversity: Labour Movements, Employers and the State in Britain and Sweden', *British Journal of Industrial Relations*, vol. 26, no. 2, pp. 246–74.

Gallaway, L. and R. Vedder (1993) 'The Employment Effects of Social-Security Tax Changes and Minimum-Wage Regulations – A Case-Study of the American Restaurant Industry', *Journal of Labor Research*, vol. 14, no. 3, pp. 367–74.

Gallie, D. (1985) 'Review of Gordon *et al.* (1982)', *Political Studies*, vol. XXXIII, no. 3, p 507.

Gallie, D. (ed.) (1988) *Employment in Britain*, Oxford: Blackwell.

Gallie, D. *et al.* (eds) (1994) *Social Change and the Experience of Unemployment*, Oxford: Oxford University Press.

Gallie, D. *et al.* (eds) (1996) *Trade Unionism in Recession*, Oxford: Oxford University Press.

Garnsey, E. *et al.* (1985) 'Labour Market Structure and Work-Force Divisions', in R. Deem and G. Salaman (eds) *Work, Culture and Society*, Milton Keynes: Open University Press.

Gelb, S. (ed.) (1991) *South Africa's Economic Crisis*, Cape Town: David Philip.

Gershuny, J. *et al.* (1994) 'The Domestic Labour Revolution: A Process of Lagged Adaptation', in M. Anderson *et al.* (eds) *The Social and Political Economy of the Household*, Oxford: Oxford University Press.

Gertler, M. (1988) 'The Limits to Flexibility – Comments on the Post-Fordist Vision of Production and Its Geography', *Transactions of the Institute of British Geographers*, vol. 13, no. 4, pp. 419–32.

Gertler, M. (1989) 'Resurrecting Flexibility – A Reply', *Transactions of the Institute of British Geographers*, vol. 14, no. 1, pp. 109–12.

Gertler, M. (1992) 'Flexibility Revisited – Districts, Nation-States, and the Forces of Production', *Transactions of the Institute of British Geographers*, vol. 17, no. 3, pp. 259–78.

Ghobadian, A. and M. White (1986) *Job Evaluation and Equal Pay*, Policy Studies Institute, Department of Employment, Research Paper no. 58.

Gilbert, A. (1994) 'Third World Cities – Poverty, Employment, Gender Roles and the Environment During a Time of Restructuring', *Urban Studies*, vol. 31, no. 4–5, pp. 605–33.

Gilbert, N. *et al.* (eds) (1992) *Fordism and Flexibility: Divisions and Change*, London: Macmillan.

Gimble, D. (1991) 'Institutionalist Labor Market Theory and the Veblenian Dichotomy', *Journal of Economics Issues*, vol. 25, no. 3, pp. 625–48.

Gindling, T. (1991) 'Labor Market Segmentation and the Determination of Wages in the Public, Private-Formal, and Informal Sectors in San Jose, Costa Rica', *Economic Development and Cultural Change*, vol. 39, no. 3, pp. 585–605.

Gittleman, M. and D. Howell (1995) 'Changes in the Structure and Quality of Jobs in the United States – Effects by Race and Gender, 1973–1990', *Industrial and Labor Relations Review*, vol. 48, no. 3, pp. 420–40.

GLC (1985a) 'Employment Institute: Charter for Jobs – GLC Officers' Response', Industry and Employment Committee of the Greater London Council, DG/IE/IU/BF 6121.

GLC (1985b) *The London Industrial Strategy*, London: Greater London Council.

GLC (1986) *The London Labour Plan*, London: Greater London Council.

Glennie, P. and N. Thrift (1992) 'Modernity, Urbanism, and Modern Consumption', *Environment and Planning D: Society and Space*, vol. 10, no. 4, pp. 423–443.

Glennie, P. and N. Thrift (1993) 'Modern Consumption: Theorising Commodities and Consumers', *Environment and Planning D: Society and Space*, vol. 11, pp. 603–6.

Glyn, A. and D. Miliband (eds) (1994) *Paying for Inequality: The Economic Cost of Social Justice*, London: IPPR/Rivers Oram Press.

Goldberger, A. (1983) 'Reverse Regressions and Salary Discrimination', *Journal of Human Resources*, vol. XIX, no. 3, pp. 293–318.

Goodman, D. and M. Watts (1994) 'Reconfiguring the Rural or Fording the Divide?: Capitalist Restructuring and the Global Agro-Food System', *Journal of Peasant Studies*, vol. 22, no. 1, October, pp. 1–49.

Gordon, D. (1972) *Theories of Poverty and Unemployment*, Lexington: Heath & Co.

Gordon, D. *et al.* (1982) *Segmented Work, Divided Workers: The Historical Transformation of Labor in the United States*, Cambridge: Cambridge University Press.

Gordon, I. (1995) 'Migration in a Segmented Labour Market', *Transactions of the Institute of British Geographers*, vol. 20, no. 2, pp. 139–55.

Gottfries, N. and B. McCormick (1995) 'Discrimination and Open Unemployment in a Segmented Labour Market', *European Economic Review*, vol. 39, no. 1, pp. 1–15.

Gough, I. (1975) 'State Expenditure in Advanced Capitalism', *New Left Review*, 92, pp. 53–92.

Gough, I. (1979) *The Political Economy of the Welfare State*, London: Macmillan.

Graham, J. and D. Shakow (1990) 'Labor Market Segmentation and Job-Related Risk', *American Journal of Economics and Sociology*, vol. 49, no. 3, pp. 307–23.

Green, F. (1988) 'Neoclassical and Marxian Concepts of Production', *Cambridge Journal of Economics*, vol. 12, no. 3, September, pp. 299–312.

Green, F. (1991) 'The Relationship of Wages to the Value of Labour-Power in Marx's Labour Market', *Cambridge Journal of Economics*, vol. 15, no. 2, June, pp. 199–213.

Greenwald, B. and J. Stiglitz (1993) 'New and Old Keynesians', *Journal of Economic Perspectives*, vol. 7, no. 1, Winter, pp. 23–44.

Gregg, P. *et al.* (1994) 'High Pay, Low Pay and Labour Market Efficiency', in A. Glyn and D. Miliband (eds) *Paying for Inequality: The Economic Cost of Social Justice*, London: IPPR/Rivers Oram Press.

Gregory, J. (1992) 'Equal Pay for Work of Equal Value: The Strengths and Weaknesses of Legislation', *Work, Employment and Society*, vol. 6, no. 3, September, pp. 461–73.

Gregory, R. *et al.* (1989) 'Women's Pay in Australia, Great Britain, and the United States: the Role of Laws, Regulations, and Human Capital', in R. Michael *et al.* (eds) *Pay Equity: Empirical Inquiries*, Washington, DC: National Academy Press.

Gunderson, M. (1989) 'Male–Female Wage Differentials and Policy Responses', *Journal of Economic Literature*, vol. XXVII, March, pp. 46–72.

Gunderson, M. (1994) *Comparable Worth and Gender Discrimination: An International Perspective*, Geneva: ILO.

Hahn, F. (1982) 'The Neo-Ricardians', *Cambridge Journal of Economics*, vol. 6, no. 4, pp. 353–74.

Hahn, F. (1995) 'Theoretical Reflections on the "Natural Rate of Unemployment"', in T. Cross (ed.) *The Natural Rate of Unemployment: Reflections on 25 Years of the Hypothesis*, Cambridge: Cambridge University Press.

Hahn, F. and R. Solow (1995) *A Critical Essay on Modern Macroeconomic Theory*, Cambridge, MA: MIT Press.

Hands, D. (1995) 'Methodological Atavism and Radical Economics: Comments on Reich', in F. Moseley (ed.) *Heterodox Economic Theories: True or False?*, Aldershot: Edward Elgar.

Hanson, C. and G. Mather (1988) *Striking out Strikes: Employment Relations in the British Labour Market*, London: IEA.

Hanson, S. and G. Pratt (1992) 'Dynamic Dependencies – A Geographic Investigation of Local Labor Markets', *Economic Geography*, vol. 68, no. 4, pp. 373–405.

Hanushek, E. (1995) 'Interpreting Recent Research on Schooling in Developing Countries', *World Bank Research Observer*, vol. 10, no. 2, August, pp. 227–46.

Harley, B. (1995) *Labour Flexibility and Workplace Industrial Relations: The Australian Evidence*, Sydney: ACIRRT.

Harris, R. (1993) 'Part-Time Female Earnings – An Analysis Using Northern Ireland', *Applied Economics*, vol. 25, no. 1, pp. 1–12.

Harrison, B. (1971) 'Human Capital, Black Poverty and "Radical' Economics", *Industrial Relations*, vol. 10, no. 3, pp. 277–86.

Harriss, J. *et al.* (eds) (1996) *The New Institutional Economics and Third World Development*, London: Routledge.

Hart, V. (1994) *Bound by Our Constitution: Women, Workers, and the Minimum Wage*, Princeton: Princeton University Press.

Harvey, P. (1983) 'Marx's Theory of Labor Power: An Assessment', *Social Research*, vol. 50, no. 2, pp. 305–44.

Harvey, P. (1985) 'The Value-Creating Capacity of Skilled Labor in Marxian Economics', *Review of Radical Political Economics*, vol. 17, no. 1/2, pp. 83–102.

Hauser, R. (1980) 'Comment on Beck *et al.* (1978)', *American Sociological Review*, vol. 45, no. 4, pp. 702–12.

Hayter, R. and T. Barnes (1992) 'Labor Market Segmentation, Flexibility, and Recession – A British Columbian Case Study', *Environment and Planning C, Government and Policy*, vol. 10, no. 3, pp. 333–53.

Heckman, J. and T. MacCurdy (1993) 'Empirical Tests of Labor Market Equilibrium', in W. Darity (ed.) *Labor Economics: Problems in Analyzing Labor Markets*, Boston: Kluwer.

Henderson, J. (1992) 'Equal Pay vs Equal Job Opportunity for Women – The Debate in Great Britain from 1891 to 1923', *International Journal of Social Economics*, vol. 19, nos 10–12, pp. 298–316.

Hernes, G. (1991) 'The Dilemmas of Social Democracies – The Case of Norway and Sweden', *Acta Sociologia*, vol. 34, no. 4, pp. 239–60.

Hiebert, D. (1995) 'The Social Geography of Toronto in 1931 – A Study of Residential Differentiation and Social Structure', *Journal of Historical Geography*, vol. 21, no. 1, pp. 55–74.

Hillard, M. and R. McIntyre (1994) 'Is There a New Institutional Consensus in Labor Economics?', *Journal of Economic Issues*, vol. XXVIII, no. 2, June, pp. 619–29.

Himmelweit, S. (1984) 'Value Relations and Divisions within the Working Class', *Science and Society*, vol. XLVIII, no. 3, pp. 323–43.

Hindson, D. (1987) *Pass Controls and the Urban African Proletariat*, Johannesburg: Ravan Press.

Hinrichs, C. and T. Lyson (1995) 'Revisiting the Role of the State Sector in the Dual Economy Paradigm – Assessing the Effects of Multiple Work Structures on Earnings', *Social Science Quarterly*, vol. 76, no. 4, pp. 763–79.

Hirsch, E. (1983) 'Review of Gordon *et al.* (1982)', *American Journal of Sociology*, vol. 89, no. 2, pp. 446–7.

Hirschmann, A. (1970) *Exit, Voice and Loyalty: Responses to Decline in Firms, Organisations and States*, Cambridge: Harvard University Press.

Hirst, P. and J. Zeitlin (1989) 'Flexible Specialisation and the Competitive Failure of UK Manufacturing', *Political Quarterly*, vol. 60, no. 2, pp. 164–78.

Hobsbawm, E. and T. Ranger (eds) (1983) *The Invention of Tradition*, Cambridge: Cambridge University Press.

Hodgson, G. (1988) *Economics and Institutions: A Manifesto for a Modern Institutional Economics*, Cambridge: Polity Press.

Hodson, R. (1978) 'Labour in the Monopoly, Competitive, and State Sectors of Production', *Politics and Society*, vol. 8, nos 3/4, pp. 469–80.

Hodson, R. and R. Kaufman (1981) 'Circularity in the Dual Economy: A Comment on Tolbert, Horan and Beck (1980)', *American Journal of Sociology*, vol. 86, no. 4, pp. 881–87.

Hofmeyr, J. (1990a) 'Black Wages: The Post-War Experience', in N. Nattrass and E. Ardington (eds) *The Political Economy of South Africa*, Cape Town: Macmillan.

Hofmeyr, J. (1990b) 'The Rise in African Wages in South Africa: 1975–1985', Economic Research Unit, University of Natal, Durban, Occasional Paper, no. 22.

Hofmeyr, J. (1993) 'African Wage Movements in the 1980s', *South African Journal of Economics*, vol. 61, no. 4, December, pp. 266–80.

Hofmeyr, J. (1994a) 'The Rise in African Wages: 1975–1985', *South African Journal of Economics*, vol. 62, no. 3, September, pp. 198–215.

Hofmeyr, J. (1994b) 'An Analysis of African Wage Movements in South Africa', Research Monograph no. 9, Economic Research Unit, University of Natal, Durban.

Horan, P. *et al.* (1980) 'The Circle Has No Close', *American Journal of Sociology*, vol. 86, no. 4, pp. 887–94.

Horn, R. (1980) 'A Case Study of the Dual Labor Market Hypothesis', *Journal of Economic Issues*, vol. XIV, no. 3, pp. 615–30.

Horner, D. and A. Kooy (1980) 'Conflict on South African Mines, 1972–1979', SALDRU Working Paper, no. 29.

Horton, S. *et al.* (1994a) *Labor Markets in an Era of Adjustment: Issues Papers*, vol. 1, Washington, DC: World Bank.

Horton, S. *et al.* (1994b) *Labor Markets in an Era of Adjustment: Case Studies*, vol. 2, Washington, DC: World Bank.

Horton, S. *et al.* (1994c) 'Labour Markets in an Era of Adjustment: An Overview', in S. Horton *et al.* (eds) *Labor Markets in an Era of Adjustment: Issues Papers*, vol. 1, Washington, DC: World Bank. Also in S. Horton *et al.* (eds) *Labor Markets in an Era of Adjustment: Case Studies*, vol. 2, Washington, DC: World Bank.

House, W. (1984) 'Labour Market Segmentation: Evidence from Cyprus', *World Development*, vol. 12, no. 4, pp. 403–18.

Humphrey, J. (1995) 'Industrial Organization and Manufacturing Competitiveness in Developing Countries: Introduction', *World Development*, vol. 23, no. 1, pp. 1–7.

Humphries, J. (1977) 'Class Struggle and the Persistence of the Working Class Family', *Cambridge Journal of Economics*, vol. 1, no. 3, pp. 241–58.

Humphries, J. (1995) 'Economics, Gender and Equal Opportunities', in J. Humphries and J. Rubery (eds) *The Economics of Equal Opportunities*, Manchester: Equal Opportunities Commission.

Humphries, J. and J. Rubery (1984) 'The Reconstitution of the Supply Side of the Labour Market: The Relative Autonomy of Social Reproduction', *Cambridge Journal of Economics*, vol. 8, no. 4, pp. 331–46.

Humphries, J. and J. Rubery (eds) (1995a) *The Economics of Equal Opportunities*, Manchester: Equal Opportunities Commission.

Humphries, J. and J. Rubery (1995b) 'Introduction' in J. Humphries and J. Rubery (eds) *The Economics of Equal Opportunities*, Manchester: Equal Opportunities Commission.

Humphries, J. and J. Rubery (1995c) 'Some Lessons for Policy', in J. Humphries and J. Rubery (eds) *The Economics of Equal Opportunities*, Manchester: Equal Opportunities Commission.

Hunter, A. and J. Leiper (1993) 'On Formal Education, Skills and Earnings – The Role of Educational Certificates in Earnings Determination', *Canadian Journal of Sociology*, vol. 18, no. 1, pp. 21–42.

Hunter, L. and S. Rimmer (1995) 'An Economic Exploration of the UK and Australian Experiences', in J. Humphries and J. Rubery (eds) *The Economics of Equal Opportunities*, Manchester: Equal Opportunities Commission.

Husby, R. (1993) 'The Minimum-Wage, Wage Subsidies, and Poverty', *Contemporary Policy Issues*, vol. 11, no. 3, pp. 30–8.

Hyman, R. (1991) 'Plus Ça Change? The Theory of Production and the Production of Theory', in A. Pollert (ed.) *Farewell to Flexibility*, Oxford: Blackwell.

ILO (1996) *Restructuring the Labour Market: The South African Challenge – An ILO Country Review*, Geneva: ILO.

Ingham, G. (1996) 'Some Recent Changes in the Relationship between Economics and Sociology', *Cambridge Journal of Economics*, vol. 20, no. 2, pp. 243–75.

Inui, A. (1993) 'The Competitive Structure of School and the Labour Market – Japan and Britain', *British Journal of Sociology of Education*, vol. 14, no. 3, pp. 301–13.

IPM (1991) *Minimum Wage: An Analysis of the Issues*, London: Institute of Personnel Management.

Itoh, M. (1987) 'Skilled Labour in Value Theory', *Capital and Class*, no. 31, pp. 39–58.

Jamal, V. (ed.) (1995) *Structural Adjustment and Rural Labour Markets in Africa*, London: Methuen.

James, W. (1992) *Our Precious Metal: African Labour in South Africa's Gold Industry, 1970–1990*, Cape Town: David Philip.

Jarman, J. (1994) 'Which Way Forward? Assessing the Current Proposals to Amend the British Equal Pay Act', *Work, Employment and Society*, vol. 8, no. 2, June, pp. 243–54.

Jenkins, R. (1984) 'Acceptability, Suitability and the Search for the Habituated Worker: How Ethnic Minorities and Women Lose Out', *International Journal of Social Economics*, vol. 11, no. 7, pp. 64–76.

Johnes, G. (1993) *The Economics of Education*, London: Macmillan.

Jones, E. (1983) 'Industrial Structure and Labor Force Segmentation', *Review of Radical Political Economics*, vol. 15, no. 4, pp. 24–44.

Joshi, H. (1990) 'Sex and Motherhood as Handicaps in the Labour Market', in M. Maclean and D. Groves (eds) *Women's Issues in Social Policy*, London: Routledge.

Joskow, P. (1995) 'The New Institutional Economics: Alternative Approaches, Concluding Comment', *Journal of Institutional and Theoretical Economics*, vol. 151, no. 1, pp. 248–59.

Kahn, P. and E. Meehan (eds) (1992) *Equal Pay/Comparable Worth in the UK and the USA*, London: Macmillan.

Kalleberg, A. and I. Berg (1987) *Work and Industry: Structures, Markets and Processes*, New York: Plenum Press.

Kaplan, D. (1990) *The Crossed Line: The South African Telecommunications Industry in Transition*, Johannesburg: Witwatersrand University Press.

Katz, H. and C. Sabel (1985) 'Industrial Relations and Industrial Adjustment in the Car Industry', *Industrial Relations*, vol. 21, no. 3, pp. 295–315.

Katz, L. and A. Krueger (1992) 'The Effect of the Minimum-Wage on the Fast-Food Industry', *Industrial and Labor Relations Review*, vol. 46, no. 1, pp. 6–21.

Kaufman, R. *et al.* (1981) 'Defrocking Dualism: A New Approach to Defining Industrial Sectors', *Social Science Research*, vol. 10, no. 1, pp. 1–31.

Kay, F. and J. Hagan (1995) 'The Persistent Glass Ceiling – Gendered Inequalities in the Earnings of Lawyers', *British Journal of Sociology*, vol. 46, no. 2, pp. 279–310.

Kelly, J. (1996) 'Does the Field of Industrial Relations Have a Future?', London School of Economics, mimeo.

Keltner, B. (1995) 'Relationship Banking and Competitive Advantage – Evidence from the US and Germany', *California Management Review*, vol. 37, no. 4, pp. 45–72.

Kenrick, J. (1981) 'Politics and the Construction of Women as Second Class Workers', in F. Wilkinson (ed.) *The Dynamics of Labour Market Segmentation*, London: Athlone Press.

Kerr, C. (1954) 'The Balkanization of Labor Markets', in E. Bakke *et al.* (eds) *Labor Mobility and Economic Opportunity*, Cambridge, MA: MIT Press.

Kessler, I. and J. Purcell (1995) 'Individualism and Collectivism in Theory and Practice: Management Style and the Design of Pay System', in P. Edwards (ed.) *Industrial Relations: Theory and Practice in Britain*, Oxford: Blackwell.

Kessler-Harris, A. (1992) *A Woman's Wage: Historical Meanings and Social Consequences*, Lexington: University of Kentucky Press.

Keyssar, A. (1993) 'Labor Economics and Unemployment: An Historian's Perspective', in W. Darity (ed.) *Labor Economics: Problems in Analyzing Labor Markets*, Boston: Kluwer.

Khan, M. (1996a) 'State Failure in Weak States: A Critique of New Institutionalist Explanations', in J. Harriss *et al.* (eds) *The New Institutional Economics and Third World Development*, London: Routledge.

Khan, M. (1996b) 'The Efficiency Implications of Corruption', *Journal of International Development*, vol. 8, no. 5, pp. 683–96.

Khosa, M. (1990) 'The Black Taxi Revolution', in N. Nattrass and E. Ardington (eds) *The Political Economy of South Africa*, Cape Town: Macmillan.

Killingsworth, M. (1990) *The Economics of Comparable Worth*, Kalamazoo: Upjohn Institute.

Kim, T. and L. Taylor (1995) 'The Employment Effect in Retail Trade of California 1988 Minimum Wage Increase', *Journal of Business and Economic Statistics*, vol. 13 no. 2, pp. 175–82.

Kirchner, C. (1995) 'Market Organization: A New–Institutional Perspective: Concluding Comment', *Journal of Institutional and Theoretical Economics*, vol. 151, no. 1, pp. 260–7.

Klein, P. (1993) *Beyond Dissent: Essays in Institutional Economics*, London: M.E. Sharpe.

Koning, P. *et al.* (1995) 'Structural and Frictional Unemployment in an Equilibrium Search Model with Heterogeneous Agents', *Journal of Applied Econometrics*, vol. 10, supplement, pp. S133–51.

Koutsogeorgopoulou, V. (1994) 'The Impact of Minimum-Wages on Industrial-Wages and Employment in Greece', *International Journal of Manpower*, vol. 15, nos 2–3, pp. 86–99.

Kraak, A. (1995) 'South Africa's Segmented Labour Markets: Skill Formation and Occupational Mobility Under Apartheid', *Work, Employment and Society*, vol. 9, no. 4, pp. 657–87.

Kraak, G. (1993) *Breaking the Chains: Labour in South Africa in the '70s and '80s*, London: Pluto Press.

Kraft, P. and S. Dubnoff (1986) 'Job Content, Fragmentation, and Control in Computer Software Work', *Industrial Relations*, vol. 25, no. 2, pp. 184–96.

Kreckel, R. (1980) 'Unequal Opportunity Structure and Labour Market Segmentation', *Sociology*, vol. 14, no. 4, pp. 525–50.

Krelle, W. and A. Shorrocks (eds) (1978) *Personal Income Distribution*, Amsterdam: North-Holland.

Kremer, M. (1995) 'Research on Schooling: What We Know and What We Don't: A Comment on Hanushek', *World Bank Research Observer*, vol. 10, no. 2, August, pp. 247–54.

Krueger, A. and L. Summers (1987) 'Reflections on the Inter-Industry Wage Structure', in K. Lang and J. Leonard (eds) *Unemployment and the Structure of Labor Markets*, Oxford: Blackwell.

Krueger, A. and L. Summers (1988) 'Efficiency Wage and the Inter-Industry Wage Structure', *Econometrica*, vol. 56, no. 2, pp. 259–94.

Kruse, W. (1977) 'An Empirical Study of Labor Market Segmentation: Comment', *Industrial and Labor Relations Review*, vol. 30, no. 2, pp. 219–20.

Kubin, I. and M. Steiner (1992) 'Labour Market Performance and Regional Types – A Conceptual Framework with Empirical Analysis of Austria', *International Regional Science Review*, vol. 14, no. 3, pp. 275–98.

LaMagdeleine, D. (1986) 'US Catholic Church-Related Jobs as Dual Labour Markets: A Speculative Enquiry', *Review of Religious Research*, vol. 27, no. 4, pp. 315–27.

Lang, K. and J. Leonard (eds) (1987) *Unemployment and the Structure of Labor Markets*, Oxford: Basil Blackwell.

Langley, P. (1978) 'Comment on Osterman (1975)', *Industrial and Labor Relations Review*, vol. 32, no. 1, pp. 86–92.

Langton, N. and J. Pfeffer (1994) 'Paying the Professor – Sources of Variation in Academic Labor Markets', *American Sociological Review*, vol. 59, no. 2, pp. 236–56.

Law, R. *et al.* (1993) 'Defense-Less Territory – Workers, Communities, and the Decline of Military Production in Los Angeles', *Environment and Planning C, Government and Policy*, vol. 11, no. 3, pp. 291–315.

Lawlor, M. (1993) 'Keynes, Cambridge, and the New Keynesian Economics', in W. Darity (ed.) *Labor Economics: Problems in Analyzing Labor Markets*, Boston: Kluwer.

Lawson, T. (1981) 'Paternalism and Labour Market Segmentation Theory', in F. Wilkinson (ed.) *The Dynamics of Labour Market Segmentation*, London: Athlone Press.

Layard, R. *et al.* (1991) *Unemployment: Macroeconomic Performance and the Labour Market*, Oxford: Oxford University Press.

Layard, R. *et al.* (1994) *The Unemployment Crisis*, Oxford: Oxford University Press.

Lazonick, W. (1983) 'Class Relations and the Capitalist Enterprise', Harvard University, mimeo.

Lee, D. (1995) 'Korea Town and Korean Small Firms in Los Angeles – Locating in the Ethnic Neigborhoods', *Professional Geographer*, vol. 47, no. 2, pp. 184–95.

Lehrer, E. (1992) 'The Impact of Children on Married Women's Labor Supply – Black–White Differentials Revisited', *Journal of Human Resources*, vol. 27, no. 3, pp. 422–44.

Leigh, D. (1976) 'Occupational Advancement in the Late 1960s: An Indirect Test of the Dual Labor Market Hypothesis', *Journal of Human Resources*, vol. XI, no. 2, pp. 151–71.

Leon, J. (1985) 'The Effects of Labor Market Segmentation on Economic Resources in Retirement', *Social Science Research*, vol. 14, no. 4, pp. 351–73.

Lever-Tracy, C. (1981) 'Labour Market Segmentation and Diverging Migrant Incomes', *Australian and New Zealand Journal of Sociology*, vol. 17, no. 2, pp. 21–30.

Lever-Tracy, C. (1983) 'Review of Gordon *et al.* (1982) and Wilkinson (1981)', *Australian and New Zealand Journal of Sociology*, vol. 19, no. 2, pp. 354–58.

Lewis, D. (1991) 'Unemployment and the Current Crisis', in S. Gelb (ed.) *South Africa's Economic Crisis*, Cape Town: David Philip.

Lewis, J. (1984) *Industrialisation and Trade Union Organisation in South Africa: The Rise and Fall of the South African Trades and Labour Council*, Cambridge: Cambridge University Press.

Light, I. *et al.* (1994) 'Beyond the Ethnic Enclave Economy', *Social Problems*, vol. 41, no. 1, pp. 65–80.

LMC (1996) *Restructuring the South African Labour Market: Report of the Presidential Commission to Investigate Labour Market Policy*, Pretoria: Government Printer.

Locke, R. *et al.* (1995) 'Reconceptualizing Comparative Industrial Relations: Lessons from International Research', *International Labour Review*, vol. 134, no. 2, pp. 139–61.

Lord, G. and W. Falk (1980) 'An Exploratory Analysis of Individualist Versus Structuralist Explanations of Income', *Social Forces*, vol. 59, no. 2, pp. 376–91.

Lord, G. and W. Falk (1982) 'Dual Economy, Dual Labour, and Dogmatic Marxism: Reply to Morrissey', *Social Forces*, vol. 60, no. 3, pp. 891–7.

Loveridge, R. and A. Mok (1979) *Theories of Labour Market Segmentation*, The Hague: Nijhoff.

Loveridge, R. and A. Mok (1980) 'Theoretical Approaches to Segmented Labour Markets', *International Journal of Social Economics*, vol. 7, no. 5, pp. 376–411.

Lowell, R. (1978) 'Testing a Dual Labour Market Classification of Jobs', *Journal of Regional Science*, vol. 18, no. 1, pp. 95–103.

Lundahl, M. and L. Petersson (1991) *The Dependent Economy: Lesotho and the Southern African Customs Union*, Boulder: Westview Press.

McClure, J. (1994) 'Minimum-Wages and the Wessels Effect in a Monopsony Model', *Journal of Labor Research*, vol. 15, no. 3, pp. 271–82.

McCrate, E. (1990) 'Labor Market Segmentation and Relative Black–White Teenage Birth-Rates', *Review of Black Political Economy*, vol. 18, no. 4, pp. 37–53.

Machin, S. and A. Manning (1994) 'The Effects of Minimum-Wages on Wage Dispersion and Employment – Evidence from the UK Wages Councils', *Industrial and Labor Relations Review*, vol. 47, no. 2, pp. 319–29.

Machin, S. and A. Manning (1996) 'Employment and the Introduction of a Minimum Wage in Britain', *Economic Journal*, vol. 106, no. 436, pp. 667–76.

McIntyre, R. and M. Hillard (1995) 'The Peculiar Marriage of Marxian and Neoclassical Labor Economics', *Review of Radical Political Economics*, vol. 27, no. 3, pp. 22–30.

McKenna, E. (1981) 'A Comment on Bowles and Gintis' Marxian Theory of Value', *Cambridge Journal of Economics*, vol. 5, no. 3, pp. 281–4.

McLafferty, S. and V. Preston (1992) 'Spatial Mismatch and Labor Market Segmentation for African-American and Latina Women', *Economic Geography*, vol. 68, no. 4, pp. 406–31.

Maclean, M. and D. Groves (eds) (1990) *Women's Issues in Social Policy*, London: Routledge.

McNabb, R. (1980) 'Segmented Labour Markets, Female Employment and Poverty in Wales', in G. Rees and T. Rees (eds) *Poverty and Social Inequality in Wales*, London: Croom Helm.

McNabb, R. (1987) 'Testing for Labour-Market Segmentation in Britain', *Manchester School of Economic and Social Studies*, vol. 55, no. 3, pp. 257–73.

McNabb, R. and G. Psacharopoulos (1981) 'Further Evidence on the Relevance of the Dual Labor Market Hypothesis for the UK', *Centre for Labour Economics*,

Discussion Paper no. 38, 1978, as reproduced in *Journal of Human Resources*, vol. XVI, no. 3, Summer, 1981, pp. 442–8.

McNabb, R. and P. Ryan (1990) 'Segmented Labour Markets', in D. Sapsford and Z. Tzannatos (eds) *The Economics of the Labour Market*, London: Macmillan.

McRae, S. (1994) 'Labour Supply after Childbirth – Do Employers' Policies Make a Difference', *Sociology*, vol. 28, no. 1, pp. 99–122.

Madsen, J. (1995) 'Inflation and Aggregate Demand Shocks', *Journal of Policy Modeling*, vol. 17, no. 6, pp. 659–66.

Magnac, T. (1991) 'Segmented or Competitive Labor Markets', *Econometrica*, vol. 59, no. 1, pp. 165–78.

Mangum, G. *et al.* (1984/5) 'The Temporary Help Industry: A Response to the Dual Internal Labour Market', *Industrial and Labour Relations Review*, vol. 33, no. 4, pp. 599–611.

Mankiw, N. (1990) 'A Quick Refresher Course in Macroeconomics', *Journal of Economic Literature*, vol. XXVIII, December, pp. 1645–60.

Mankiw, N. (1993) 'Symposium on Keynesian Economics Today', *Journal of Economic Perspectives*, vol. 7, no. 1, Winter, pp. 3–4.

Manning, A. (1992) 'Multiple Equilibria in the British Labour Market', *European Economic Review*, vol. 36, no. 7, pp. 1333–65.

Manning, A. (1995) 'Developments in Labour Market Theory and Their Implications for Macroeconomic Policy', *Scottish Journal of Political Economy*, vol. 42, no. 3, August, pp. 250–66.

Manning, A. (1996) 'The Equal Pay Act as an Experiment to Test Theories of the Labour Market', *Economica*, vol. 63, no. 250, May, pp. 191–212.

Marceau, N. and R. Boadway (1994) 'Minimum-Wage Legislation and Unemployment-Insurance as Instruments for Redistribution', *Scandinavian Journal of Economics*, vol. 96, no. 1, pp. 67–81.

Marglin, S. (1974) 'What Do Bosses Do? The Origins and Functions of Hierarchy in Capitalist Production', *Review of Radical Political Economics*, vol. 6, no. 2, pp. 60–112.

Martin, B. (1994) 'Understanding Class Segmentation in the Labour Market – An Empirical Study of Earnings Determination in Australia', *Work, Employment and Society*, vol. 8, no. 3, pp. 357–85.

Marx, K. (1976) *Capital*, Volume I, Harmondsworth: Penguin, original of 1867.

Marx, K. and F. Engels (1975) *Selected Correspondence*, Moscow: Progress Publishers.

Massey, D. *et al.* (1994) 'An Evaluation of International Migration Theory – The North-American Case', *Population and Development Review*, vol. 20, no. 4, pp. 699–751.

Mavroudeas, S. (1990) *Regulation Approach: A Critical Assessment*, PhD Thesis, University of London.

May, J. (1990) 'The Migrant Labour System: Changing Dynamics in Rural Survival', in Nattrass and Ardington (eds) (1990).

Mayhew, K. and B. Rosewall (1979) 'Labour Market Segmentation in Britain', *Oxford Bulletin of Economics and Statistics*, vol. 41, no. 2, pp. 81–107.

Meng, R. (1985) 'An Empirical Test for Labor Market Segmentation of Males in Canada', *Industrial Relations*, vol. 24, no. 2, pp. 280–7.

Merrilees, W. (1982) 'Labour Market Segmentation: An Econometric Approach', *Canadian Journal of Economics*, vol. XV, no. 3, pp. 458–73.

Merton, R. (1957) *Social Theory and Social Structure*, New York: Free Press.

Meulders, D. and L. Wilkin (eds) (1987a) *Labour Market Flexibility*, special edition of *Labour and Society*, vol. 12, no. 1.

Meulders, D. and L. Wilkin (1987b) 'Labour Market Flexibility: Critical Introduction to the Analysis of a Concept', in D. Meulders and L. Wilkin (eds) *Labour Market Flexibility*, special edition of *Labour and Society*, vol. 12, no. 1, January.

Michael, R. *et al.* (eds) (1989) *Pay Equity: Empirical Inquiries*, Washington, DC: National Academy Press.

Michie, J. (1997) 'Developing the Institutional Framework – Employment and Labour Market Policies', in J. Michie and V. Padayachee (eds) *The Political Economy of South Africa's Transition – Policy Perspectives in the Late 1990s*, London: Dryden Press.

Michie, J. and V. Padayachee (eds) (1997) *The Political Economy of South Africa's Transition – Policy Perspectives in the Late 1990s*, London: Dryden Press.

Miliband, R. *et al.* (eds) (1987) *Socialist Register*, London: Merlin.

Mill, J.S. (1929) *Principles of Political Economy with Some of Their Applications to Social Philosophy*, London: Longmans, Green & Co, original of 1848.

Miller, J. (1992) 'Gender and Supervision – The Legitimation of Authority in Relationship to Task', *Sociological Perspectives*, vol. 35, no. 1, pp. 137–62.

Millward, N. and M. Stevens (1986) *British Workplace Industrial Relations 1980– 1984: The DE/ESRC/PSI/ACAS Surveys*, Aldershot: Gower.

Millward, N. and S. Woodland (1995) 'Gender Segregation and Male/Female Wage Differences', in J. Humphries and J. Rubery (eds) *The Economics of Equal Opportunities*, Manchester: Equal Opportunities Commission.

Moens, G. and S. Ratnapala (1992) *The Illusions of Comparable Worth*, CIS Policy Monograph no. 231, Centre for Independent Studies, Australia.

Montgomery, D. (1983) 'Review of Gordon *et al.* (1982)', *Business History Review*, Spring, pp. 116–18.

Moore, R. (1981) 'The UK Building Industry', in F. Wilkinson (ed.) *The Dynamics of Labour Market Segmentation*, with Introduction, London: Athlone Press.

Morgan, G. and D. Hooper (1982) 'Labour in the Woollen and Worsted Industry: A Critical Analysis of Dual Labour Market Theory', in G. Day *et al.* (ed.) *Diversity and Decomposition in the Labour Market*, Aldershot: Gower.

Morishima, M. (1978) 'S. Bowles and H. Gintis on the Marxian Theory of Value and Heterogeneous Labour', *Cambridge Journal of Economics*, vol. 2, no. 3, pp. 305–10.

Morris, P. (1996) 'Asia's Four Little Tigers – A Comparison of the Role of Education in Their Development', *Comparative Education*, vol. 32, no. 1, pp. 95– 109.

Morrison, A. (1994) 'Are Institutions or Economic Rents Responsible for Inter-Industry Wage Differentials', *World Development*, vol. 22, no. 3, pp. 355–68.

Morrison, P. (1990) 'Segmentation Theory Applied to Local, Regional and Spatial Labor Markets', *Progress in Human Geography*, vol. 14, no. 4, pp. 488–528.

Morrissey, M. (1982) 'The Dual Economy and Labour Market Segmentation: A Comment on Lord and Falk', *Social Forces*, vol. 60, no. 3, pp. 883–90.

Moseley, F. (ed.) (1995) *Heterodox Economic Theories: True or False?*, Aldershot: Edward Elgar.

Muntaner, C. and P. Parsons (1996) 'Income, Social Stratification, Class and Private Health Insurance – A Study of the Baltimore Area', *International Journal of Health Services*, vol. 26, no. 4, pp. 655–71.

Muscatelli, A. and L. Hunter (1995) 'Editors' Introduction: Contemporary Labour Market Issues', *Scottish Journal of Political Economy*, vol. 42, no. 3, August, pp. 250–66.

Natti, J. (1990) 'Flexibility, Segmentation and Use of Labour in Finnish Retail Trade', *Acta Sociologia*, vol. 33, no. 4, pp. 373–82.

Nattrass, N. (1990) 'The Small Black Enterprise Sector – A Brief Note of Caution', in N. Nattrass and E. Ardington (eds) *The Political Economy of South Africa*, Cape Town: Macmillan.

Nattrass, N. and E. Ardington (eds) (1990) *The Political Economy of South Africa*, Cape Town: Macmillan.

de Neubourg, C. *et al.* (1982) 'Dual Labour Market Theories in the Netherlands: Some Empirical Evidence', *Institute of Economic Research*, University of Groningen, Research Memorandum no. 69.

Neuman, S. and A. Ziderman (1986) 'Testing the Dual Labor Market Hypothesis: Evidence from the Israel Labor Mobility Survey', *Journal of Human Resources*, vol. 21, no. 2, pp. 230–7.

Neumark, D. and W. Wascher (1992) 'Employment Effects of Minimum and Sub-minimum Wages – Panel Data on State Minimum-Wage Laws', *Industrial and Labor Relations Review*, vol. 46, no. 1, pp. 55–81.

Neumark, D. and W. Wascher (1995) 'Minimum-Wage Effects on Employment and School Enrollment', *Journal of Business and Economic Statistics*, vol. 13 no. 2, pp. 199–206.

Nickell, S. (1990) 'Unemployment: A Survey', *Economic Journal*, vol. 100, June, pp. 361–439.

Nickell, S. (1996) 'Sectoral Structural Change and the State of the Labour Market in Great Britain', *The Labour Market Consequences of Technical Change and Structural Change*, Discussion Paper no. 2, Centre for Economic Performance, London School of Economics.

Nishibe, M. (1996) 'A Rivalous and Dispersive Market-Image – Hayek's Theory on a Spontaneous Order', mimeo.

Nolan, P. (1996) 'Industrial Relations and Performance since 1945', in I. Beardwell (ed.) *Contemporary Industrial Relations*, Oxford: Oxford University Press.

Nolan, P. and P. Edwards (1984) 'Homogenise, Divide and Rule: An Essay on *Segmented Work and Divided Workers*', *Cambridge Journal of Economics*, vol. 8, no. 3, pp. 197–215.

Nolan, P. and K. O'Donnell (1987) 'Taming the Market Economy? An Assessment of the GLC's Experiment in Restructuring for Labour', *Cambridge Journal of Economics*, vol. 11, no. 3, September, pp. 251–63.

Nolan, P. and K. O'Donnell (1995) 'Industrial Relations and Productivity', in P. Edwards (ed.) *Industrial Relations: Theory and Practice in Britain*, Oxford: Blackwell.

Nolan, P. and J. Walsh (1995) 'The Structure of the Economy and Labour Market', in P. Edwards (ed.) *Industrial Relations: Theory and Practice in Britain*, Oxford: Blackwell.

North, D. (1993) 'Institutions and Credible Commitment', *Journal of Institutional and Theoretical Economics*, vol. 149, no. 1, March, pp. 11–23.

North, D. (1996) 'The New Institutional Economics and Third World Development', in J. Harriss *et al.* (eds) *The New Institutional Economics and Third World Development*, London: Routledge.

Olson, M. (1965) *The Logic of Collective Action*, Cambridge, MA: Harvard University Press.

Ong, N. (1980) 'Marx's Classical and Post-Classical Conceptions of the Wage', *Australian Economic Papers*, vol. 19, no. 35, pp. 264–77.

Osberg, L. *et al.* (1987) 'Segmented Labour Markets and the Estimation of Wage Functions', *Applied Economics*, vol. 19, no. 12, pp. 1603–24.

Oster, G. (1979) 'A Factor Analytic Test of the Theory of the Dual Economy', *Review of Economics and Statistics*, vol. 61, no. 1, pp. 33–9.

Osterman, P. (1975) 'An Empirical Study of Labor Market Segmentation', *Industrial and Labor Relations Review*, vol. 28, no. 4, pp. 508–23.

Osterman, P. (1977) 'Reply to Kruse (1977)', *Industrial and Labor Relations Review*, vol. 30, no. 2, pp. 221–4.

Osterman, P. (1978) 'Reply to Langley (1978)', *Industrial and Labor Relations Review*, vol. 32, no. 1, pp. 92–4.

Osterman, P. (ed.) (1984) *Internal Labor Markets*, Cambridge, MA: MIT Press.

Paci, P. *et al.* (1995) 'Pay Gaps Facing Men and Women Born in 1958: Differences within the Labour Market', in J. Humphries and J. Rubery (eds) *The Economics of Equal Opportunities*, Manchester: Equal Opportunities Commission.

Panico, C. (1988) *Interest and Profit in the Theories of Value and Distribution*, London: Macmillan.

Patchell, J. and R. Hayter (1995) 'Skill Formation and Japanese Production Systems', *Tijdschrift voor Economische en Sociale Geografie*, vol. 86, no. 4, pp. 339–56.

Patinkin, D. (1965) *Money, Interest and Prices: An Integration of Monetary and Value Theory*, New York: Harper & Row, second edition.

Peck, F. and I. Stone (1993) 'Japanese Inward Investment in the Northeast of England – Reassessing Japanisation', *Environment and Planning C, Government and Policy*, vol. 11, no. 1, pp. 55–67.

Peck, J. (1989) 'Reconceptualising the Local Labour Market – Space, Segmentation, and the State', *Progress in Human Geography*, vol. 13, no. 1, pp. 42–61.

Peck, J. (1992a) 'Labor and Agglomeration – Control and Flexibility in Local Labor Markets', *Economic Geography*, vol. 68, no. 4, pp. 325–47.

Peck, J. (1992b) 'Invisible Threads – Homeworking, Labour Market Relations, and Industrial Restructuring in the Australian Clothing Trade', *Environment and Planning D, Society and Space*, vol. 10, no. 6, pp. 671–89.

Penn, R. (1982) '"The Contested Terrain": A Critique of R.C. Edwards' Theory of Working Class Fractions and Politics', in G. Day *et al.* (eds) *Diversity and Decomposition in the Labour Market*, Aldershot: Gower.

Penn, R. *et al.* (1994a) 'Gender, Technology, and Employment Change in Textiles', in A. Scott (ed.) *Gender Segregation and Social Change: Men and Women in Changing Labour Markets*, Oxford: Oxford University Press.

Penn, R. *et al.* (eds) (1994b) *Skill and Occupational Change*, Oxford: Oxford University Press.

Penn, R. *et al.* (1994c) 'Technical Change and the Division of Labour in Rochdale and Aberdeen', in R. Penn *et al.* (eds) *Skill and Occupational Change*, Oxford: Oxford University Press.

Perlman, R. and M. Pike (1994) *Sex Discrimination in the Labour Market: The Case for Comparable Worth*, Manchester: Manchester University Press.

Phelps, E. (1992) 'A Review of *Unemployment*', *Journal of Economic Literature*, vol. XXX, September, pp. 1476–90.

Phelps, E. (1994) *Structural Slumps: The Modern Equilibrium Theory of Unemployment, Interest, and Assets*, Cambridge, MA: Harvard University Press.

Phelps, E. (1995) 'The Origins and Further Development of the Natural Rate of Unemployment', in T. Cross (ed.) *The Natural Rate of Unemployment: Reflections on 25 Years of the Hypothesis*, Cambridge: Cambridge University Press.

Pietrykowski, B. (1995) 'Fordism at Ford – Spatial Decentralisation and Labor Segmentation at the Ford Motor Company, 1920–1950', *Economic Geography*, vol. 71, no. 4, pp. 383–401.

Piore, M. (1970) 'Jobs and Training', in S. Beer and R. Barringer (eds) *The State and the Poor*, Cambridge, MA: Winthorp.

Piore, M. (1974) 'Discussion', in M. Wachter (1974) 'Primary and Secondary Labor Markets: A Critique of the Dual Approach', *Brookings Papers on Economic Activity*, vol. 3, pp. 637–80, and Discussion, pp. 681–94.

Piore, M. (1975) 'Notes for a Theory of Labor Market Segmentation', in R. Edwards *et al.* (eds) *Labor Market Segmentation*, Lexington: Heath & Co.

Piore M. (1978) 'Dualism in the Labor Market: A Response to Uncertainty and Flux, the Case of France', *Revue Economique*, vol. 26, no. 1, pp. 26–50.

Piore, M. (1979a) *Birds of Passage: Migrant Labor and Industrial Societies*, Cambridge: Cambridge University Press.

Piore, M. (1979b) 'A "Sociological" Theory of Wages', in M. Piore (ed.) *Unemployment and Inflation: Institutionalist and Structuralist Views*, with Introduction, White Plains: Sharpe.

Piore, M. (1979c) 'Unemployment and Inflation: An Alternative View' in M. Piore (ed.) *Unemployment and Inflation: Institutionalist and Structuralist Views*, with Introduction, White Plains: Sharpe.

Piore, M. (ed.) (1979d) *Unemployment and Inflation: Institutionalist and Structuralist Views*, with Introduction, White Plains: Sharpe.

Piore, M. (1983) 'Labor Market Segmentation: To What Paradigm Does it Belong?', *American Economic Review*, Paper and Proceedings, vol. 73, no. 2, pp. 249–53.

Piore, M. (1986) 'Perspectives on Labor Market Flexibility', *Industrial Relations*, vol. 25, no. 2, pp. 146–66.

Piore, M. and C. Sabel (1984) *The Second Industrial Divide: Possibilities for Prosperity*, Basic Books: New York.

Pollert, A. (ed.) (1991a) *Farewell to Flexibility*, Oxford: Blackwell.

Pollert, A. (1991b) 'The Orthodoxy of Flexibility', in A. Pollert (ed.) *Farewell to Flexibility*, Oxford: Blackwell.

Poole, M. *et al.* (eds) (1984) *Industrial Relations in the Future: Trends and Possibilities in Britain over the Next Decade*, London: Routledge & Kegan Paul.

Posel, D. (1991) *The Making of Apartheid, 1948–1961: Conflict and Compromise*, Oxford: Clarendon Press.

Prasch, R. (1996) 'In Defence of the Minimum Wage', *Journal of Economic Issues*, vol. 30, no. 2, pp. 391–7.

Psacharopoulos, G. (1977) 'Market Duality and Income Distribution: The Case of the UK', *Centre for Labour Economics*, Discussion Paper no. 5, reproduced in W. Krelle and A. Shorrocks (eds) *Personal Income Distribution*, Amsterdam: North-Holland.

Psacharopoulos, G. (1996a) 'A Reply to Bennell', *World Development*, vol. 24, no. 1, p. 201.

Psacharopoulos, G. (1996b) 'Designing Educational Policy: A Mini-primer on Values, Theories and Tools', *International Journal of Educational Development*, vol. 16, no. 3, pp. 277–9.

Purdy, D. (1988) *Social Power and the Labour Market: A Radical Approach to Labour Economics*, London: Macmillan.

Rebitzer, J. (1993) 'Radical Political Economy and the Economics of Labor Markets', *Journal of Economic Literature*, vol. XXXI, September, pp. 1394–434.

Rebitzer, J. and L. Taylor (1995) 'The Consequences of Minimum-Wage Laws: Some New Theoretical Ideas', *Journal of Public Economics*, vol. 56, no. 2, pp. 245–55.

Rees, G. and T. Rees (eds) (1980) *Poverty and Social Inequality in Wales*, London: Croom Helm.

Reich, M. (1984) 'Segmented Labour: Time Series Hypothesis and Evidence,' *Cambridge Journal of Economics*, vol. 8, no. 1, pp. 63–81.

Reich, M. (1993) 'Radical Economics in Historical Perspective', *Review of Radical Political Economics*, vol. 25, no. 3, pp. 43–50.

Reich, M. (1995) 'Radical Economics: Successes and Failures', in F. Moseley (ed.) *Heterodox Economic Theories: True or False?*, Aldershot: Edward Elgar.

Ressler, R. *et al.* (1996) 'Full Wages, Part-Time Employment and the Minimum Wage', *Applied Economics*, vol. 28, no. 11, pp. 1415–19.

Reynolds, L. (1956) *The Evolution of Wage Structure*, New Haven: Yale University Press.

Rhoads, S. (1993) *Incomparable Worth: Pay Equity Meets the Market*, Oxford: Oxford University Press.

Rich, B. (1995) 'Explaining Feminization in the US Banking Industry, 1940–1980 – Human Capital, Dual Labor Markets or Gender Queuing', *Sociological Perspectives*, vol. 38, no. 3, pp. 357–80.

Riveros, L. (1994) 'Chile', in S. Horton *et al.* (eds) *Labor Markets in an Era of Adjustment: Case Studies*, vol. 2, Washington, DC: World Bank.

Roberts, B. *et al.* (eds) (1985) *New Approaches to Economic Life*, Manchester: Manchester University Press.

Roemer, R. and J. Schnitz (1982) 'Academic Employment as Day Labour: The Dual Labour Market in Higher Education', *Journal of Higher Education*, vol. 53, no. 5, pp. 514–31.

Rogerson, C. (1994) 'Flexible Production in the Developing World: The Case of South Africa', *Geoforum*, vol. 25, no. 1, February, pp. 1–17.

Romer, D. (1996) *Advanced Macroeconomics*, New York: McGraw-Hill.

Rosenberg, S. (1977) 'The Marxian Reserve Army of Labor and the Dual Labor Market', *Politics and Sociology*, vol. 7, no. 2, pp. 21–64.

Rosenberg, S. (1981) 'Occupational Mobility and Short Cycles', in F. Wilkinson (ed.) *The Dynamics of Labour Market Segmentation*, London: Athlone Press.

Rosenblum, G. and B. Rosenblum (1990) 'Segmented Labor Markets in Institutions of Higher Learning', *Sociology of Education*, vol. 63, no. 3, pp. 151–64.

Rosenblum, G. and B. Rosenblum (1996) 'The Flow of Instructors Through the Segmented Labour Markets of Academe', *Higher Education*, vol. 31, no. 4, pp. 429–45.

Rosenfeld, R. (1992) 'Job Mobility and Career Processes', *Annual Review of Sociology*, vol. 18, pp. 39–61.

Rowthorn, R. (1980) *Capitalism, Conflict and Inflation*, London: Lawrence & Wishart.

Rowthorn, R. and H. Chang (eds) (1995a) *The Role of the State in Economic Change*, Oxford: Clarendon Press.

Rowthorn, R. and H. Chang (1995b) 'The Role of the State in Economic Change: Entrepreneurship and Conflict Management', in R. Rowthorn and H. Chang (eds) *The Role of the State in Economic Change*, Oxford: Clarendon Press.

Rozen, M. (1983) 'Review of Gordon *et al.* (1982)', *Journal of Economic Issues*, vol. XVII, no. 1, pp. 215–24.

Rubery, J. (1978) 'Structured Labour Markets, Worker Organisation and Low Pay', *Cambridge Journal of Economics*, vol. 2, no. 1, pp. 17–36.

Rubery, J. (1994) 'Internal and External Labour Markets: Towards an Integrated Analysis', in J. Rubery and F. Wilkinson (eds) *Employer Strategy and the Labour Market*, Oxford: Oxford University Press.

Rubery J. and F. Wilkinson (1981) 'Work and Segmented Labour Markets', in F. Wilkinson (ed.) *The Dynamics of Labour Market Segmentation*, London: Athlone Press.

Rubery, J. and F. Wilkinson (eds) (1994) *Employer Strategy and the Labour Market*, Oxford: Oxford University Press.

Rubery, J. *et al.* (1984) 'Industrial Relations Issues in the 1980s: An Economic Analysis', in M. Poole *et al.* (eds) *Industrial Relations in the Future: Trends and Possibilities in Britain over the Next Decade*, London: Routledge & Kegan Paul.

Rubery, J. *et al.* (1987) 'Flexibility, Marketing and the Organisation of Production', in D. Meulders and L. Wilkin (eds) Labour Market Flexibility, special edition of *Labour and Society*, vol. 12, no. 1, January, pp. 131–51.

Rubinstein, M. (1984) *Equal Pay for Work of Equal Value*, London: Macmillan.

Rumberger, R. and M. Carnoy (1980) 'Segmentation in the US Labour Market', *Cambridge Journal of Economics*, vol. 4, no. 2, pp. 117–32.

Ryan, P. (1981) 'Segmentation, Quality and the Internal Labour Market', in F. Wilkinson (ed.) *The Dynamics of Labour Market Segmentation*, London: Athlone Press.

Sabel, C. (1982) *Work and Politics*, Cambridge: Cambridge University Press.

Sabel, C. and J. Zeitlin (1985) 'Historical Alternatives to Mass Production: Politics, Markets and Technology in Nineteenth-Century Industrialisation', *Past and Present*, 108, pp. 133–76.

Saintpaul, G. (1995) 'Do Labor-Market Rigidities Fulfil Distributive Objectives – Searching for the Virtues of the European Model', *International Monetary Fund Staff Papers*, vol. 41, no. 4, pp. 624–42.

Sakamoto, A. and M. Chen (1991) 'Inequality and Attainment in a Dual Labor Market', *American Sociological Review*, vol. 56, no. 3, pp. 295–308.

Sakamoto, A. and D. Powers (1995) 'Education and the Dual Labor Market for Japanese Men', *American Sociological Review*, vol. 60, no. 2, pp. 222–46.

Sales, W. and J. Davies (1957) 'Introducing a New Wage Structure into Coal Mining', *Bulletin of the Oxford University Institute of Statistics*, vol. 19, no. 3, pp. 201–24.

Samoff, J. (1966) 'Which Priorities and Strategies for Education?', *International Journal of Educational Development*, vol. 16, no. 3, pp. 249–72.

Samuels, W. (1995) 'The Present State of Institutional Economics', *Cambridge Journal of Economics*, vol. 19, no. 4, August, pp. 569–90.

Samuelson, P. (1971) 'Understanding the Marxian Notion of Exploitation: A Summary of the So-Called Transformation Problem Between Marxian Values and Competitive Prices', *Journal of Economic Literature*, vol. 9, no. 2, pp. 399–431.

Sapsford, D. and Z. Tzannatos (eds) (1990) *Current Issues in Labour Economics*, London: Macmillan.

Sapsford, D. and Z. Tzannatos (1993) *The Economics of the Labour Market*, London: Macmillan.

Schatz, R. (1985) 'Labor Historians, Labor Economics, and the Question of Synthesis, Review of Gordon *et al.* (1982)', *Journal of American History*, vol. 71, March, pp. 93–100.

Schiller, B. (1977) 'Relative Earnings Mobility in the United States', *American Economic Review*, vol. 67, December, pp. 926–41.

Schiller, B. (1994a) 'Moving Up – The Training and Wage Gains of Minimum-Wage Entrants', *Social Science Quarterly*, vol. 75, no. 3, pp. 622–36.

Schiller, B. (1994b) 'Below-Minimum-Wage Workers – Implications for Minimum-Wage Models', *Quarterly Review of Economics and Finance*, vol. 34, no. 2, pp. 131–43.

Schiller, B. (1994c) 'State Minimum-Wage Laws – Youth Coverage and Impact', *Journal of Labor Research*, vol. 15, no. 4, pp. 317–29.

Schoenberger, E. (1989) 'Thinking about Flexibility – A Response to Gertler', *Transactions of the Institute of British Geographers*, vol. 14, no. 1, pp. 98–108.

Schreuder, Y. (1989) 'Labor Segmentation, Ethnic Division of Labor, and Residential Segregation in American Cities in the Early Twentieth Century', *Professional Geographer*, vol. 41, no. 2, pp. 131–43.

Schuld, T. *et al.* (1994) 'Allocation and Wage Structure – Differences between Men and Women', *Applied Economics*, vol. 26, no. 2, pp. 137–52.

Scott, A. (1992) 'Low Wage Workers in a High Technology Manufacturing Complex – The Southern Californian Electronics Assembly Industry', *Urban Studies*, vol. 29, no. 8, pp. 1231–46.

Scott, A. (ed.) (1994a) *Gender Segregation and Social Change: Men and Women in Changing Labour Markets*, Oxford: Oxford University Press.

Scott, A. (1994b) 'Gender Segregation and the SCELI Research', in A. Scott (ed.) *Gender Segregation and Social Change: Men and Women in Changing Labour Markets*, Oxford: Oxford University Press.

Scott A. (1994c) 'Gender Segregation in the Retail Industry', in A. Scott (ed.) *Gender Segregation and Social Change: Men and Women in Changing Labour Markets*, Oxford: Oxford University Press.

Scott, F. *et al.* (1989) 'Effects of the Tax Treatment of Fringe Benefits on Labor Market Segmentation', *Industrial and Labor Relations Review*, vol. 42, no. 2, pp. 216–29.

Sengenberger, W. (1981) 'Labour Market Segmentation and the Business Cycle', in F. Wilkinson (ed.) *The Dynamics of Labour Market Segmentation*, with Introduction, London: Athlone Press.

Shaheed, Z. (1994) 'Minimum-Wages and Low Pay – An ILO Perspective', *International Journal of Manpower*, vol. 15, nos 2–3, pp. 49–61.

Shaiken, H. *et al.* (1986) 'The Work Process under More Flexible Production', *Industrial Relations*, vol. 25, no. 2, pp. 167–83.

Shergold, P. (1983) 'Review of Gordon *et al.* (1982)', *Economic History Review*, vol. 36, pp. 658–60.

Siltanen, J. (1981) 'A Commentary on Theories of Female Wage Labour', in Cambridge Women's Studies Group *Women in Society*, London: Virago.

Siltanen, J. (1994) *Locating Gender: Occupational Segregation, Wages and Domestic Responsibilities*, London: University College Press.

Sisson, K. and P. Marginson (1995) 'Management: Systems, Structures and Strategy', in P. Edwards (ed.) *Industrial Relations: Theory and Practice in Britain*, Oxford: Blackwell.

Sloane, P. (1994) 'The Gender Wage Differential and Discrimination in the Six SCELI Local Labour Markets', in A. Scott (ed.) (1994a) *Gender Segregation and Social Change: Men and Women in Changing Labour Markets*, Oxford: Oxford University Press.

Sloane, P. and I. Theodossiou (1996) 'Earnings Mobility, Family Income and Low Pay', *Economic Journal*, vol. 106, no. 436, pp. 657–66.

Sloane, P. *et al.* (1993) 'Labour Market Segmentation – A Local Labour Market Analysis Using Alternative Approaches', *Applied Economics*, vol. 25, no. 5, pp. 569–81.

Smit, M. (1995) 'Wages and the Structure of Product Markets', *South African Journal of Economics*, vol. 63, no. 1, pp. 1–25.

Smit, M. (1996) 'Inter-Industry Wage Differentials: The Wage-Gap in South Africa', *South African Journal of Economics*, vol. 64, no. 1, pp. 43–73.

Smith, A. (1937) *The Wealth of Nations*, New York: Random House, original of 1776.

Smith, M. *et al.* (1995) 'External Flexibility in Sweden and Canada – A Three Industry Comparison', *Work, Employment and Society*, vol. 9, no. 4, pp. 698–718.

Smith, R. (1988) 'Comparable Worth: Limited Coverage and the Exacerbation of Inequality', *Industrial and Labor Relations Review*, vol. 41, no. 2, January, pp. 227–39.

Smith, R. and B. Vavrichek (1992) 'The Wage Mobility of Minimum-Wage Workers', *Industrial and Labor Relations Review*, vol. 46, no. 1, pp. 82–8.

Snell, M. *et al.* (1981) *Equal Pay and Opportunities: A Study of the Implementation and Effects of the Equal Pay and Sex Discrimination Acts in 26 Organisations*, Department of Employment, Research Paper no. 20.

Snower, D. (1995) 'Evaluating Unemployment Policies: What Do the Underlying Theories Tell Us?', *Oxford Review of Economic Policy*, vol. 11, no. 1, Spring, pp. 110–35.

Snyder, D. *et al.* (1978) 'The Location of Change in the Sexual Structure of Occupations 1950–1970: Insights from Labour Market Segmentation Theory', *American Journal of Sociology*, vol. 84, no. 3, pp. 706–17.

Solinas, G. (1982) 'Labour Market Segmentation and Workers' Careers: The Case of the Italian Knitwear Industry', *Cambridge Journal of Economics*, vol. 6, no. 4, pp. 331–52.

Solow, R. (1987) 'Unemployment: Getting the Questions Right', in C. Bean *et al.* (eds) *The Rise in Unemployment*, Oxford: Blackwell.

Solow, R. (1990) *The Labour Market as a Social Institution*, Oxford: Blackwell.

Sorenson, B. (1994) *Comparable Worth: Is It a Worthy Policy?*, Princeton: Princeton University Press.

South African Foundation (1996) *Growth for All – An Economic Strategy for South Africa*, Johannesburg: South African Foundation.

Spandau, A. (1980a) 'A Note on Black Employment Conditions on South African Mines', *South African Journal of Economics*, vol. 48, no. 2, June, pp. 214–17.

Spandau, A. (1980b) 'Mechanization and Labour Policies on South African Mines', *South African Journal of Economics*, vol. 48, no. 2, June, pp. 167–82.

Staples, C. (1984) 'Review of Gordon *et al.* (1982)', *Sociology and Social Research*, vol. 68, no. 2, pp. 281–2.

Steedman, I. *et al.* (1981) *The Value Controversy*, London: Verso.

Steele, R. (1979) 'The Relative Performance of the Wages Council and Non-Wages Council Sectors and the Impact of Incomes Policy', *British Journal of Industrial Relations*, vol. 17, no. 2, pp. 224–34.

Steinberg, R. (1987) 'Radical Challenges in a Liberal World: The Mixed Success of Comparable Worth', *Gender and Society*, vol. 4, December, pp. 466–75.

Steinberg, R. (1992) 'Gendered Instructions – Cultural Lag and Gender Bias in the Hay System of Job Evaluation', *Work and Occupation*, vol. 19, no. 4, pp. 387–423.

Stiglitz, J. (1993) 'Post Walrasian and Post Marxian Economics', *Journal of Economic Perspectives*, vol. 7, no. 1, pp. 109–14.

Stock, J. and M. Watson (1988) 'Variable Trends in Economic Time Series', *Journal of Economic Perspectives*, vol. 2, no. 3, Summer, pp. 147–74.

Streeck, W. (1992) *Social Institutions and Economic Performance: Studies in Industrial Relations in Advanced Capitalist Countries*, London: Sage.

Swedberg, R. (1993) 'On Custom: Comment', *Journal of Institutional and Theoretical Economics*, vol. 149, no. 1, pp. 204–9.

Sweetland, S. (1996) 'Human Capital Theory – Foundations of a Field of Inquiry', *Review of Educational Research*, vol. 66, no. 3, pp. 341–59.

Swinnerton, K. (1996) 'Minimum Wages in an Equilibrium Search Model with Diminishing Returns to Labor in Production', *Journal of Labor Economics*, vol. 14, no. 2, pp. 340–55.

Taplin, I. (1996) 'Rethinking Flexibility – The Case of the Apparel Industry', *Review of Social Economy*, vol. 54, no. 2, pp. 191–220.

Tarling, R. (1981) 'The Relationship between Employment and Output: Where Does Segmentation Lead Us?', in F. Wilkinson (ed.) *The Dynamics of Labour Market Segmentation*, London: Athlone Press.

Telles, E. (1993) 'Urban Labor Market Segmentation and Income in Brazil', *Economic Development and Cultural Change*, vol. 41, no. 2, pp. 231–49.

Theodossiou, I. (1995) 'Wage Determination for Career and Non-Career Workers in the UK: Is There Labour Market Segmentation?', *Economica*, vol. 62, no. 246, pp. 195–211.

Thompson, E.P. (1979) *The Poverty of Theory*, London: Merlin Press.

Thompson, P. (1983) *The Nature of Work: an Introduction to Debates on the Labour Process*, London: Macmillan.

Thurow, L. (1975) *Generating Inequality: Mechanisms of Distribution in the US Economy*, New York: Basic Books.

Tickell, A. and J. Peck (1995) 'Social Regulation *after* Fordism: Regulation Theory, Neo-Liberalism and the Global-Local Nexus', *Economy and Society*, vol. 24, no. 5, August, pp. 357–86.

Tokman, V. (1989) 'Economic Development and Labor Market Segmentation in the Latin American Periphery', *Journal of Inter-American Studies and World Affairs*, vol. 31, nos 1–2, pp. 23–47.

Tolbert, C. (1982) 'Industrial Segmentation and Men's Career Mobility', *American Sociological Review*, vol. 47, pp. 457–77.

Tolbert, C. *et al.* (1980) 'The Structure of Economic Segmentation: A Dual Economy Approach', *American Journal of Sociology*, vol. 85, no. 5, pp. 1095–116.

Tool, M. (ed.) (1993) *Institutional Economics: Theory, Method, Policy*, Boston: Kluwer Press.

Torres, A. (1991) 'Labor Market Segmentation – African-American and Puerto-Rican Labor in New York City', *Review of Black Political Economy*, vol. 20, no. 1, pp. 59–77.

Toye, J. (1996) 'The New Institutional Economics and Its Implications for Development', in J. Harriss *et al.* (eds) *The New Institutional Economics and Third World Development*, London: Routledge.

Truu, M. (1983a) 'Comment on Cassim (1982)', *South African Journal of Economics*, vol. 51, no. 4, pp. 567–73.

Truu, M. (1983b) 'Final Comment on Cassim (1982)', *South African Journal of Economics*, vol. 51, no. 4, p. 579.

Valkenburg, F. and A. Vissers (1980) 'Segmentation of the Labour Market: The Theory of the Dual Economy', *Netherlands Journal of Sociology*, vol. 16, no. 2, pp. 150–70.

Vanhophem, H. (1987) 'An Empirical Test of the Segmented Labour Market Theory for the Netherlands', *Applied Economics*, vol. 19, no. 11, pp. 1497–514.

Vansoest, A. (1994) 'Youth Minimum-Wage Rates – The Dutch Experience', *International Journal of Manpower*, vol. 15, nos 2–3, pp. 100–17.

Vietorisz, T. and B. Harrison (1973) 'Labor Market Segmentation: Positive Feedback and Divergent Development', *American Economic Review*, Papers and Proceedings, May, pp. 366–83.

Villa, P. (1981) 'Labour Market Segmentation and the Construction Industry in Italy', in F. Wilkinson (ed.) *The Dynamics of Labour Market Segmentation*, London: Athlone Press.

Wachter, M. (1974) 'Primary and Secondary Labor Markets: A Critique of the Dual Approach', *Brookings Papers on Economic Activity*, vol. 3, pp. 637–80, and Discussion, pp. 681–94.

Waddoups, J. (1991) 'Racial Differences in Intersegment Mobility', *Review of Black Political Economy*, vol. 20, no. 2, pp. 23–43.

Waddoups, J. and D. Assane (1993) 'Mobility and Gender in a Segmented Labor Market – A Closer Look', *American Journal of Economics and Sociology*, vol. 52, no. 4, pp. 399–412.

Wallace, M. and A. Kalleberg (1981) 'Economic Organisation of Firms and Labor Market Consequences: Towards a Specification of Dual Economic Theory', in I. Berg (ed.) *Sociological Perspectives on Labor Markets*, New York: Academic Press.

Wallace, M. *et al.* (1993) 'Positional Power, Class, and Individual Earnings Inequality – Advancing New Structuralist Explanations', *Sociological Quarterly*, vol. 34, no. 1, pp. 85–109.

Webster, E. (1985) *Cast in a Racial Mould: Labour Process and Trade Unionism in the Foundries*, Johannesburg: Ravan Press.

Weeks, J. (1989) *A Critique of Neoclassical Macroeconomics*, New York: St Martin's Press.

Weingast, B. (1993) 'Constitutions as Governance Structures: The Political Foundations of Secure Markets', *Journal of Institutional and Theoretical Economics*, vol. 149, no. 1, pp. 286–311.

Wessels, W. (1993) 'The Minimum-Wage and Tipped Employees', *Journal of Labor Research*, vol. 14, no. 3, pp. 213–26.

Whalley, P. (1984) 'Deskilling Engineers? The Labour Process, Labour Markets, and Labour Segmentation', *Social Problems*, vol. 32, no. 2, pp. 117–32.

Whaples, R. (1996) 'Is There a Consensus Among American Labor Economists – Survey Results on 40 Propositions', *Journal of Labor Research*, vol. 17, no. 4, pp. 725–34.

Wilkinson, F. (ed.) (1981) *The Dynamics of Labour Market Segmentation*, with Introduction, London: Athlone Press.

Wilkinson, F. (1983) 'Productive Systems', *Cambridge Journal of Economics*, vol. 7, no. 4, pp. 413–29.

Wilkinson, F. (1992) *Why Britain Needs a Minimum Wage*, London: Institute of Public Policy Research.

Williams, N. (1993) 'Regional Effects of the Minimum-Wage on Teenage Employment', *Applied Economics*, vol. 25, no. 12, pp. 1517–28.

Williamson, O. (1975) *Markets and Hierarchies: Analysis and Antitrust Implications*, New York: Free Press.

Williamson, O. (1993a) 'Contested Exchange versus the Governance of Contractual Relations', *Journal of Economic Perspectives*, vol. 7, no. 1, pp. 103–108.

Williamson, O. (1993b) 'The Evolving Science of Organization', *Journal of Institutional and Theoretical Economics*, vol. 149, no. 1, pp. 36–63.

Williamson, O. *et al.* (1975) 'Understanding the Employment Relation: The Analysis of Idiosyncratic Exchange', *Bell Journal of Economics*, vol. 6, Spring, pp. 250–78.

Wilson, F. (1972a) *Migrant Labour in South African Gold Mines, 1911–1969*, Cambridge: Cambridge University Press.

Wilson, F. (1972b) *Migrant Labour in South Africa*, Johannesburg: Christian Institute of South Africa.

Wilson, F. and M. Ramphele (1989) *Uprooting Poverty: The South African Challenge*, Cape Town: David Philip.

Wilson, F. *et al.* (1995) 'Race and Unemployment – Labor Market Experiences of Black and White Men, 1968–1988', *Work and Occupations*, vol. 22, no. 3, pp. 245–70.

Wimmer, B. (1996) 'Minimum Wage Increases and Employment in Franchised Fast-Food Restaurants', *Journal of Labour Research*, vol. 17, no. 1, pp. 211–14.

Winship, C. and R. Mare (1992) 'Models for Sample Selection Bias', *Annual Review of Sociology*, vol. 18, pp. 327–50.

Wood, S. (ed.) (1982) *The Degradation of Work: Skill, Deskilling and the Labour Process*, London: Hutchinson.

Wray, K. (1984) 'Labour Market Operation, Recruitment Strategies and Workforce Structures', *International Journal of Social Economics*, vol. 11, no. 7, pp. 6–31.

Wright, R. and J. Ermisch (1990) 'Male–Female Wage Differentials in Great Britain', Birkbeck Discussion Paper in Economics no. 10/90.

Wright Mills, C. (1959) *The Sociological Imagination*, New York: Oxford University Press.

Zabalza, A. and Z. Tzannatos (1985) *Women and Equal Pay: The Effects of Legislation on Female Employment and Wages in Britain*, Cambridge: Cambridge University Press.

Zagorski, K. (1992) 'Occupational and Industrial Contextual Indicators in Income Determination Models for Australia', *Social Indicators Research*, vol. 26, no. 1, pp. 61–91.

Zucker L. and C. Rosenstein (1981) 'Taxonomies of Institutional Structure: Dual Economy Reconsidered', *American Journal of Sociology*, vol. 46, no. 6, pp. 869–84.

Index